W9-APF-650

A NARRATIVE
TEXTBOOK OF
PSYCHOANALYSIS

A NARRATIVE TEXTBOOK OF PSYCHOANALYSIS

Peter L. Giovacchini, M.D.

Jason Aronson Inc.
Northvale, New Jersey
London

Copyright © 1987 by Jason Aronson Inc.

10 9 8 7 6 5 4 3 2 1

All rights reserved. Printed in the United States of America. No part of this book may be used or reproduced in any manner whatsoever without written permission from *Jason Aronson Inc.* except in the case of brief quotations in reviews for inclusion in a magazine, newspaper, or broadcast.

Library of Congress Cataloging-in-Publication Data

Giovacchini, Peter L.
  A narrative textbook of psychoanalysis.

  Includes bibliographies and index.
  1. Psychoanalysis.   2. Psychoanalysis—History.
I. Title. [DNLM: 1. Psychoanalysis—history.   2. Psycho-
analytic Theory. WM 460 G512n]
RC504.G55   1987   616.89'17'09   87-1495
ISBN 0-87668-964-0

Manufactured in the United States of America.

CONTENTS

Part II. Mapping the Unconscious

Part III. Clinical Uses of Psychoanalysis

PREFACE

When an area of knowledge is expanding and changing as rapidly as psychoanalysis is, it is impossible to write a standard textbook. In recent years there have been no attempts to provide a text dealing solely with a clinical and theoretical perspective that is directed to all levels of the psychic apparatus. Brenner (1957), Fenichel (1945), and Waelder (1960) have written excellent and concise summaries of Freud's concepts, but psychoanalysis in the past two decades has shifted its focus, because of clinical necessity, to the operations of the psyche as it relates and adapts to the external world, and so it has moved away from an exclusive focus on instinctual forces.

Recent approaches belong to the realm of ego psychology, which some psychoanalysts consider to be a separate and distinct frame of reference. To write a textbook, however, that includes ego psychology as an extension of classic psychoanalytic theory and technology may be premature because our concepts regarding this approach are not sufficiently solidified. Even our categories, such as object relations theory, the British school, and self psychology are not yet well defined; all we can definitely state is that we are dealing with intraego psychic processes as the mind relates to external reality. We also agree that we are emphasizing psychic structure rather than instinctual forces.

Nevertheless, as we review the concepts that are derived from classic psychoanalytic theory, it becomes apparent how much they remain the foundation of modern clinical orientations. Indeed, in disagreement with Kohut (1971, 1977) and Gedo and Goldberg (1976), as well as other followers of Kohut, I have concluded that classic analytic theory has made possible the findings and formulations of ego psychology, and the latter, in turn, has enriched and extended our concepts regarding the deeper instinctual forces of the id.

Although Freud was primarily involved with the instincts and their development and vicissitudes, as well as their significance in determining the types and manifestations of psychopathology when they clash with one another, he was also the first psychoanalyst to discuss psychic development and structure. In his classic paper "The Ego and the Id," Freud (1923a) introduced the structural hypothesis and postulated a tripartite model of the mind: the id, ego, and superego. This structural scaffold still represents the fundamental building blocks of the ego-psychological perspective, and much of what Freud stated in his metapsychological papers is still pertinent to many of our current concepts. I have already discussed in some detail (Giovacchini 1982) how the bases of some of our "modern" ideas can be found in Freud's writings.

Another problem in writing a textbook is the difficulty in integrating modern theories with classical psychoanalysis. As implied, there is no comprehensive theory of ego psychology because, as I stated, it is not an autonomous theoretical system that stands apart from the general body of psychoanalysis. Furthermore, attempts to integrate ego psychology into Freud's formulations, beyond tracing the evolution of some supposedly new concepts to them, are difficult because ego concepts have not been precisely defined.

Thus, I direct my attention to the current diversity of the ego-psychological focus, that is, the various facets of the ego that have been emphasized by different psychoanalysts. Some

clinicians have focused on ego subsystems, a microscopic anatomical approach, whereas other investigators have concentrated on the dynamic relations between parts of the ego and
external objects and various facets of the external world. These
are not essentially different approaches; rather, they deal with
the many factors that underlie phenomena that we all encounter
in our clinical observations. At the present, ego psychology is
attached to the body of psychoanalysis, but it is not totally
integrated. It is not entirely split off, either; at most it is somewhat fragmented.

In this book, I cover standard psychoanalytic theory, di-
gressing occasionally to make connections between early and
later formulations. My purpose in doing this is to trace a conceptual continuum, as I attempted to do with Freud's theories
(Giovacchini 1982). Here I amplify this continuum between id
and ego psychology. I also discuss ego psychology in a separate
section, stressing an orientation derived from studying ego concepts in the classic analytic tradition.

I do not include the topic of applied psychoanalysis; instead, the orientation that I emphasize leads to the exploration
of technical factors that pertain to the treatment of patients,
since the focus of this volume is clinical.

This clinical focus is stressed in every chapter and, as a
consequence, some repetition is unavoidable, but I try as much
as possible to make cross-references. As similar clinical phenomena are studied from various frames of reference, I sometimes
discuss principles and concepts that have already been covered
in a different context. Furthermore, because this volume attempts to approximate a textbook, the reader may choose to
select only a particular section to study and may not want to
refer to another chapter to acquaint himself with concepts that
he needs to know to understand what he is reading. So for the
sake of completion, repetition is necessary. This applies especially to ego psychology, which is discussed in many chapters as
well as in a special final section.

Textbooks have required the author to be more or less
nonexistent, to report the facts in as unobtrusive a manner as
possible. Psychoanalysts should be quite adept at remaining
unobtrusive. When it comes to writing, however, I do not find it

a pleasant prospect. Granted, it is not the purpose of a textbook to be entertaining, but if a subject is presented in a lively style, the reader will be more involved. Furthermore, if authors clearly identify their opinions, whether they are innovative, extensions of standard doctrines, or a critical evaluation, this should add a soupçon of spice. Readers can form their own opinions if doxology is separated from commentary.

I recall how I struggled over chapters I have written for textbooks. The editors insisted that I not use the first person singular pronoun. If I would venture an opinion, it could only be tolerated if I began my sentence with "the author believes." Such a beginning often leads one into a sentence whose structure—for example, the passive voice—lacks force and clarity.

Since I will not be following the usual conventions of textbook style and exposition, this is not a standard, orthodox textbook. My publisher has encouraged me to pursue my own approach. This means that I will not avoid interjecting my opinions or making connections that go beyond a comprehensive presentation of the psychoanalytic viewpoint.

Peter L. Giovacchini, M.D.

A NARRATIVE
TEXTBOOK OF
PSYCHOANALYSIS

Part I

FREUD'S DISCOVERY OF THE UNCONSCIOUS

Chapter 1

HISTORICAL ELEMENTS

DEFINITION OF PSYCHOANALYSIS

Can psychoanalysis be defined in the same way as other sciences can? Can its essence be expressed in a few simple sentences? No, it cannot, for such a simplification would be too limiting. Even though the object of investigation—the psyche—seems clear, it is the emphasis on the method of study and its basic assumptions, rather than on the object of investigation itself, that distinguishes psychoanalysis from other disciplines.

At first psychoanalysis was a conceptual system constructed to explain certain types of psychopathology, mainly the hysterical neuroses, but rather quickly it became a technique of treatment. Finally, it expanded into a theory of personality that applied to both normal and abnormal development. Psychoanalysis has not as yet achieved the goal of becoming a comprehensive general psychology.

Psychoanalysis was "invented" by Sigmund Freud (1856–1939), and for many years he was virtually its only proponent. Because he derived many of his insights from his self-analysis and had to defend himself against his detractors, his theories contain many of his biases, which have been carried on to the present. Nevertheless, although still controversial, psychoanalysis is the most comprehensive and influential of all the personality theories.

Psychoanalysis, primarily a depth psychology, views the mind as containing hierarchically ordered primitive and sophisticated mental elements. The primitive end of the psychic spectrum is known as the *id*. The id consists of biologically based instincts seeking gratification and striving to express themselves against the more-structured reality elements found in the higher levels of the mind, a region known as the *ego*. The ego determines whether it is appropriate to satisfy the id—the biologically based instincts—in terms of reality. Within the realm of the ego resides the *superego*, which imposes moral standards and prohibitions on the ego, which, in turn, decides which instincts should be gratified.

The psychoanalytic model of the mind emphasizes clashes of various psychic elements as being characteristic of its standard operations. As it also decides the outcome of these conflicting intrapsychic forces, the psychoanalytic orientation is considered a psychodynamic approach.

Psychoanalysis is, as well, a system based on strict determinism. Its foundations rest on the concept of causality; that is, even the most irrational and nonsensical behavior can be explained by rational premises. The clashing forces within the personality are, for the most part, unconscious, but, even though they are beyond conscious awareness, they affect feelings and behavior. These unconscious forces affecting the conscious, higher levels of the personality are said to be part of a *dynamic unconscious*. This assertion of the existence of a dynamic unconscious is the most fundamental and distinctive hypothesis of psychoanalytic theory.

The treatment method is based on the analyst's interpretations of unconscious motivation. Freud encouraged his patients to *free associate*, that is, to tell the therapist everything that occurs to them, no matter how trivial or embarrassing their thoughts and feelings may seem to them. Patients are expected to suspend their judgment and say everything that comes to mind. As they become more skillful at free associating, they will begin to ascribe infantile attitudes and feelings to the analyst, a process known as *transference*. The classical analyst confines interpretations to the interpretation of the transference.

Today, interpretations are not confined to the conflictual strivings of instinctual impulses; now the therapist also refers to the structure of the psychic apparatus, which includes parts of the self and a variety of internalized representations of persons and situations in the outer world. These are referred to as *self* and *object representations*. Their concentration on psychic structure has enabled psychoanalysts to extend the range of their therapeutic applications.

Other than the immutability of a few fundamental issues, such as the dynamic unconscious and working within the transference context, psychoanalysis is far from a closed system. This is partly a result of the unique interplay of both observation, which includes learning and research, and application, which refers to treatment. The relationship with a patient can be viewed as an experiment from which the investigator can confirm or augment, modify, and even discard previously held hypotheses. This theory building benefits both psychoanalysis and the patient.

A HISTORICAL OUTLINE

Psychoanalysis started as an offshoot of psychiatry and followed the medical orientation of the mid-nineteenth century. Psychiatry, in turn, incorporated the attitudes of science. At the time, science was delving deeper into fundamental causes. The intellectual atmosphere was suffused with positivism, and the outlook had changed from romanticism and mysticism to a practical, mechanistic orientation. This atmosphere thus influenced the education that Freud received in France and Austria and helped him to decide to go into the practice of psychiatry as a profession.

In 1845, Mayer, a physician, postulated the first law of thermodynamics, the law of conservation of energy, which emphasized constancy and balance. Helmholtz and his colleagues adhered to the principle of strict determinism, believing that every problem could be solved and understood in terms of its basic etiology. Medicine also incorporated this theory regarding etiology and began searching for the causes of diseases. The medical profession therefore had advanced from the goal of ameliorating symptoms to the goal of eradicating diseases by discovering and eliminating their causes. The germ theory, as hypothesized by Pasteur and Koch, and the momentous discoveries of pathology, under the leadership of such giants as Virchow, led doctors to become enthusiastic and hopeful that all diseases would be conquered. Such ideals were founded on a purely physicochemical, materialistic approach.

The study of emotional illness, which was largely confined to the major psychoses, lagged behind the research in general medicine, especially in regard to those diseases that had a bacterial etiology. Psychiatry at this point was confined to description and classification. Psychiatrists found all kinds of clues in their patients' gestures, posture, facial expressions, modes of dress, and innumerable other details that enabled them to make inferences about character structure as well as prognoses. Today, psychoanalysts concentrate on their patients' verbal discourse, and few pay much attention to the nonverbal aspects of their patients' behavior.

Psychiatrists, who in the late 1800s were known as *alienists*, considered mental illness to have organic causes, usually neurological disorders. This approach was useful for understanding some of the dementias and mental aberrations associated with intracranial pathology, but it was not particularly useful in understanding the neuroses and the majority of the psychoses. Steeped as they were in the medical tradition, psychiatrists remained optimistic that those etiologies that could not be understood as yet would be discovered in time, given enough research.

Freud, himself a neurologist and anatomist (1877a, b) also sought an organic cause, or causes, for emotional disorders and spent eight years in Brücke's laboratory doing basic research on the nervous system. He wrote important treatises on aphasia (1891) and cerebral diplegia and nearly discovered the neuron.

Because salaries for pure research were low and Freud needed money so that he could marry and raise a family, he decided to pursue a more lucrative career as a private practitioner.

Despite his extensive experience in the basic sciences, Freud concluded that he could not obtain the insights he needed to understand his patients if he adhered to his colleagues' assumption that organic causes would eventually explain all diseases. Although he continued to believe that organic and constitutional factors might play a role, Freud evaluated his patients primarily according to a psychological frame of reference, at least for the psychoneuroses. He had decided on a career in psychiatry, and he was not pleased with the prospect of treating patients with the current therapies—massage, electrotherapy, baths—methods that did not reach the etiological core. Freud was too much of a scientist to be satisfied with treatment procedures he could not justify, nor could he be content to remain ignorant of processes that might underlie symptomatic manifestations.

Freud focused instead on psychic processes, and by the end of the nineteenth century, he had made some important discoveries about mental life in general. His ideas were not generally accepted, however, because of his emphasis on sexual etiology and his formulation of infantile sexuality, although the opposition to his ideas may not have been as strong as he stated (Ellenberger 1970); that is, his psychological approach was not totally disparaged.

Nevertheless, an important discovery set back dynamic psychiatry for many years. Just when some scientists were beginning to consider the intrapsychic factors in emotional problems, in 1904 Noguchi found that general paresis, then a fairly common disease often characterized by states of grandiosity associated with insanity, was caused by the bacteria *Treponema pallidum*, a spirochete. What was beginning to be regarded as a functional psychosis turned out to be a neurological disease, syphilis of the brain. The organic-mechanistic approach then was intensified, and the belief was rekindled that other psychoses could be explained in a similar fashion. The only psychiatrist to receive a Nobel Prize was Julius von Wagner-Jauregg, for his fever treatment of general paresis. He generated high fever by injecting into his patients attenuated strains of the malarial parasite, with the hope of killing the spirochetes. Some of his patients did, in fact, improve, but this was a dangerous and usually ineffective treatment. Nevertheless, the search for medical and even surgical procedures continued.

Since the supposed breakthrough concerning the role of a bacillus as a cause of major psychosis, little of consequence has been discovered regarding the organic etiology of mental disorders. Some investigators in the early 1900s thus returned to a psychological approach, and a few gathered around Freud.

Freud isolated himself from the medical community and developed psychoanalysis. In the first decade of the twentieth century, he formed his own group, which met on Wednesday afternoons in his waiting room (Nunberg and Federn 1962). He and his colleagues attempted to understand the mind and its aberrations in a purely psychological frame of reference. Not all of the members of his group were physicians; Freud accepted any educated person who was interested in psychoanalysis, including art historians, lawyers, and even a music critic. But they all were consumed by their desire to know what was happening in people's minds, rather than simply controlling their behavior or symptoms. They needed a conceptual system to restore order to the chaotic confusion that their patients presented. Freud thus offered his patients order; he was able to make sense of the seemingly irrational. That is, he was able to explain the irrational by means of the rational.

Freud moved away from the taxonomic profile approach, as he was able to respond to his patients' feelings. Contemporary psychoanalysts have added a new dimension, by including the patient's feelings in their formulations and viewing the patient as a three-dimensional being who does not fit into a simple mold. The analyst accepts the patient's unique and individual emotional makeup rather than trying to fit it into behavioral stereotypes and other surface characteristics. Lately, analysts have further expanded their evaluations of their patients to include their own (that is, the analysts') feelings in the process of trying to understand the patients' emotional problems. Patients today are therefore frequently examined in terms of a relationship and interaction in which the reactions of both the therapist and the patient are given equal consideration. The analyst's reactions, often known as *countertransference*, add yet another dimension to the psychoanalytic clinical viewpoint.

This type of progression is not unique to psychoanalysis. Something similar has happened in the physical sciences that also began with categorization but during the Renaissance focused upon the underlying laws that governed various phenomena. The discovery of these laws involved clever observation and mathematical manipulation. Physics reached many conclusions about events and structures that cannot be directly observed. Physicists made inferences and derived conclusions from observations far removed from the subatomic phenomena they were studying. With the advent of quantum mechanics, physical scientists, like psychoanalysts, had to add another dimension to their observational frame. They had to take the measuring instrument into account inasmuch as the very act of observing changed the phenomenon they were examining. In a simplified fashion, this is a statement of Heisenberg's *Uncertainty Principle*, which is analogous to the influence of countertransference feelings in affecting the psychic balance between patient and therapist in the psychoanalytic setting.

Before Freud, neither the mode and technique of examination nor the underlying reasons for the patient's symptomatic behavior were considered. As early as 1895, much had been accomplished in constructing a conceptual system and laying down the ground rules of the therapeutic process (Breuer and Freud 1895). Even though Freud later had to revise some of his early concepts—for example, the seduction theory as a traumatic cause of neuroses, a subject that has recently gained considerable notoriety (see Malcolm 1981)—much of Freud's early postulates have endured. Within the last two decades some analysts have attempted to modify the superstructure of Freud's metapsychology, such as the energic hypothesis; however, his few fundamental formulations and assumptions remain unchanged.

ORIGINS

Psychoanalysis is concerned with the functioning of the mind, a subject that has long fascinated mankind. It is impossible to specify when in history mental phenomena and behavior began to be viewed in terms of intrapsychic forces, some of them even below the level of awareness. In medicine it seems that everything can be traced back to Hippocrates, and accordingly, he had much to say about the connection between mental and somatic processes. Likewise, throughout history, physicians, scientists, and philosophers have considered the operations of the mind, and their ideas have been incorporated into the main body of psychoanalysis. Indeed, the first chapter of *The Interpretation of Dreams* (Freud 1900) emphasizes how strikingly modern, in psychoanalytic terms, some of Freud's predecessors were in regard to the structure, origin, and function of dreams.

I will not go into detail about the forerunners of psychoanalysis, as this topic has been covered by others, such as Alexander and Selesnick (1966), Zilboorg and Henry (1941), and, in particular, Ellenberger (1970), whose monumental scholarly treatise deserves special praise. I will outline here only some general principles concerning the approach to mental aberrations that Freud might have used to construct some of his hypotheses.

Mankind has always been fascinated with mental aberrations and have usually been able to concoct a cure for or ascribe some particular significance to psychic events such as dreams and hallucinations. Madness, in particular, has been held in awe through the centuries. Other elements, such as dreams, exert a similar influence, as can be seen from the references to dreams in the Bible and other ancient historical works such as that by Herodotus (1952). Many ancient therapies, unlike some today, also had a rationale, often being based on demonology and the exorcism of demons and devils. The aim of ancient therapies was to discharge such forces and liberate the psyche. An *incubus* or *succubus* was made responsible for a person's insanity (Sprenger and Kraemer 1486), and such destructive influences had to be purged. These early treatments, based on restoring psychic equilibrium by eliminating causes outside the sphere of immediate awareness, are in fact similar to psychoanalysis.

The methods used to eradicate noxious forces residing in the psyche have varied from exorcism by torture to the trephining of the skull. We may be horrified by the cruelty and barbarism of such procedures, but we still administer shock therapy and continue to rationalize its use, and until recently, frontal lobotomies were considered a valid scientific treatment procedure. In fact, Egas Moniz, who was the first to perform psychosurgery, was awarded a Nobel Prize.

Psychoanalysis is highly dependent on the therapist–patient relationship. Known as the talking cure, the procedure, at first, involved no more than the analyst's listening to the patient's associations, an interaction, however, that was not entirely new. For example, in one of Aristophanes' comedies (Aristophanes 1955), a merchant approaches Socrates with a request as to how he might be able to better cheat his customers. Socrates suggests that the merchant lie down on a couch and freely tell him what comes to his mind. The merchant puts up some resistance to Socrates' instructions, but Socrates persists and forces the merchant to reveal himself. At this point, however, this episode deviates from the psychoanalytic relationship because Socrates is judgmental and uses what he hears against the merchant to criticize and admonish him. This must be one of the earliest, if not the earliest, reference to using the couch in therapy. Free association, on the other hand, was a fairly common theme, and so Freud was familiar with the idea of free association and with the major writers who wrote about this method of communication. For example, he quoted Börn, who advised would-be writers to write down, for three days, every thought that occurred to them, without any regard for organization, coherence, or relevance (Jones 1953). Börn apparently believed that this procedure would release the writer's creative potential, leading Freud to conclude that this also represented a means of gaining access to the hidden recesses of the mind.

The mind has elements that cannot immediately be known; that is, parts of it are unconscious, or below the level of conscious awareness. An awareness of an unconscious mind, in one fashion or another, has frequently been mentioned in literature and also dates back to antiquity. Freud was an extensive reader and so was acquainted with the numerous references to hidden mental phenomena. He was aware that reaching into the depths of people's souls preoccupied poets and philosophers as well as physicians and scientists. He was fascinated with unconscious mental phenomena, as evidenced by his early interest in and practice of hypnosis. Freud also recognized that such unconscious phenomena were related to his patients' problems and became ever more convinced of this during the year he spent in Paris attending Charcot's lectures.

As Freud developed his concept of the unconscious, he openly acknowledged his debt to Nietzsche (1937) and Spinoza (1952). He also was greatly influenced by Herbart (Jones 1953), whose concepts were strikingly similar to those that Freud proposed. Freud, unlike Herbart, however, derived his formulations from clinical events and applied them to the study of psychopathology.

The procedure of free association, the concept of psychic determinism, and the unconscious mind were not controversial. No one before Freud, however, had put them together, and in doing so, Freud liberated psychic determinism from demonology and developed free association as a vehicle to explore the unconscious mind. That is, he created a conceptually consistent frame of reference that enabled him to understand and treat his patients. Often creative accomplishments consist of a synthesis of seemingly unconnected and disparate enclaves of data. Freud was able to draw from the unconnected insights of predecessors who speculated about various facets of the mind, but who were not able to extend them sufficiently so that they could be clinically useful.

Indeed, the construction of psychoanalysis is the work of a single person, Sigmund Freud. Freud had no mentors and, at the beginning, very few colleagues and students. He had to work alone for many years, years that he referred to as "splendid isolation" (Freud 1914d, 1925a).

OPPOSITION

Any great idea or new paradigm creates opposition, according to Kuhn (1962). In fact, Kuhn stated, no new model or system of thought gains acceptance from the older scientific generation. Rather, each innovation foments a "revolution" and has to wait for integration into the accepted body of knowledge until the younger generation gains ascendency. The problem with psychoanalysis may have been even more complicated because those opposing it were not confined to a well-defined group of professionals; instead, its critics came from many different groups, including physicians, psychologists, psychiatrists, educators, and intellectuals, many of whom had no training, experience, or expertise in psychoanalysis.

By postulating the existence of an unconscious mind, Freud made people's inability to know themselves a basic tenet of psychoanalysis: Only a small portion of the mind is knowable, even though critics of psychoanalysis often insist that they do know themselves or that there is nothing beyond their self-appraisal that exists or requires knowing, but Freud (1914c) felt that his new perspective of human nature made inroads into such narcissism, and he compared this aspect of his work with the discoveries of Copernicus and Darwin:

1. Copernicus's demolition of the geocentric theory threatened man's omnipotence by placing him on a planet that does not represent a central position around which the rest of the world revolves. Therefore, the inhabitants of earth do not occupy the most important position in the universe.
2. Darwin's theory of evolution, in a similar manner, shook man's belief in his uniqueness. Instead of being specially created by God, the human species had evolved from lower beasts and is not fundamentally different. Our species can be understood as being part of a continuum rather than being a divine breed separate and distinct from all the beasts that roam the earth.
3. Now psychoanalysis asserts that man is not even in control of his mind. There are hidden, unknown forces within him that dictate his thoughts and behavior.

It is easy to understand why Freud would be unpopular, and no matter how convincing his arguments may be on an intellectual level, they pale when pitted against a reactive sense of personal humiliation and indignation.

FREUD'S BACKGROUND AND TRAINING

Because the beginnings of psychoanalysis are exclusively connected with Freud, we should know something about his background. Freud was born in Moravia in 1856, but when he was very young his family moved to Vienna. Freud did well in school, where he was repeatedly the first in his class. He showed a great interest in history, classical literature, and languages. He spoke French, English, and Spanish and had a working and reading knowledge of other languages, including Latin and Greek. Some of his early letters are truly remarkable for their sophistication and erudition (Freud 1969). Despite his interest in the humanities, he pursued science as a profession.

After graduating with honors from the Gymnasium, Freud went to medical school. However, he was not particularly interested in treating patients (Freud 1925a, 1950), as he did not feel comfortable with the current therapeutic approaches, most of which did not have a scientific rationale. Freud's main interest, instead, was research. When he graduated from medical school, he did not relish the prospect of private practice, and so he postponed his final clinical training in order to work for the world-renowned neurophysiologist Brücke, spending the next eight years doing research in Brücke's laboratory.

Freud's interest in experimentation and investigation dated back to his adolescence. The discoverer of the Oedipus complex and castration anxiety wrote his first published article about his having found the hidden testes of a particular species of eel, an animal whose testes had never been previously located. This work was done when Freud was only 21 (Freud 1877b).

Freud was a serious, hard-working person. From his letters and autobiographical articles (Freud 1914d, 1925a), he appears to have had a single-minded ambition to become famous. He was the antithesis of the gay, carefree, romantic seeker of truth and conqueror of the mysterious unknown, comparing himself to a conquistador and identifying with Hannibal struggling against tremendous odds.

While working in Brücke's laboratory Freud fell in love with Martha Bernays. Indeed, his letters to Martha are the only evidence, and it is only indirect evidence, that Freud had sexual feelings. These letters were passionate but by no means erotic. It is ironic that the man who made *sex* a household word did not seem personally preoccupied with the subject. Still, it was during his courtship and early years of marriage that Freud began making inferences about the sexual etiology of the neuroses.

After completing his clinical training as a neurologist and psychiatrist, Freud started his private practice. At that time, most of the people who consulted neurologists were psychoneurotics. Because of his scientific background and the natural bent of his mind, however, Freud was not content with the superficial therapies currently being employed, such as massage, hydrotherapy, and Faradic stimulation. Indeed, we would classify these today as nondynamic behavioristic approaches that had no relevance to the underlying psychic processes. Drug treatment was strictly palliative and often was founded on no rationale whatsoever, such as prescribing tincture of Valerium as a remedy for hysteria.

Freud was familiar with hypnosis, but as a therapeutic method it had little respectability because of the cult created around it by Mesmer. Although Mesmer was a scholar (see Ellenberger 1970), his activities were considered, at that time and later, to be melodramatic, magical manipulations associated with charlatans. Nonetheless, the French school, under the leadership of Charcot in Paris and Liebault and Bernheim in Nancy, began using hypnosis to treat hysterical patients, and in many instances, they were able to relieve them of their symptoms.

Freud was eager to learn more about this treatment of hysterical patients, as many of the patients seen in a psychiatrist's private practice were suffering from hysteria with dramatic somatic symptoms. When he was in his late twenties, therefore, he decided to go to France and attend the great Charcot's popular demonstrations. He was able to obtain a grant to spend approximately one year with French neurologists and psychiatrists (the distinction between a psychiatrist and a neurologist was then by no means clear-cut). Charcot was a good teacher and greatly influenced Freud. Freud was also impressed by the Nancy school, especially by Bernheim's demonstrations of posthypnotic phenomena. The energy the French put in their therapeutic endeavors stood in sharp contrast with the detached, emotionally uninvolved approach of Freud's German colleagues, who apparently confined their observations to only surface phenomena.

Freud derived many hypotheses from his stay in France that benefited the first patients he treated. The main proposition that he formulated, based on Bernheim's experiments with posthypnotic suggestion, was that part of the mind is largely unknown and can be understood only by inference or through hypnosis. This part of the mind, known as the unconscious, nevertheless, affects both feelings and behavior, and Freud was quick to perceive that it was responsible for the formation of symptoms.

Even though the existence of an unconscious mind had been known for centuries, an unconscious that is active and influences the psyche was Freud's discovery, and became the fundamental hypothesis of psychoanalysis. This principle of a dynamic unconscious and the concept of psychic determinism represent the foundations of psychoanalysis. These unique and fundamental assumptions enabled Freud to view his patients, especially hysterics, from a different viewpoint. These new hypotheses also appealed to his scientific outlook because he could envision a series of rational process connections between the deeper recesses of the personality and seemingly irrational, purposeless symptoms. Freud believed that everything, even painful and apparently self-defeating symptoms, had a purpose. He was, even in the early days of psychoanalysis, espousing the adaptive viewpoint.

When his stay in France ended, Freud returned to Vienna, and because he had been supported by a grant, he had to report his findings to the medical society. He was disappointed with the reception of his ideas and never again attended a meeting of that society. Ellenberger (1970), however, produced data, such as some of the discussions in that meeting, that seem to indicate that Freud had been overly sensitive. Nevertheless, whatever the medical society's reactions were, Freud encountered considerable opposition from both the public and the scientific community. He evoked strong, impassioned responses, many of them hastily contrived without deliberation. Much of the opposition he stimulated was based on emotional and personal factors rather than rational evaluation. He had, indeed, threatened his world's narcissistic complacency.

Although the emotional responses of Freud's medical colleagues can be interpreted differently, their reactions to his report are much more certain. First, hysteria was at that time an emotional illness exclusively confined to women. This is, in itself, an interesting example of primary-process thinking, that is, thinking that follows the laws of the unconscious rather than the laws that govern coherent, rational, logical thought processes. The physicians at that time based their conclusions on the fact that *hysteria* is a Greek word meaning "wandering uterus." Only a woman has a uterus, and so how could a man develop hysteria? Freud dispelled this notion by citing clinical examples of male hysteria with dramatic somatic symptoms, and his audience was not pleased with the prospect of having to change their firmly entrenched attitudes.

Freud must have further threatened his audience when he indicated that he was not viewing psychoneurotic patients from a purely descriptive viewpoint. Having ignored the significance of a label such as hysteria, he continued his discourse by emphasizing that there were unconscious conflicts behind the flamboyant symptoms. Although Freud meant by this that he was introducing a new perspective, he went beyond the limits of propriety when he suggested that these unconscious forces contained sexual feelings. Some of the then-current literature indicates that this was not entirely a new theory, but Freud elaborated on it, incorporating these new ideas about sexuality into a consistent conceptual system that became the basis of his psychodynamic approach.

I cannot help but believe that Freud's youth (he was hardly 30) did not make the situation any easier for him. He was reporting to his elders in order to justify the money that he had received for his trip. Instead, I conjecture that he must have sounded like an authority lecturing to his students. Of course, it is impossible to know exactly how Freud related to his audience, but we know from many of his letters and articles that he could be very proud of his ideas and expected others to treat them with the same respect. I doubt that he paid much attention to age differences or his lack of clinical experience when compared with that of his elders. It must be remembered, too, that this was the same Freud who gratefully accepted the task of translating into German the charismatic Charcot's textbook and then had the temerity to make annotations and add footnotes expressing his own opinions and criticisms. As might be expected, Charcot was not pleased.

Some years later, Freud further offended the mid-Victorian scientific community when he postulated the existence of infantile sexuality (1905b). He had already attacked his colleagues' narcissistic complacency and feelings of superiority by demonstrating his ability to see far beyond his mentors' sphere. Indeed, it is a wonder that he was not completely ostracized. Nevertheless, he must have had some friends, and one of them, Joseph Breuer, became a very important person in Freud's life.

Breuer was a prominent Viennese internist who apparently liked and respected Freud. He even lent him money to help him get started in practice and to set up a household. Breuer was also interested in treating hysterical patients by dealing with the basic causes of their disorders. To that end, he used hypnosis as a method of uncovering underlying conflicts, rather than simply suggesting away the symptoms, as Charcot and Janet had done (Ellenberger 1970).

EARLY PSYCHOANALYTIC CONCEPTS

Freud also used hypnosis as his main therapeutic tool, but before he conferred with Breuer, he had not as yet formulated a therapeutic approach or rationale. Though he was not completely satisfied with Charcot's methods, Freud also used suggestion, though indirectly. In an early paper on hypnotherapy (1892), Freud described therapy as a "clashing of wills." The patient's will was responsible for her clinging to her symptoms. Freud conceptualized treatment as a struggle in which he attempted to help the patient develop a counterwill against the symptoms, so to speak. This line of reasoning appears somewhat bizarre, but it is, nevertheless, interesting, because a few years later he discussed resistance, an invariant response to treatment, in similar terms. To some measure, this struggle of wills, whether the patient's will and counterwill or the patient's will and the analyst's counterwill, remains part of many current, so-called classical, analyses.

Freud was intrigued by some of Breuer's ideas. Breuer treated a patient, known as Anna O., by administering hypnosis daily. He believed that her illness, which had many bizarre symptoms—such as fugue states, amnesia, visual and auditory hallucinations, and somatic symptoms such as a persistent cough and occasional paralysis—could be traced back to psychic trauma. The patient, however, could not recall the trauma, and so it had to be unearthed in the hypnotic trance.

Breuer reasoned that when the trauma occurred, the anxiety that would ordinarily be felt, was not, for some reason. It had become "strangulated," according to Breuer, and so the therapeutic task was to release it, to discharge it so that the trauma would not remain pent up in the psyche and create deleterious effects. This process introduced new words into the technical vocabulary, such as *catharsis* and *abreaction*, which refer to discharging blocked affects. In the now-classic volume coauthored by Breuer and Freud—a book that Freud considered to be the first psychoanalytic publication (Breuer and Freud 1895)—they described the treatment of patients considered to be hysterics, by bringing to consciousness their hidden complexes and feelings.

Reichard (1956) questioned whether these early patients were actually hysterics. Their symptoms, especially those of Breuer's Anna O., were so bizarre that they seemed to be suffering from a more severe condition than a psychoneurosis. There are considerable data regarding Anna O., who was the well-known Bertha Pappenheim and the founder of the social work movement (see Pollack 1973).

Freud concluded that the traumas underlying neuroses that had to be brought into consciousness were sexual traumas, a point that Breuer at first accepted but later questioned. Breuer preferred to believe that because the affect was strangulated, the traumatic memory had become encapsulated in what he called a *hypnoid mental state*. Today, we would interpret this to mean that the ego has undergone fragmentation—a split—and that the trauma is retained in the portion of the ego that is dissociated from the main psychic stream. Though it was not recognized at the time, this is a formulation of psychopathology based on structural changes—splitting—and it is similar to current formulations regarding character disorders that are chiefly concerned with defects in structure. Freud, however, believed that Breuer's ideas represented a throwback to the antiquated and judgmental formulations regarding patients suffering from emotional illness, particularly hysteria, as being degenerate. Janet viewed hysterics as having weak egos because of their tendency to dissociate; they did not have the strength and cohesion to maintain a unified whole, and this was considered a sign of moral inferiority.

Freud also became dissatisfied with the use of hypnosis as the main therapeutic modality. He learned that he could not hypnotize all the patients that came to see him, and he was not comfortable with its magical implications and melodramatic features. He was also unhappy that what his patients revealed during a deep hypnotic trance they could not remember when awake, and so whatever insight the therapist might have gained was not emotionally available to them.

In "Studies on Hysteria" (Breuer and Freud 1895), Freud related an interesting and significant episode with one of his female hysteric patients. Apparently she had just had a massage and was relaxing on the table when Freud dropped in to inquire how she was getting along. Not explicitly acknowledging his presence, she started talking in a seemingly random fashion. When reading these passages, I could almost see Freud as it dawned on him that he was gathering valuable information that helped him understand many aspects of her psychopathology that had previously eluded him. But this time he was collecting data while listening to a patient who was fully conscious and not in a hypnotic trance. He thus could now discard hypnosis. In this way, free association was discovered, a treatment method that has become the hallmark of psychoanalysis.

According to "Studies on Hysteria," Freud had devised a clinically useful system that enabled him to understand and treat those patients that he considered to be psychoneurotic. He had formulated both a conceptual system to explain psychopathology based on sexual traumas—which he determined as having occurred during childhood (Freud 1894, 1896)—and a method of treatment that no longer required hypnosis but instead relied on the patient's free associating (the uninhibited, noncritical expression of thoughts and feelings). In "Studies on Hysteria," Freud also discussed transference and resistance.

It is amazing how many of the essential features of psychoanalysis can be found in this first volume. In a moment of generosity and perhaps sentimentality, Freud credited Breuer as being the discoverer of psychoanalysis, but later (Freud 1914d), he withdrew this tribute and emphatically stated that he had been its sole innovator as well as its only practitioner for many years.

Breuer's enthusiasm for the subject cooled after Anna O. developed a pseudocyesis, naming him the father. Though Freud viewed Anna O.'s reaction as the outcome of a sexual trauma, Breuer was still upset. Breuer, in turn, made public the fact that he had changed his mind about the sexual etiology of the neuroses, and his close relationship with Freud dissolved.

Part II

MAPPING THE UNCONSCIOUS

Chapter 2

METAPSYCHOLOGY: THE POINTS OF VIEW OF PSYCHOANALYSIS

Metapsychology is a term coined by Freud to indicate a psychology that embraces different points of view, a psychology that makes investigations in different frames of references simultaneously. Freud's intention was to understand psychopathology, but the metapsychological approach is not limited to psychic aberrations, as it encompasses all mental functioning. Freud's first mention of the word *metapsychology* occurs in *The Psychopathology of Everyday Life* (1901). In this book he discussed behavioral phenomena that are the obvious manifestations of unconscious processes but are not necessarily the outcome of emotional illness, for example, familiar occurrences such as lapses of memory and slips of the tongue which indicate more the power of the unconscious than defective functioning.

Freud's greatest insights, as well as his first model, were derived from this study of nonpathological phenomena, especially those in his *Interpretation of Dreams* (1900). From his study of the dream process, Freud drew a picture to describe it that has been frequently referred to as the *picket fence model*. This was a simple diagram of a horizontal line with perpendiculars at each end, one representing the sensory end of the psychic apparatus and the other the motor end where discharges take place. Between these two lines is a series of other lines that depict memory traces. Freud also described in the *Interpretation of Dreams* another model which could be called the *topographic hypothesis* and which he elaborated on later in "The Unconscious" (1915c).

THE TOPOGRAPHIC HYPOTHESIS

As we have stated, psychoanalysis began with the assumption of the existence of the dynamic unconscious, an unconscious that belongs to levels below those concerned with awareness but that continues affecting these higher levels. To construct the conceptual foundations of psychoanalysis, Freud needed to locate the unconscious somewhere in the psychic sphere; that is, he needed a basic anatomy of the mental apparatus before he could deal with dynamic psychic processes. This anatomical analogy must have suited Freud, as he was somewhat of an anatomist when he worked in Brücke's laboratory, and in fact one of the chapters of "New Introductory Lectures on Psychoanalysis" (1933) is entitled "The Anatomy of the Psychic Apparatus."

To locate the unconscious in the psyche required a juxtaposition with other psychic structures that could somehow be placed on a continuum with consciousness. Freud wanted to base his "anatomy" on an hierarchical continuum connecting the lower, unstructured levels with the higher, more-structured organizations. To achieve this, Freud made the phenomenon of consciousness an axis around which he could organize the various structures included in the structural hypothesis.

In his topographic hypothesis Freud did not explain the concept of psychic structure. Rather, he was more interested in topography, that is, the landmarks, locations, and positions of various structures relative to one another. To complete this model, he had to include something about the functions of various structures, as is commonly done in anatomy, for example, when describing the origins and insertions of muscles or blood vessels, or cardiac chambers and their valves. Freud therefore concentrated on the act of a psychic element's becoming conscious.

The topographic hypothesis divides the mind into three parts, but Freud did not specify their sizes nor did he separate, by rigid boundaries, one from the other. He proposed a spectrum beginning with a level consisting of the *unconscious*, moving up to the *preconscious*, and finally reaching the highest level of the *conscious*.

Though Freud was inexact as to the extent of each of these areas, it is clear that the realm of the unconscious is much larger than that of the conscious. This can be easily inferred from Freud's iceberg analogy (1916–1917), in which he compared the mind to an iceberg, four-fifths of which is hidden under water and only one-fifth appears above the surface. The relative size of the preconscious thus remains obscure, although by inference it is probably much smaller than that of the unconscious. However, as Freud (1925c) later indicated, the preconscious must be substantial when placed alongside consciousness, whose content is extremely limited (1900, 1916–1917, 1924b, 1925c).

The topographic hypothesis also clarified and simplified various phenomena. In this model, Freud distinguished between the unconscious as an area of the mind and as a quality of mental processes. To emphasize this distinction, when the unconscious refers to a part of the mind and a system, it is designated as *Ucs*, the preconscious as *Pcs*, and the conscious as *Cs*. When the unconscious refers to a quality of a mental event, it is abbreviated as *Unc*. However, consciousness is a quality that belongs only to the conscious system (Cs) and, therefore, does not require a distinguishing abbreviation. This is further justified in that the act of becoming conscious elevates a psychic element into the area of the conscious. Thus, the quality of consciousness is restricted to just one part of the mind, in contrast with the quality of unconscious, which can occur in both the unconscious (Ucs) and the preconscious (Pcs).

Freud noted that his patients often found it impossible to recall emotionally traumatic events, to bring to the surface material that might help explain the patient's symptoms or lead to abreactions that involved the reenactment of significant conflicts. The same resistance to bringing some memory or thought to consciousness was also prominent in nonpathological circumstances as well, what Freud called the *psychopathology of everyday life* (1901). The familiar phenomenon of lapses of memory, often described as having something on the tip of the tongue, is an excellent example. The harder we try to remember under such circumstances, the more difficult it is to recapture what we have lost. This inaccessibility to consciousness is a quality that Freud attributed to the system Ucs. The pathway to Cs is blocked.

The Pcs is somewhat different in that it has easy access to the Cs. A Pcs thought or memory quickly becomes conscious when attention is focused on it. The Pcs contains what psychoanalysts call *memory traces*. Sensory impressions, thoughts—that is, whatever occurs in the external world—or sensations originating in the internal world of the psyche after passing through the system Cs are registered and stored in the Pcs as memory traces. This does not mean, however, that everything that a person experiences is kept in the Pcs or, for that matter, slips into the Ucs if it is not used. Certain bits of information may no longer be relevant in the present, such as an old address or a telephone number of many years ago. For a memory trace to remain in the preconscious, therefore, it has to be periodically revitalized (see section on psychoeconomic hypothesis).

Freud has been misunderstood to have stated that nothing is ever lost to the psyche. Rather, it is either retained and stored in the system Pcs, or it is confined to the depths of the Ucs where it remains chained, though it struggles to reach the upper levels of the systems Pcs and Cs. (Freud often depicted psychic operations by anthropomorphizing the inner processes as doing battle with one another.) In any case, Freud did not mean that everything experienced is always preserved in the psyche: some things may be lost because they are no longer significant.

The topographic hypothesis emphasizes the connections among the three systems, Ucs, Pcs, and Cs. The Pcs creates a barrier between itself and the Ucs, but as I stated, it communicates freely with the Cs. Between the Pcs and the Ucs, Freud postulated a *censor* that guards the Pcs against the intrusions or assaults of the Ucs. This is another example of Freud's vivid anthropomorphizing. However, the pathway between the Pcs and the Cs is not entirely open either. Freud (1915c) formulated the existence of a second censor that prevents the Pcs's content from entering the Cs. He did not expand on this theme but seemed to indicate that this second censor is not as strict or rigid as is the first censor. I believe that these almost parenthetical remarks about a second censor are important because they imply that *there may be a certain intrinsic psychic inertia that restricts the free movement of mental elements from the less-structured to the more-structured psychic strata.*

This inhibition is based on hierarchical differences of psychic structure, in contrast to the censor that blocks the Ucs content from pushing into the Pcs and eventually into the Cs. The latter is based on a conflict between the Pcs and the Ucs, conflicting vectors being the essence of the psychodynamic hypothesis. The second censor that Freud described can be found at every stratum of the psychic apparatus that is further structuralized than the preceding one. Freud conjectured that the mind may have many censors.

Freud wrote very little about the system Cs. The editors of the *Standard Edition* believe that at least one of his papers on metapsychology that has been lost dealt with the psychology of conscious processes. It is interesting that Freud first wrote about the Cs in his *Interpretation of Dreams* and later in "A Note on the Mystic Writing Pad" (Freud 1925c), neither of which discuss either psychopathology or clinical issues. Most likely, Freud wanted to study both the phenomenon and the topography of consciousness in the context of a general psychology that went beyond psychopathology.

Freud did not conceptualize the system Cs as a definitive one, as he had with the Ucs and the Pcs. Rather, he viewed it as a sort of mirror that illuminates elements in the adjoining Pcs. Its range, however, is narrow in that it can include only a limited number of impressions at any one time. This makes sense if we consider that we can think of only one thing at a time and that the number of sensory impressions of which we are aware at any given moment is restricted.

Does the system Cs have a location similar to those of the Ucs and Pcs, in that elements from these lower levels eventually enter a specific area? Freud wrote about the movement of the Ucs content into the Pcs (1915c), but he was vague about something similar occurring between the Pcs and the Cs. He liked optical and camera analogies that minimized the lens or mirror as a material entity in favor of its capacity for reflection and illumination, consciousness being the manipulation of such an illumination. Freud could not adequately conceptualize consciousness as a mental quality simply in terms of topography. We need energic factors to understand what is more a function than a location.

Freud had a penchant for dealing with polarities, and his formulation of the topographical hypothesis is an excellent example of his dualistic thinking. Even though this is a tripartite model, it is nevertheless based on the dual polarity of consciousness and unconsciousness. Freud broke away from the traditional unified view that dominated psychology, a psychology that considered only conscious phenomena. If academicians did acknowledge that there were unconscious factors operating in the mind, they viewed them as representing different gradations of consciousness rather than as being qualitatively different. Freud commented that this attitude was tantamount to stating that there was no darkness, only different shades of light. Nevertheless, it was difficult for psychologists to accept that mental processes, such as feelings and thoughts, were not in some way felt and recognized.

The topographical hypothesis served Freud well for many years as he focused his attention on the role of unconscious factors in the production of hysterical and obsessional symptoms. He wrote much about the operations of the system Ucs, what he called *primary process operations*, in contrast with those of the higher systems Pcs and Cs, which are ruled by *secondary process operations*.

What is the pragmatic significance of the topographical hypothesis? As a theoretical system, it is consistent and simple, but for clinicians struggling to understand and treat their patients, the question remains as to how such a model can be used to explain phenomena that otherwise make no sense. Such phenomena, with the exception of the parapraxes (memory lapses and slips of the tongue), are usually manifestations of psychopathology. Under ordinary circumstances, there are few data that justify distinguishing between unconscious and conscious processes. Indeed, this would weaken the feasibility of the mind's tripartite organization that Freud suggested, if it were constructed primarily on a psychopathological axis.

Freud first postulated the topographic hypothesis in *The Interpretation of Dreams*. He also included in this book fairly lengthy discussions of regression and primary process operations, in order to understand dreams. He had to explore the lower recesses of the mind, and yet dreams, because of their universality, cannot be considered to belong exclusively to the domain of psychopathology. The dream represents a psychic event that is far removed from the influence of reality and logical, rational, secondary process mental operations. It is the product of a primitive mental state, and yet it is not necessarily a manifestation of psychopathology.

In order to construct models that reflect the structure of the mind as it ordinarily functions, mental operations had to be intensified, as occurs with psychopathology, so that they could be observed. By establishing the tenets of metapsychology, Freud demonstrated that inferences regarding the mind can be made from studying patients suffering from emotional disorders. The validity of these psychoanalytic formulations has often been challenged, however, as the basic models were derived from the study of patients. As clinicians continue gaining experience, especially with patients fixated at the levels of primitive mental states, they learn that the distinctions between psychopathological and nonpathological processes become increasingly blurred. Studies of emotional development and psychic adaptation, such as longitudinal studies and neonatology, have indicated that Freud's ideas hold up well in regard to their findings and that some of his models serve as useful conceptual scaffolds for their observations.

Inasmuch as psychoanalysis is a depth psychology and focuses on processes of which a person is only partially or perhaps totally unaware, the topographical hypothesis offers the therapist a useful clinical approach. I am referring to distinguishing between unconscious and preconscious elements. For example,

I recall a patient, a young lady in her middle twenties, who had an extraordinary capacity to ignore situations or events that could cause her psychic pain and embarrassment. For example, she had had two bad marriages, but I did not learn about them until she had been in treatment for about 6 months, and then I had to infer their existence from a dream. When I confronted her with not having told me about these obviously important segments of her life, she naively responded in a typically hysterical fashion that she never thought about her former husbands, that they never came to mind. Because I had not specifically asked her about any previous marriages, although I had inquired about emotional attachments, she saw no reason for dwelling on these unpleasant moments in her life.

We could debate whether this patient was deliberately suppressing information for defensive purposes. Was she purposely being evasive and thereby defying the rules of free association? This is possible, but the topographical hypothesis offers us another explanation without forcing us to be critical and judgmental. She could have stored the memories of those marriages in her preconscious and simply not directed the attention of her consciousness to them. Freud (1911a) wrote about consciousness's meeting the preconscious halfway, a "notational" function of attention. My patient apparently directed her attention to current rather than past events. However, she could easily recall past experiences if she wanted to, but with me, she chose not to. This could be an example of a censor between the Pcs and the Cs, as described in the topographical hypothesis. Why this patient did not direct her attention inwardly toward preconscious memory traces is another question that cannot be answered in terms of the topographical hypothesis. Freud devised a metapsychology because he was aware of the mind's multiple dimensions, which require different frames of reference, but to explain motivation he required a psychodynamic hypothesis.

Explaining my patient's not revealing her past marriages as not directing attention to her preconscious is, in a sense, not different from saying that she was suppressing material for defensive reasons. However, the latter, as I mentioned, has critical implications and does not place the patient's reactions in a perspective that illuminates all levels of the psyche. The patient was not remembering—an example of the quality of being unconscious without being part of the system Ucs. Nevertheless, elements in the preconscious, when threatened by the outside world's attempts to unearth them and to bring them into the sphere of conscious awareness, could be drawn into the system unconscious where they could better resist exposure.

The following clinical excerpt from the same patient illustrates the interaction between the system Ucs and the system Pcs. The patient dreamed of being at a ball when a man in a gray suit asked her to dance. As he held her tightly, he backed her against a wall, and she felt his erect penis pressing against her. She was overwhelmed with anxiety and suddenly awakened. After describing the dream, she continued talking but made no reference whatsoever to it. I waited, wondering whether she was free associating to the dream, but as yet I had not been able to establish any connections. As she continued, I felt that she was getting further and further away from the dream or, more precisely, that she was completely disconnected from it. Consequently, I decided to intervene and to ask her about the dream. She replied, "What dream?"

I was convinced that she had blotted the dream out of her memory, and so I gently reminded her that about ten minutes ago, she had told me about a very interesting dream. She again affirmed that she did not recollect telling me about a dream, and so I gave a brief account of what she had reported to me. With some encouragement, she was finally able to remember having had the dream, but not of having talked about it during the session. Still, she did remember the dream, and so I asked her to tell me her associations to it.

She repeated the same sequence of wandering in a seemingly aimless fashion with her associations, again ignoring the dream. Once more, I asked her about the dream, and I received the same response, "What dream?" I confess I was startled at this woman's inability to hold a memory or, rather, her capacity not to remember; in any case, I again told her about the dream and with some difficulty she remembered it for the second time. As might be expected, she continued in the same manner, with the result that the dream was eventually out of sight. In repeating the dream this final time, I added a transference interpretation, pointing out that the man in the gray suit was I. I had planned adding this interpretation while listening to her not talk about the dream, as it was reasonable to assume that she would continue forgetting it. I reasoned that introducing a transference focus might help her anchor the unconscious elements in the here and now of the therapeutic setting, but nothing could have been further from her intention.

At first, the patient blushed. Then she sat up on the couch, tightly grasping its sides. In a shaky voice, she indicated that she was being overwhelmed by a powerful surge of dizziness. She described herself as sitting on the couch, which was rapidly twirling around as it was being sucked into a whirlpool. She felt herself being dragged into its depths. However, she rapidly recovered and gained her composure. She then went on as before in her usual calm manner. I persevered and confronted her with the dream, but this time, no matter how much I dwelled on it, she could remember nothing. I felt as if I were pulling teeth and getting absolutely nowhere. At most, I succeeded in getting her to admit that what I was describing was vaguely familiar, but she was no longer able to feel that the dream belonged to her.

This extraordinary course of events, in my opinion, can be best conceptualized in the framework of the topographical hypothesis, although other views of metapsychology are also applicable. At the level of phenomenological sequences, the topographical approach is the most suitable because it easily explains the movement from remembering to forgetting. When my patient came to her session, her dream resided in her Pcs, and she could easily bring it into consciousness, as she was able to tell me about it. She knew that she was expected to free associate to the dream, with the intention of bringing to consciousness its underlying unconscious content. However, the censor between the Ucs and the Pcs that would have had to be overcome or bypassed, because of internal conflicts, increased its vigilance. This was done in an interesting fashion because I was covertly trying to break it down with my expectations of analyzing the dream. Therefore, in order to reinforce the censor by weakening the impact of elements in the system Ucs that would force their way past the censor to the Pcs, the patient pushed the preconscious dream into the system Ucs, a process we call *repression* (see Chapter 6). Because the dream was outside, that is, below the system Pcs, the patient would not be able to free associate to it, nor would she be able to remember it. The Pcs no longer contained the dream's manifest content, and so the patient could not bring derivatives of the Ucs to attach them to Pcs dream content that, in turn, would pass through the Cs and be communicated to the therapist.

The patient was clearly resisting my efforts to examine the dream, which would require that she remember it. When I interrupted her, so as to get her on the track of dream analysis, she was safe because the dream was not at her disposal. When I seized the transference element by interpreting the erotic transference, however, this momentarily upset her psychic equilibrium. Recognizing the underlying unconscious impulses that were responsible for the dream content and for introducing them to the patient's consciousness—that is, having them reflected in the system Cs—the censor weakened, releasing the sexual impulses that had been banished to the system Ucs in the dream package. My interpretation took her by surprise, inasmuch as it unlocked the gates of her unconscious and allowed the impulses responsible for the dream's manifest content to rush out and overwhelm her. Her reactions depicted her inner turmoil, her sensations of dizziness and of the couch spinning around, and her being sucked into a whirlpool. The latter might have been the sensory manifestation of the psyche's attempts to push back what had escaped from the Pandora's box of her unconscious.

Of course, these explanations are incomplete and do not tell us anything about the patient's conflicts, her sexual feelings, the types of defenses she used, and other features that would help us understand her character structure and the problems that caused her to seek treatment. Still, this initial view of metapsychology helps put many phenomena into a coherent perspective. Today, many years after Freud's first attempts to understand his patients, the topographical hypothesis can again be useful, as we study patients who can be best understood in terms of defective "anatomy" rather than psychodynamic disequilibrium.

Another patient, a middle-aged housewife, often forgot her appointments, even though she had a fixed four-times-a-week schedule. She would always be quite dismayed about her forgetfulness, explaining that she might have forgotten to note the appointment times on her weekly calendar or might have started doing something, like reading a book or writing a letter, and simply continued with the task on hand, never thinking about the appointment. It would have been easy to interpret her failure to keep appointments as a resistance to treatment or an acting out of hostile feelings toward me, and this would have been correct, except that it would have missed some essential features of this patient's character structure.

I noted a discontinuity from session to session. She would, during a particular session, work herself into a frenzy about certain social injustices that she was working hard on committees to correct. She seemed totally absorbed by this particular project, and her feelings were so strong that I wondered whether she was somewhat paranoid. She also promised me that the next day when she came to her session she would bring me letters and transcripts that would reveal the insidious totalitarian forces threatening our society. Some of the arguments obviously had merit, but the intensity of her involvement betrayed her underlying psychopathology. Because of my previous experiences with similar patients, I expected a long and persistent preoccupation with these issues. My therapeutic efforts would be constricted by a state of siege as the patient threw herself into battles in the external world that would protect her from my attempts to make inroads into her inner mental world. I could not have been more mistaken.

To my surprise, she brought no literature to the next session, and she did not even mention the issues with which she had been involved on the previous day. Instead she talked about all the injustices that she had suffered from her father as a child, and indeed, there were many. She saw her father as emotionally and, to a lesser extent, physically brutalizing her while her mother stood by doing nothing, either being unable or unwilling to protect her. Again, I had the impression that she would focus on this theme for a long time, but she did not.

During the next session she talked about her marriage, not

mentioning her father once. Again she focused on injustices in the sense that her husband was inconsiderate and insensitive, but unlike her father, he was not brutal. She felt no support from him. During another session, she might spend the whole time discussing her adolescent children, sometimes in a similar vein, emphasizing their selfishness, rudeness, and rebellion, or she might concentrate in a concerned and warm, empathic manner on their need for help. Each session seemed to be a self-contained unit with little connection with the previous one. Perhaps a thread of feeling assaulted or exploited, a paranoid flavor, ran through many of her sessions, but even this was not a consistent pattern.

Understandably, I often felt that I was seeing a different patient each time that I saw her. I began viewing her as a fragmented character who presented different facets of herself at different times. She functioned adequately in her daily life, but she was wealthy and had maids to take care of her house; her children were more or less self-sufficient; and her husband made no demands. She spent most of her time writing congressmen, attending meetings, or serving on committees, and so even if her personality were poorly synthesized, it would not necessarily be apparent.

This patient's approach to life appeared superficial. She gave the impression of being shallow and removed from deeper feelings, if indeed she had them. She was not close to anyone, and she was not involved with anything but her projects. I felt that I was facing only the upper layer of her personality and seldom heard any derivatives from her unconscious; for example, she never reported a dream.

Although many explanations of her behavior are possible, I believe that this was another instance that can be explained by the topographic hypothesis. We might envision this patient as having a disorganized preconscious in which memory traces were not efficiently categorized. The dates and times of her appointments were haphazardly thrown around rather than being neatly filed so that they could be easily found when needed. In other words, consciousness could have been easily directed toward them if it had some knowledge of their location. This phenomenon has been described as a freely mobile quality of the perceptual system, as preconscious content meets consciousness halfway.

In addition to the Pcs's being disorderly, it is rigid and immobile in regard to the beacon of consciousness (Freud 1900). When my patient's attention was focused on a specific task, she was unable to turn away from it to revive the memory of an appointment time. The searchlight of her consciousness was somewhat frozen in that it could not turn. It could not turn away from a fixation on the outer world to illuminate an aspect, even a superficial aspect, of the internal world, the memory traces of the Pcs. Later in analysis, I was able to ascertain that to a lesser extent, this patient used these defects in the systems Cs and Pcs to defend against access to the content of the Ucs (see Chapter 6), but this was a manifestation of the analytic interaction rather than an intrinsic factor of her psychopathology. Still, by avoiding her appointments, she could effectively curtail any efforts of the treatment interaction to make contact with the deeper levels of her personality. I do not believe, however, that this was a primary motive.

Nevertheless, there are many patients, perhaps the majority of those seen in analysis, who directly resist the analyst's attempts to reach down into the Ucs. They may resist the analyst's request that they free associate, as Freud described in the "Studies on Hysteria" (Breuer and Freud 1895). Patients use a variety of defenses to protect their psyches from encroachments from the Ucs (see Chapter 6), but the most elemental defense, as demonstrated by the patient who repeatedly forgot her dream during a session, is *repression*, which simply means that some psychic forces (in the topographic hypothesis, referred to as *censors*) directly bar, turn away, or push back derivatives from the Ucs trying to break through into the Pcs.

The phenomenon of repression made Freud aware of the limitations of the topographic hypothesis. He found that the rigid compartmentalization of mental systems that characterizes the topographical hypothesis makes it difficult to find the psychic location of a process such as repression. Clinical observation reveals that patients are usually not aware of repressing. They may feel some tension or uneasiness, but except for lapses of memory—which Freud called *parapraxes* and described in

The Psychopathology of Everyday Life (Freud 1901)—most patients are not aware of repressing. This means that this defense, as is true of all defenses, contains the quality of being unconscious but is located in the system Pcs rather than in the Ucs. It must be positioned in the Pcs because it guards the Pcs from the intended onslaughts of the Ucs. There are also other reasons that repression must be attributed to the preconscious levels of the personality that concern the production of anxiety, and I shall discuss these later in Chapter 5.

Regarding the topographic hypothesis, Freud discovered that he was faced with an inconsistency. If the phenomenon of repression belonged to the Pcs but possessed qualities of the Ucs, then how could it be counted among the other preconscious elements? True, the contents of the preconscious usually possess the quality of unconscious, but unlike unconscious elements, they can usually be made conscious. It is characteristic of the processes or elements relegated to the Ucs that they cannot, without intense effort, be made conscious. Repression, as I stated, is usually not a conscious phenomenon and cannot, without considerable struggle, become conscious. Therefore, it should properly belong to the Ucs, but it cannot if it is to guard the Pcs. The situation becomes even more confusing when we note that the reason that unconscious elements do not have access to consciousness is because they are repressed, the outcome of repression. These conceptual inconsistencies are difficult to resolve.

Perhaps the site of repression could be placed adjacent to the Pcs but not within it. The censor could be standing at the border, barring the entrance to the Pcs. Freud was particularly fond of such metaphors, especially those that depicted the psyche as a military outpost (Freud 1909b, 1916–1917). To pursue the metaphor further, the instigator of repression would be placed in a type of "no man's land," an outpost on the outskirts of the Pcs. This model presents difficulties because (1) as discussed, the repressive process possesses qualities found only in the Ucs but, according to this metaphor, it is located neither in the Ucs nor in the Pcs and (2) the psyche is now chopped up into fragments rather than being viewed as a smooth continuum in which the lower layers gradually become structuralized as psychic elements move toward upper levels. This formulation thus requires a view of the mind as discontinuous, a movement from the Ucs to an intermediate area that is merely a receptacle for processes that cannot be placed anywhere else, to the Pcs, and finally to the Cs. This is an *ad hoc* and clumsy model that has little explanatory value.

Freud (1923a) faced another problem with the topographic hypothesis when he tried to understand the *unconscious sense of guilt* on the basis of such a model. He had encountered patients in his practice whose actions were self-defeating, although they were not particularly aware of it. In treatment such unconscious guilt causes a *negative therapeutic reaction*, which means that the patient attempts to foil the analyst's efforts to help him resolve his conflicts. Just when an analytic resolution seems likely, that is, when the patient is making significant progress, he does something to defeat what has been accomplished, or he blocks further progress, perhaps by terminating treatment.

There are many factors involved in the unconscious sense of guilt, which I shall discuss later. Here, I merely wish to emphasize that as with repression, Freud was facing a similar dilemma with unconscious guilt. Guilt both encompasses higher levels of the personality and possesses qualities that are characteristic of the system Ucs. Once again, the topographical hypothesis does not provide a location in which to place such a complicated process.

Both repression and the unconscious sense of guilt are associated with psychopathology. However, in his explorations of the unconscious, Freud began to understand that the unconscious participated significantly in all mental activity and was not confined simply to psychopathology. Freud (1901) had written about the unconscious when discussing parapraxes, and he also concentrated on the role of unconscious factors in the production of great works of art and in the character structure of geniuses (Freud 1910b, 1914a, 1917a). The psychoanalytic viewpoint focuses on unconscious processes and attempts to understand and interpret behavior, activities, and even ways of thinking in terms of unconscious derivatives. This view emphasizes that when studying mental processes, there is no clear-cut distinction between conscious and unconscious factors, which becomes especially clear when examining creative endeavors.

Freud did not study creativity per se. If he had, he might have had difficulty, as he did with repression and the unconscious sense of guilt, placing it in the perspective of the topographic hypothesis. The creative act is a mixture of mental operations that are characteristic of both unconscious and preconscious processes, that is, a combination of primary process thinking that uses primitive thinking mechanisms (see Chapter 4) and logical thought operations that emphasize etiological sequences, synthesis, categorization, and other types of organization that Freud discussed as examples of *secondary elaboration* (1900), or secondary process. During creative accomplishments, all levels of the personality participate, and at moments, the lower levels are dominant in that they come to the surface. The topographical hypothesis implies a rigid, unalterable sequence that does not have the flexibility or mobility essential to the creative act.

Consequently, Freud needed another model to depict the structure of the mind that would enable psychoanalysis to include phenomena that went beyond its initial field of observation. He required a conceptual scheme that stressed hierarchies of structure, as the treatment of patients repeatedly brought to light, because of therapeutic regression to early phases of psychic development. Psychoanalysts (Abraham 1924, Ferenczi 1955) were beginning to understand that the stages of emotional development that Freud had outlined (Freud 1905b, 1916–1917) were more than just theoretical abstractions. They represented the content of fixations and regressions (see Chapter 3) that characterize the analytic process as the patient becomes more deeply involved in treatment. Clinicians appreciate that there are no clear-cut boundaries between the various levels of the personality; rather, these various levels blend with one another. Freud had to construct the structural hypothesis.

THE STRUCTURAL HYPOTHESIS

The *structural hypothesis* is also a tripartite model consisting of the now-familiar id, ego, and superego. The id corresponds to the system Ucs whereas the ego also has elements of the system Ucs as well as the Pcs and Cs. The superego is a part of the ego, with specific functions that correspond to those of the censor in the typographic hypothesis. It also contains elements of the systems Ucs, Pcs, and Cs (Freud 1923a).

The topographic hypothesis is a linear model. It could be represented by an arrow, a vector, that depicted a structural progression, based exclusively on how difficult or how easy it is for a psychic element to achieve conscious representation. By contrast, the structural hypothesis is not a simple longitudinal extension from the lower to the higher levels of the personality but both personifies character in breadth and emphasizes stratification.

I purposely used *personify* because this model, more than the topographical hypothesis, is anthropomorphic. The id is viewed as a demon seeking to overwhelm the ego; the superego can be a "tyrannical" taskmaster; and the ego "serves three masters," the id, the superego, and the demands of the external world.

The structural hypothesis is the most comprehensive of all the frames of reference of psychoanalysis and cannot be isolated from the other metapsychological viewpoints, as Freud's more sophisticated concepts of structure cannot be discussed comprehensively without involving some developmental and energic factors. It is therefore difficult to understand the id, ego, and superego without knowing something about their origins and dynamic interrelationships.

According to Freud, the psyche's initial neonatal state consists of an unorganized (not disorganized) amorphous state designated as the id. Freud borrowed the term from Groddeck (1923) because he felt that it had an impersonal quality. In German the word is *das Es*, which in English literally means "it." The translators of Freud's works preferred the Latin version. I believe that it is consistent with the psychoanalytic perspective to view the earliest developmental phases as impersonal, in that feelings, affects, and all the emotional qualities that define humanness gradually develop through interactions with the outer world, beginning with the nurturing and soothing maternal relationship.

This seems clear enough if our purpose is to construct a structural hierarchy. The ego develops from the periphery of the id as it receives stimuli from the external world (Freud 1920). However, Hartmann (1939), an innovator in ego psychology, took issue with Freud's concepts regarding the structural origin of the psychic apparatus. He preferred to believe that the initial stage of the psyche consists of an id–ego undifferentiated matrix that evolves in two directions, one leading to the id and the other to the ego. I shall again refer to Hartmann's ideas when discussing ego psychology (see Chapter 8). Here I shall attempt to demonstrate that Freud's ideas about the development of psychic structure have been useful to our understanding of patients suffering from characterological defects. Freud also undoubtedly saw such patients but formulated them as hysterics or dismissed them as narcissistic neuroses (1914c).

Proposing an undifferentiated id rather than an id–ego matrix as the beginning of psychic life emphasizes the progressive evolution of psychic structure from an unstructured state—defined as the id—into higher structures and functions that retain elements of their origin. As id becomes structuralized, it is no longer id but becomes ego, or rather, it contains a larger proportion of ego elements.

Ego elements are associated with the qualities of mentation existing in a psychological context, whereas the id comprises biological interactions and processes that can be classified as *premental* (Giovacchini 1979b). Although Freud did not make this point, he was opening the way in his sequence of structural development for understanding another attribute of the unconscious, by making it possible to postulate a primeval id that has not yet acquired the quality of mentation: it has not developed sufficient structure to acquire the potential for consciousness or to enter conscious spheres.

The primeval id, as an amorphous undifferentiated mass, can be compared with the blastula stage in embryology. According to embryologists, the surface of the blastula sphere undergoes changes that lead to structuralization and differentiation, eventually resulting in the construction of the various organ systems that are responsible for a well-functioning mind and body. The structural hypothesis thus provides a developmental model of the mind that is compatible with the findings of embryology.

Psychoanalysts frequently ask when the infant's psychological birth begins. Mahler (1968, 1972) believes that it occurs around the time of *separation–individuation*, that is, when the child recognizes the existence of the external world, distinct and apart from the self. It is not clear when this actually happens, but estimates place it somewhere between age 3 and 5 months. This is still a controversial and unsettled issue. Spitz (1959) implied that the infant acquires some degree of mentation at the age of 2 months, which is when the smiling response develops. Neonatologists (Brazelton 1963, 1980, Emde 1980, Klaus and Kennel 1982) have made observations that keep pushing psychological awareness further and further back.

I shall examine developmental factors in Chapter 3. The theoretical issue that we face here when discussing psychological birth is how to define this phenomenon in the context of the structural hypothesis. Does it involve the acquisition of consciousness as a sufficiently developed sensory discrimination of both internal and external stimuli that goes beyond a simple reflex sequence? The structural hypothesis can support a view of consciousness that does not require the distinction of internal from external stimuli. It merely presupposes the development of an ego that can perceive, without necessarily knowing about the source of those perceptions or possessing sufficient structure to store them as memory traces. These attributes, however, develop with further structuralization.

Returning to the impersonal nature of the id, the "it" that Groddeck (1923) wrote about, confronts us with psychic states that antedate psychological awareness. Does the knowledge of such states have clinical relevance? Such a primitive orientation probably was not particularly meaningful to Freud, who studied psychopathology as it affected higher psychic levels. He dealt with ego-level defenses as they protected the psyche from the onslaught of the id and the potentially disruptive effects of anxiety. Today we are also concerned with primitive structural configurations.

We sometimes encounter patients who are not able to discriminate inner sensations; these are commonly children, some of whom are autistic. This also occurs in adults, either as part of their psychopathology that is the outcome of a developmental arrest or as a regression during treatment. Such patients also have problems in experiencing affects in general, such as anger, erotic feelings, and even anxiety. Their most bitter feeling is the inability to feel. This group of patients can be viewed as being dominated by id forces, but in an entirely different fashion than are impulse-ridden persons with poor superego control. The id in these "un-feeling" patients is dominant, but not because it is threatening to break through to better-structured, mentational levels; rather, it occupies most of the psychic apparatus because there is not much else. The ego in these patients, from this viewpoint, is both undeveloped and maldeveloped. The structural hypothesis therefore is an exceptionally good model to use to investigate patients suffering from character disorders, patients often described as having ego defects.

In discussing the development of the ego in the context of the structural hypothesis, Freud (1923a) made two profound statements that are pertinent to our current understanding of the majority of our patients: "The ego is first and foremost a body ego" (p. 26) and "The ego is a precipitate of past object cathexes" (p. 29). The first remark emphasizes the primitive origins of the ego and how it evolves from the id. More subtly, however, it implies how a structure such as the ego, which regulates, controls, and adapts to the external world—that is, serves three masters—retains its prementational antecedents, in this instance in the form of a body ego. This statement also contains several implications regarding the development of the mind and its psychopathological vicissitudes.

Freud's second statement more specifically indicates how the ego develops. In "The Ego and the Id," he wrote about the role of identification as a structure promoting psychic mechanisms. By internalizing object relationships, the ego acquires what I have called the "functional modalities of object relationships" (Giovacchini 1984) and what Freud referred to as the "precipitate of past object cathexes."

Conscious awareness is a function of the ego that becomes elaborated through interactions with the external world, thus increasing the ego's capacity for sensory discrimination and adaptive capabilities which, in turn, lead to further identifications. The latter then add to the ego's differentiation into a variety of subsystems and functional units.

According to the structural hypothesis, the phenomenon of

consciousness is no longer simply part of a duality of awareness and nonawareness. Consciousness has become endowed with other dimensions that involve a hierarchy of sensory discriminations and a sense of being. Consciousness is also an overall ego quality, and its qualitative components depend on what aspect of the mind is being experienced, including relationships with external objects.

As much as the id is a prementational, impersonal "it," the ego is a psychological structure containing various levels of differentiation. At the upper levels we encounter personal elements that are manifestations of the identity sense. The word Freud used for ego is *das Ich*, which means "I." Ego means "I" in Latin and Greek. Freud, however, did not use pedantic classic Latin or Greek vocabulary. The feeling one gets from reading Freud's works in German, however, is of a more personal ego, than one gathers from the English translation. The concept of ego is thus indispensable to the clinical investigation of patients who have identity problems because of specific types of traumatic infantile environments. The original, incomplete formulations of consciousness in the topographic hypothesis are incorporated in the identity sense in the structural hypothesis. When treating patients suffering from identity problems, we note parallel disturbances in their stream of consciousness, which also pertains to reality testing.

There are certain types of adaptations, usually referred to as *splitting* and *fragmentation*, in which consciousness is split or compartmentalized (see Chapter 6). The various qualities of consciousness are, to a large measure, determined by the cohesiveness of the ego. Perceptions and the evaluation of perception are markedly affected by the organization of ego subsystems such as the self representation responsible for the identity sense. The structural hypothesis, as originally formulated, however, did not deal with the various components that are the building blocks of the tripartite model. A more detailed approach belongs to the realm of *ego psychology which, in essence, represents an extensive elaboration of the structural hypothesis*. Still, many commonly observed disorders of the identity sense can be explained on the basis of ego fragmentation which, in turn, is associated with disturbances in perception, the stream of consciousness, and evaluation. The latter also encompasses the superego, or what Freud referred to as the *ego-ideal* in his first paper dealing with the structural hypothesis (1923a).

When describing splitting mechanisms, Freud (1938) stated that psychic elements became dissociated from the "main ego current." He also acknowledged that a split-off portion of the psyche may develop an independent, autonomous existence. This may be what has happened to those patients diagnosed as having multiple personalities, but it can also apply to a large, less-striking group of patients who have been evaluated as borderlines or as having character neuroses. The same structural lack of synthesis is also common among psychotic patients. I offer a clinical illustration that has some dramatic features but did not show the degree of fragmentation present in cases of multiple personalities. Nonetheless, this patient was hovering on the edge of psychosis.

The patient sought treatment because he was having a severe identity problem which manifested itself by such plaguing questions as to who he was, where he was going, and what the purpose of his life was. At moments, he felt so miserable and depressed that the only solution he could think of was to kill himself. He also experienced intense tension and anxiety, bitterly complaining that he was "neither fish nor fowl." His disruption had become acute after his girlfriend left him to become engaged to another man, which was the precipitating cause that led him to therapy.

When he regressed in treatment, he had moments when he literally did not know who he was. He had lapses of memory in which he "forgot" his name, address, and other identifying data. He was disturbed by this, but not to the degree of panic. Gradually, he was able to derive some comfort, some calming, from the treatment, and he seemed to begin functioning more efficiently and cohesively.

Because he appeared to be doing better, he announced that he had moved to a new apartment and, with some enthusiasm, briefly described the building and his living quarters. I tended to dismiss this information, except to be somewhat pleased that he could feel some enthusiasm rather than being overwhelmed by a constant and pervasive depression. Several weeks later he once again referred to his apartment, and I recall that I felt somewhat puzzled and uneasy. Something he said seemed inconsistent with what he had told me several weeks before, but I could not specify exactly what, and so I made no comments about it.

During the next several months, the patient made more and more references to rooms, furniture, apartment layouts, and other details about his apartment. I then realized that he could not be describing the same place, and so I tried to understand his discrepancies in terms of his psychopathology and the looseness of his psychic structure. I came to discover, however, that what he was reporting was accurate, but he was, nevertheless, demonstrating how fragmented his ego was. Still, he was attempting to hold himself together and to maintain a precarious identity sense rather than displaying the manifestations of psychic disintegration.

As I stated, this patient's descriptions were correct, but he was telling me about different apartments, something that he had failed to reveal until I faced him with what would have been irreconcilable contradictions, such as being on the first floor and the next reference being to his penthouse. In a period of slightly over a month, he had rented about a dozen apartments, each one serving a particular function. For example, one apartment would serve primarily as a bedroom, being the place he chose to sleep in. Another apartment would serve as a study and library. This is where he would study and read, and another would be where he would eat. He had a place to entertain guests, seduce women, watch television, and so on. All of these apartments had several rooms, but the patient selected only one room to identify his purpose for being there.

He could not use one apartment to fulfill the various needs that are usually served by a single dwelling: his ego did not have the unity and synthesis that would permit him to live comfortably in one place. As was evident in the difficulties he was having in maintaining a cohesive self representation, he was unable to relate to the external world, except as he was able to fragment it, a reflection of the fragmentation of his mind.

The structural hypothesis is a useful model to help us understand introjective-projective processes. The patient just discussed was able to construct an external world, one of many apartments, that supported a fragmented ego. He was fortunate in that he had the financial resources to maintain such an expensive adaptation. In a sense, he was projecting, or as I prefer, externalizing (Giovacchini 1967) aspects of his self representation (its lack of cohesion) into the external world. Something similar occurs in the transference that is part of psychoanalytic treatment. This formulation, however, is somewhat different from Freud's, in that he focused on the projection of instinctual impulses, whereas I am referring to the projection of psychic structures, a subject that also concerned Winnicott (1954) and Klein (1946).

Freud (1923a), however, was the first investigator to suggest that interactions with the outer world, what we commonly call *object relationships,* lead to the formation of psychic structure, stating that the "ego is a precipitate of past object cathexes" (p. 29). In the same monograph, he also explained the origin of the superego, or the ego ideal, the two being synonymous at that time. Like the ego, the superego is a precipitate of a past object cathexis and represents the end result of a series of rather complex identifications.

The superego upholds moral standards. It is our conscience, but it is much more than that. The little boy of 3 or 4 incorporates prohibitions in order to appease his father. There are certain things he cannot do, such as sexually possess his mother, because such behavior would be punishable by castration (see Chapter 3). This is, of course, a description of the *Oedipus complex.* These prohibitions become internalized and integrated into the child's psyche, which continues to have influence by dictating the limits of the child's behavior. According to Freud, the superego is "the heir of the Oedipus complex" (1923, p. 36), and it contributes significantly to the formation of character. The superego, however, is more than just a conglomerate of prohibitions, as it also contains positive elements.

Before discussing further the components of the superego, we should ask where it is located. Freud placed it in the ego area as an appendage. He drew it in the shape of an ear, an auricular appendage, because he believed it was incorporated primarily through the auditory sphere. Although in his drawing of the psychic apparatus (1923a, 1933) it sits on the ego, Freud also stressed that it "dips" deep into the id. In other words, he was once again pointing out that the superego can also be viewed in terms of a hierarchical stratification, the more primitive, tyrannical edicts residing at the deeper id levels and the benign regulatory factors at the upper ego levels (Schafer 1960).

In "The Ego and the Id," these different qualities and the location of the superego are confusing because the term *ego ideal* has become differentiated from the superego. Piers and Singer (1953), for example, believe that transgressions against the ego ideal cause shame, which is to be distinguished from superego violations, which are experienced as guilt. Freud (1914c) himself had, for years before he formulated the superego, referred to the ego ideal as representing a person's ideal, inner aspiration. Today we think of the ego ideal as an extension of the superego by which we determine our level of self-esteem, dependent on how close we come to achieve its aims. Thus, the ego ideal would fit into the higher levels of the personality, which also include artistic interest, creative endeavor, and aesthetic sense. The spectrum of this psychic agency is broad.

Considering the ego ideal as an upward hierarchical extension of the superego indicates that the content of what is internalized is more than just prohibitions, the "thou shalt nots" that Freud described. It also includes many "thou shalts," which help shape the character. The boy identifies with many of the father's personality traits, although he cannot share some of the paternal prerogatives, such as his sexual privileges. There thus is a balance between what is and is not allowed.

The structural hypothesis is especially helpful in understanding structure-building psychic processes and, to a certain extent, obliterates the distinctions between psychopathological and nonpathological mental functioning. I do not believe it was Freud's intention to pursue the mechanisms of building psychic structures as much as he was concerned with constructing a setting in which he could place conflicting intrapsychic forces. Nevertheless, for that purpose, the topographic hypothesis would have been adequate, but Freud went far beyond such a theoretical need.

From time to time, Freud remarked parenthetically how outside elements become part of the personality and how the process could reverse itself in special circumstances. He described the sequence from external prohibitions to the establishment of moral restraints as the conscience becomes integrated into the psyche. He also mentioned a similar integration of self observations which he felt occurred prominently in those persons who had a philosophical bent (1914c). He did not include himself in this group. The reexternalization of such self-observations also frequently occurs among paranoids.

A scientist in his late twenties had the extraordinary talent of being able to literally hear himself think. This was similar to eidetic imagery, except that it was auditory. It served him well in helping solve the problems he encountered in his research and in his hobby of playing a musical instrument.

When playing his musical instrument, this young man would hear a voice that made helpful suggestions about his technique. Often it would praise him for doing well and correct him when he made mistakes. It would tell him what to do, and he would improve and learn from this interaction. It did not seem important, during these moments, whether he believed the voice stemmed from an outside source or represented a part of himself. Most of the time he realized that he was talking to himself, but the idea that he had a concerned "genie" hovering nearby delighted him.

During regressed periods, the "genie" became further externalized and transformed. The voice would gradually lose its gentle quality, and what had been benign criticism became harsh and severe. The voice started to attack the patient verbally and eventually assumed the typical hostile attitude of a persecutor. Now the young man definitely perceived this as an outside voice, which he degraded to an auditory hallucination.

I believe this sequence can be easily and elegantly conceptualized in terms of the structural hypothesis, especially that part of the tripartite model that contains the superego. When the patient was relatively well balanced emotionally, he could enjoy

the upward ego ideal extensions of the superego. He knew that
what he heard was part of himself, that he was experiencing a
talent based on an extremely sensitive auditory apparatus. He
could hear his thoughts clearly, something that ordinary persons
cannot do, and he could allow himself the freedom to play with
the notion that someone was talking to and looking after him.
His self-observing functions were at their keenest.

As he succumbed to the psychotic process, what had been
previously well integrated into his ego became dislodged and
projected into the external world. During a phase of decompensation the patient had the delusion that he was being persecuted,
as is typical for the paranoid. This externalization is a psychopathological variant of a reversal of the normal developmental
process in which an external relationship becomes integrated in
the ego sphere as the superego. To repeat, as a newly formed
psychic structure, this superego "dips" into the id.

In addition to externalization, the superego's pathological
degradation is also evidenced by the dominance of sadistic,
tyrannical elements that suppress its benign, loving aspects
(Schafer 1960). My patient was reviled in that he was depre-
ciated, called a homosexual, and showered with obscenities.

It was interesting that at other times he had projected the
helpless, vulnerable parts of his self representation into the outer
world, where the voice would multiply into voices, and he
would hear a chorus of crying babies, sometimes plaintive and
sometimes screaming, but whatever their tone, they were hungry babies who had been ignored and abandoned. Their distress
reflected his inner turmoil, but during these psychotic moments
these various parts of his psyche were disconnected from one
another.

The structural hypothesis provides us with a good model to
understand how psychic structure evolves as a consequence of
object relationships. It can help explain introjective-projective
processes, mechanisms that also refer to internalization and
externalization, which will be discussed in the section on defenses and adaptations with the specific purpose of distinguishing them from other similar processes, such as incorporation and
identification. Regarding the superego, there is much confusion
as to what psychic processes are involved in its formation. For

example, Sandler (1960) and Sandler and Rosenblatt (1962) reserve the term *introjection* only for the internalization of prohibitions and controlling interactions that define the superego.

Many clinical disorders can be explained by defects in the superego. Johnson and Szurek (1952, 1964) wrote about superego *lacunae* that are responsible for amoral, antisocial behavior. They concluded that many such patients have incorporated their parents' superego standards, but not those that dictate their conscious behavior. Rather, the children identify with the unconscious, primitive elements of the parents' superegos that are corrupt and defective. The prohibitive, limit-setting functions of the parents' superegos have gone awry, which is reflected in their children's behavior: the parents are living vicariously through them.

There are many types of behavior that are based on different superego organizations. A harsh superego, for example, can lead to depression, guilt feelings, and constricted relationships that repress or deny instinctual needs. On the other hand, this same superego can lead to sadistic and cruel attitudes and actions, or in a seemingly paradoxical fashion, it can be responsible for antisocial acting out. Alexander (1927, 1956, 1961) wrote about such patients "bribing" the superego, that is, seeking punishment in the outside world to appease a conscience that demands retribution.

When Freud first established the structural hypothesis, it did not exclude the concept of conflict in favor of defective structure. By anthropomorphizing, he was able to continue conceptualizing in terms of conflicts, but instead of drive conflicts, he now wrote about conflicts between psychic structures, such as I have been discussing, primarily conflicts between the id and the ego, between the ego and the superego, and between the ego and the outer world. The last one marks the beginning of object relations theory, by stressing the importance of object relationships for both emotional maturation and the development of psychopathology.

Freud (1924a, 1924b) wrote two papers explaining how the ego retreats from the outer world when it is in conflict with it, when it perceives it as dangerous. He had already pointed out such withdrawal in his analysis of Judge Schreber (1911b) as the beginning of a paranoid psychosis. In these latter papers, he concentrated more on the "loss of reality," focusing on structural factors rather than energic shifts and libidinal redistributions. Consequently, Freud was able to maintain his emphasis on both intrapsychic conflict and structure. However, his interest in instincts and their vicissitudes never diminished, and the psychodynamic hypothesis remained his most important frame of reference when making clinical formulations.

THE PSYCHODYNAMIC HYPOTHESIS AND INSTINCTS

The psychodynamic hypothesis is a natural extension of the concept of the dynamic unconscious. I am referring to forces within the mind of which a person is not aware, that in topographic terms belong to the system Ucs, and yet have palpable effects on thoughts, feelings, and actions. What do these unconscious forces consist of, and how are they accepted by other parts of the psyche? Obviously, if they are banished to the Ucs, they must, in some way, be unacceptable to other strata of the personality. Freud described the content of the Ucs or the id as consisting mainly of instinctual impulses. (I shall discuss instinct theory in Chapter 5). In describing the psychodynamic hypothesis it is essential, however, that instincts be defined and that we understand some of their unique characteristics. The psychodynamic approach is based on forces clashing between different layers of the mind, a conflict between an impulse from the id—an instinct—struggling for expression and opposing strivings designed to prevent it from reaching the higher levels of the psyche. Breaking through the barriers of inhibiting, defensive forces leads to what Freud called *discharge*, or satisfaction. The psychodynamic hypothesis is chiefly based on the concepts of conflict and defense. What is defended against is a forbidden impulse—an id impulse or an instinct—seeking gratification.

Freud (1915a) defined an instinct operationally as an impetus, a propelling force having a source, an aim, and an object. The source is the id or the system Ucs. The aim is satisfaction or instinctual discharge, and the object is the person or means that will achieve this satisfaction. Thus, an instinct is associated with an inner need and is considered a borderland concept between the psychic and somatic areas.

Freud used the concept of instinct in a different way than zoologists or ethologists do. Actually, the translation in English of "instinct" is unfortunate, as Freud used the German word *Trieb*, which literally means "drive," whereas *Instinkt* corresponds more closely to the English "instinct," referring to innate, predetermined behavioral patterns. On the other hand, from a psychoanalytic viewpoint, "drive" refers to the conscious representation of an instinctual need. In other words, the instinct that manifests a biological need and thus cannot, as such, reach consciousness, is psychologically elaborated and perceived in the ego sphere as a drive. As a drive, it has achieved mental representation. These terminological confusions are unfortunate, and the psychodynamic hypothesis leaves us with some fundamental unanswered questions. For example, if we accept that instinct, or drive, as Freud prefers, is the outcome of biological needs, such as the need for nurture, protection from disruptive stimuli, and soothing, why should such basic requirements conflict with other levels of the personality?

According to Freud, conflict occurs throughout the course of emotional development. The newborn is an instinctual creature, uninhibitedly expressing needs and not feeling any shame or guilt. Rather, inhibitions and conflict are the results of the process of acculturation and the internalization of the caretaker's values (Freud, 1923a). Freud was quick to point out, however, that biological factors also contribute to the development of inhibitions and defenses against certain instinctual impulses, that there will be inevitable taboos that are an intrinsic part of normal development and are inherited from our ancestors in a collective unconscious (1913c): Freud's ideas about evolution were Lamarckian.

As instincts become sexualized, they become more and more subject to prohibiting factors. The ultimate taboo enters the psychic sphere at the height of the Oedipus complex when the child has incestuous feelings toward the parent of the opposite sex. For boys, this is when they want to kill their fathers but fear retaliatory castration (see Chapter 3). This course of psychological events is innate and developmentally predetermined according to classic psychoanalytic theory. The universality of the Oedipus complex and its vicissitudes has been challenged by some analysts and has led to dissension, splits, and the formation of other schools of psychoanalysis that emphasize sociocultural rather than biological factors.

There has always been controversy as to how many instincts are part of the human condition. Man's needs have developed away from their biological roots, and as civilization flourishes, so do our needs multiply. Whatever instinct theory is in the forefront, however, the conflicting qualities of the instinctual forces—whether biologically predetermined and inherited or acquired through the limitations imposed by authority figures—are a dominant factor.

The psychodynamic hypothesis represents a frame of reference that is inextricably related to reality testing and to the establishment of limits. Indeed, the evolution of the *pleasure* and *reality principles* cannot be understood without using some of the assumptions of the psychodynamic hypothesis, inasmuch as intrapsychic conflict can be traced back to these polarities.

Freud simply meant that the organism seeks pleasure through instinctual discharge and strives to avoid pain, which is the result of the internal tension caused by needs that have not been satisfied. The pleasure ego refers to an ego that uninhibitedly pursues pleasure, whereas the reality ego constrains itself as it conforms to the limits imposed by reality.

In "Instincts and Their Vicissitudes," Freud (1915a) outlined the sequence of development that leads from the pleasure ego to the reality ego, a sequence that can be considered to be responsible for the origin of conflict. It is interesting that in this monograph Freud asserted that the formation of the reality ego precedes that of the pleasure ego and that instincts are the vehicle that enable us to distinguish the inner world of the psyche from external reality as both instincts and external percepts lead to actions that seek discharge.

An external stimulus has a momentary impact on the psyche, whereas an inner, instinctual need leads to a continuous state of tension. This brings us to a controversial point, as exemplified by the following conclusion: Freud wrote that the "almost entirely helpless living organism as yet unoriented in the world" (1915, p. 119) (I assume he was describing the neonate) would soon be able to differentiate internal from external percepts by means of muscular action. Freud did not specify how soon, but we assume this occurs sometime during the neonatal period. In effect, if the baby can remove the stimulus by means of muscular action, that is, by flight or active avoidance, then the stimulus has an external source. If it cannot be removed, then it has an internal, that is, an instinctual origin. Freud was pointing out the organism's need to reestablish equilibrium, but he did lose sight of the structural factors that have to be accounted for when explaining how psychodynamic equilibrium is attained.

We might question what "inside" and "outside" mean to an "almost entirely helpless living organism as yet unoriented in the world." The earliest phases of psychic life are largely amorphous and undifferentiated, in which distinctions between inner and outer do not yet exist, as ego boundaries are poorly, if at all, established. Therefore, the distinction between inner drives and external percepts could not be sustained by such a primitive psychic organization.

This does not mean, however, that neonates do not have regulatory mechanisms and may not have disturbing feelings. The infant, even the neonate, develops some capacity to make connections between certain disruptive feelings and reactions that bring relief. For example, if a bright light causes pain, infants will soon learn that shutting their eyes will bring relief, but they do not have to know anything about the source of the stimulus. This protective action is practically, if not actually, a reflex. If infants are hungry, such a simple muscular maneuver will not be enough, but they can cry and then be fed. Early in life, children become aware of needs and discomforts and "know" that certain responses will bring relief. This occurs without any knowledge of sources or any distinctions between the inner and outer world.

Nevertheless, Freud stated that such a distinction was acquired when a child could abolish external impingements by means of muscular action. This heralds the formation of the *reality ego,* a beginning ego state designed to maintain psychic equilibrium. Next, as the ego falls under the sway of the pleasure–pain principle (see "The Psychoeconomic Hypothesis and Repression), the psyche strives for maximum pleasure without necessarily taking into account the possibility of painful consequences. Freud (1915a) called this psychic state the *pleasure ego*, which *follows* the formation of the reality ego. In an earlier article (Freud 1911a) he contrasted this ego, which he then called the *purified pleasure ego*, with the ego that was dominated by the reality principle. Finally, as the pleasure ego becomes increasingly under the sway of the reality principle—that is, as the limits imposed by reality are gradually understood and the prohibitions of the newly formed superego are integrated into the psyche—it is transformed into what Freud referred to as the *final reality ego*.

The movement from an initial reality ego to a pleasure ego and then a final reality ego is a curious sequence. I believe that this is evidence that Freud placed psychodynamic balance in the forefront, even ahead of pleasure seeking, which he emphasized later in his monograph "Beyond the Pleasure Principle" (1920).

Whatever the actual developmental sequence of the pleasure and reality egos, the role of instincts in creating conflict becomes more distinct as the psyche becomes aware that certain desires and actions are at variance with the norms and values of the external world. The pleasure ego is an early ego state that seeks gratification and cannot tolerate delay or waiting. It demands immediate satisfaction, but the impulses involved are primitive instinctual needs.

As all the points of view of metapsychology emphasize, especially the structural hypothesis, the psyche is constructed as a hierarchical stratification and contains its antecedents. Freud repeatedly asserted that primitive mental states exist side by side with later-acquired sophisticated psychic structures. The pleasure ego, although superseded by the reality ego, continues to make itself felt. Because the orientation of these two egos differs, they often create conflict. Thus, conflict is an intrinsic quality of the psyche.

Even though this type of conflict implicates the structural hypothesis, the pleasure ego and the reality ego nevertheless refer to instincts and how they are reacted to: The distinction between instinctual need and psychic structure is blurred when we discuss primitive antithetical ego states. The ego is fashioned around its reaction to a need, a response that is also determined by interactions with the outer world. The ego's *reaction* defines the ego state and determines its structural characteristics. This is an excellent example of how one frame of metapsychology blends into another, in this case the structural into the psychodynamic hypothesis.

As Freud constantly demonstrated, psychoanalytic theory was the outcome of clinical necessity. That is, the psychodynamic hypothesis was the natural consequence of Freud's formulation of the dynamic unconscious. He was confronted with patients suffering from somatic symptoms that he wanted to explain on a psychogenic basis, as they could not be fit in any organic pattern. The psychodynamic hypothesis thus is especially well suited to explain how the psyche converts intrapsychic processes into somatic symptoms, as occurs with conversion hysteria. Regardless of whether Freud's early cases were actual hysterics (see Reichard 1956), he described a psychological constellation that explained the symptoms in terms of conflicting impulses, minimizing the effects of defective structure and stressing the contribution of aberrant instinctual impulses. In fact, Freud at first did not want to focus on psychic structure, because members of the French school, especially Janet, condemned hysterics by viewing them as morally degenerate: The "weakness" of the ego responsible for the hysteric's propensity to dissociate was a sign of constitutional deficiency and inferiority.

Freud (Breuer and Freud 1895, Freud 1893, 1905a) postulated that in hysteria a forbidden sexual impulse is activated and seeks gratification. Invariably there has been a premature stimulation of sexual impulses brought about by trauma. At first Freud thought that this was an actual childhood seduction (1894, 1896), but later he revised his thinking and decided that the memory of seduction was based on fantasy rather than fact (1905a and letter 69, Freud 1950). The important point is that in hysteria, certain impulses seeking gratification are unacceptable to the upper, more reality-oriented, levels of the personality.

That is, the superego passes moral judgments and prohibits the expression of sexual feelings.

More can be said about how the superego develops its moral code and how instinctual impulses become dangerous and "noxious stimuli," *schädlich*, as Freud described them. Infantile traumas definitely play a role, but these need not be specific events or episodes with molesting adults. Rather, the child's general environment during the early vulnerable months and years of emotional development determines how the mind adapts to both the inner and the external world. As psychopathology develops, instinctual impulses do not become integrated with one another and with other parts of the psyche but instead clash with other instincts and with other psychic agencies, a viewpoint based on the psychodynamic hypothesis. Freud also believed that there were constitutional incompatibilities among various parts of the psyche.

In "Studies on Hysteria," Freud described several patients, but he had not developed the psychodynamic hypothesis sufficiently to use it to explain their symptoms. Later (1904) he described an adolescent girl, whom he called Dora, in terms of intrapsychic conflicts, interpreting her somatic symptoms as symbolic representations of forbidden sexual impulses and the struggle to block their expression. Her symptoms represented *compromise formations* (see Chapter 6). In the famous case of a 5-year-old child known as "Little Hans," Freud continued with the theme of conflict, defense, and symbolic representation (1909a).

Although I shall later discuss defenses in general, I must now explain the particular defense of conversion in order to outline how intrapsychic conflicts produce the final clinical picture. Conversion is a process by which an intrapsychic conflict is converted into a physical symptom. However, this cannot happen unless the somatic disturbance is a symbolic representation of that conflict. If it is not, then it is not hysteria. In these instances, physical symptoms that are related to psychogenic factors are thought of as *functional* or *psychosomatic* in nature.

For a clinical illustration, I call attention to a hysterical anesthesia. If it affects a limb, it may be an example of a stocking or glove anesthesia. This means that the area of sensory deficit does not correspond to any known peripheral nerve distribution. Instead, if it affects the hand, the boundaries of the anesthesia will be similar to an area covered by a glove and, in the case of a leg, it will resemble a stocking. The hysterical conversion process ignores anatomy. Rather than corresponding to organic factors, the symptom reflects how folklore might conceptualize sensory loss.

Freud always looked for the sexual factor that determined the symbolic meaning of a somatic symptom. Pursuing the situation of hysterical anesthesia, if it affects the hand, it may be a reaction to forbidden masturbatory impulses. Combined with a paralysis, it further protects the patient from the urge to masturbate, inasmuch as the hand cannot be used, and the lack of feeling may represent an inhibition of sexual sensations. At the same time, the attention that the affected limb receives—its examination and its manipulation—points to the disguised gratification of the masturbatory impulse that is being defended against. Thus, the symptom is a symbolic representation of the forbidden sexual impulse and the forces that are in conflict with this impulse, a compromise formation.

The weakness of the psychodynamic hypothesis is its emphasis on instinctual impulses as if they were operating in isolation. It more or less ignores psychic structure. At the beginning of psychoanalytic clinical explorations, this hypothesis was useful in making sense out of dramatic but seemingly senseless somatic symptoms that defied an organic explanation. This was another example in which irrational phenomena could be explained rationally, the hallmark of the psychoanalytic approach. Still, the psychodynamic approach ignores the breadth and complexities of character structure, which can include conflict. That is, in the psychodynamic hypothesis, conflict is studied in isolation. Although Freud also constructed the topographical hypothesis and later the structural hypothesis, he did not use them simultaneously when studying emotional disorders. This multidimensional frame, which was responsible for the creation of metapsychology, is just beginning to be used and has been subsumed under the rubric of ego psychology.

The usefulness of the psychodynamic hypothesis can also be questioned in view of the types of patients we encounter today in our clinical practice. The conversion hysterics about which Freud and the French school of psychiatry wrote are now rarely seen, especially in cities. Conversion hysterics may be found in minority groups and in some less-developed nations but almost never in sophisticated circles. It also has been frequently asserted that hysterical symptoms can be a cover for an underlying schizophrenic core or a severe character disorder.

Although Freud developed a scheme of emotional development, he concentrated on the elaboration and progression of what he labeled *sexual impulses*, a theory of libidinal development (see "The Psychoeconomic Hypothesis and Repression"). If we study inner needs and impulses from a hierarchical perspective and trace them back to their antecedents, we will learn that some needs that were appropriate during an early stage of development are no longer acceptable later when the psyche is more sophisticated. Needs or instinctual impulses undergo progressive refinement, that is, secondary process revision, throughout the course of psychic growth. Thus, conflict is the outcome of the structuralizing process. Early primitive needs are at variance with the more reality-oriented requirements of the mature psyche. Previously (see section of structural hypothesis), I have discussed how within the framework of a structural hierarchy, different levels of the personality clash with each other. Here, I am emphasizing something similar, but since I am now discussing the psychodynamic hypothesis, I am focusing on an intrinsic propensity for conflict that is the outcome of the development of instincts. As instincts or drives strive for expression, they clash with other drives, leading to states of pent-up tension. These drives are propelled (impetus) by psychic energy, which Freud dealt with in the psychoeconomic hypothesis.

THE PSYCHOECONOMIC HYPOTHESIS
AND REPRESSION

Psychoanalysis requires a concept of psychic energy to explain the various movements of the psychic apparatus, those involved in action, problem solving, reestablishment of emotional equilibrium, and growth. An energic hypothesis must be based on certain general principles that dictate the distribution and production of energy and how it is to be used. Freud was familiar with the science of his times, but whether he was acquainted with the most recent principles, that is, the laws of thermodynamics, is not certain, although I suspect he was. If not, he was at least well acquainted with psychologists, such as Fechner, who incorporated thermodynamic concepts in their theoretical models.

Freud relied on two principles on which he built his concepts of psychic energy, the *principle of constancy* and the *pleasure principle* or, more specifically, the *pleasure–pain principle*. The constancy principle is based on the hypothesis that the function of the nervous system and the psychic apparatus is to keep the level of excitation at its lowest point. The pleasure principle is related to the constancy principle in that it asserts that lowering the level of excitation, which connotes release and relief, leads to pleasure, whereas increased excitation creates tension and disruption and is experienced as pain.

The psychoeconomic hypothesis is the most controversial of all the points of view and assumptions of metapsychology. For example, observations of the nervous system indicate that it does not necessarily seek lower states of excitation. Indeed, rather than avoiding stimuli, the organism seems to crave stimulation. In fact, sensory deprivation is an unpleasant state in which internal percepts become disorganized and disruptive. Many psychoanalysts reject the psychoeconomic hypothesis because it is based on erroneous assumptions that conformed to the perspective of mid-Victorian science. I am referring to the tension–discharge axis characteristic of the operations and shifts of psychic energy postulated by this hypothesis. The constancy and pleasure principles, which also are dependent on tension-discharge vectors, are questioned because the data of neurophysiology do not support them.

In regard to the pleasure principle, excitement is often pleasurable, sometimes ecstatic, whereas low levels of energy frequently accompany boredom, apathy, and withdrawal. However, pleasure and pain cannot be reduced to such simple quantitative fluctuations.

Freud characterized the pleasure principle as the tendency

of living organisms to avoid what he called unpleasure (*Unlust*). In "Beyond the Pleasure Principle" (Freud 1920), he indicated that it was the rhythmic changes of excitation that generate pleasure, and he concluded, therefore, that the principles of constancy, pleasure, and pain are identical. In that same monograph he equated the constancy principle with the *Nirvana principle*, the organism's striving to attain what was supposedly the bliss and calm of the intrauterine state. This specifies a lack of tension but not necessarily an absence of stimuli.

Obviously, Freud was struggling with the concepts of excitation, pleasure, and constancy. He insisted that pain is related to the intensity of excitation but that it is not directly proportional to it. He wrote about this as early as 1905 in his "Three Essays on Sexuality," adding that there is some association with time, but he was cryptic and not at all clear. Perhaps he meant that a rise or lowering of excitation must occur during a particular interval of time in order to be perceived as pleasure or pain. For instance, an increase in stimulus intensity during a short period of time would have a greater effect than would the same increase over a longer period of time.

Freud (1920) quoted Fechner, who stressed stability and instability as the significant elements in producing pleasure or pain. Fechner believed that as feelings reach consciousness, they tend toward either states of stability, which produce pleasure, or states of instability, which lead to unpleasure. Fechner stated, ". . . every psychophysical motion rising above the threshold of consciousness is attended by pleasure in proportion as, *beyond a certain limit*, it approximates to complete stability" (Freud 1920, p. 8, italics added). Fechner added that the same limit applies to unpleasure as the impulse approaches instability. What he meant by "beyond a certain limit" is vague and confusing. It could be understood if consciousness were operationally defined as quantities of energy that may increase beyond a limit and be disruptive to the system Cs, leading to a disruption of sensory input. On the other hand, sensory systems must be energized in order to function. The function of the reticular system in the pons supports theories regarding the levels of energy required for "acknowledgment" by higher centers of sensory input. In any case, Fechner concluded that between the limits of stability and instability lies an area of "aesthetic indifference."

These concepts are difficult to understand because they are not clearly stated and cannot be integrated with the knowledge of the nervous system acquired since Freud's time. These reasons have therefore caused many critics to label the psychoeconomics hypothesis as an anachronistic theory. Still, we must have some force, some source of energy that operates the psychic apparatus.

The energic hypothesis can be modified so as to be compatible with our current knowledge of the central nervous system. We need not think in terms of increasing and decreasing excitation, as Freud did. Other than proposing an innate tendency toward low levels of excitation, we can think of an inherent striving toward equilibrium. Many years ago, Bernard (1865) concluded that the organism seeks a state of equilibrium, which he formulated in his principle of internal constancy. Later, Cannon (1932) used the same principle in regard to a living system's need to establish homeostasis. These principles focus primarily on integration rather than quantities of energy.

The psychoeconomic hypothesis is, in essence, a tension–discharge hypothesis. As I have already stated, the increase in excitation is equated only with the production of tension and unpleasure. Instinctual impulses contain what we might consider to be potential energy, which, according to Freud, becomes kinetic energy when that impulse is set in motion to seek discharge. The impulse itself, in the psychoeconomic hypothesis, represents a unit of energy that grows as it remains unsatisfied, which means that its energy is not discharged. As long as it is not discharged, it combines with more units of energy until it reaches a state of maximum tension.

As an inner need—which I am considering as being synonymous with an instinctual impulse—strives for discharge (gratification), it gathers momentum. I mentioned that an instinct is a *borderland concept* between the soma and the psyche. In seeking gratification, an instinct moves from the psyche's deeper biological levels to the mentationally higher, reality-oriented levels. While traversing the psyche, what began as a raw biological disruption, conceived as a packet of energy, gathers accretions, further quanta of energy during its upward journey. The need as it receives these additions is felt as a need and is not necessarily experienced as disruptive tension.

As early as in his "Project for a Scientific Psychology" Freud (1895b) wrote about quanta of energy. Later he wrote about the potential energy of an instinctual impulse or other psychic structures as *Besetzung*, which has been translated into English as "cathexis." *Besetzung* literally means "to occupy." From the energic viewpoint, inner needs are thought of as being ruled primarily by the amounts (cathexis) of psychic energy they contain that push them to seek discharge.

It is difficult to understand what discharge means. In the "Studies on Hysteria" (Breuer and Freud 1895), the behavior of patients during hypnosis sometimes resembled an explosion. The patient often attained a crescendo of tension, anger, or anxiety that, after reaching a peak and being dramatically and intensely expressed, subsided into a state of calm and eventually insight. These states of abreaction and catharsis phenomenologically fit well with the slightly more abstract entity of discharge.

The psychoeconomic hypothesis, more than any other point of view of metapsychology, is based on a series of abstractions and metaphors. Some, such as concepts of discharge, seem suitable to describe phenomena as abreaction and catharsis, but the basic question that remains unanswered is what is psychic energy. Obviously to answer this question we have to leave the domain of psychology and enter the realm of neurophysiology and neurochemistry. Freud could not do this because not enough was known then, or even today, to answer this question. Still, he had to establish a fairly definitive concept of psychic energy because he needed to explain the operations of the mind in terms of the power that enables it to carry out its various functions—executive, sensory, and integrative.

At the same time, Freud was developing his theory of sexuality that, along with catharsis and abreaction, could be neatly fit in a psychoeconomic tension–discharge context. The sexual act reaches a peak of excitation and then a discharge (literally), in which there is a sudden diminution of need or, stated differently, the sexual drive loses its impetus. It was this progression that enabled Freud to define psychic energy. Because he viewed the majority of drives as sexual (see Chapter 3), he dealt primarily with their energic component. He called the energy of the sexual drives *libido*, and his theory of emotional development was based on the *libido theory*.

Quanta of energy were now quanta of libido, and they could be bound or unbound (analogous to potential and kinetic energy) or projected, displaced, or repressed (see Chapter 6), as in some instances, libido could be freely mobile. The psychoeconomic hypothesis allows for two types of energy, libidinal and aggressive, although whether these are qualitatively different is debatable.

The concept of aggressive energy needs to be expanded and further differentiated from sexual and hostile impulses, but again, this can best be done in the context of the development of instinct theory. However, when explaining how various parts of the mind function, we must consider types of energy other than libido. I am referring primarily to the function of consciousness and the act of becoming conscious, which involve various distributions of energy. Freud (1925c) vividly described these shifts of cathexis in his imaginative paper "On the Mystic Writing Pad." The energy involved at these higher levels is, according to Freud, nonsexual.

The mystic writing pad, sometimes called the magic slate, is a pad on which one can write or draw with a stylus. The pad is covered by a thin outer layer or sheet. The writer presses the stylus on this sheet, making an impression or an indentation on the slate, but once the sheet is pulled away from the slate, the writing is erased and the slate can be used again. These slates are usually sold as toys and have two outer sheets, one next to the slate and the other protecting the inner sheet. The marks of the stylus are registered on the inner sheet, but immediately beneath it is a corresponding indentation on the slate. The latter is permanently registered, whereas whatever impression is made on the inner sheet disappears once it is detached from the indentation on the slate.

This mystic writing pad is a made-to-order model for the relationship of the preconscious to consciousness as they both react to stimuli from the outer world. The slate represents the Pcs, the inner sheet the Cs, and the outer sheet, if any, a stimulus barrier that monitors incoming stimuli that otherwise might be disruptive. These interactions are easily placed in a topographical perspective, but it is the energic factors that interest us here.

First, however, we must consider briefly the structural alterations. As stated, a stimulus (the stylus) will leave a permanent trace on the slate. This constitutes a memory trace, indicating that there has been an addition to the Pcs. There is a change, therefore, a greater organization, in the structure of the Pcs. For this memory trace to have an adaptive significance, it requires energy; that is, it must be cathected.

Freud used the mystic writing pad model to illustrate how the phenomenon of consciousness occurs and to demonstrate that conscious impressions are not registered in the system Cs, but are evanescent. The role of the preconscious is important because once the "sheet" of consciousness is detached from the Pcs, the stimulus is no longer perceived. Emphasizing the energic factors, Freud concluded that the incoming stimuli are met halfway by consciousness.

Attention is an attribute of consciousness and indicates that consciousness directs itself toward certain stimuli, in a sense reaching out to meet them. This is determined by "feelers" from the Pcs. The memory traces become cathected once consciousness is involved in the act of perception. They move forward as energic shifts to the adjacent system Cs. As external stimuli corresponding to the memory trace meet at the spot where the preconscious cathexis joins consciousness, the memory trace is visibly or otherwise recorded as a sensory impression.

The act of becoming conscious emanates therefore from both the system Cs and Pcs. The Pcs energizes the Cs with certain memory traces that have been cathected because they correspond to or are associatively connected with the incoming stimuli. Freud then went beyond the mystic writing pad and conjectured that the Cs, because of the Pcs cathexis, reaches into the external world to meet the incoming stimuli. In other words, Freud reminded us that perception does not occur in a vacuum. To emphasize the perceptual function of consciousness, he revised his designation of consciousness to that of perceptual consciousness, *Pcpt-Cs*. To perceive, however, requires some idea of what is to be perceived. He thus referred to *notation*, a function of attention that relies on cathected memory traces in order to organize incoming stimuli so that they can reach higher levels of awareness (1911a).

The energic factors involved in the act of becoming conscious are complicated, especially if we attempt to understand them primarily in psychoanalytic terms. In the model I have just presented, consciousness proceeds from the periphery; that is, external stimuli directly enter the system Cs at the same time that Pcs stimuli also impinge on it. Is this progression compatible with the data of neurophysiology? A stimulus first enters the organism through receptors that have no mentational attributes. These receptors, through intermediary pathways, carry the stimulus—which can be thought of as a movable energic configuration, an impulse—to higher centers which eventually achieve conscious representation. This may be an oversimplification, partly because many of the intermediary pathways between the sensory receptors and final conscious perception are complex and not definitely known.

Nevertheless, it is important to the psychoanalyst to know whether the act of becoming conscious involves the participation of the primitive levels of the personality. Does an impulse, for example, enter the psyche through the id and proceed to higher ego levels, eventually reaching the system perceptual consciousness? Or in an antithesis of this sequence, does a stimulus enter the Pcpt-Cs directly from the outside world, as presented in the model of the mystic writing pad? This is important because as a basic biological need acquires accretions as it strives for gratification, so does a sensory stimulus accumulate features of the psychological system it passes through on the pathway to achieve a perceivable representation. What becomes associated with it determines a sensory impulse's fate and how it will be perceived or not perceived.

According to the psychoeconomic hypothesis, there are distributions and redistributions of energy that establish the outcomes of both instinctual needs and external stimuli. A stimulus may be distorted, misperceived, or even not registered, depending on its energic state. Whether or not it is perceived depends on its energic status, that is, the amount of cathexis it contains. Distortions are the outcome of associative connections with the id's content, for what is relegated to the id is forbidden conscious expression.

The concept of the *day residue* is pertinent to these issues. When discussing dreams, Freud (1900) postulated that a day residue—an indifferent, perhaps trivial, event that occurred on the day, or even two days, before the dream—has some similarity to a repressed id element and so attaches itself to that element and carries it along to higher psychic levels where it becomes elaborated into a dream (see Chapter 4). The act of dreaming is thus indicative of a state of psychic awareness that must involve consciousness to some degree. A dream is a conscious experience that contains the day residue in a disguised and distorted form.

The tachistoscope is an instrument that permits an investigator to demonstrate the pathway within the psyche of certain types of external stimuli. The subject is exposed to visual stimuli, usually a picture or a number or perhaps some sentences, on a card for a fraction of a second. Its duration is so brief that it is not consciously registered. This is a subliminal stimulus that, from a psychoeconomic perspective, leads us to conclude that a certain threshold of cathexis is required for a stimulus to be elevated to the level of conscious awareness. However, tachistoscopic experiments indicate that even hypocathected or subliminal stimuli somehow enter the psychic apparatus, but because they are not directly perceived, they must come in at lower levels. In some experiments the subjects were asked to make drawings, and in others, to describe their dreams. Both the drawings and dreams revealed that the stimulus had not been lost, that it could be found in a distorted form in the drawings and the manifest content of the dreams. Somewhere during its travels through the psyche, as does the ordinary day residue, the stimulus acquires content and momentum (energy) from the lower levels, propelling it toward the Pcpt-Cs. In other words, the hypocathected stimulus acquires cathexis as id content becomes attached to it.

Freud stated that the act of becoming conscious requires that a preconscious element become *hypercathected*. It is difficult to know precisely what hypercathexis is, as the quantitative elements of the psychoeconomic hypothesis are purely impressionistic and there is no calibrating scale. All we know is that some impulses and elements contain more energy, that is, are more highly cathected than others are. A psyche element in the Pcs acquires additional energy from the preconscious and then passes over into the Pcpt-Cs.

This progression of a hypercathected preconscious element into the Pcpt-Cs is usually orderly and helps make distinctions between the inner world of the mind and the outer world of reality. Ego boundaries must be sufficiently cathected if they are to maintain this differentiation between the mind and reality. This differentiation, however, must be understood further in regard to the psyche's distinguishing inner from outer stimuli and discovering the source of stimuli beyond their cessation or continuation following an action designed to avoid stimuli (Freud 1915a).

For the moment, let us assume that an external stimulus first enters the psychic apparatus at the level of the Pcpt-Cs, as Freud assumed in his model of the mystic writing pad, rather than having to travel up through the id to the pcs and then the Pcpt-Cs. This external stimulus is met halfway by perconscious "feelers" that stem from memory traces, which are residues from previous experiences with similar stimuli from the external world. Thus, every perception is cathected from two directions. As the stimulus resides for a brief stay in Pcpt-Cs, it is energized from the Pcs and the system Pcpt-Cs itself. If the stimulus emanates from the inside, that is, if it is a manifestation of an instinctual need, then the cathexis it carries with it into the Pcpt-Cs will be acquired chiefly from the internal world of the mind. Apparently when the stimulus reaches the Pcs and receives additional energy from that system, it is felt as belonging to the inside rather than the outside. Pcs cathexis is the decisive factor that identifies a sensory impression as belonging to the self. The proportion of Pcs cathexis to energy received from the Pcpt-Cs or other sources determines whether a stimulus is perceived as internal or external. An inner need from the id is hypercathected in the Pcs and passed into the Pcpt-Cs. It contains a large proportion of Pcs energy, compared with the cathexis it receives from the Pcpt-Cs, and thus it is felt as internal. By contrast, an external stimulus contains a small amount of cathexis from the preconscious "feelers," compared with the amount it gathers from the Pcpt-Cs, and thus it is experienced as external.

The psychoeconomic hypothesis can be extended to the understanding of psychopathological phenomena. For example, Freud explained hallucinations as the consequence of a lack of preconscious cathexis. Essentially, a hallucination is created by an id impulse's moving directly into the Pcpt-Cs without cathecting or minimally cathecting a memory trace in the system Pcs. This would mean that id cathexis is freely mobile and does not have or does not retain sufficient attachment to the psyche, to its site of origin, to indicate that it belongs to the internal world. Consequently, once it reaches the Pcpt-Cs, it is perceived as belonging to the external world, as it has passed, in a relative sense, over the Pcs.

These energic shifts and distributions can also be applied to the more general issue of *repression*, a mental mechanism that constitutes a defensive psychopathological adaptation, or it may be simply an adaptation that belongs to the "psychopathology of daily life." The concepts of cathexis, hypercathexis, and decathexis are especially useful for explaining the phenomenon of repression. Repression (see Chapter 6) is a core defense that is basic to the psychoanalytic understanding of the psychoneuroses, which in the classical tradition, represent the clinical field suitable for the psychoanalytic approach. This is a controversial topic that will be discussed in the section on ego psychology. In this context a repressed element represents an impulse that has become decathected and therefore is not able to reach the Pcpt-cs.

Again, impulses are not allowed access to discharge because of various internal conflicts, usually brought about by superego prohibitions. In this case, the roles of opposing forces, such as censors, are at the forefront. In energic terms, Freud referred to these censors as having *countercathexis*, opposing the cathexis toward discharge of the forbidden impulse and the impetus to make it conscious. The concept of repression demonstrates the interrelatedness of the psychodynamic and the psychoeconomic hypotheses.

Whatever factors account for the unacceptability of the impulse destined for repression, there is always a sexual component that is at variance with the other parts of the psyche and, in some instances, with what the outer world will permit. External and internal prohibitions have a synergistic effect on each other. In other words, the forbidden drive contains libido as its dominant, if not exclusive, source of energy. Repression consists of delibidinization; libido is detached from the impulse and is used to push it back, to repress it. Freud (1915b) stated that the energy of repression was derived from a withdrawal of libido from a sexual impulse formed in the id, one that has been banished to the id and is now trying to escape from this "seething cauldron" (1916–1917). Because the combination of the content of the impulse and the libido is unacceptable to the higher levels of the psyche, the libido is withdrawn, leading to a decathexis of the impulse. Depriving the impulse of its energy inactivates it and renders it harmless, because it no longer has the impetus pushing it toward conscious awareness and discharge. A repressed impulse is a deactivated impulse.

Freud (1915b) wrote about two types of repression, *repression proper*, which I have already described as repressing forces stripping the impulse of its energy and using it against it, and *primal repression*, which is somewhat more difficult to understand. Freud commented that the id contains two groups of content, one consisting of elements that have been repressed but are capable of becoming conscious and at one time were, whereas the second group has never been conscious. Freud did not explain further and left us puzzled, especially because he went on to describe primal repression as the banishment of percepts from the Pcpt-Cs to the Pcs and then, the Ucs, because elements in the id that are associatively connected to the percepts have some kind of attractive force that draws them into the id. Freud did not clarify this, but I believe he meant that this magnetic-like force belongs to id elements that have never been conscious. These elements are difficult to conceptualize, however, because up to this point, he had described psychic energy only as a buildup of tension, discharge, or forces opposing that discharge. In primal repression, therefore, Freud introduced another dimension to psychic energy, a capacity to pull as well as to push. From the discharge vantage point, this would be negative energy.

This new dimension has other implications that apply to psychic structures as well as impulses and percepts. We are accustomed to think of the psyche's higher levels having inhibitory effects on the lower levels, but Freud's ideas teach us that it is not that simple. The lower levels, in turn, "resist" permitting psychic content that is appropriate to that level travel into realms that operate in a more sophisticated fashion. Moreover, if what is connected to these elements, in either content or organization, enters the psychic apparatus from the periphery of the Pcpt-Cs, it will be "pulled" back into the system to which it properly belongs.

In regard to external percepts having direct access to the Pcpt-Cs without traversing the lower levels, what would be the theoretical consequences of giving up this assumption in favor of the hypothesis that an external percept similar to an internal need travels the same path within the mental apparatus? Obviously, this does not happen in the nervous system because apart from different receptor areas, various sensory neurons, synapses, and locations in different parts of the brain and nervous system are involved in the complex act of perception. These are different from the structures involved with inner needs and the conduction of visceral impulses. Consequently, there is no reason to suppose that the psyche cannot be viewed in a parallel fashion. However, we can continue to assume that an external stimulus first gains access to the mind by traveling through biological, prementational levels before being elaborated in a psychological sense.

Nevertheless, this pathway of conduction from the lower to the upper levels does not necessarily invalidate Freud's formulations about external stimuli directly entering the Pcpt-Cs. We can distinguish between the biological factors involved in sensory conduction from the psychological elaboration and the process of conscious awareness. The former emphasizes a passage through various levels of the nervous system, leading from the peripheral structures to the central areas of the brain stem and cerebral cortex. The latter have been considered to be the sites of mentational constructions.

As mentioned, a sensory stimulus, for example, a visual or auditory one, enters the nervous system at a receptor site, in these instances the retina or the auditory nerve, and is then carried by nerve fibers to specific synaptic junctions where other connections (relays) are made and eventually are brought to the appropriate areas of the brain such as the visual area of the occipital cortex. There is much that remains unknown about what happens at these locations pertaining to associative pathways and the act of becoming conscious. The noteworthy point here is that the sensory impulse created by an external stimulus travels through conductor pathways without being significantly modified. Presumably, the conduction of sensory impulses involves changes in electric potential. How these become elaborated into subjective experiences remains largely unknown, but it is certain that this occurs only in the higher brain centers and not in the conducting pathways that carry the stimulus to these centers. So even though the external stimulus first gains access to the mind's inner world through the so-called lower levels of the nervous system (peripheral nerves), it does not become mentationally elaborated until it reaches centers that could be considered to be in context with the Pcpt-Cs.

I do not believe that it is necessary here to pursue connections with neuroanatomy and neurophysiology, except to point out that perceiving an internal stimulus is complicated, perhaps much more complex than perceiving an external stimulus. The sensory peripheral network is part of the vegetative nervous system which has features different from those of the voluntary nervous system, as well as specific qualities dependent on the organ or organ system to which it is connected. The motor sympathetic and parasympathetic nervous pathways evoke different responses in various organs, as the messages they receive from subcortical layers of the brain dictate. In other words, a good deal is going on within the organism without any significant contributions from stimuli from the outer world. Energic distributions are, in these instances, the outcome of internal processes rather than changes primarily effected by interactions with and impressions from the outer world.

Thus, whatever the final pathways of perception specific for the vegetative nervous system, they help elevate visceral processes to mentational levels. This does not always occur with clarity. Many internal feelings are vague, indefinite, and difficult to describe, although most of us know what is meant by hunger, sexual feelings, a need to defecate, or a full bladder. Nevertheless, these sensations are different from external percepts. They lack sharpness in the same way that a visual conjuring of a fantasy differs from looking at something similar in the outer world. The quality of vividness seems to be connected with sources of energy that are stimulated by external percepts.

Apparently, Freud was not altogether certain about the source of libido. He vacillated between believing (1) that the "seething cauldron" of the id was its initial source and (2) that the ego was its primary site. In working out the complexities of narcissism, instinct theory, and anxiety theory, Freud (1914c, 1920, 1923a, 1926) tried to understand the various distributions of libido in terms of its origin. Libido, as the energic power of an instinct and similar to an instinct, has a source, aim, and object. It is, in fact, the impetus of a drive. Thus it first must be attached to a psychic system and, when sufficiently developed, seeks and finds an object.

It is interesting that some of Freud's earlier ideas are more applicable to present-day formulations than are what we might call an intermediary phase of psychoanalytic concepts. In his papers "On Narcissism" (1914c) and "Beyond the Pleasure Principle" (1920), he made the ego the generator of libido, whereas in "The Ego and the Id" (1923a), he assigned this function to the id.

In Appendix B of "The Ego and the Id," the editors of the *Standard Edition* pointed out that in the third edition of the "Three Essays" (1905b) published in 1915 but written in 1914, Freud wrote: "Narcissistic or ego libido seems to be the great reservoir from which the object-cathexes are sent out and into which they are withdrawn once more; *the narcissistic libidinal cathexis of the ego is the original state of things,* realized in earliest childhood, and is merely covered by the later extensions of libido, but in essentials persists behind them" (p. 218, italics added). In his paper "On Narcissism" (1914c) he conveyed the same idea in his famous amoeba analogy: "Thus we form the idea of there being an original libidinal cathexis of the ego, from which some is later given off to objects, but which fundamentally persists and is related to the object-cathexis much as the body of an amoeba is related to the pseudopodia which it puts out" (p. 75).

The editors of the *Standard Edition* also emphasized that the amoeba analogy, apparently a favorite of Freud's, recurs in later writings. For instance, in his paper "A Difficulty in the Path of Psycho-Analysis" (1917b), Freud stated: "The ego is a great reservoir from which the libido that is destined for objects flows out and into which it flows back from those objects. . . . As an illustration of this state of things we may think of an amoeba, whose viscous substance puts out pseudopodia . . ." (p. 139). Freud also mentioned the amoeba in the "Introductory Lectures" (1916–1917), and in "Beyond the Pleasure Principle" he again affirmed "that the ego is the true and original reservoir of libido" (p. 51).

Shortly afterward in an encyclopedia article (1923c) Freud made a similar statement, but in "The Ego and the Id" he reversed his position: "Now that we have distinguished between the ego and the id, we must recognize the id as the great reservoir of libido . . ." (p. 30). In the "Autobiographic Study" (1925a) he returned to his earlier view of the ego's being the reservoir, and he repeated this position in the "New Introductory Lectures" (1933) as well as in the "Outline of Psycho-Analysis" (1940).

In these latter two works, however, Freud considered the source of libido from a developmental viewpoint and regarded the psychic apparatus as first consisting of an id–ego undifferentiated matrix. Any libido attached to the ego during this beginning rudimentary stage would also be part of the id, as the ego and id are not separated from each other. When differentiation occurs, libido becomes detached from the id, as it remains with the ego in the beginning developmental phase of primary narcissism (see Chapter 3).

The editors of the *Standard Edition* apparently did not want to believe that Freud might have been inconsistent. Consequently, they interpreted his remarks about the libidinization of the id–ego matrix as resolving a seeming contradiction. The id acts as a storage tank, and the ego is a reservoir that distributes libido, either keeping it for itself as narcissistic libido or sending it into the external world as object libido. The ego draws libido from the id as its supplies become depleted. That libido is involved with the id–ego matrix seems somewhat puzzling if we retain Freud's definition of libido as the energy of the sexual instincts. Sexuality then would be present from the beginning, even before mentation has been achieved. Like Athena bursting forth from the head of Zeus, there are no developmental antecedents for libido. It is simply there as the psyche is structured from early amorphous states.

I believe that Freud's inconsistency regarding the source of libido highlights, in general, the inconsistencies of the psychoeconomic hypothesis. Kardiner and colleagues (1959) wrote an extensive critique of this hypothesis which they could not get published in a psychoanalytic journal, as at that time papers criticizing Freud were not very popular. One of the authors told me that Kardiner had predicted that in ten years there would be many articles in the psychoanalytic literature that would repeat their arguments without giving him credit. This prediction has turned out to be accurate. There have been, indeed, many papers criticizing the psychoeconomic hypothesis; in fact, it became fashionable to attack it, but Kardiner's arguments, although repeated many times, have seldom been acknowledged.

In summary, psychoanalysis must include a concept of energy as a driving power, but it need not be attributed to a particular psychological system. It can be part of the body's general metabolism and diurnal variations that extend into the psychic sphere. Perhaps energy, similar to drives, can be considered a borderland area between the biological and the psychological. Its fluctuations are readily recognizable in affective states and their pathological variants such as depression and mania.

OTHER FRAMEWORKS

Clinicians have always felt the need to expand Freud's three metapsychological views. New hypotheses evolved when clinical material focused on certain issues that could not be fully explained by these three approaches. Two of these new frames of reference are especially relevant to the psychoanalytic clinical approach, the *adaptive* and the *genetic hypotheses*.

It is debatable whether these two hypotheses are at the same conceptual level as are the three classical viewpoints of metapsychology. For example, if structure and function were placed in an interrelated network, then the adaptive viewpoint could easily be incorporated into the structural hypothesis as an extension. This, to a large extent, has been done and is included under the rubric of ego psychology. The genetic approach emphasizes the significance of the past, which is basic to all psychoanalytic clinical formulations.

The Adaptive Hypothesis

Adaptation is a psychic function that has been located in the ego's executive apparatus. From a structural viewpoint, the ego's activities have been divided into three areas, (1) sensory, (2) integrative, and (3) executive. Adaptation pertains to the motor end of what is essentially a sensory-motor sequence.

The acquisition of adaptations entails introjective processes. The child has needs, and under optimal conditions, those needs are met. During the early months of life, the infant gradually internalizes various aspects of the nurturing relationship, forming an endopsychic registration of a gratifying relationship. At most, this must be subjectively perceived as a state of comfort, one characterized by calm and feeling soothed at this very early stage of development. Perhaps the infant experiences a sequence of tension and relief as inner needs are met. At some point, the child begins to recognize that the source of nurture resides outside the self. Nevertheless, he continues to internalize the comfort-producing, satisfying aspects of the caretaking relationship.

These first introjects are what I call *functional introjects*, which means that rather than a person being internalized, only those aspects of the external object that are directed to satisfying the child's needs are intrapsychically registered. With greater emotional development, other attributes of the outside world are made parts of the self as the identifying process becomes progressively elaborated. Included in the interactions of assimilating various aspects of the external world are skills and techniques that enable the ego to cope with its environment and eventually sustain itself independently. In summary, adaptive techniques are acquired through interactions with the outside world as the psyche reaches higher levels of psychic structure. There is a parallel structural sophistication of sensory and integrative ego systems. The caretaking experience becomes integrated into the ego's executive system and also becomes part of the self represenation. The identity sense is, to a large measure, determined by how one adapts to the external world.

The adaptive view has gained prominence because clinicians often see patients whose main problem is that they cannot cope with the exigencies of daily life and do not know who they are. They do not know where they are going and the purpose of their lives. They feel empty, futile, and without roots. They seem to be lacking in adaptive techniques. These patients must be distinguished from the psychoneurotic patient who has a variety of inhibitions caused by intrapsychic conflict. Such patients are not repressing techniques designed to gratify inner needs. Rather, they simply do not know how to accomplish tasks that, for most people, would be relatively simple and pedestrian (see Chapters 8 and 9).

For example, a student in his late teens sought therapy because nothing in life "worked" for him. In college he had to do assignments and write papers, and he became extremely anxious because he did not know where to begin. Although bright, as evidenced by test scores and the fact that he had been accepted in a school known for its rigorous academic standards, he was unable to function academically. In high school, he was, according to him, "spoon-fed" and because he had a good memory, he could follow instructions. At the university, he had to rely on his own resources, which he felt were nonexistent.

His problems, however, were not confined to just academic difficulties. He did not know how to function in general. At first, he believed that it was because he was not used to big cities, having been raised in a small town, but it soon became evident that throughout his life, he had been sheltered and never had had to do anything on his own. Now he was distressed whenever he had to do something. As I have found to be true for several adolescents, he was particularly perplexed about his clothes. For example, he did not know that wearing Bermuda shorts in the main part of the city during the winter was not appropriate. He wondered what type of shoes were proper for specific occasions. Could he wear sneakers with a tuxedo? He literally did not know how to make a telephone call, but more important was his lack of knowledge of interpersonal relationships. He was in a complete quandary as to how to ask for a date. He could not make a call, but even if he could have, he would not know what to say.

I wondered whether it were possible that anybody could be so ignorant. This patient's inability to function may have been caused by anxiety, or he may have had to repress and inhibit courses of action because of various intrapsychic conflicts based on past traumas. However, after having seen him for about a year, I concluded that he really did not have the adaptive techniques to carry out the daily routines of everyday living. To wit, he never had a dream indicating that he was repressing an activity that was part of the ego's executive system. Instead, he lacked those experiences that would have taught him how to move easily and smoothly in his cultural milieu.

He was not only socially clumsy and inept but also physically awkward and mechanically incompetent. For many months, I was apprehensive each time he walked into my consultation room. He would stumble in and move his arms about in such an uncoordinated fashion that I feared for the safety of breakable items such as table lamps and pictures on the wall. He would invariably knock pillows off the couch and drag my throw rugs from their usual position. On several occasions, he stumbled over them, tripping and nearly falling. He never commented about his clumsiness and near-accidents, making me suspect that this awkwardness was a familiar part of his life. It seemed that he had accepted an ego defect that affected his motoric functioning, but in general, he felt miserable.

There were large gaps in his knowledge. Similar to Coppolillo's (1967) patient, he was unfamiliar with the traditional fairy tales. Until recently, he had never heard of Cinderella, Pinocchio, Snow White and the Seven Dwarfs, and many other fairytale characters familiar to practically every literate person in our culture. This unfamiliarity with our folklore represented a significant lacuna in his memory system, which made difficult his relating to the outer world in terms of human interactions. What became apparent was that he had received only a minimum of soothing and did not experience the early nurturing relationship beyond simply having his basic needs met. No one ever played with him or seemed to take any delight in his mere presence.

The patient's father had died when he was 2 years old, and so he had no conscious recollection of him. His mother, who had inherited a sizable sum of money, spent most of her time traveling and, from what I could gather, probably having a series of affairs. The patient had a succession of indifferent maids who apparently knew how to take care of his material needs but were either not able or did not want to give him anything beyond that. His childhood was emotionally impoverished and drab, his mother being absent most of the time. He insisted that he grew up like Topsy without anyone playing with him or assuming the role of a mentor. Even Topsy was someone he had just recently learned about in a class.

This patient reminded me of another patient who summarized his dilemma by stating that he lived in a world of calculus complexity but he had only an arithmetic mentality. He felt crass, stupid, and embarrassed, but the patient I have been discussing was not aware of his social transgressions until afterwards when someone told him about them, and then he would feel terribly humiliated. He told of two seemingly trite situations for which he had been severely reprimanded by his classmates. He recalled an episode in the dormitory lunch hall when he buttered a slice of bread and ate it without tearing it in half. On another occasion, a classmate pulled out a pack of cigarettes and offered them to his friends before taking one himself. Some refused and others accepted, including the patient. Later the patient took out a pack of his own, and he was severely criticized for having accepted a cigarette previously when he had his own.

He felt embarrassed, but as I stated, he was often unaware of the significance of his behavior and circumstances. For example, I was struck by the fact that he took public transportation to come to my office, even though he owned both an expensive sportscar and a motorcycle. They were never in running order, always lacking some part. I also learned from a colleague who was treating one of his friends that my patient would have ranked among one of the worst drivers in the world. Driving with him was reported as sheer agony. Though he professed to be knowledgeable about automobiles, he was unable to shift gears smoothly, to steer without making wide swerves, or to stay in his lane and maintain a proper distance from the cars in front of him. The patient would wryly remark when his automobile was not running that it had suffered from "psychosomatic failure." He had a dream of being in a Volkswagen, a Beetle, but he was unable to get it to run. This dream and his associations indicated that he viewed himself as a nonfunctioning, inadequate being. The Volkswagen in the dream indicated that he did not value himself, as it was a considerable notch below the expensive sportscar he actually owned, even though it did not seem to run any better than did the cheap Beetle he dreamed about.

There is much that could be said about this patient's psychopathology, but here I merely wish to stress his lack of adaptive techniques that made him feel ashamed and inadequate. He had not had the early experiences that would have given him a cultural breadth and sophistication to deal with the more subtle aspects of his interpersonal relationships. There was little evidence to indicate that his inability to cope was the result of repressive defenses because of intrapsychic conflict, although there may have been some repressive mechanisms. The latter and a defect in the ego's executive apparatus are not mutually exclusive, but I believe his psychopathology can be better explained in terms of the adaptive rather than the psychodynamic hypothesis.

The Genetic Hypothesis

Freud always thought in terms of the past's influencing later adaptations and the construction of psychopathology (Breuer and Freud 1895, Freud 1894, 1896), and the basis of the genetic hypothesis is that the earliest experiences are the most signifi-

cant for the construction of character. Freud quoted the em-
bryologist Roux, who observed that a pinprick at an embryolog-
ical phase, such as the blastula stage, will have profound effects
on the developing organism, perhaps producing serious birth
defects and monsters, whereas a similar pinprick in a child or
adult will be inconsequential (Freud 1920). Freud felt that something similar happens with psychic experiences.

The two most important subjects in the context of the
genetic hypothesis are *infantile sexuality* and *traumas*, which are
closely linked together, inasmuch as Freud considered psychic
traumas to consist of childhood seductions, a topic that has been
receiving more recognition.

According to Freud, early childhood experiences consist of
levels of gratification that involve sexual satisfaction. These
developmental phases are called *psychosexual* stages. Note,
however, that Freud's concept of sexuality was much broader
than the one conventionally held and entailed many areas beside
those generally associated with the sexual act. That is, he emphasized *pregenital* sexuality which is related to both bodily
needs and functions included in the realms of *orality* and *anality*. Children have sexual feelings that can lead to intrapsychic
conflict.

After publishing the "Studies on Hysteria" Freud (1895)
clarified types of sexual traumas. He divided them into active
and passive and then related various forms of psychopathology
to whether the traumas were active or passive and when they
occurred during childhood. In hysteria, the most commonly
studied neurosis in Freud's time, the trauma supposedly occurred early in childhood between ages 2 and 4 or 5 and was pas-
sively experienced. This meant that an adult seduced the child,
usually a relative such as an uncle, although in regard to one case
(Katharina) that Freud reported (Breuer and Freud 1895) he
later admitted that he disguised the seducer as an uncle, whereas
he was really the father. For the obsessional patient, Freud
placed the trauma's occurrence somewhat later, after the age of
6 or 7. He referred to the obsessional's trauma as an active
trauma, in that the patient seduced a younger child. Here Freud
referred only to males, but the child who is seduced is a girl. He
called such a seduction a trauma because the future obsessional

would be plagued with self-reproaches. However, underneath the obsessional neurosis, the clinician often discovers a hysterical core, for as a child, the obsessive may have been seduced earlier as a hysteric and then later became the seducer.

Freud (1905a) concluded that his patients had misled him, that these were not actual occurrences but wish-fulfilling fantasies. Freud was at first stunned by this discovery, and he felt betrayed by his patients. But he then realized how powerful a fantasy can be, and in terms of neurosogenesis and psychoanalytic treatment, it was not particularly important what actually happened.

Freud's early ideas about psychic trauma are subsumed under the rubric of *seduction hypothesis*. For the most part, psychoanalysts were content to accept that their patients' reports were the outcome of fantasy or distorted *screen memories*. The latter are memories that cover up important childhood events that can be traumatic for the developing personality (Freud 1899) and that are important to the therapeutic interaction (Freud 1914e). Recently, there has been a movement asserting that the original seduction hypothesis—that is, that there was an actual rather than a fantasied seduction—is correct, but because of Freud's own background and personal problems, he revised his theory (see Malcolm 1981). Few analysts have supported these later assertions, and although we are learning that the incidence of child molesting and incest is astonishingly high, it is difficult to accept that every psychoneurotic patient who seeks psychoanalytic help was seduced in childhood.

The genetic hypothesis is highlighted in Freud's (1918) discussion of his famous patient, the *Wolf Man*. Although the patient was an adult when he sought treatment, Freud concentrated on the patient's childhood, on what he called the *infantile neurosis*. He carefully traced the patient's symptoms to a series of past experiences as well as to his relationship with his parents, particularly his father. Freud mentioned childhood seduction but stressed the importance of the child's witnessing, at a very early age, his parents having sexual intercourse. Apparently, the Wolf Man—so named because as a child he had a phobia of the wolves he saw in picture books—slept for some years in a crib in his parents' bedroom.

Freud discussed the *primal scene*, which is what he called the child's observation of parental intercourse. He concluded that this event had a profound influence in determining character structure and psychopathology. He deduced the existence of a primal-scene trauma from a study of the Wolf Man's dreams and associations. Freud further surmised that every adult neurosis is preceded by an infantile neurosis, although in later childhood it may not be manifest, remaining in a latent state.

Since then, psychoanalysts continue to focus on the influence of the past. However, we tend to think less in terms of specific traumas, seductions, and primal scenes. Rather, the understanding of the total infantile environment has gained importance, and now we take into account its general traumatic potential when assessing psychopathology. Sometimes we encounter dramatic childhood episodes of trauma, but usually we are presented with an environment that can be viewed in terms of continual and cumulative traumas (Khan 1964). In treatment, the infantile environment suffuses the consultation room as the patient attempts to pattern the analytic ambience after what he or she knew in childhood as well as to convert the therapist into an important figure from the past. These phenomena, the hallmarks of the transference interaction, belong in the context of the genetic hypothesis.

Chapter 3

DEVELOPMENTAL FACTORS AND INSTINCT THEORY

Although psychoanalysis began as a clinical discipline and treatment method, it soon expanded to the study of stages of emotional development. Our understanding of psychopathology and therapeutic techniques require a sequential scheme of psychic development. In psychoanalytic treatment, the patient regresses and recapitulates, in a modified form, early developmental phases. Both neuroses and psychoses are based on a series of fixations on and regressions to these past ego states and orientations (see Chapter 5). Freud was well aware of the influence of the past on the formation of character structure and the production of emotional illness, and so early in the history of psychoanalysis he postulated the *psychosexual stages of development*. These stages define the sequence of normal development.

Developmental theory was established in tandem with sexual theory. In fact, they are not only closely related, but from one viewpoint, they are the same. Psychosexual theory represents the developmental antecedents of sexual impulses which are elaborated into instinct theory. Thus, psychosexual development, sexuality, and instinct theory can be viewed as different facets of essentially the same processes.

Instinct theory, as discussed in Chapter 2, is also known as libido theory. Because Freud made sexual factors fundamental to the etiology of psychic disturbances and emotional development, he was accused of being a "pansexualist." His opponents attacked him because he stressed infantile sexuality and considered early infantile activities as erotic. There is some merit in his adversaries' contention that psychoanalysis gave sex a prominent position, perhaps to the exclusion of other needs. For example, Freud (1905b) also considered pregenital elements as being sexual. That is, his concept of sex went beyond what is ordinarily considered as belonging to the realm of sex, beyond the activities of the genitals or other organs in foreplay that eventually lead to intercourse or a perversion of the sex act (see "Three Essays on Sexuality," Freud 1905b).

Although Freud postulated other instincts beside sexual, essentially he acknowledged other types of strivings, those seeking to satisfy basic survival needs. Still, his psychosexual stages of development blur the distinction between nurturing and sexual strivings; that is, the two seem to be blended together.

PSYCHOSEXUAL STAGES

Freud described a sequential progression of methods of obtaining gratification and linked them with various bodily zones. In regard to the body and pleasure, Freud preferred to consider these activities as sexual in a pregenital sense. They are also necessary for the infant's survival and as an impetus for growth and development. This sequence of psychosexual development is based on the acquisition of progressively sophisticated modes of gratification. As the psyche differentiates, it turns to the outer world to satisfy these better-structured needs. The psyche thereby becomes capable of relating to external objects and of profiting from the interaction in an increasingly pleasurable fashion. Finally the psyche becomes capable of experiencing genital sexual pleasure. Thus, the theory of psychosexual development is also an object relations theory, although external objects are not its chief focus.

The Autoerotic Stage

The beginning, or *autoerotic*, stage of psychosexual development is characterized by a psyche that has not yet attained unity and cohesion. Freud confined his description of this stage to instinctual activity, but he also implied that the autoerotic stage could be viewed as an amorphous psychic state in which there is little, if any, ego and the outside world is not sufficiently differentiated to be recognized as a separate entity.

The neonate's orientation is primarily biological, and there is a minimal awareness of feelings and needs based on a psychological orientation. I have referred to this stage as a *prementational* stage, stressing that this first stage precedes mentation, that is, feelings, perceiving and interacting from both an affective and a conscious perspective.

Despite such a primitive organization, Freud believed that autoerotic gratification and pleasure were possible in this stage. In keeping with the psychoeconomic hypothesis, he conceptualized the inner needs as being accompanied by a buildup of tension, and pleasure as resulting from the discharge of accumulated tension.

An instinct has a source, aim, and object (see Chapter 2). Although instincts are poorly differentiated during the autoerotic stage, they nonetheless possess these three attributes. The aim is, as always, satisfaction; the object is a part of the self; and the source is a libidinized organ. The libidinized organ explains how Freud allowed sexuality to enter at the beginning of the developmental scheme, as the word *autoerotic* indicates. The tension that seeks discharge consists of libido, or energy, which belongs to the sexual drive.

The discharge of energy in connection with an organ produces *organ pleasure*, and the part of the body that leads to such pleasure is known as an *erogenous zone*. The mouth is an example of an erogenous zone, and the oral mucosa is the organ that produces tension. By means of thumb sucking, the infant discharges tension and supposedly achieves pleasure. Whether the child really does feel pleasure is debatable, for to experience a structured affect requires a level of psychic integration that a neonate may not yet have attained. In any case, the autoerotic stage is one that precedes well-constructed needs and responses.

Freud (1905b) proposed that instincts first express themselves as *component instincts*. He referred to sucking and rubbing various parts of the body as examples of component instincts seeking satisfaction, but he did not offer more specific examples.

If we do not separate structure from instinctual activity, an equation that is particularly justified during the early developmental stages, the concept of component instincts will fit into a spectrum of psychic differentation, a hierarchy from states of lesser organization to those of greater organization. Before the ego acquires cohesiveness and unity, it can be viewed as various bits and pieces operating somewhat independently or at least not in synchrony with one another. Glover (1930) stated that the psyche first consists of groups of ego nuclei. As the mind strives to achieve cohesiveness, what Nunberg (1932) called the synthetic function, these ego nuclei coalesce and form the ego. Nunberg believed that a force within the ego impels it to pull together disparate phenomena, leading to integration and the formation of psychic structures. However, it is this same impetus toward synthesis that is responsible for the establishment of the ego as a psychic organization that regulates and leads to further structure.

In accordance with our assumption that instinctual activity and psychic structure are related, we can equate component instincts with ego nuclei. Initially, these component instincts can be pictured as separate forces, vectors moving in different directions, unconnected with one another. These disparate forces are part of an amorphous psyche. Gradually, as with ego nuclei, these forces come together, blending with one another and moving in a particular direction as a unit. The setting in which this occurs is also better organized, and the instinctual vector, a composite of component instincts, seeks contact with other parts of the self and eventually with the outer world. This setting, which is the mind, thus becomes differentiated from the id and forms the ego.

Primitive Mental Functioning and
Regressed Ego States

The beginning of mental life is characterized by an impetus to unite, to synthesize, and to integrate. The primary process, the characteristic functional mode of primitive mental states, is defined in terms of its operations, which are condensation, displacement, and symbolism. Condensation refers to the pulling together of two or more psychic currents by binding them with each other. Displacement will be discussed in more detail in Chapter 6, but it also is the combining of two psychic elements. They do not remain combined, however; one takes over and substitutes for the other, which is repressed. Symbolism is a product of displacement and condensation in which something concrete and part of the external world represents a wish, a need, or some other psychic element, perhaps associated with a part of the body such as the breast or the genitals.

The manifestations of the primary process are often bizarre, especially when the mechanism of condensation has been dominant. Nothing is added to the psychic elements being subjected to primary process operations. They do not acquire further structure or integration, but in the bringing together of disparate elements, the inherent impetus of the psychic apparatus to synthesize and integrate is facilitated by primary process operations. During these early stages, the mind's integrative capacity is enhanced and is set in motion by condensation and displacement. Thus, new psychic structures are formed, and so the primary process represents a *modus operandi*, which in the context of what we might call a *developmental drive* causes the mind to progress to higher developmental levels.

At these higher levels, the secondary process prevails. This is characterized by logic and analysis combined with self-evaluation and reality testing. Whereas the primary process pulls things together, the secondary process separates, analyzes, and differentiates. The ego, which is based on a secondary process approach, has both cohesiveness and various subsystems differentiated from one another but capable of working together.

The primary and secondary processes do not oppose each other in content or as functions. They do not represent polarities. In a healthy person, they can operate simultaneously, leading to creative accomplishment and psychic growth. Primary process material is refined and rearranged by means of secondary process revision; for example, a perhaps bizarre idea is modified in the light of reality and made to conform to an established context.

During psychopathological regression, secondary process thinking and reality testing break down. Ordinarily, there is a balance between primary process and secondary process mental operations, but in emotional illness, primary process operations predominate without the supraordinate organization of secondary process synthesis. A regressed ego state is different from its corresponding early stage of development. Such states have retained the organization and adaptive techniques acquired later in development. In the early stages, this organization and these adaptive techniques are not yet developed, whereas in the regressed state they persist or are damaged and defective. The regressed state is *dis*organized, whereas early developmental stages are *un*organized. In the early developmental stages, both primary and secondary process operations contribute to emotional growth and the acquisition of psychic structure. In contrast, in the regressed state, primitive and advanced modes of relating deteriorate. Both, in some measure, have lost their adaptive capabilities.

In summary, the autoerotic stage is one of relative unorganization, and most behavior during this stage is the outcome of reflex activity. Autoerotic satisfaction gradually diminishes as the psyche attempts to distinguish and make contact with the external world.

Primary Narcissism

The ego develops at the periphery of the id as it experiences the stimuli of outer reality (Freud 1920). In the infant, these stimuli are mitigated by the protective shield of the mother, but they cause the amorphous id to organize itself defensively and thereby to acquire some structure. This initial structure represents the embryonic ego that is not yet able to recognize the external world as being separate and apart from the psyche.

At this early stage of intrapsychic differentiation between the id and the ego, psychic energy can be viewed as originating in the id and flowing into the newly formed ego. As I pointed out, Freud vacillated between the id and the ego as the original site of libido, which is often equated with psychic energy. In most of his papers, however, he referred to the id as being the libidinal reservoir. The flow of libido from the id to a rudimentary ego is known as *primary narcissism*. This is merely a transfer of psychic energy from one part of the mind to another, slightly more structured part. The psyche is self-contained in that it is unable to recognize anything outside its boundaries. In fact, it cannot even discern boundaries, for the perceptual system, as is true of the ego in general, is only minimally developed.

Balint (1937, 1959) did not see any purpose in formulating a stage of primary narcissism, as it does not have any mentational representation and can only be inferred. We could raise the same objection about the autoerotic stage, as the clinician cannot obtain data that are directly related to the processes that Freud postulated. From a theoretical perspective, these early prementational stages are logically consistent antecedents of later developmental stages that can be determined from the observation of behavioral data and a person's fantasies, dreams, and free associations. Balint, however, would not have found it necessary to form any hypotheses regarding psychic processes and structure that cannot be reconstructed from the analytic interaction. Still, in addition to broadening the spectrum of emotional development, the study of primitively fixated and regressed ego states in various psychopathological situations reveal configurations and intrapsychic and interpersonal reactions that contain autoerotic features and energic distributions apparently oriented along a primary narcissistic axis. Severely regressed psychotic patients, such as catatonics and those suffering from autistic states, furnish us with prominent examples of autoerotic behavior and an oblivious attitude toward the external world that defines primary narcissism.

Secondary Narcissism

The psyche both enters into and admits the external world into its domain through the process of *secondary narcissism*. As mentioned in Chapter 2, Freud used the metaphor of an amoeba to describe how object relationships are first formed. This also is a description of secondary narcissism (Freud 1914c). The amoeba moves by expanding and contracting armlike and leglike protoplasmic extensions known as pseudopodia. When it encounters a small object, it wraps its pseudopodia around it and then absorbs the particle and the limb into its body. The particle thus becomes embedded in the protoplasm. Infants react similarly by putting objects into their mouth, treating them as if they were food. That is, they learn about the external world by trying to incorporate objects and make them part of themselves. Consequently, they do not at first precisely distinguish between the inner and outer world and actually relate to objects, but as with the amoeba, there is a back and forth movement between inside and outside, a movement that finally enables the psyche to become aware of direction and that helps establish the subjective state of position. What is central and what is peripheral is gradually recognized, and by means of spatial rearrangements and manipulation, inner and outer are eventually differentiated. What has been made part of the self is redeposited in the external world and acknowledged in its own right rather than as just a part of the self.

Secondary narcissism is an important developmental stage, but it is also a character trait that may or may not have psychopathological implications. Clinicians speak of narcissistic personalities who do not relate to persons in the outer world as separate. Such personalities deal with external objects only in terms of their needs, ranging from the need to be nurtured to self-esteeming interactions of praise and admiration. They view the outer world as belonging to them; it has become a part of the self, a slave or handmaiden possessing no autonomy of its own.

In adults, when this narcissistic orientation is this extreme it is indicative of severe psychopathology. If such persons have specific talents, they may be well compensated, enjoy considerable success, and gain the admiration they desperately need. But these are fragile personalities and may easily decompensate, as we have so frequently noted among many celebrities in the entertainment industry.

In children, however, these same needs and traits noted in narcissistic personalities can be simply an aspect of normal development. This phase occurs ordinarily at around 3 months and lasts until 6 or 7 months (Mahler 1968). The child's narcissism is not offensive, as is the adult's. Instead, we are entranced by it, and Freud wrote of "his majesty, the baby" sitting on a throne ruling the emotions of admiring and devoted parents. Freud conjectured that the baby represents our lost infantile narcissism that we try to recapture, much as we try to recapture our lost youth.

Other than the baby's almost instinctive tendency to explore the external world by incorporating it into the self, do we have direct observational data that support a concept of secondary narcissism? Today the term secondary narcissism is used synonymously with *self object*, a term that I believe was first used by Modell (1963, p. 285, footnote) and then by myself (Boyer and Giovacchini 1967, p. 269). Although Balint questioned the feasibility of the concept of primary narcissism, from a theoretical viewpoint, primary narcissism is more logically consistent within the psychoanalytic developmental framework than is secondary narcissism.

It makes sense to have an early stage when the mental apparatus, especially the perceptual system, becomes sufficiently energized so that it can begin to function. Before it can function, however, it has to accumulate a certain amount of energy, and it is this process of accumulating energy that can be subsumed under the rubric of primary narcissism. Secondary narcissism, on the other hand, is not a process that logically follows primary narcissism. Wrapping parts of the self, so to speak, around objects in order to perceive them seems at first mechanistic and fanciful. It appears that such a formulation is based on a concrete acceptance of what was intended to be just a metaphor, the amoeba metaphor.

Nevertheless, patients in a state of regression during analytic treatment often reveal material indicating that they feel fused with the analyst. Often this is the outcome of psychopathology or the manifestation of an early developmental stage, or both. It usually represents a developmental stage somewhat advanced beyond primary narcissism, in which object relations have been fairly well established. Even the fusion states of psychotic and autistic patients indicate that they have some capacity for object contact, but it may be based on delusions.

The Oral Stage

As is true for most psychoanalytic formulations based on a hierarchical sequence, distinctions among different levels are never clear-cut. This is especially true of secondary narcissism and orality. The amoeba's pseudopodia reaching out and incorporating segments of the outer world as a metaphor for secondary narcissism and the child's exploring and discovering the outer world by trying to eat it leads us to ask how such activities can be distinguished from what we call oral behavior. Certainly the mouth is dominantly involved.

The child's patterns of behavior must be placed in a context before we can differentiate the various psychosexual stages. Infants can crawl and put objects in their mouth without being particularly aware of the objects themselves. Thus, they have not yet reached the oral stage. Orality represents a method of relating to the external world and has many implications. It means that the ego is now able to deal with its environment on a part–object basis. The child recognizes the mother as a nurturing source, as someone separate from the self.

When the infant begins to smile at a person, it is considered to be the time that the child begins to recognize objects in the external world as separate from the self. The smiling response is an indicator that an affect, such as pleasure, can be generated as a result of an interaction with the external world. At first, that interaction is not too specific, but it eventually becomes related to the mother.

The recognition of the mother is initially confined to her role as a nurturing caretaker. The child's percept of her is that of a *part–object breast* that will feed and soothe. The child now knows that the source of nurture is on the outside, and is oriented toward the world as if he or she were a hungry mouth. Thus, the child's outlook during this very earliest stage of part–object relationships is oral.

As is true of all developmental stages, the passage from one stage to another does not mean that the previous one completely disappears or is totally incorporated into the next level. Freud (1915a) pointed out it persists as layers of lava do, for even though they are pushing forward and being modified by what lies in front of them, the layers that lie behind remain as they were when they erupted. The mind contains all its antecedent stages. Some of them have been modified because of developmental advances, and others remain as they were when they were first formed.

Thus, the oral stage both persists in its primitive form and is modified by later developmental accretions. Clinicians refer to orally dependent patients, indicating that such extreme dependency is caused by a predominance of oral elements in the adult object-related and reality-adapted ego state. This means that the orally dependent person tends to relate to the world in terms of being nurtured. In contrast with the child, the adult does not seek actual nurture; he does not literally want to be fed. However, he wants to be taken care of and looked after. He wants to be nurtured and soothed in a psychological sense. This personality orientation has therefore been designated as an *oral character*.

Freud also wrote about *oral drives*, and today we still think in similar terms, although we usually add the word *dependent* and call them *oral-dependent drives*. These needs are part of our instinctual endowments, but if they exceed certain quantitative limits (keeping in mind that there is no quantifying scale in psychoanalysis), they will become involved in intrapsychic conflict, meaning that the psyche's higher levels will have to institute defenses against them, such as rationalization, displacement, and reaction formation. These intense oral-dependent needs are psychopathological exaggerations that stem from primitive, unmodified oral ego states that dominate because the psyche has regressed to their level.

According to Abraham (1916, 1924a, 1924b), there are two types of oral needs that are characteristic of the oral stage and that vary in their relative strength. Abraham divided oral impulses, or instincts, into oral-dependent impulses, which he considered to be passive, and oral-cannibalistic impulses, which are actively destructive. The former are associated with passive intake, as exemplified by sucking, and the latter are characterized by the impetus to bite, tear apart, and devour.

Unless there has been a trauma associated with oral intake, passive-dependent oral personalities expect to be taken care of, and their outlook toward life is often optimistic. Abraham designated this attitude as *preambivalent*, which means that the mind is reverting to a state preceding the formation of intense affects of love and hate directed toward the same person or object. Oral-dependent characters are capable of loving and hating, but they have special persons or situations that they unequivocally hate and, similarly, other persons whom they unconditionally love. This is an exaggerated example, because again, I want to emphasize that elements of later ambivalent stages are always operating in all personality types. However, these are the textbook qualities associated with passive-dependent characters that are never seen in their pure form. During regression, patients sometimes reveal ego states that approximate preambivalent orientations and the splitting of objects into good and bad (see Chapter 6)—those that are loved and those that are hated. Everything is black or white, with no in-between groups.

By contrast, oral-cannibalistic characters are highly ambivalent. They attack those they love, relating to their loved ones in an *oral-sadistic* fashion. This puzzling and self-defeating attitude is associated with tremendous guilt and is often an underlying factor in patients suffering from agitated depressions.

As patients, the oral-sadistic or oral-cannibalistic character reveals a traumatic oral stage and a disturbed maternal relationship. Their mothers felt ambivalent toward their children, and so the mothers' acts of loving care and nurture became fused with destructive urges. These mothers frequently leave their infants for long periods of time, often because they have been incapacitated by depression or psychosis. Such children feel intense frustration and then rage. This is when ambivalence enters the psychic sphere, because the person that the children need and crave is the same person who causes them pain, anxiety, and rage.

Freud (1915a) felt that ambivalence, a term first coined by Bleuler, was a fundamental quality of instincts, whereas I believe that it manifests itself in object relationships. Freud distinguished three types of ambivalence: (1) emotional ambivalence, which refers to coexisting feelings of love and hate toward the same person; (2) voluntary ambivalence, which is characterized by indecision: a person cannot decide what course of action to follow; and (3) intellectual ambivalence, which permits the psyche to tolerate antithetical ideas. These types represent different developmental levels: the first, emotional ambivalence, is associated at the oral-aggressive stage; the second is characteristic of the anal stage; and the third is a quality of mature thinking.

In the sequence of normal development, it is more appropriate to divide the oral stage into an initial passive stage and a later aggressive stage, that is, aggressive rather than oral cannibalistic or oral sadistic. Oral cannibalistic and oral sadistic refer to emotional disturbances, whereas passive and aggressive are terms that need not have psychopathological connotations.

Freud explored various character types, especially anal characters, but he continued stressing the role of instincts. Instinctual forces are incorporated into the various ego subsystems and determine the quality of psychic structure: what can be recognized as a character type depending on which instincts are involved. Freud must have been emphasizing, however, the primitive elements participating in the formation of character, because he believed that instincts are oriented in the direction of the primary process.

Freud believed that archaic instincts, that is, the instincts of primitive man, were more ambivalent than are those of modern man. He contended that initially, instincts were very active and intense. Then as man became more civilized, his instincts were tamed and transformed into less-intense and less-active impulses. These later impulses were passive compared with the initially strong instincts, and Freud postulated a fundamental ambivalence inherent in instinctual activity, since earlier instinctual modes persist alongside later acquired tamed impulses. Apparently, the dichotomy of active and passive are polarities that are part of ambivalent attitudes, especially voluntary ambivalence in which the alternatives involved in reaching a decision are active and passive, the former consisting of positive action while the latter might consist of doing nothing. This is reflected in the oral stage between the passive, expectant attitude and the aggressive attitude involved in actively seeking nurture.

To summarize, in normal development, psychoanalysts (primarily Freud and Abraham) subdivide the oral stage into a preambivalent passive-dependent phase and an ambivalent active-aggressive phase. The latter can become psychopathologically accentuated into an oral-cannibalistic or an oral-sadistic phase.

The sequence from preambivalence to ambivalence is not necessarily confined to emotional disturbances but is part of emotional development. Pathological oral sadism and nonpathological oral aggressiveness are difficult to distinguish, however, because they are based on impressionistic and imprecise quantitative factors. The problem is further complicated because all of these phases are also considered descriptive of both ego states and qualities and types of instincts.

The Anal Stage

Unlike the oral stage, the anal stage does not directly pertain to nurture. It is not connected with a basic survival function. I would conjecture that this might have been what caused Fairbairn (1941, 1954) to omit it from his normal developmental sequence (see Chapter 9). He viewed anality as a mode of relating but did not give it the status of a developmental stage. Freud, on the other hand, saw control of the anal sphincter—toilet training—as an important accomplishment in the child's development that contributed to adult character structure. Traumas during the anal stage may lead to an obsessive-compulsive neurosis.

Again, Abraham's (1921, 1927) ideas are important. As with the oral stage, he divided the anal stage of development into two subphases, the *anal retentive* and the *anal expulsive*. Similar to the two types of orality, the anal-retentive phase refers to a passive stance, and the anal-expulsive phase represents an active, sadistic, attacking orientation. These orientations are not just rebellious and attacking. To the infant, feces are valuable products and are offered as gifts. Thus, the combination of hostile and loving impulses gives the anal stage a characteristically ambivalent stamp.

Freud's scheme of psychosexual development concentrates on a sequential dominance of various bodily zones, what he considered to be a progression from the mouth to the anus and finally the penis. Freud has been criticized for pushing female developmental psychology into the background, not distinguishing it from that of the male. Still, the importance of the mouth and the genitals appears self-evident in that they both are involved with self-preservation, the mouth with the preservation of the individual and the genitals with the preservation of the species (Freud 1920). The anal region does not seem to belong in the same frame of reference, at least from a biological viewpoint.

Psychologically, the role of the anal sphincter becomes increasingly important as the mind develops and ego boundaries are established. In a sense, the first demands that the external world makes concern excretory functions. Usually until the time of toilet training, children are in relative control of their destiny. The external world either has sensed their needs and responded to them or has been receptive to their demands, as occurs in the two types of orality that Abraham described. By contrast, during the anal phase someone else makes demands, expecting the children to behave in a fashion that threatens their sense of control and mastery.

I again wish to caution against the dangers of adultomorphization and absolutism, two attitudes that are not foreign to psychoanalytic theory. However, as mentioned, if we do not attribute too-complex and sophisticated reactions to infants and think in terms of states of calm satisfaction or disruptive frustration, we need not modify some of these classic psychoanalytic formulations. The child's state of homeostatic equilibrium is upset when made to conform to someone else's demands at the expense of his own needs, one particular need being to feel unequivocally accepted and taken care of. This belief is contradicted during the anal phase, as the child is expected to curb the expression of a biological process. Of course, there have been other restrictions, but these were designed to protect the child.

From the child's viewpoint, controlling the anal sphincter has nothing to do with his welfare. The child has to please someone else in order to remain in favor and to continue to have his needs met. During normal development, this may be the time, that is, at the beginning of the second year of life, that the child feels resentment and is aware of a sense of opposition. The child must renounce a mode of gratification and can no longer indulge in the pleasure and abandonment of soiling.

The anal-retentive phase is associated with stubbornness. It characterizes the child's refusal to give up excrement because it is expected that he do so at a prescribed time and in a particular fashion. It is a direct rebellion against toilet training, an assertion that the child will give up feces when and how he pleases. The child will not let himself be controlled or compromised by rules.

The anal-expulsive phase represents an attack, a sadistic reaction to the external world, which is perceived as depriving and manipulative. Toilet training and dictating where and how excrement will be handled also determine when feces can or cannot be released from the body. During the anal-expulsive phase, the child defies the prohibitions against defecation, and the fantasies accompanying the act are destructive and murderous.

In view of the sadistic nature of these descriptions, we can well question whether these are part of the normal developmental sequence or whether we are dealing with psychopathological variations or extensions, a question that has often been posed in reference to most of Klein's ideas (see Chapter 9). This question can be asked about all of Freud's psychosexual stages of development, but it is especially pertinent to the anal stage because it is not simply a structural extension of increasingly differentiated inner needs. It is also the outcome of demands of the outer world, and conflict is intrinsic to its development.

Perhaps in ideal development, the role of conflict can be

minimized, as there is a parallel development of the limitations imposed by reality and the pride in gaining control over instinctual forces. Children certainly are proud when they have been successful in producing feces in a fashion that gains the approval of the adult world. Feces then become valuable gifts rather than noxious destructive forces.

Although Freud's main focus was not on character structure, he was interested in the so-called anal character (1907, 1908, 1916, 1917d). The child's attitude toward control and authority becomes an important attribute of the adult character structure and contributes significantly to the style of adaptation to both the inner and the outer world. These attitudes are formed by reaction formations against many of the features associated with anal-retentive and anal-expulsive ambivalent impulses. The outcome of the anal stage is a series of character traits that have been shaped by the process of overcompensation or reaction formation and displacement. Scrupulousness, cleanliness, and parsimony are three such character traits that are the consequences of complex reactions to soiling and rebellious impulses. The tight anal sphincter of stubbornness manifests itself in rigid behavioral patterns and an inability to experience warm and tender feelings. These are usually emotionally constricted persons.

On the other hand, if modulated, anal character traits, can be useful and fulfilling adaptations. Orderliness and organization can be channeled in such a way that they lead to mastery but do not stifle imagination or feeling. Here again we are faced with a question that will be raised in Chapter 6 dealing with defenses, and that is whether these traits are the products of reaction formation or sublimation.

The Phallic Stage

The phallic stage was introduced as part of the developmental sequence relatively late in the psychoanalytic literature. From the beginning, Freud (1923b) stressed the importance of the penis as an organ that could lead to heightened self-esteem and also could be a source of concern associated with castration anxiety.

It is interesting that the formulations of the different stages of psychosexual development were not made in the same chronological sequence as they appear on the developmental timetable. Freud (1905b, 1950) wrote about the Oedipus complex early in his career, first mentioning it in letter 69 to Wilhelm Fliess. He next wrote about anality, then orality, and finally he introduced the phallic stage as immediately preceding the oedipal constellation.

The phallic stage today, as might be expected, is controversial because it mentions only the penis and there is no comparable developmental pattern for females. As man is missing a rib in *Genesis*, woman lacks a developmental way station in classic psychoanalytic theory.

During the phallic stage, the little boy is concerned mainly with his penis. He is proud of it and delights in the strength and length of his urinary stream. These preoccupations entail considerable masturbatory activity, not as an erotic activity as during puberty, but as something that creates diffuse pleasure and soothing. The penis becomes the part of the body that receives the most attention, and the mouth and the bowels recede into the background. We are now dealing with a child between 18 months and 2 to 3 years of age. This does not mean that the earlier zones, such as the mouth, have been abandoned, for we encounter many children in this age group that still spend considerable time sucking their thumbs. All the erotogenic zones, as Freud (1905b) called them, remain active, but the concentration on the penis is the most intense.

In "Three Essays on the Theory of Sexuality," Freud (1905b) introduced the term *pregenital* to designate any bodily zone or activity that precedes genital dominance. The phallic stage, however, is also pregenital, as the derivatives of phallic preoccupation are not sexual in a purely erotic sense. The penis has become a symbol of power, prestige, ambition, and competitiveness, traits that can become connected with sexual activity but are not necessarily intrinsically tied to it. Thus, the phallic stage, like the previous stages, gives its specific stamp to the character organization. The phallic character is also distinct and is responsible, more than is any other psychosexual, pregenital stage, for qualities that have been typically associated with masculinity, particularly aggressiveness and competitiveness. To repeat, the oral and anal contributions to character structure are not submerged by those of the phallic stage.

Which stage eventually dominates depends on specific elements of the infantile environment that will favor one psychosexual stage's mode of relating over another. Fixation and regression are processes that are also instrumental in determining the personality's final organization.

Freud believed that his sequence of psychosexual stages was based both on an intrinsic developmental current propelled by biological forces and on a predetermined maturation of needs. He did not consider that some of the stages he observed might have been cultural artifacts, as did some analysts who later left the mainstream of psychoanalysis, formed their own groups, and became known as neo-Freudians.

The Oedipus Complex and Beyond

The child progresses to the oedipal phase at around age 3. Again, it is difficult to trace the steps sequentially for little girls, because, according to Freud, the penis plays a central role during the oedipal phase. Thus, I shall first relate what Freud said about boys' development, although he did also consider girls' emotional progression.

During the oedipal phase the boy's object relationships achieve greater depth and breadth. Until then, object relations were confined to a two-person system, usually a mother–child interaction. Now the father enters the picture, and the child becomes involved in a triangle known as the *Oedipus complex*. That is, emotional development proceeds from the phallic stage to the oedipal phase. During the oedipal phase we encounter the Oedipus complex, probably the best known of all psychoanalytic formulations.

The penis remains the central erotic zone during the oedipal phase. According to Freud, it is not, however, just a symbol of power and ambition, as it had been in the previous phallic stage. In addition, it becomes a sexual organ in that the little boy wants to possess his mother sexually; he is striving for an incestuous relationship. In the natural course of maturation, these needs become increasingly structured until their goals become truly sexual in the context of genital intercourse. Before the oedipal phase, although such needs are still considered to be sexual, they are sexual in a pregenital sense; they are not seeking genital discharge.

Because the child has sexual impulses in the adult sense, the oedipal phase is also known as the *genital stage*, all earlier stages being pregenital. This is a crucial period of development, a milestone, because the sexualization of drives evokes definitive, if not overwhelming, responses from the outer world. Children learn during the anal phase, when they have to relinquish control of their bowels to the demands of significant external objects, that the world is not a passive support system. With the emergence of sexual feelings toward the mother, the father makes a thunderous, threatening, forbidding appearance. Previously, when the issue was control, the child was not attacking anyone or being otherwise destructive. He wanted to maintain sovereignty over the domain of his own body, but during the oedipal phase he wants to usurp the father's exalted position and steal his wife, as occurs in the Oedipus legend. Incestuous feelings are combined with patricidal impulses.

The child fears retaliation, the father's reactive wrath leading to *castration anxiety*. Inasmuch as the penis is the attacking organ, in that it seeks an incestuous relationship, the father's retaliation will also be directed against the penis. Because of forbidden feelings toward the mother and murderous impulses toward the father, the child is afraid that the father will exact revenge by castrating him. This constellation, a triangle, constitutes the Oedipus complex, and as explained in the last chapter, the superego is its heir. Castration anxiety and the father's prohibitions are internalized and become the basis for moral control. According to Freud (1913c), incest and patricide are handed down from generation to generation as a hereditary pattern in the unconscious. Consequently, from the viewpoint of classic psychoanalytic theory, the appearance of the Oedipus complex is inevitable. Just as the phallic stage has been disputed, the universality of the Oedipus complex has also been challenged.

As has been mentioned, some analysts and anthropologists believe that the Oedipus complex is a cultural phenomenon. It is based on a closely knit family system that is ostensibly patriarchal but covertly and subtly matriarchal. With the relative break-down of the family there now seems to be less of an oedipal basis for the emotional disturbances we see, although incest is a more commonly observed phenomenon. Nonetheless, son-mother incest is not too frequently seen.

Another objection to the assumption that the Oedipus com-plex is universal is the time of the superego's appearance. Freud viewed the superego as a psychic structure that was the direct outcome of the resolution of the conflicts caused by the oedipal triangle. The threat of castration as a reaction to incestuous feelings is internalized and becomes a part of the psychic appa-ratus, a prohibiting, controlling part and the foundation of mo-rality. Investigators, however, have often observed that children commonly develop self-regulating prohibitions much earlier during their childhood, often before the age of 1 and, as dis-cussed, frequently associated with elements of the anal stage.

Still, regardless of the controversy about the universality of the Oedipus complex, the child does become a much more civilized and socially acculturated person around the age of 3 or 4, and this might have been especially noteworthy in the world that Freud lived in. I make this conjecture because, following the Oedipus complex and the formation of the superego, chil-dren supposedly enter a *latency* period in which their sexual feelings are held in abeyance. This period is presumably low-keyed in that instinctual tension is at its lowest ebb. Children are not as inner directed as they had been, as their attention is focused principally on the outer world, school, peers, play, and sports. They are less concerned about interpersonal relation-ships as gratifying needs, except perhaps as maintaining self-esteem. The next instinctual upheaval after the Oedipus com-plex occurs at puberty.

Because children are chiefly fixed on the external world during latency, they have a sparse fantasy life, and the ego keeps its distance from the unconscious. Apparently the psyche has experienced a wave of repression brought about by castra-tion anxiety. Incestuous and all related sexual feelings are re-pressed, and latency-age children appear to be asexual crea-tures. Their relationships are shallow and superficial without passion or deep sensitivities.

At puberty all of this changes suddenly and drastically.

Along with the bodily changes that accompany sexual maturation, young adolescents are almost overwhelmed by fantasies
and sexual feelings. Freud (Breuer and Freud 1895, Freud
1905b, 1916–1917) described the *return of the repressed* that in
some instances can lead to neurosis and even psychosis. Adolescents must construct defenses and adaptations that will enable
them to cope with sexual feelings that in part are generated by
the recently developed gonads and the return of the repressed.
The latter is also stimulated by hormonal changes and genital
maturation.

Freud viewed the female as essentially a castrated male, at
least from a psychological viewpoint. She did not suffer from
castration anxiety because she did not have a penis to lose.
Instead she would fear loss of love if she pursued her incestuous
feelings toward her father. According to Freud, women always
want a penis, and so penis envy is a persistent problem (Freud
1937). Modern developmental theorists, however, do not accept
these theories as being valid for ordinary development, although such orientations can be found in psychopathology.

The little girl values parts of her body and has goals that are
different from the boy's. Some investigators believe that the
vagina might hold a position similar to that of the penis and that
the wish to give birth and have a child is a major goal that
defines a woman's femininity and establishes her self-esteem.
Certainly, these wishes are commonly seen in the female Oedipus complex, which has also been called the *Electra complex*, a
term that is hardly ever seen in the current psychoanalytic
literature.

The existence of the latency period has also been questioned. Prepuberty children are not as instinctually quiescent as
Freud believed. They seem to have rich fantasy lives and to be
quite preoccupied with sexual themes. There are no data to
support the thesis of massive repression.

In treatment, the repression that led to the latency period is
the same repressive process that causes infantile amnesia. The
task of psychoanalytic treatment is to lift infantile amnesia and
recover repressed memories. However, this seems to be a rare
experience among modern practitioners of psychoanalysis. The
dramatic moments of recovering significant and traumatic mem-

ories hardly ever occur in the analysis of our patients, most of whom suffer from character disorders (see Chapter 7).

Perhaps the absence of the latency phenomenon is another example of cultural influence. Because the polarities of right and wrong are not so rigidly fixed as they once were, repression does not occur as frequently or as intensely as it might have in the past. There is little in the realm of inner feelings or outer reality that is shocking to us. We have faced, with relative equanimity, atrocities that were unthinkable in the past generation. We may be outraged, but we are not surprised. We are not overwhelmed or caught unaware. Consequently, perceptual systems of our patients seem to have a high threshold of tolerance for painful and terrifying experiences. They do not need to shut out unpleasant stimuli, and so other defenses beside repression are prominent (see Chapter 6).

For example, witness the recent freedom to use four-letter words. Although obscenities have always been frequently used, they were, in the past, restricted to certain settings and usually to males. It was unladylike for women to swear. Certain words in mixed settings were simply never used. If a man, or more rarely a woman, said *fuck* in mixed company, it usually was consciously unintentional, a slip of the tongue, as if repressed material had broken through the cordon of censorship. *Fuck* was considered a taboo word. Some men could not even use such words with their male peers and had difficulty in saying them out loud even when alone. Now, the situation is different. In fact, in some social situations it seems that both men and women go out of their way to punctuate their language with expressions once reserved for longshoremen or truck drivers. The movies also reflect this change in that both language and sexual behavior are made quite explicit.

Erotic material therefore no longer has the same shock value that it once did. Ostensibly it does not provoke conflict, shame, or embarrassment. It is dealt with openly and need not be defended against. Thus, there is no longer an almost-reflex aversion and avoidance of sexual situations and feelings. The Oedipus complex may still be centered on incestuous drives, but the fear of castration as a retaliatory, punitive measure does not seem to be sufficient to lead to defenses, especially repression.

I do not mean, however, that sex is no longer an issue in the production of illness or that everybody is at ease with their sexuality. I am merely stating that there is greater openness regarding sexual matters, and ostensibly they are not treated as if they were a taboo or dangerous subject. Sexual topics are not barred from consciousness, but at deeper levels of the personality, there can still be considerable conflict regarding sexual drives. However, as seems to be the situation generally with psychopathology, the contribution of psychic structure has become equal in importance with—if it has not actually overshadowed the significance of—the drives, and this also applies to sexual drives. Gender identity is an important aspect of the self representation, a psychic structure whose defects determine various types of emotional illness known as character disorders.

Sexual problems are now more apt to be acted out than they seem to have been in Freud's time. From our experience during just the last two decades, persons who would have hidden their sexual actions and perversions because of public censure and, in some instances because they were illegal, are now openly declaring themselves. The gay liberation movement is widespread, and even politicians running for and holding public office proudly affirm their homosexuality.

Our environment in regard to sex is phenomenologically almost the total antithesis of Freud's mid-Victorian society. Does this mean that Freud's sequence of psychosexual development is not applicable to our contemporary culture? I do not believe that we have to abandon what Freud postulated, perhaps just modify some elements of his progression. His scheme can be subdivided into two general categories, an early sequence that is based mainly on biological factors and a later period that is sociologically or interpersonally oriented. The so-called pregenital stages—oral, anal, and phallic—all are based on the dominance of various bodily zones and the activities associated with them. Even the earlier autoerotic and narcissistic stages are principally concerned with the body and the maintenance of homeostasis by reestablishing states of comfort. During and following the oedipal period, the child's focus shifts from an almost-exclusive preoccupation with what is happening inside the body to the outside world. True, the child is still concerned about inner feelings, in this instance, sexual feelings, but the presence of an external object is both acknowledged and required. It was required during the pregenital stages, too, but only as a means to provide whatever was necessary to achieve psychic equilibrium. The presence of the parent of the opposite sex has become, by itself, a source of satisfaction and security. The child develops concern for a relationship and has moved beyond an exclusive desire to have inner, biologically based needs met. Perhaps these latter stages are more subject to modification by cultural influences, whereas the earlier biologically oriented stages are relatively immutable.

DEVELOPMENT OF INSTINCT THEORY

Freud had to struggle with developmental theories so that they would remain compatible with clinical discoveries and other aspects of psychoanalytic theory. Throughout his lifetime, he had to make significant revisions as he modified his concepts regarding major psychic currents. His aim was to keep his ideas about instinct development consistent with psychosexual progression. As stated, the stages of psychosexual development were the outcome of the maturation and increasing integration of instincts. Freud focused on the basic needs characteristic of the oral and phallic stages of development. Consequently, he first proposed two types of instincts, sexual and self-preservative instincts (1910c). This is his first instinct theory, the first of two theories.

In his 1910 paper, Freud called the self-preservative instincts *ego instincts*, but he asserted that sexual instincts remained attached to ego instincts. Only during illness do they become detached from the self-preservative instincts, but they still may seek the same person for gratification. Freud (1914c) called this type of object choice *anaclitic*, in that the sexual instincts "lean on the ego instincts." Freud also stated that the choice of objects for the self-preservative instincts was considerably more restricted than was that for the sexual instincts. It is conceivable that at some early stage of development, sexual and ego instincts can be directed toward the same object, as might occur during the oedipal period in which the mother becomes a sexual object and yet still remains a nurturing source. However, keeping sexual instincts attached to ego instincts, as Freud did, can create conceptual difficulties if we insist on retaining a dual instinct theory.

To repeat, Freud clung to dualism. This might have been in keeping with the scientific atmosphere of the time, or it may have been intrinsic to his cultural milieu in which polarities were sharply defined. In any case, he thought in terms of polarities such as ego and outer world, unconscious and conscious, and now sexual and ego instincts. By outlining intrinsic patterns, he constructed dualistic hypotheses to explain the processes involved in psychic development. At the same time, he investigated what we might call the reverse direction, the course of regression and the genesis of psychopathology.

Freud (1915a) focused on the basic changes in elemental instinctual forces. The editors of the *Standard Edition* translated the title of Freud's seminal paper on instincts as "Instincts and Their Vicissitudes" from the German "Triebe und Triebschicksal." *Schicksal* means "fate," and so a more literal title would have been "Drives and Their Fates." Vicissitudes implies that actions in the external world have a major influence in determining the course and development of drives, whereas Freud thought more in terms of a predetermined sequence. Instincts are subjected to four "fates" as they progress forward on the developmental scale and reach their final integrated state. Freud enumerated the following: (1) reversal of content, (2) turning toward the self, (3) repression, and (4) sublimation. He examined repression as a separate topic (see Freud 1915 and Chapter 6), and he supposedly wrote a separate paper on sublimation, but it has never been found. I believe that Freud was describing what we may call directions in the psyche, as the mind becomes better integrated and differentiated from the outer world.

The reversal of an instinct's content can, according to Freud, occur only in the transformation of love into hate, two fundamental polarities of mental life that I shall discuss shortly. The turning of an instinct toward the self means changing activity into passivity, that is, an internal object changing into an external object. Freud examined this process in two pairs of instincts, sadism–masochism and scopophilia–exhibitionism.

At first, Freud stated that sadistic feelings were initially directed toward another person, an external object. But as he further developed his instinct theory, he changed his mind and proposed an earlier state in which sadistic impulses are directed toward the self, the stage of *primary masochism*, a formulation that is basic to his final instinct theory, which contrasts death instincts with life instincts.

When first directed toward another person, sadism consists of the exercise and control of aggressive feelings; the impulse does not include violence or the desire to inflict pain. This is in keeping with the observation that children can be quite destructive in their play, even though this is not their intent. Rather, they are mainly interested in exploring their environment and establishing a sense of autonomy. Following this stage of outwardly directing the instincts, the external object is once again replaced by the self. The subject from whom the instinct emanates becomes the object of the instinct. The instinct has changed from being active and outwardly directed to being passive and inwardly directed. In the final step it is once again directed toward an external object. The destructive qualities of sadism are acquired when the instinct is directed back toward the self after being directed toward an external object. Freud did not explain why this should happen, but presumably something happened to the instinct after it was directed toward the external world.

The same developmental sequence can be outlined for scopophilia–exhibitionism. Freud proposed a preliminary phase of looking at the self, using the development of this pair of instincts. As we noted with other formulations, he described this sequence only as it occurs in males. First, the child looks at his penis, and then he looks at another person's penis. Similar to the sequence attributed to sadism, the self next becomes the external object—the object being looked at—by identifying with it. Thus, Freud traced a sequence from initially looking at the self, a narcissistic phase, to looking at someone else, voyeurism or scopophilia and, finally, exhibitionism, that is, looking at the self or being looked at. The motion from activity to passivity is similar to that of the instinctual pair of sadism–masochism, first looking at the self which could be considered passive, followed by voyeurism which would indicate activity, and then, finally and once more, a passive orientation.

Active and passive in the context of scopophilia–exhibitionism impulses are hard to define. Freud viewed these qualities only in terms of one vector, the direction of the instinctual impulse, subject to object being active and object to subject being passive. Ordinarily we think of voyeurism as being passive, although the impulse proceeds from the self to the outer world. Looking is the activity of the spectator rather than of the active participant. Exhibiting oneself, however, is often equivalent to an active assault. Activity and passivity thus are complex reactions that cannot be described on the basis of just one variable.

Freud's descriptions of these instinct pairs is an especially interesting sequence that, if looked at closely, does not support his developmental progression of autoerotism, primary narcissism, secondary narcissism, and then object relationships that begin as part–object relationships. He began by describing the instinct as first being directed toward the self. This could easily be an example of primary narcissism, as the libido does not yet extend itself toward the outer world. Furthermore, this self-directed activity is pleasurable, indicating that it can also be considered autoerotic. The next step is an extension of the instinct beyond the self to an external object. *There is no intermediary stage of fusion with that object, a stage that in another context Freud* (1914c) *called secondary narcissism.* It is *after* the instinct attaches itself to another person that the subject becomes the object, an identification that indicates fusion. In Chapter 6, I distinguish among such psychic processes as fusion, identification, and incorporation.

The role of the object as separate and distinct is negligible for these primitive instinctual components. There is a connection between the drive's organic source and the qualities required to achieve instinctual discharge. Freud might have been commenting about functional modes, in that certain instinctual needs are associated with specific adaptive processes characteristic of particular developmental stages. For example, some anal activities and male sexuality are expulsive, whereas the hungry stomach is introjective. These modalities are associated with various instinctual discharge patterns. External objects complement these patterns; for example, in response to male sexuality, the gratifying object is receptive, a quality that Freud related to femininity.

Thus, the vicissitudes of turning toward the self gives us a broad outline of how the psyche moves from an exclusive preoccupation with the inner world to an orientation in which it is able to distinguish itself from the external world of reality. As we have seen, Freud used specific instinct pairs to demonstrate the process of structuralization and development. He also had some interesting thoughts about the reversal of content.

As stated, the reversal of content applies only to the transformation of love into hate. Love and hate, however, are not equivalent instincts because they do not belong to the same frame of reference. Love, in contrast with hate, is not a component instinct. Rather, it is "the expression of the whole sexual current of feeling" (Freud 1915a, p. 133). It is a highly complex, structured feeling or attitude associated with mature relationships with whole objects. Hate, on the other hand, appears early in psychic development, and according to Freud, is the first response that accompanies the distinction between the inner and the outer world. He referred to a child's first learning of the external milieu when being fed something that has an unpleasant taste. The child reflexively spits it out, an act that Freud (1915a) believed was the forerunner of hate.

Nevertheless, even though love is not a component or, better still, an elemental instinct, it can still be studied in terms of polarities. Freud postulated three polarities: (1) love–indifference, (2) love–hate, and (3) love–being loved. He was describing sweeping developmental trends that are fundamental to structuralizing processes. These polarities can be linked with the vicissitudes that I have just described.

Love–indifference corresponds to the antithesis of the ego and the outer world and represents the earliest differentiation made by the developing psyche. Either the child loves or does not love an external object which, in psychoeconomic terms, means that either libido flows outwards and cathects the object or remains attached to the self and is indifferent to the person in the outside world.

Love and hate represent an antithesis of feelings. Although they stem from different levels of the psyche, according to Freud, these feelings represent polarities. They are also associated with pleasure and pain, also polarities that are fundamental to the psychoeconomic hypothesis. The psyche operates according to the pleasure principle, seeking objects that are pleasurable and rejecting those that are unpleasurable. Freud preferred the word *unpleasure* (*Unlust*) to pain because he was emphasizing the absence of pleasure rather than the presence of pain. These inherent tendencies propel the ego toward certain segments of the outer world and cause it to withdraw from other aspects. Instincts become less narcissistically fixated as the psyche finds its interactions with the surrounding milieu gratifying and pleasurable.

Loving–being loved is another example of the vicissitude of the instinct's being turned toward the self. It is closely related to the two polarities just discussed, love–indifference and love–hate. The child can either love or be indifferent to the external object, as has been emphasized. This is the active stance. The opposite occurs when the infant is or is not loved (indifference), a passive position. The acquisition of pleasure and the infliction of pain can also be correlated with loving and being loved, for pleasure is given or received and equated with loving feelings. Unpleasure can also be included in the context of indifference.

These polarities are also characteristic of early narcissistic phases. Instincts are initially directed toward the ego; the outside world is not cathected. Freud added that the ego coincides with what is pleasurable and that the outside world is viewed as indifferent or perhaps as unpleasurable.

Although classical psychoanalytic theory is primarily id oriented, the importance of the external object to psychic development is still acknowledged. Returning to his first instinct theory, Freud explained that part of the sexual drive is autoerotic, as it can obtain pleasure within the boundaries of the self, whereas another part is dependent on external objects for gratification, a dependence that is also characteristic of the ego instincts. The dependence of both the sexual and the ego instincts on external objects disturbs the original narcissism of the early developing psyche and so is an impetus for emotional development and later the establishment of the reality principle (Freud 1911a).

Thus, at first, the sources of pleasure are located within the psyche, and everything else is initially perceived with indifference. When external objects become the gratifying source, the ego acknowledges their presence and role. However, the satisfaction of the self-preservative drives—the ego instincts—does not lead to love: the ego needs but does not at first love the caretaker. By contrast, the satisfaction of sexual needs does lead to love.

What is not pleasurable is initially perceived as indifferent and as being outside the self. Later, everything that produces unpleasure—and here we can add pain—is hated. In regard to hate and unpleasure, it makes no difference whether sexual or ego instincts are involved, but the prototype of hate is not related to the sexual instincts. Instead, it is connected to the ego's struggle to survive, to the ego instincts. Love, on the other hand, is derived from the satisfaction of the sexual instincts. Thus, love and hate develop from different sources. They become opposites when the influence of the pleasure–pain principle becomes effective.

In Freud's first instinct theory, the dichotomy of ego and sexual instincts is conceptually inconsistent if we juxtapose love and hate at the same early level of psychic development. If hatred is a reaction to frustrated ego instincts and if love is the consequence of satisfied sexual instincts, the latter—because love is a complex structured feeling—cannot have its origins at the same primitive level as hate does. The only way that Freud could overcome this difficulty inherent in the first instinct theory is by postulating the existence of feelings that are forerunners to love. Even the most complex feelings must have their antecedents, and this also applies to hate. The first instinct theory becomes more plausible if we again return to concepts that stress structural hierarchies and assume that the ego and sexual instincts, as well as their reaction to satisfaction and frustration, are initially precursors of needs and feelings that later acquire sensitive and sophisticated qualities associated

with intimate and tender emotions. Perhaps it would have been
better if Freud had not used the word *love* in reference to the
early pregenital stages.

For example, Freud made the vague statement that love is
the outcome of the ego's ability to satisfy its instinctual needs
autoerotically. Then he added that love is initially narcissistic.
The ego loves itself. Next, the ego becomes directed toward
pleasure-giving objects that have become incorporated into it;
that is, the ego loves its introjects. This is secondary narcissism.
Finally, love becomes part of later more-developed sexual instincts which when synthesized become incorporated into genital sexuality. Freud was careful to point out that in his theories
of early development, he was not discussing mature love; rather,
he was conceptualizing "preliminary stages of love" that are
connected with "provisional sexual aims."

As was customary with Freud, he made the stage of secondary narcissism follow primary narcissism, a sequence that I have
emphasized is not clinically valid or conceptually consistent. I
believe that Freud also demonstrated that this is not a feasible
sequence. He did not dwell on what happens between primary
narcissism and loving introjects. Obviously the ego would first
have had to relate to external objects in a pleasurable fashion
before it would make such objects part of the self. Only the
good is taken into the self, and so external objects that become
introjects must have been experienced as gratifying and, therefore, loved. Consequently, between primary narcissism and secondary narcissism there must be an in-between phase in which
external objects are recognized and then related to in a need-
satisfying fashion. Whether we are referring to the gratification
of sexual or self-preservative instincts is problematic. Freud
outlined this sequence for sexual instincts, but these were precursors of genital sexuality and could easily have included self-
preservative elements. He tried to keep sexual and ego instincts
separate because he wanted to maintain dualism, but as we shall
soon see, he was unable to do so without transforming the first
instinct theory into what he considered to be the second instinct
theory.

Freud's first instinct theory has many interesting facets,
although as will be soon evident, it could not endure as a
theoretical construct. He initially justified it because it explained

both individual survival and that of the species. That is, the ego instincts are directed toward the survival of the individual, and the sexual instincts guarantee the survival of the species. The duality of ego and sexual instincts is further supported by the fact that such instincts reflect the two fundamental needs of hunger and sex.

The term *ego instinct*, however, created difficulty from the time it was first coined (Freud 1910b). As I pointed out in Chapter 2, Freud vacillated between the ego and the id as being the reservoir of libido. We can raise a similar question regarding ego instincts. Ordinarily, we would think of an ego instinct as emanating from the id seeking gratification from appropriate objects in the outer world. If that is the case, then the distinction between sexual and ego instincts becomes blurred, because Freud defined early needs as libidinal strivings, categorizing them as sexual instincts that had "preliminary sexual aims." If ego instincts seek similar gratifications, then how are they different from sexual instincts? But if they emanate from the ego, as Freud once postulated for libido, then it is impossible to maintain the hierarchical organization that characterizes the structural hypothesis. Freud was aware of these problems and finally abandoned the first instinct for his final theory that divides instincts into life and death instincts, a theory that has become even more controversial than the first instinct theory.

In tracing the development from the first to the second instinct theory, Bibring (1941) outlined four stages. He emphasized how difficult it was to maintain a dichotomy between sexual and ego instincts if both groups are cathected with libido. At that time, Freud had not yet proposed a nonlibidinal or nonsexual form of psychic energy. Bibring offered the following four stages:

1. The first phase is the division of ego (self-preservative) instincts and sexual instincts. Because sexual instincts are included in pregenital activities and also pursue self-preservative activities, this separation is difficult to maintain. There is also no energic basis enabling us to differentiate one instinct from another, as Freud defined psychic energy only in terms of libido.
2. The introduction of narcissism (Freud 1914c) further

complicated the issue of separating sexual and ego instincts. Freud referred to the phenomenon of treating one's body as a love object when he first described narcissism. He understood the process underlying such self-love as a libidinization of the egoism of the self-preservative drive. This implies that he believed that the self-preservative drive is directed toward the ego, as the expression *ego instinct* indicates.

Nevertheless, Freud also stated (1915a) that the self-preservative instincts require an external object, whereas some sexual instincts do not. The latter may be auto-erotic or directed toward the self, as in narcissism which, according to Freud, always has a sexual component. Even though an external nurturing object is required for an infant's survival, is the neonate aware of a nurturing source outside the self? Both ego and sexual instincts would be directed toward a rudimentary ego that has not yet achieved the capacity to distinguish between the self and the external world. During these early stages, we cannot think of any drive as being object directed. Object direction is achieved later.

When Freud discussed the egoism of the self-preservative drive, he was referring to the part of the drive that cathects the ego. Up to this point, he had said nothing about egoism in terms of energic factors. In defining narcissism he wrote about the libidinization of this egoism of the self-preservative drive, and by so doing, he destroyed the dualism of the first instinct theory. In fact, he described three types of instincts on the basis of their operations: (1) self-preservative or ego instincts directed toward external objects; (2) a libidinization of the egoism of the ego instincts, known as narcissism (Freud [1914c] also defined narcissism as the flow of sexual instincts toward the ego, ego libido); (3) sexual instincts directed toward external objects. As can readily be seen, the discovery of narcissism makes it impossible to maintain a dualism based on sexual versus nonsexual, especially when Freud acknowledged only one type of psychic energy, libido.

To maintain some type of dichotomy Freud temporarily resolved his dilemma concerning narcissism by hypothesizing two different directions of libidinal currents, ego libido and object libido. It is difficult to view this dichotomy as supporting a dual-instinct theory. Rather, Freud seems to have formulated a monistic theory, as it contains only libido, which would mean sexual instincts and nothing else. Where this libido flows, either toward the ego or external objects, does not change the nature of the instinct.

3. Freud was not satisfied with the division of ego libido and object libido as a basis for a dual-instinct theory. He recognized that to maintain dualism, he had to propose the existence of another type of energy beside libido, a nonsexual energy attached to ego instincts. He called this energy *interest* (Freud 1920). At this transitional point in the development of instinct theory, we can again state that Freud was describing three types of instincts or instinctual currents: (1) ego libido, again narcissism; (2) ego interest, a nonlibidinal narcissism; and (3) object libido. Freud did not carry this revision further by including a fourth type which would have been object interest, to balance ego interest, as ego libido balances object libido. It is also puzzling why he did not take this obvious step, because he could have preserved a dual-instinct theory contrasting libidinal with nonlibidinal (interest) cathexes rather than basing his distinctions on the object of the instinct, whether it be the ego or an external object. The problem, nevertheless, remains because Freud was struggling between accepting a nonlibidinal narcissism, what he called *ego interest*, or what he had postulated earlier, self-preservative instincts directed toward the outer world. He seemed to prefer self-preservative instincts directed toward the outer world, but then he felt that these instincts had to be libidinized when they became narcissistic.

We can surmise that Freud was not comfortable in separating fundamental instincts on the basis of whether they are sexual or nonsexual. He wanted to maintain both dualism and sexuality, if instincts were to remain connected with needs and developmental factors. Apparently he was unable to achieve this aim, because his final instinct theory dealt with global and inherent tendencies that are immutable and not susceptible to developmental vicissitudes.

As we have already learned, Freud gave sadistic impulses a central position in instinct theory, as instinctual impulses are directed toward the outer world. He may have believed that he could preserve sexuality and duality by arguing for different types of sexual instincts reaching toward the ego and external objects. He first considered sadism as a component instinct of the sexual instinct. I have described how in outlining the steps involved in instinctual vicissitudes, the sadistic instinct is initially aimed toward the self before being directed to the outside world. At that time, Freud considered sadism to be a component instinct of sexual instincts, and this attitude was in keeping with his formulations regarding instincts becoming libidinized when they become narcissistic. If an instinct is initially narcissistic before becoming related to external objects, then all instincts, including self-preservative ones, belong in the domain of sexuality.

This, however, destroys the duality of hunger and love, and Freud did not return to these two different but connected basic needs. Instead he decided to give sadism a separate status rather than viewing it simply as a component sexual instinct. He postulated two fundamental instincts, aggressive and libidinal. It must be remembered that sadism represents an attempt at mastery and is not characterized by destructiveness and the need to inflict pain. This occurs only later when the instinct turns toward the self. At that time it is libidinized; that is, it is fused with the sexual instincts.

In the context of this instinct theory, sadism is chiefly an attempt at mastery and an aggressive adaptation. According to Freud (1920), during the oral stage, sadism leads to the destruction of the object, and later, during genital sexuality, it satisfies the sexual instinct by subduing the sexual object. The aim of the aggressive instinct during the oral stage is not to destroy the satisfying nurturing product; it simply seeks gratification and is not concerned about destruction. Freud perhaps meant something similar when he wrote about subduing the sexual object. In order to achieve sexual gratification, the sexual object has to be found, pursued, and conquered. This requires aggression. According to these formulations, the aggressive instinct is a servant to the sexual instincts in that it represents a modality by which the latter can be gratified. It is not exactly a sexual instinct, but it is closely involved in how such instincts relate to the outer world.

Many analysts are content to stop at this point and accept an instinct theory that divides drives into the two categories of sexual and aggressive. Still, if we accept Freud's formulations, the self-preservative needs of the organism will be ignored. Freud's hypotheses have been often modified and extended, however, and the aggressive instinct has become associated with both the achievement of self-preservative and destructive urges.

This again creates a contradiction. Aggression and sexuality are not similar, and they do not belong in the same frame of reference. Sexuality concerns a need, a need for sexual discharge, whereas aggression is a modality similar to activity, as contrasted with passivity. Freud stated that aggression was a primary drive, with the peripheral musculature as its organic source. In children, there seems to be evidence for a separate need for aggression, an aggressive drive, but with increasing age it becomes more of an attitude than simply a motoric discharge, as it is connected with sexual and self-preservative needs.

There are other objections to this theory. The more obvious one refers to the use of the aggressive instinct to master and subdue the sexual object. This is, of course, a chauvinistic, masculine viewpoint in which the sexual instinct is restricted to males. In fact, as Freud formulated it, this instinct theory applies only to males. Taken to its extreme, females have no sexual needs of their own; they have to be subdued because they renounce sexuality.

This theory is also inconsistent in another respect. Freud (1914c) asserted the existence of anaclitic object relations, in which the sexual instincts "lean" on dependent instincts. Although at that time he was writing about ego or self-preservative instincts and sexual instincts, he described later how aggressive instincts found their way into the external world through sexual instincts. Here he was emphasizing the opposite—aggressive instincts leaning on sexual instincts.

Ego interest, aggressive instincts, and self-preservative instincts become combined and constitute the aggressive instinct which is set alongside the sexual instinct. As mentioned, many analysts are content to accept this formulation.

4. As Freud pursued his concepts further, he was not content to let rest the question of instinct theory. Now with the formulation of the aggressive drive, he was able to accept that the ego can relate to objects on a nonsexual basis, that is, in terms of aggression, although it quickly offers itself for sexual mastery. Still, how can the vicissitudes of such a drive be formulated? The answer to this question led to a further revision of his instinct theory.

He outlined the development of the sexual drive in the following fashion: Autoerotism—primary narcissism—secondary narcissism—object relations. A similar pathway for the aggressive instincts would necessitate the following sequence: Autoaggression—primary masochism—secondary masochism—sadistic control of objects.

A primary instinct of aggression that is destructively directed toward the self during an early stage of development supports Freud's concept of the existence of a death instinct. In "Beyond the Pleasure Principle" (1920), he stressed that the organism is driven by a self-destructive drive, a death instinct. Because of an innate tendency to strive toward lower levels of excitation and a natural inertia, all living matter operates on the basis of this death instinct. The only exceptions are the germ or reproductive cells that seek life through conjugation.

Basically, Freud viewed all species as being governed by two opposing forces that ordinarily achieve a balance and lead to biological equilibrium. There exists a death instinct that is balanced by a life instinct. Freud emphasized that the death instinct is basic and that the life instinct is one of its vicissitudes, a point that created considerable controversy. These are different processes, or opposite tendencies, that he termed "constructive or assimilatory, and . . . destructive and dissimilatory" (1920, p. 49).

Freud discussed an interesting metaphor (although I wonder whether he considered it a metaphor) in which all the cells of a multicellular complex organism are endowed with both life and death instincts. Certain cells give up their life instincts to other cells in order to neutralize their death instinct. This is an example of the operations of the death instinct being interrupted by the life instinct. The germ cells, in particular, require this fresh impetus of life instinct in order to carry on the immense task of reproduction.

The evolution from previous instinct theories to the fourth instinct theory is interesting but is difficult to follow and is characterized by paradoxes. Freud began by stating that the concept of the self-preservative instinct had lost its theoretical importance. It seems to pursue life-sustaining forces, but its real aim is to permit the organism to seek death in its own fashion.

As we have learned, the self-preservative instincts become the aggressive instincts which, in turn, become the death instincts. This is an interesting paradox, for what were once strivings for life, self-preservation, are, in the final instinct theory, transformed into death instincts. Freud traced this development through the vicissitudes of the aggressive instinct that led him to postulate primary masochism, which is in keeping with his philosophy concerning the existence of a death instinct. The existence of primary masochism as a vicissitude of the aggressive instinct paves the way for making the aggressive instinct into the death instinct.

The life instinct is the outcome of the sexual instinct and

also presents an interesting paradox. As Freud maintained, the purpose of the sexual instinct is to lower the level of excitation, which he equated with the pleasure principle. However, the lowering of excitation also represents a tendency toward death. The sexual instincts seeking death have now become the life instincts, clearly a contradiction.

Libido has been traditionally associated with life. There is no similar expression for the energy of the death instinct. Some years ago Federn (1933) suggested the term *mortido*, and later Weiss (1950) coined the expression *destrudo* to distinguish the energy of the death instinct from libido. Because the concept of the death instinct, which in the thirties was a heated and controversial issue, has gradually withered away through attrition, the type of energy involved is also now of little interest.

Instinct theory, however, is still important to both classic and modern psychoanalytic theory. Although as this book constantly emphasizes, there has been a shift in focus from instincts to structural factors, the role of instincts, or, internal needs, has to be recognized both in psychopathology and as an impetus for psychic development.

Chapter 4

DREAMS

Freud considered "Interpretation of Dreams" (1900) to be his most important work. From the beginning of his psychoanalytic explorations, dreams had a central position in both his clinical and theoretical pursuits, and in his psychological works, the word *dream* appears 6113 times, more than any other term does (Guttman et al. 1980).

Dreams have always fascinated mankind and they were frequently mentioned in the ancient literature. In an extensive review, Freud remarked that for the most part, the ancients dealt with dreams as if they were visitations from gods and possessed mystical and spiritual qualities. They were used to forecast the future, predict the outcome of battles, and determine when it would be propitious to take some definitive action. This reasoning was the outcome of magical thinking and religious fervor.

Today, the same fascination with dreams persists, although we no longer approach them with mystical awe. Freud considered them to be mental phenomena that could be scientifically studied. Many others before him had used similar approaches, but Freud's work in this area was monumental, and as he himself admitted, it led to insights that "disturbed the sleep of the world." He achieved this by fitting the dreams' unconscious determinants into a psychoanalytic context.

Freud's unique achievement was to place dreams in the domain of psychic determinism. In other words, like all other mental products, he viewed them as having purpose and meaning and not merely as being the breakdown phenomena of the natural regression associated with sleep. Freud's insistence that dreams could be understood in the same fashion as could other products of the unconscious both helped him understand their structure and meaning, and advanced his treatment techniques by interpreting dreams for therapeutic advantage. In the technical psychoanalytic armamentarium, dreams indeed became the "royal road to the unconscious."

Thus, dreams can teach us about psychic structure, psychopathology, and unconscious mental processes. Their study has contributed to psychoanalytic theory, and their analysis has become part of the psychoanalytic treatment setting. Consequently, the exploration of dreams represents a convenient transition between classical metapsychology and clinical theory.

THE MEANING OF DREAMS

Freud recognized that philosophers and scientists were attracted to dreams because they were expressions or manifestations of the unconscious mind. Any activity that refers to a hidden portion of our mental makeup is, of course, intrinsically appealing and piques our curiosity. Freud used his technique of free association to explore those parts of our minds not readily accessible to consciousness and also used it to explore dreams. To do this he had to make only a few assumptions, the same ones that he had made about the unconscious mind in general, that is, that dreams themselves are the outcome of unconscious mental processes and are knowable in that they have meaning that can be understood at higher psychic levels.

Early in his explorations, Freud asked what a dream's purpose is, and he quickly concluded that they occurred in order to protect sleep. During sleep there are many internal and even some external stimuli that are sufficiently intense that, if left unchecked, would awaken the sleeper. Dreams can somehow incorporate these stimuli into their content so as to protect sleep. There are many examples of such dreams.

Especially common are those dreams that handle inner pressures. A full bladder may lead sleepers to dream that they are urinating and thereby permit them to remain in bed a little longer. Freud referred to his own experience, of dreaming of drinking water from a carafe after having eaten anchovies that evening and feeling particularly thirsty.

Interruptions from external stimuli may produce such familiar dream responses as that to alarm clocks, in which the sleeper dreams about getting up, bathing, and otherwise preparing for the day. By dreaming about awakening, the sleeper can continue sleeping a while longer. Some of these dreams may become quite complex and elaborate.

Having established a general purpose for dreams, Freud continued looking for various motivations that might further elucidate the dream process. By analyzing his own and his patients' dreams, he concluded that all dreams represent *wish fulfillments*. That is, every dream embodies the fulfillment of a wish, even if on the surface, it does not seem to refer to a fulfilled wish.

To illustrate this thesis, Freud used the dreams of children, which contain little if any disguise and naively reveal their obvious motives. For example, Freud's daughter, Anna, went to bed craving strawberries, and that night she dreamed of eating strawberries. Wish fullfillment is easily illustrated by fairly simple dreams, especially when they are concerned with somatic needs such as hunger. In these instances, we are dealing with conscious wishes. The situation is, however, considerably more complex when we deal with unconscious and conflicting wishes. In these circumstances, the unconscious wish is far from apparent, and the chain of events leading to the final dream can contain many experiences and thoughts, traversing a complicated and circuitous route.

From his studies, Freud decided that every dream must have a *day residue* that begins the process of forming a dream.

The day residue is usually a trivial event that occurred on the day before the dream, although in some instances it can occur on the previous day. Freud stressed the triviality of the day residue, although in another instance, he referred to it as some thought or action that has not been disposed of. Regardless of its exact nature, it has an associative connection to some thoughts or feelings residing in the system Ucs or the id.

As the day residue is internalized, it becomes fused with those id elements that are associatively similar, although such similarities may be purely superficial. The fact that it is superficial facilitates the pathway to dream formation. Freud commented that the id can more easily attach itself to a trivial or insignificant experience or day residue than to an emotionally meaningful event. The latter would more likely attract the attention of the censor which in turn would mobilize defenses. The day residue is the vehicle by which an unconscious wish is expressed as fulfilled in the manifest dream content.

The latter conclusion rests on the assumption that the id contains repressed, unexpressed wishes that are released in dreams during the sleep state when inhibiting mental forces are relaxed and the access to motility and acting out is blocked. The fact that these id impulses remain within the context of a dream renders them harmless. We all are familiar with the reassuring reflection that after all, "it was only a dream." Indeed, these forbidden wishes are barred access to the external world because they are contained in dreams.

The dictum that all dreams are wish fulfillments requires us to look further into the nature of the underlying wishes that are, according to Freud, responsible for constructing dreams. As mentioned, children's dreams are often naive, and the wishes that they contain are usually apparent. Such wishes should not disturb the child's psychic equilibrium. To dream of strawberries when she craved them, as Anna Freud did, seems to be a fairly typical child's dream. The wish does not seem to spring from deep id levels, thus indicating that some dreams come from the surface, as Freud believed (1900).

By contrast, other dreams depict deeply repressed, primitive, infantile wishes. Often the wish-fulfillment properties of such dreams are far from obvious, as the dream is heavily disguised. All dreams seem to have two components, a *manifest* and a *latent content*. The manifest content refers to the actual remembered dream. The latent content refers to the hidden aspects of the dream, those parts that are not within the sphere of conscious awareness or easily brought into it, or the unconscious underlying elements responsible for constructing the manifest content. The latent content contains the meaning of the dream, which can be discovered through the process of free association and which lends itself to therapeutic exploration and interpretation. The purpose of dreams, therefore, is to preserve sleep by representing inner needs as wish-fulfillments. The sleeper remains satisfied and undisturbed as internal wishes are depicted as gratified.

Freud referred to the dream of Irma, which has become known as the *specimen* dream of psychoanalysis. Freud dreamed that he was at a social gathering where he met his patient Irma. Apparently she was still ill. Freud reproached her for not having accepted his "solution" and told her that if she still had pain, it was her fault. Freud wondered whether he had missed an organic illness and so looked at her throat. He saw a big white patch and some gray scabs. He called Dr. M. for a consultation; he examined Irma and confirmed Freud's findings. Freud had two other friends, Otto and Leopold, both standing beside her. Leopold was percussing her through her bodice, and he noted that she had a "'dull area down on the left." He also concluded that the skin of her left shoulder was infiltrated. Dr. M. then remarked that Irma undoubtedly had an infection but that dysentery would supervene and the toxin would be eliminated. Otto, in the past, had given Irma an injection of a formula that Freud saw printed in heavy type in the dream. In the dream Freud also conjectured that one should be careful with such injections because the syringe probably was not clean.

As is obvious from the length and number of details, this was a complex dream. Freud, nevertheless, chose this dream because it gave him a good opportunity to demonstrate both the participation of day residues in forming dreams and the wish-fulfillment properties of dreams. The events of the previous day provided the starting point for this dream.

Freud explained that he had treated Irma that summer with

only partial success. She had been relieved of her hysterical anxiety, but she still had many somatic symptoms. Because Freud was not completely certain as to what constituted a successful resolution of a hysterical problem, he had proposed a consultation, but she refused. Consequently, they discontinued the treatment for the summer vacation. Otto, Freud's junior colleague, had remarked on the day before the dream that Irma was "better, but not quite well." Freud was aware that Otto's tone of voice had annoyed him, as he had detected in it a note of reproof. The evening before the dream, Freud wrote up Irma's case history in order to show it to Dr. M. so that he could justify his formulations and treatment approach.

It was obvious to Freud that the dream stimuli were the news that Otto had given him of Irma's condition and the letter that he wrote which occupied him far into the night. Although he was able to make such connections, this shed no light on the dream's meaning, which on the surface appeared to be incomprehensible and nonsensical.

Today, we can consider the dream of Irma's injection as if it were an experimental dream. I doubt that if we encountered such a dream in the treatment setting that we would subject it to the detailed analysis that Freud did. He used the individual elements of the manifest content as stimuli for free association. He then combined his associations, discovering a dominant thread that enabled him to uncover the wish fulfillment, which was disguised and hidden in the manifest content. Freud was trying to create a hypothesis about dreams, whereas we would have no such intention when analyzing patients.

Some dreams can lead to a virtually inexhaustible number of interpretations, depending on the level being studied. The associations stemming from any dream element can wander in many different directions and lead to various meanings. They can also join other currents of thoughts and feelings and thereby emphasize certain themes. Freud stressed wish fullfillment, but for clinical purposes, therapists would want to concentrate on a dream's transference significance. Thus, dreams have many meanings that are not mutually exclusive and that serve different purposes.

To illustrate the dream's many meanings, I shall return to

Freud's dream and begin with those elements of the manifest dream in which Freud reproached Irma for not having accepted his solution, blaming her because she still had pains. When analyzing his dream of Irma's injection, Freud chose to deal with the dream's events chronologically. This is only one approach. For example, the analyst may be struck by some detail or obvious transference allusion in the manifest content and so ask the patient to associate first to that.

Freud acknowledged that he may actually have complained to Irma about her not being well. At the time, he believed that his therapeutic task was achieved when he was able to inform the patient of the hidden meaning of his or her symptoms. He now knew better, but he had been anxious not to take responsibility for Irma's continuing pains. Thus, if they were her fault, he could not be blamed for them. Freud reasoned that therefore he might have been on the right track in pursuing the purpose of the dream.

We can already see a wish-fullfillment motive for at least the first part of Freud's dream. In real life, Irma still had symptoms. Freud, apparently, felt guilty that his therapeutic efforts had not been entirely satisfactory. To assuage his conscience, in the dream, as also in waking life, he disavowed his responsibility for her bad health and blamed her for the treatment's lack of success. Thus, the wish fulfillment was that Freud had behaved conscientiously and competently, and if that had not been adequate, it was because Irma had been uncooperative. Freud was exonerated.

The question remains, however, that if Freud had such thoughts in waking life, why did he have to construct such an elaborate and, superficially at least, such a nonsensical dream? Otto's remarks and the need to justify himself, as evidenced by his writing a letter the evening preceding the dream, indicated that Freud was feeling agitated, perhaps enough that such feelings would interfere with his ability to sleep. He therefore might have needed such a dream to be able to remain asleep, the dream containing the wish fulfillment that resolved his conflict regarding Irma's treatment. Still, why did it have to be such a convoluted dream? Could not Freud have been able to stay asleep with a much simpler dream? He seemed to be dealing with wishes that were well within his sphere of conscious awareness.

Freud felt that he was moving in the right direction with his interpretation, but he suspected that there was much more to the dream that was hidden in the unconscious recesses of his mind.

He examined his reaction in the dream that he was alarmed at the idea that he might have overlooked an organic illness. Missing a physical disease is the fear of all psychiatrists, who deal primarily with functional disorders. This is especially true with patients who present somatic symptoms, because we can never be certain that we have exhausted all organic possibilities.

On the other hand, Freud confessed that a faint doubt crept into his mind that his alarm was not entirely genuine. He emphasized that he did not know where this doubt came from, but he was immediately able to put it in context by means of the earlier wish he had expressed about Irma's illness. He surmised that if Irma's condition were organic, then he would not be responsible for curing it, as his treatment was designed to treat only hysterical symptoms. He concluded that he was wishing that he had made a wrong diagnosis, for then he could not be blamed for his lack of success. This latter wish was recognized only as he free associated to certain elements in the dream. It was not self-evident as his propensity to want to blame Irma. In fact, it was somewhat startling and unexpected and perhaps conflict-laden.

Freud discovered that he had been comparing Irma with two other persons, Irma's friends, whom he believed would also have resisted treatment. This represented an elaboration of the theme that this dream was a reaction to Freud's dissatisfaction with Irma's progress or lack of progress. One of her friends would have accepted Freud's solution sooner because she was wiser, and Freud wondered whether he might have wished to exchange Irma for this friend.

This part of the dream offers an example of how a concrete action in the manifest content can be an allusion to a metaphor or an idiomatic expression. In the dream, Irma was reluctant to open her mouth when Freud wanted to examine her throat. Her friend would have "opened her mouth properly" and have told him more than Irma did.

Freud touched on many related themes dealing with various facets of Irma's supposed illness. He indicated his ambivalence toward the various persons in his dream, such as Dr. M., whom he identified with his elder brother. He was annoyed with Dr. M. and this brother because they both had rejected a "certain suggestion I had recently laid before them." He gave this as a reason for linking Dr. M. to his brother.

Freud had also partially linked himself to Irma in that the dream examination revealed that a portion of the skin of her left shoulder was infiltrated. In real life, Freud suffered from rheumatism of the shoulder which especially bothered him when he sat up late into the night. Apparently some sexual feelings toward Irma were stimulated at this point, as Freud's associations led him to further thoughts about examining female patients and how some doctors insisted that the patient not undress. Freud did not want to pursue this line of inquiry, however, stating, "Frankly, I had no desire to penetrate more deeply at this point" (1900, p. 113).

In the dream, Dr. M. had said, "It's an infection, but no matter. Dysentery will supervene and the toxin will be eliminated." In reaction to this sentence, Freud made an important point about the technique of dream interpretation. He observed that if there is something ridiculous in the manifest content, such as this pronouncement, then it especially deserves to be analyzed. Such material has meaning that may be crucial to understanding the dream. As we can see, Freud approached dreams as a detective might, looking for clues that would help unravel the secret that lay buried somewhere in the dream thoughts. If something on the surface of the dream appeared nonsensical, it might have special significance. In this instance, Freud also dwelled on the fact that Dr. M. in the dream had to console Freud, as evidenced by the expression "no matter."

Freud's associations led him to believe that Irma might be suffering from diphtheria, a severe organic disease. This again can be linked to the dream's wish-fulfillment quality. Freud once more saw his attempt to shift the blame away from himself. His psychotherapy could not be expected to cure pains that were caused by diphtheria, but Freud's conflict concerning this attempt to exonerate himself became more apparent. He admit-

ted that he felt awkward—we might say guilty—about giving
Irma such a severe illness so that he could feel blameless. He
was aware of being cruel. Here again, Freud was emphasizing
something important about the dreamer. The dreamer is responsible for everything that occurs in a dream. Although this
would seem to be self-evident, as the dreamer has created all the
elements of the dream, both the dreamer and the analyst often
lose sight of this fact. Indeed, the defense mechanism of negation is often used as a defense against accepting responsibility
for what occurs in dreams (see Chapter 6).

Freud acknowledged his cruelty in his dream version of
Irma's illness, and this aggravated his conflict. Consequently, he
needed some assurance that everything would turn out well, and
so this was Dr. M.'s role in the dream, to console Freud, another
facet of the dream's wish-fulfillment function. Still, the question
of why this consolation took such a nonsensical form has not
been answered.

Freud's attention turned to his feelings about Dr. M. He
asked himself whether he were making fun of him. He could
have been ridiculing him by having him produce far-fetched
explanations and making unexpected pathological connections.
Through a series of associations, Freud decided that he was
deriding physicians who were ignorant of hysteria. Dr. M.
would not have been able to discover the hysterical basis of
Irma's symptoms and therefore would not have agreed with
Freud's formulations. So the wish fulfillment in the dream could
now be expanded to include revenge against two persons. He
was attacking Irma by blaming her for her symptoms, and he
was attacking Dr. M. by the nonsensical statement that he had
attributed to him. This is an example of *overdetermination*, a
characteristic of dreams in which several related wish-fulfilling
motivations come together in the manifest dream and are represented by the same element. Often an overdetermined dream
element stands out from the rest of the dream; for example, it
may be especially visually intense, bizarre, or absurd, as was
Dr. M's pronouncement.

We have information beyond what Freud gave us about Dr.
M. (see Jones 1953). He was Freud's mentor and erstwhile
friend Dr. Josef Breuer, a successful and highly respected Vien-

nese internist. As we know, Breuer's work with his patient Anna O. inspired Freud to develop his theories about hysteria, especially its sexual etiology. Breuer, on the other hand, became increasingly doubtful about Freud's emphasis on sex, and apparently, he had reacted badly to his patient's sexual transference, which made her believe that he had made her pregnant. Breuer thus gradually dissociated himself from Freud's ideas, and there is no question that Freud resented Breuer's "defection." It seems reasonable, then, that this would have been reflected in the dream.

There are many further paths to pursue in this dream, such as the appearance of the formula of trimethylamin in such a vivid fashion. It was printed in heavy type indicating that it was an important factor involved in the latent dream thoughts. Freud stated that it was an allusion to sexuality and to a friend who supported his opinions when he felt most isolated. Freud was referring to Fliess, but we need not pursue this aspect of the dream further which, as I have repeatedly stressed, runs in many directions.

Freud's anger was also represented in the dream, as he produced many associations indicating his annoyance with his younger colleague Otto. He concluded that the dream fulfilled various wishes which were stimulated by the events of the previous evening, particularly Otto's reproachful remarks about Irma's health and the writing of the case history for Dr. M. The dream asserted that Freud was not responsible for the persistence of Irma's pain. Through a series of associations, he discovered that he was getting revenge on Otto by throwing the reproach back on him. The dream exonerated Freud of blame by demonstrating that Irma's condition was due to other factors. Freud thus expressed his wrath toward Irma, Otto, and Dr. M., and the dream can thus be viewed as the fulfillment of hostile wishes.

As is true of dreams in general, there was a recurring thread that ran through this dream. As a beginning practitioner, Freud was eager to treat his patients successfully and to validate the theories and concepts on which he based his therapeutic procedure. He was much involved with the sexual etiology of the neuroses, having met with considerable opposition to his ideas about the role of sex in neurosogenesis. Apparently, Freud felt insecure, and on the evening before the dream, he must have felt particularly vulnerable. Thus, the dream was an attempt to deal with the disturbing feelings that Otto had stimulated, by taking revenge on him and other skeptics, such as Dr. M. Within the context of revenge, Freud's ideas were also vindicated.

This explanation asserts that the motive for dreaming is a wish and that the content of the dream is a wish fulfillment. The wish on which Freud concentrated is fairly sophisticated: he was struggling for the acceptance of his theories and his scientific viewpoint. Most dreams, however, are not so intellectual but deal with more elemental and basic feelings. Freud knew this, and he indicated it many times in his associations to Irma's dream, by his repeated assertions that he did not want to pursue one or another line of inquiry. Obviously, he was beginning to encounter personal feelings that he did not want to reveal. Still, he was indirectly emphasizing that a dream has many levels of meaning, but he would have insisted that at whatever level a dream is being discussed, it represents a wish fulfillment.

Freud recognized, however, that some dreams do not appear to be wish fulfillments. These have been called *traumatic dreams*, which contain large amounts of anxiety. Often we refer to them as nightmares, although Freud (1920) was referring to particular types of traumatic dreams in which the sleeper dreams about a specific traumatic event. He wondered whether if dreams are wish fulfillments, why anyone would want to dream about something so unpleasant and frightening. We would think that the dreamer's wish would be to avoid such painful situations. What then is the purpose of such dreams, and what has happened to their wish-fulfilling properties?

Freud did not easily give up his hypotheses. He was able to see the adaptive elements of these dreams. The repetition of the traumatic event in the dream represented the wish to master the trauma. The dreamer creates the trauma and by so doing changes his position from passive vulnerability to active mastery. Such dreams could therefore be considered to be the dream equivalents of the repetition compulsion (see Chapter 7). There is an innate tendency to repeat infantile traumas in actions, symptoms, and dreams. The purpose is to resolve the trauma, and many factors are involved in these attempts at resolution, as discussed in Chapter 2 in regard to discharge phenomena and the release of anxiety in catharsis and abreaction. This type of wish fulfillment is different, however, in that the wish does not comprise specific feelings or needs but is a global wish intended to establish general psychic equilibrium.

This raises the question of what wish fulfillment means. How do we define a wish? If phrased in a certain way, could we make just about anything into a wish? If the dream were painful, then the wish would be an attempt to master the pain, or it could be a wish emanating from the superego, which wished to punish the dreamer because of some transgression. Guilt could be behind the wish fulfillment.

Certainly, dreams have meaning and are the pictorial expression of unconscious processes. That they contribute to the maintenance of psychic stability and the preservation of sleep also seems to be beyond question. Experiments in dream deprivation bear out this point, but to state that all dreams are wish fulfillments especially if we think in terms of specific wishes, might constrict our viewpoint to the extent that we ignore other features of the dream process and the special features of specific types of dreams that may be associated with structural disintegration or its antithesis, creative integration.

DISGUISE IN DREAMS

Freud was concerned with how latent dream thoughts became transformed into manifest content. He was thinking about such processes in a psychodynamic context which means that various parts of the personality oppose one another. As with the formation of symptoms, censors between the system Ucs and the system Pcs necessitate certain modifications and disguise if various unconscious impulses and orientations are to be woven into the manifest-dream fabric. The same psychodynamic clashes that lead to the construction of defenses and the formation of symptoms are responsible for the formation of dreams. Still, this does not mean that anyone who dreams suffers from a psychoneurosis. It simply asserts that intrapsychic conflict is inherent in, but not necessarily associated with, psychopathology.

The censor—today we would say superego barriers—contributes to the disguise in the dream work. It attacks the dream wish, changing and distorting it until it is acceptable to the higher psychic levels. This aspect of the dream work occurs alongside those processes responsible for transforming feelings and impulses into pictorial images. These are complicated psychological processes that are still imperfectly understood.

Most of us, however, are somewhat familiar with *hypnogogic phenomena*, in which we are partially awake and yet are dreaming. This happens when we are going to sleep, but before slipping into a state of complete sleep, we experience sensory distortions of the surrounding world. The furniture may change shape or color, or strange things may happen in the room as unconscious elements achieve pictorial representation. Silberer (Freud 1900) described how if he fell asleep or into a state of somnolence while working on an intellectual problem, he might dream of a picture of wood with different layers. Freud cited the example of the snake with its tail in its mouth, curled like a hoop and rolling down a hill, Kekulé's famous dream that he reputedly had just before he discovered the benzene ring. Another dream is of a piece of wood being sawed, but the saw is working on its own without human intervention, representing intense intellectual activity. These are concrete, metaphorical, and symbolic representations of abstract processes. Because they are pictorial and their significance is not obvious, we might consider them to be disguised, and so their meaning is not always immediately clear to the dreamer. When, however, these are higher-level activities and apparently not associated with conflict, they usually can easily be deciphered.

This is not always the case with hypnogogic states, especially when what is being pictorially represented stems from instinctual levels rather than intellectual activity. One patient, after having had sexual intercourse, thought that he had had a hallucination. As he was lying in bed, he saw a man walk out of the wall to the foot of his bed, lean over, and touch his penis. He was petrified with fear and began screaming. He became aware of his screaming when his wife awakened him from what seemed to be a nightmare. The patient was not aware of even being asleep, as evidenced by the fact that he labeled this frightening experience a hallucination. His wife, however, insisted that he was sound asleep, as he was breathing deeply and snoring loudly. The patient also had no idea what this "dream" could mean, although the material in his analysis was concentrating on oedipal wishes and castration anxiety. Nevertheless, we can guess that the disguise in this pictorial representation of guilt feelings and castration anxiety was not very effective, as the sequence from intercourse to the touching of his penis does not seem to be that far removed in form or content from sexual feelings and retaliatory castration fears. Undoubtedly, that is why the experience became a nightmare and a panic state.

Thus, the transformation from a mental element to a visual image—a process that Freud called regressive—contains some element of disguise. As would be expected, the more primitive or conflict-ridden the element is, in that it is attached to deeper unconscious levels, the less recognizable it will be. Interestingly enough, Freud was not particularly interested in experiments in which conscious mental activity is changed into visual images; he was concerned with how unconscious factors gain access to higher levels, as occurs in the formation of the manifest dream.

The mechanisms in forming disguises and dreams, to repeat, are similar to those forming defenses. Perhaps the differences are a matter of degree. The main purpose of defenses is to maintain repression (see Chapter 6), although defenses contain some elements of the return of the repressed. The repressed wish in dreams gains more access to the preconscious and conscious levels and plays a greater role in the dream content and formation than in the achievement of psychic equilibrium that is maintained by defensive processes. The repressive forces play a relatively greater role in a defensive equilibrium than do those striving to express unconscious impulses in dreams. In most dreams, the elements from below, rather than those from above, seem to have the dominant part, although Freud (1900) also described "dreams from above," the latter are comparatively rare when placed alongside "dreams from below."

Freud emphasized, in effect, the processes at work in the construction and disguise of "dreams from below." The day residue becomes attached to associatively connected unconscious elements that are energized by this attachment. The primary process enters the picture at this point. That is, the inter-

meshing of the day residue with unconscious schemas follows
the laws of the primary process, displacement, condensation,
and symbolization (see Chapter 2). The product of this fusion
takes a regressive course within the psyche because there is no
access to motor discharge: the pathways to the outer world are
blocked, as the environment is shut out during sleep.

This degree of blocking varies, as indicated in the discussion of hypnogogic states. It seems that in such states the psyche
attempts to maintain some contact with its surroundings as it
sinks into the sleep state, and the result is the depiction of an
outer world that is distorted or imbued with unconscious elements. The aspects of the outer world that are drawn into the
dream simultaneously undergo regressive changes as they become incorporated into the manifest content.

In the more ordinary dream, however, the path of unconscious elements is reversed. Instead of proceeding to the
psyche's higher levels until they reach the ego's interface with
the outer world, they go in the opposite direction. That is how
Freud described it in one of his early models of the mind, the
picket fence model. This is a linear model, based on a reflex arc,
with a sensory mode at one end and a motor mode at the other.
Between them is a series of lines perpendicular to the base,
representing memory traces. The unconscious complex travels
from the motor end through the memory traces to the sensory
side, which, when reached, is experienced as a dream.

The path through the psyche is not unidirectional. If the
dream process begins with stirrings from the id, striving for
expression because the censorship has relaxed during sleep, then
there must be a movement seeking discharge as the unconscious
elements travel up through higher psychic levels. Because the
motoric discharge, that is, access to the outer world, is blocked,
the psychic forces cannot seek expression through external interactions. Instead, they move backwards, that is, sink deeper into
the psychic apparatus. They do not move very far backwards,
however; for the most part they remain in the preconscious as
they activate associatively connected memory traces. After having done so, they once again travel to a somewhat higher level,
but not much higher. They finally reach the perceptual consciousness system where they are elaborated into a dream.

Distortion and disguise of the dream occur at different

levels of the psyche as the unconscious seeks expression and the remainder of the mental apparatus wants to continue sleeping. The day residue and the unconscious complexes join within the context of the primary process. The day residue introduces a segment of the external world and gives the unconscious something to which it can attach itself. It permits unconscious feelings to acquire a visible form, but their form will be determined by such processes as condensation, displacement, and symbolization.

The process of dream formation continues as these psychic currents pass through a series of memory traces in the system preconscious. They gather accretions during this passage which are also organized around the axis of the primary process. However, secondary elaboration is also occurring simultaneously throughout the dream formation. The secondary elaboration rearranges the products of the primary process operations so that they can attain sensory representation, that is, so that they can be registered in perceptual consciousness. The final dream product will be a disguised and distorted manifest content, but it will usually be patterned after the sleeper's world. The amount of distortion is, according to Freud, determined by the amount of conflict inherent in the unconscious dream elements, the latent thoughts, and how deeply they had been repressed before they attached themselves to the day residue.

This process applies to the majority of dreams, which are dreams from below. The dominance of latent unconscious elements over the reality features of the day residue determine how disguised or bizarre the manifest-dream content will be. The work of secondary elaboration is correspondingly more difficult and ineffective, as the day residue is in a sense pushed into the background. Secondary elaboration, or secondary process, is a reality-oriented activity and operates on the basis of logical principles. It also occurs in the part of the mind that is closest to the external world or internal representations of that world. Thus, dreams from below are usually less reality organized than are dreams from above, although this depends on the relative strength of the primary and secondary processes.

Disguise is required to maintain the state of sleep. As elements in the unconscious strive for expression when they are stimulated by the day residue, they may disturb or disrupt sleep.

Therefore, to establish harmony so that sleep can continue, these aspects of the unconscious are elaborated into a dream, sufficiently disguised so that the ego is not threatened and has to summon sufficient energy to repress them once again. This would require a state of wakefulness. For example, we know that nightmares are insufficiently disguised so that sleep cannot be maintained.

Disguise is also needed so that the dream can be perceived. The sensory system can deal only with content that has some degree of secondary process organization, so that it can be perceived. Disguise helps achieve mental representation and perceptual registration. It may distort certain secondary process connections, but the gaps in logic and absurdities may contribute to the dream's becoming perceivable. In sleep, the system perceptual consciousness is operating with low levels of energy; it is hypocathected. To pursue this argument in terms of the psychoeconomic hypothesis, we can assume that in order for perception to occur, there has to be a certain level of psychic energy attained in the system perceptual consciousness. The energy is derived from both the content of perceptual consciousness and the residual energy it contains. These two sources of energy are additive, and a certain threshold must be reached before the dream can be visualized. Perhaps the dream is formed while raising energy levels and achieving sensory representation. A bizarre or disguised configuration stands out—in energic terms it can be considered hypercathected.

These formulations are made within the context of the psychoeconomic hypothesis, and as pointed out in Chapter 2, it has been severely criticized. The same objections to this hypothesis could also apply to these theories of dream formation. Nevertheless, some of these theories fit well with patients' subjective reactions to their dreams and observations such as those of Silberer. They can also be useful in a clinical context.

TYPES OF DREAMS

Dreams from above and traumatic anxiety dreams can be useful clinically, for they both may focus on a central traumatic core that has been aroused because of some recent experience. These dreams also reveal much about the traumatic infantile environment. Other types of dreams are also clinically useful and are frequently presented by patients in psychoanalytic treatment.

Typical Dreams

So-called typical dreams are commonplace and supposedly have the same meaning for all dreamers. Anxiety and examination dreams are familiar examples of this genre. In a typical examination dream, the dreamer is a student who is taking or has taken an examination that he is failing or has failed. The dreamer feels a moderate amount of anxiety because he feels totally unprepared for the examination. The dream is unpleasant, and the dreamer usually feels relieved when it is over, relieved to learn that this was just a dream. The experience in the dream feels quite real.

When Freud (1900) first discussed these dreams, he asked the obvious question of how wish fulfillment can be part of these painful dreams; that is, it is difficult to link the manifest content of unpreparedness and failure to any latent wish-fulfilling thoughts. Freud finally concluded that these dreams were dreams of reassurance, because he discovered that the examination in these dreams was actually of subjects in which patients excelled. It is as if the dreamer were saying, "All of my failures should be like this one." If the dreamer's feared failures are really successful experiences, then he can feel secure and content. In this connection, it is interesting that frequently when a student dreams of failing an examination before taking it, it is likely that he will pass and do well. The underlying dynamics are similar to those just discussed. The student knows that he is well prepared, and so to be anxious about this examination is putting this anxiety into a setting in which he does not feel vulnerable.

For older persons having such dreams, Freud discovered another wish-fulfilling motive. He was referring to dreams in which the dreamer has returned to school and is not doing well. I recall one patient, a successful physician, who had recurrent dreams of being back in medical school. In his dream, he had not attended classes, and in some instances he did not know the courses he was taking or, if he did, where they were meeting or what they were covering. In the dream, he felt anxious because he had to take comprehensive examinations in these subjects, for which he was totally unprepared. The dream would usually depict his frantically seeking a textbook or notes in order to study, despite knowing that the task in front of him was so formidable that he could not possibly succeed. Still, in real life, as is generally true for typical dreams, these all were subjects in which he was at the head of his class.

Freud commented that such dreams also represent the wish not to grow old. In his dream, my patient was still in medical school, although in reality he was a well-known and successful physician. The problems he was having in his dream were the problems of his youth. He was struggling with his subjects and was anxious that he would not pass some crucial examinations. These insecurities are typical of young men, not established physicians whose problems are not the same as those of medical students. If he had such problems, then he would be young again, and according to Freud, that is the wish-fulfilling quality of typical dreams.

Freud included certain exhibitionistic dreams in the category of typical dreams. He was referring to the commonly reported dreams of walking around naked, often in crowds or on moderately populated streets. This is another instance in which the dreamer, if he is an older person, is expressing the wish to remain young. Children and infants run around without clothes, and they and the surrounding world are not particularly concerned about their nakedness. Such exhibitionism is a prerogative of childhood, and so the dreamer is yearning for his lost childhood. Some clinicians are wary of generalizations about this class of dreams.

Freud's theory about not wishing to be old is often correct, but usually this is an incomplete explanation. The motives behind exhibitionistic behavior can be quite complex and the product of intense conflict. The dreamer frequently feels ashamed of and embarrassed by his nakedness and sometimes may also experience intense anxiety. Furthermore, the underlying dream thoughts of a woman having such a dream may be quite different from those of a man whose dreams may seem similar. These dreams are frequently reported by young patients and depict types of wish fulfillments other than the ones that Freud described. Still, there is some uniformity to the manifest content of many exhibitionistic dreams, and Freud's ideas are often appropriate.

Freud also discussed flying dreams, which he believed represented sexual excitement. Again, this explanation has been repeatedly confirmed, but because it is so broad and general, it can be expected to be relevant to most flying dreams in which the excitement is clearly discernible and vividly described by the dreamer. When we study flying dreams in greater detail, we may learn that there are other threads in the dream thoughts that cannot be generalized to all such dreams and that are characteristic of the dreamer's unique psychic constellations. From this viewpoint, we are examining the "typical" aspects of so-called typical flying dreams. Most dreams reflect the dreamer's individual psyche, but common qualities and similarities are found in all human minds.

Dreams of Psychic Structure

Dreams of psychic structure are in some ways similar to those that Silberer described. They concentrate on depicting psychic structure in favor of dealing with conflicting instinctual drives. Clearly, these two qualities are not mutually exclusive. Dreams of psychic structure, however, emphasize the architecture of the psyche, and to the extent that they do, they differ from dreams from below.

Dreams of psychic structure differ from Silberer's examples, which dealt primarily with psychic processes and functions, although in psychoanalytic theory, structure and function cannot be arbitrarily separated but blend with each other.

Dreams of houses or the interiors of houses are the most typical dreams of psychic structure. The arrangement of rooms, the various floors, ceiling, attic, and basement refer to different levels and segments of the psychic apparatus. The basement most often represents the unconscious, that is, the deepest layer of the mind, whereas the upper parts of the house such as the attic or ceiling depict the superego. The various rooms may refer to ego subsystems; for example, the kitchen or dining room alludes to the nurturing modality or maternal introject, and the library represents the preconscious system, the various books depicting memory traces. These are not static dreams but contain some specific action that informs us about emotional integration and what is happening to psychic equilibrium.

In this regard, these dreams are much like those Silberer described except that they encompass all of the mind rather than the mind's involvement in a particular activity. For example, a patient in a state of frightening regression dreamed of being in a room in which the floor collapsed. In a nightmarish fashion, he fell to the next floor. On awakening, he felt that he was "falling apart," that is, in a state of psychic disintegration, which soon necessitated a short hospitalization. The dream action consisted of the patient's spatial position: He moved downward, falling from the higher levels of his psychic apparatus to the lower ones, when the floor, his support, caved in. This is a graphic example of topographical regression (see Chapter 2). The house, however, did not completely collapse; the patient did not fall into the basement, and the foundation remained firm. The fact that he was able to return to treatment after a brief hospital stay indicates that the regressive process was contained and that his ego was resilient enough to reestablish psychic equilibrium.

Does this dream contradict the wish-fulfillment theory of dreams? I do not believe so; I have simply approached this dream from a different direction. We can consider this to be an ego-psychological approach rather than an id-oriented investigation. The former has been criticized because it relies on understanding the manifest content in terms of its form and the changes in that form. The id-oriented approach is based on primary process id impulses that can be discovered through their derivatives as they appear in the patient's free associations.

The patient's associations, however, also make direct or indirect references to psychic structure, and the interpretations of these dreams are also derived from examining the patient's associations and their transference implications. In fact, the dream just described was the outcome of feeling abandoned by the analyst. It represented a regressive, disintegrative reaction to feeling rejected, but it was also a cry for help. The patient felt that only by "falling apart" could he get anyone to relate to him, to rescue him. This transference interaction could be considered to be the dream's wish-fulfilling property, although this is admittedly a fairly broad view of wish fulfillment.

Dreams of structure are not simply limited to a pictorial representation of the psychic apparatus. My patient's dream also contained a transference interaction. Most of such dreams also involve feelings—perhaps frightening, conflicting feelings—and tell us something about the dreamer's object relationships.

Another patient, a college student, presented a brief and anxiety-laden dream that is fairly often encountered in an analytic practice. He dreamed that he was exerting all of his strength to hold down the lid of a manhole cover. Apparently, there was a monster underneath that was struggling to get out so that he could devour the patient. This dream occurred during the first two weeks of analysis, and its meaning was clear to both of us. This young man was intensely ambivalent about becoming involved in an analytic relationship. He had seen several analysts in the past and was always able to find some rationalization for believing that the relationship would not work out. With me, he had decided that no matter what happened, he would not run away from treatment. He presented this dream because he was determined not to give in to his resistance. He was now able, however, to recognize how frightened he was and could understand why this dream was a reaction to beginning treatment, the fear that what would emerge from his unconscious could destroy him.

In his daily life, this patient was controlled to the extent that he found it difficult to cope with the exigencies of his surrounding world, and he could not form an intimate relationship with anyone, man or woman. He felt that his emotions were "frozen," and this was his reason for seeking treatment. He understood that the dream was a reflection of his intense anxiety and explained why he was so ambivalent about getting involved in a therapeutic relationship. The manhole cover represented repressive forces that were literally maintaining a lid on his unconscious. He expected that the analysis would somehow either strengthen his unconscious feelings and impulses or loosen the lid, or both.

These dreams have also been called *representational* because they represent structural configurations and their stability or instability. However, as is evident in the preceding dream, the ego's reaction to instinctual impulses can be incorporated in the manifest content. This dream was still a depiction of the psyche as it was displayed in a state of precarious equilibrium. As such, it was simply a pictorial translation of anxiety caused by the anticipated threat of treatment to intrapsychic defensive adaptations, mainly repression and the maintenance of tight controls so that repression can be rigidly enforced.

Again, the question about the dream's wish-fulfilling purpose can be raised, as the representational factors seem to be in the foreground. The fact that this patient's dream was related to his beginning treatment and his resolve not to give in to his defense of withdrawal emphasizes that there is a strong transference element responsible for its production. The patient's associations indicated that he made the analysis the reason for the dilemma he dreamed about. Still, he was not paranoid: the final responsibility was still his because he had chosen to be analyzed, and so he himself was responsible for, and had created, the predicament he dreamed about. Later, a convoluted wish-fulfillment aspect emerged. The patient believed that he was telling me what he feared might happen in treatment if it proceeded too quickly. Therefore, he was asking me to go slowly so that the monster under the manhole cover would not be unduly aroused. By showing me the possibly disastrous consequence of moving too rapidly, which meant attacking and weakening his defense, he was asking me to let him keep his controls and possibly to reinforce them with my capacity for control.

This dream, like the first dream of structure reported, can be considered a wish fulfillment in a transference context. The dream's manifest content, however, as it represents the struggle between the ego and the id, must be examined in a different frame of reference. Because the dream's transference implications came to the fore later in treatment and were retrospectively reconstructed, we can ask whether these feelings were created after the dream and then attributed to it, that they were not really involved in creating the dream.

This question can be asked about all dreams, and perhaps it cannot be answered, at least by means of the psychoanalytic method. It is also a question that is not particularly relevant to clinicians, because they are interested in the development of the transference, and if dreams can help determine how it is evolving, it does not matter if such feelings were actually participating in some aspect of the dream work.

We can also ask whether the dreams that patients report are the same as what they actually dreamed. That is, perhaps they are fresh associations and images that are strung together in a sequence, and the reported dreams are the product of current thoughts and feelings that are then moved back in time to the sleep state. This, too, is of little consequence in treatment, as the patients are still revealing the state of their mind and the conflicts that plague them. Furthermore, it is possible that a person's impressions when waking up determine the dream's form, rather than its being a definite picture while asleep. The dream's final form that is reported does not mean that our ideas about its function, such as preserving sleep, have to be modified.

As stated, these representational dreams contain other mental elements besides psychic structure. They can be compared to a stage, a scene in which various actions can occur. As in a play, the scenario has become a means of unfolding the plot. The scenery may dominate in some instances and may evolve so that what was at first the background becomes the foreground. As the reported dreams demonstrate, patients can concentrate on instinctual impulses within a structural context, or they can dream about changes in structure, such as collapse and loss of integration.

My college-student patient reported a dream that was a reflection of his object relations which, in turn, revealed how inhibited he felt. He dreamed that he was in a house wandering through its various rooms. He noted that some of the rooms contained a slab with a body on it. The bodies were neither dead nor alive but were in a state of suspended animation. In his associations, the patient was able to identify the bodies as his mother, father, and older siblings, all of whom had related to

him as parents, as he was the "baby" of the family. He emphasized at this time, as he had in the past, how inept all of these
persons were, especially when they were put in the position of
caring for him.

He stressed his mother's incompetence in relating to his
needs. He did not see her as a live, vital person. He felt, rather,
that she was frozen—not in the sense that she was cold and aloof
but frozen as a machine might be when its gears become stuck.
He believed that his mother was functionally paralyzed (Giovacchini 1984). She was frightened and timid when she tried to
feed or otherwise care for him. She admitted that she did not
know what to do and was eager to hand him over to others to
care for him. These other caretakers were equally incompetent
and indifferent.

The patient had been clumsy and inept throughout his
childhood. He had also been "delicate" and suffered from enco-
presis, a condition that had caused much concern to his family
and for which they had sought numerous medical consultations.
He had received psychotherapy from the age of 5 up to the
present, when he started seeing me.

He recalled an episode with his mother when he was about
5 years old. He asked what she would do if he stopped soiling.
Her eyes filled with tears, and in a tremulous voice, she replied,
"I don't know." Then she rushed upstairs and locked herself in
her room and sobbed.

The emphasis in his associations—and it was depicted in his
dream by the bodies in a state of suspended animation—was
that nothing worked. His mother could not function as a mother
who could respond to her child with joy and pride when he
became able to regulate and control his bodily functions. She
"didn't know" how to react to a functioning being, and as the
patient introjected her, he also felt paralyzed. He could not
work, play, or relate to people.

The lack of executive techniques was manifest in this patient's behavior, dreams, and view of himself. He lacked a firm
identity sense, and when he dreamed of rooms in his houses,
these rooms were furnished in a bizarre fashion. He had a bed in
the kitchen in which he slept. He ate in the living room and used
the bedroom as a study. When I questioned him, he claimed that

he did not know that certain rooms were assigned particular functions. When he told me about the arrangement of the rooms, I had to question him about their location to determine what they actually were.

The patient's dream indicated that each room was filled with a "frozen introject." For the patient, all the rooms were the same, because he did not have enough experiences with external objects to help him make intrapsychic differentiations. Introjects, the outcome of object relationships, are assimilated into the psyche and help structure various ego subsystems such as the executive system which, in turn, enables the person to relate to external objects in a productive and satisfying fashion.

As I have stressed, this dream—especially the bodies in a state of suspended animation—can be studied from many different angles. Destructive and sexual feelings also were part of this dream, but its construction from the internalization of vital object relationships is its centerpiece.

Dreams Within Dreams

Dreams within dreams are easy to describe and recognize. They are, as the name indicates, dreams in which the sleeper dreams of having a dream. This can occur in many different circumstances, which can be considered as belonging to the first dream level. In treatment, the patient frequently has forgotten the dream within the dream, which led Freud to conclude that the latter represented deep unconscious, strongly repressed conflicts.

These dreams are, in a sense, multilayered and need not necessarily involve dreaming about dreaming. There are other varieties of such dreams in which the sleeper, instead of having a dream within a dream, dreams of a play or a movie that has a plot differing from the background in which it is observed. The play depicted within the dream has a significance similar to that of the dream within the dream.

A middle-aged man dreamed that he was going to make love to his secretary. He was, in fact, sexually attracted to her, but he felt too inhibited to make overtures, although he believed that she would be receptive to his advances. In the dream, he was in bed with her and was preparing to have intercourse with her. However, he then fell asleep and dreamed that he was visiting his dentist. This was a painful, frightening scene in which his dentist told him that he had to extract all of his wisdom teeth. The patient awakened from this dream within a dream feeling intense anxiety, but he was no longer in bed with his secretary. He was now back in his office, working on some difficult problems. When he finally awakened, he was relieved to discover that what had happened was just a dream.

It was strange that the whole dream was experienced as oppressive, as most of the manifest content was not overtly unpleasant. In the beginning of the dream, he was in bed with his secretary whom he found sexually attractive. Likewise, the latter part of the dream was simply a routine and familiar work situation that should not have been the source of any concern. The dream within the dream, however, was extremely frightening.

I present this dream because its oedipal elements are fairly obvious and were clearly demonstrated by the patient's associations. He expressed considerable guilt about his extramarital sexual urges, which was portrayed in the dream by the dream within the dream and by the somewhat modulated later part of the dream, which can be considered to be on a higher psychic level than was the dream within the dream.

The dream began with an attempt to gratify what he viewed as illicit sexual feelings. He was trying to recapture certain adolescent strivings that were never satisfied during adolescence. He had been shy, withdrawn, and a virgin as an adolescent. Now moderately successful, he had acquired some self-confidence and felt reasonably certain that he could have a sexual relationship with his secretary. Similar to when he was an adolescent, he was shy about approaching her. He also felt guilty about what, to him, were unacceptable feelings. He had never been unfaithful, and consciously he did not want to hurt his wife. These attitudes were connected with his fear of incest.

In the dream, he momentarily overcame his conflict and proceeded to get involved in a forbidden sexual situation. This was similar to a "wet" dream in which biological sexual pressures gain ascendancy. Conflicting forces, however, soon dominated the dream picture. He left the sexual setting by falling asleep and dreaming that he was in a dentist's office. This scene symbolically represented castration anxiety. Freud (1900) often mentioned that a tooth is a symbol for the penis. In this dream within a dream, the patient was afraid to lose his wisdom teeth, which were equated with potency and adulthood. He thus was going to be castrated by their extraction, be reduced to a sexless childhood status. He resolved the problem by returning to the office, that is, by reassuring himself that he was an adult, but his secretary was nowhere to be seen.

This is a fairly straightforward oedipal interpretation that was pieced together from the patient's associations, a knowledge of his past history, and the sequence of the dream's manifest content. If, however, the dream within the dream is the manifestation of intense and deeply repressed conflict, why was this dream so transparent at the manifest-content level?

This patient was concretely oriented and not at all psychologically minded. He approached dream material, as he did everything else in his life, in an obsessional-literal manner. He could understand that going to bed with his secretary was an expression of sexual wishes, but he was completely puzzled as to why he would dream of being in a dentist's office, especially as there was no occasion for such a visit. Working in his office was a pedestrian occurrence, and so he was not surprised that he would dream about it, but he did not wonder or know about the connection of these three fragments.

In view of his concreteness, it is interesting to note how this dream was organized and stratified. As I indicated, it is convenient to divide this dream into three segments, the beginning sexual fragment, the middle dream within a dream, and the finale in which he was working in his office. The first and last fragments belong to an upper level and are concretely organized. They seem to be dominated by a secondary process in that they were fairly faithful replicas of reality, and the intentions and actions in these settings were both plausible and possible. By contrast, the middle segment is not connected to either the patient's inner desires or the external world. He also pointed out that the whole scene was blurry and unreal. The dentist was not a person that he knew, and his features were somewhat satanic. He could not imagine any reason that this scene should have entered his dream, except that he knew that people dreamed about "crazy things," whereas his dreams were usually well organized and reality oriented. The dream within a dream belonged to another level, a deeper level than that housing the other two sections of the manifest content.

In addition to the stratification inherent in such dreams, the dream within a dream—at least with my patient—seems to have had more primary process and symbolic elements than the general dream context does. This agrees with Freud's assertion that the second dream contains deep, frightening material. The fact that my patient had had such a dream emphasized that he had to keep primitive feelings and impulses deeply buried, as evidenced by his dull, unimaginative behavior. It also indicated, however, that he did have emotions and primitive passions; he simply could not get in touch with them. As he progressed in analysis, he proved to be a person of deep sensitivities and imagination.

Elusive Dreams

Elusive dreams are dreams in which the sleepers know that they are dreaming. Usually these are highly pleasurable experiences because of narcissistic gratification and the realization of omnipotence. The dream is experienced as a fantasy come true.

Because such dreamers know that they are dreaming, they feel perfectly safe in doing whatever they please. If they wish to jump off a tall building or fly through space, as a superman might, they need not hesitate. Usually such dreams involve flying, which is felt as highly pleasurable and is associated with a sense of power. Occasionally the gratification of oral impulses may be prominent. Such dreamers, especially if they are trying to lose weight and are on a diet, may dream of a sumptuous banquet with all of their favorite dishes. They know that they are dreaming, and so they can eat all they wish, with impunity. It is interesting that the gratification of sexual impulses is not included in these dreams of uninhibited wish fulfillment, indicating that they deal with the more primitive pregenital levels of personality.

A scientist in his early thirties had had many elusive dreams, but he remembered one in particular that he had first had at the age of 6 and that periodically recurred until puberty. He dreamed that he was flying amidst skyscrapers, and he finally found himself in the lobby of the apartment building he lived in. He delighted himself by getting underneath the elevator and pushing it up to the top floor. He was exhilarated by his superhuman strength and the fact that he could disobey the laws of gravity. As he was enjoying himself to the utmost, he said, "I must be dreaming," whereupon a voice from above said, "Of course you are dreaming, but this is the best part of the dream." He awakened, feeling a little letdown because reality was not as exciting as what he had dreamed about. Nevertheless, even at the early age of 6 he was amused by the dream and thought of it as an accomplishment.

These dreams are unusual in that they appear to be free of conflict. Unlike the stratification of dreams within dreams, elusive dreams seem to have no boundaries, perhaps indicating that the psychic level being depicted is fairly undifferentiated. The dominant feeling is one of power and omnipotence, accompanied by actions and achievements that could be fantasies attached to infantile narcissism. Elusive dreams are pictorial representations of megalomanic fantasies, experienced with satisfaction and in a relatively comfortable fashion. The dreamer is able to get in touch with early narcissistic phases and reenact the wishes attached to them.

Ordinarily, when patients regress to such early stages, they are overcome by anxiety—in some instances panic—because they feel that they are losing control; they anxiously complain that they are falling apart. The loss of psychic structure characteristic of such regressions is threatening, and so many patients have to construct fairly elaborate defenses to maintain control of their inner primitive feelings. During elusive dreams, such defenses do not appear to be necessary.

I have treated several scientists and some artists. All of them had numerous elusive dreams. From my data and that of some of my colleagues, I believe that these dreams are apt to occur in creative persons. This conclusion contradicts the dictum that dreams cannot tell us much about character structure. The cor-

ollary conclusion that particular dreams cannot be correlated
with specific types of psychopathology, however, is not challenged by these observations.

The persons I have known who are often aware that they
are dreaming while dreaming seem to have an extraordinary
capacity to dig deep into their unconscious and can rather easily
relax repressive barriers. This ability to make contact with the
primitive aspects of the self and at the same time to maintain a
modicum of secondary process is the essence of the creative act.
The same process seems to be operating in elusive dreams; that
is, the primitive infantile parts of the self are found to be
enjoyable rather than frightening.

THE CLINICAL USE OF DREAMS

For the clinician, dreams can be helpful in understanding unconscious processes and the patient's hidden feelings. Indeed,
Freud called them the "royal road to the unconscious." In treatment, they can forecast the course of treatment, clarify the
status of the transference, and sometimes predict some of the
impasses that may arise within the framework of resistance.

Some patients do not bring any dreams to treatment, claim-
ing either that they do not dream or that they do not remember
them. It is difficult to draw any definitive conclusions from this
phenomenon. In some instances, these patients keep their feelings repressed and deal with life in a rigid, concrete manner.
This might mean that they will be difficult to treat. On the other
hand, other such patients do not present any special difficulties
even if they do not produce dreams. They free associate comparatively easily and are able to benefit from the insights they
gain from interpretations.

By contrast, some patients present numerous dreams. For
instance, one of my patients brought me 500 dreams a month.
His sessions were dominated by the recitation of dreams, to the
point that I was overwhelmed by their manifest content. Because of the number of dreams he reported, there was no time
for free association. When I finally interrupted him, picked out
the last dream he had mentioned, and asked him to free asso-

ciate to it, he went completely blank; he had nothing to say. Obviously, this patient was using dreams as a means of resistance. Later in treatment he was able to relax and brought in only a few dreams, and he could free associate to them.

Apart from their number, are there other qualities of dreams that are related to a patient's treatability or psychopathology? I have repeatedly stated that we cannot equate particular dreams with specific types of psychopathology. Dreams are depictions of the primitive aspects of the personality, levels that recapitulate early developmental phases common to all of us. When the best-adjusted persons regress in the dream state, they can produce bizarre dreams. Are there types of bizarreness, however, that may cause us to think of severe psychopathology? At present, this question has not been answered, but some dreams may lead the therapist to suspect a psychotic process.

For example, one patient dreamed of dead bodies that could easily be seen under water in a clear pond. All the therapists who heard this dream reported an eerie feeling, and the patient turned out to be schizophrenic. It was impossible to determine why we all felt as we did, but there was something about this dream that made it out of the ordinary.

Another patient, a young woman, dreamed that she was holding a baby in her arms. The baby began gradually shrinking in size. It finally became as small as and looked like a beetle. She slowly pulled off its appendages and then dashed it to the ground. This dream was reported to me by a supervisee, and I immediately thought of schizophrenia, which proved to be correct. There was nothing unique about my diagnostic guess, as it was a rather common reaction to this kind of dream.

Dead bodies under water and dismembering a beetle that had once been a baby are, indeed, bizarre preoccupations that might be associated with primitive thought disorders. Still, there are patients who present similarly bizarre dreams who are emotionally stable and who demonstrate logical thought processes and appropriate abstractions and symbols, all in the context of good reality testing. For example, a woman in her late twenties had the following dream: She walked into an obstetrical delivery room, feeling that she was a fraudulent woman. She was not certain what this meant but was inclined to believe that it was concerned with whether she were a real woman or a real person. Her face was wrinkled and grotesquely ugly. As she was standing there, someone unrecognizable pulled the skin off her face, stripping it completely away. As this mask was pulled off, she gave birth to a baby, a baby who was in fact a doll and about 3 inches long. Underneath the woman's mask was another grotesque face that was identical with the one that had been ripped off. This procedure was repeated a second time, and she gave birth to an identical baby doll.

This patient showed no signs or symptoms of severe psychopathology. She was emotionally sensitive and psychologically minded and had a keen sense of intuition. Her evaluations of the external world were realistic, and her responses to other persons were often empathic. In other words, she seemed to have good ego strength. This was her current state, but one that reached such stabilization after many years of intensive treatment.

I need not go into any great detail about the underlying factors that motivated the formation of this dream. Briefly, the tearing away of this woman's mask represented that she currently viewed the analytic interaction as stripping away her false self, but there was nothing different underneath it. The doll babies referred to herself, who was treated as a transitional object and who had been named for her mother's favorite doll. Her self representation was tenuous and beset by intense destructive inner forces. She could be easily understood in terms of a psychotic core which at the beginning of treatment was quite manifest. Now there was a considerable overlap of psychic structure.

Rather than its actual structure and content, the importance of this dream was the message that the patient was trying to convey to me. She was reminding me of how emotionally disturbed she had been and also not to ignore her remaining helplessness and vulnerability. I had to be careful about taking her for granted and expecting more of her than she felt capable of achieving.

Though she functioned well, part of her still believed that she was operating on the basis of a false self; that is, her contact with the outer world was not based on anything substantial. She therefore wore a mask to hide her belief that there was nothing underneath it and that her self representation was empty and amorphous. These attitudes had been especially intense when she first started treatment many years ago.

As bizarre as this dream appeared to be, its manifest content contained features that were not just the outcome of ego defects and a malformed self-representation. It is puzzling that what was functioning as a mask was itself amorphous and ugly and resembled a monster. The patient's description and associations emphasized these characteristics. This was a dream, but we can still ask why what was to be hidden was portrayed as being on the surface, which in turn was hiding something identical. To rephrase this, what was to be defended against became the defense. In literature, Edgar Allen Poe's "The Purloined Letter" could be a parallel situation, but in that story, no one recognized the letter being sought because they did not think of looking for it where it could easily be found. In this woman's dream, the mask was how the world viewed the patient, and I was ripping it off.

Her associations stressed that there were at least two factors behind the stripping off of the mask. As I stated, she wanted me to understand how empty she still felt, as indicated by there being nothing different under the mask, just the same amorphous monster. This was a transference message. However, she was also demonstrating a psychodynamic shift brought about by changes in her psychic structure. The weak, hateful, inadequate parts of her self were no longer buried by her false self and psychotic constellations. Instead, she had elevated them to the spatial position and status of a defense. This could mean that they had acquired organization and cohesiveness, although on the surface they appeared to be unstructured. This would be similar to the distinction that Deutsch (1942) made between a true as–if and a pseudo as–if personality. The true as–if types feel empty because they are empty, whereas the pseudo as–if types believe that they lack an identity because they want to keep the structured aspects of the self hidden because of some inner conflict. My patient was indicating a transformation from a true structural defect to a character organization in which the former defect was being used defensively to protect other parts of the self.

Giving birth to the dolls was also connected to protecting her good parts; even though the babies were dolls, as she was treated as a child, these births represented an attempt to transform the dolls into human beings under her maternal care. The two dolls to which she gave birth were herself and her daughter, rebirths with the prospect of a better outcome than that of the past.

Although this dream is bizarre, it incorporates progressive elements as well as a psychotic core that had been much more active in the past. Again, this shows that we cannot generalize about psychopathology and character structure from dreams' manifest contents. Dreams, however, are especially useful in understanding the overlapping of defenses with various types of character constellations. To some degree, dreams portray some elements of the infantile traumatic environment and recapitulate in a disguised form the sequence of early development.

Panoramic Dreams

Clinicians occasionally encounter panoramic dreams at the beginning of treatment, often the first dream. These dreams are usually lengthy but fairly coherent, although the degree of coherence varies. I call them panoramic dreams because they cover a wide expanse of the dreamer's psyche. Consequently, they are particularly important dreams and reveal what direction the treatment will take and how the transference will develop. A young man in his middle twenties provided a good example of a panoramic dream.

During the second session, he had the following dream: He was walking up the stairs to the bedroom of a house similar to one he had lived in as a child. He knocked on the door. An elderly man opened the door, obviously angry for having been interrupted. He had apparently been making love. With an angry gesture he slammed the door in the patient's face. The patient was both intimidated and amused as he left the house. He then found himself on a sidewalk near a beach and started jogging. While running, he felt exhilarated as he looked at the bulging muscles of his thighs. He was proud of his manliness, but this feeling was short-lived. For some unknown reason, his mood suddenly changed and he was overcome by depression and ravenous hunger. He noticed that there were many food stands on the beach. Nevertheless, despite his hunger, he was inhibited about buying something to eat. When he turned toward a food stand, his legs felt as if they were paralyzed, and he was unable to reach the stand. He then gazed at the sea and felt desperately lonely and sad.

Despite the richness of the material, the patient was unable to free associate to any segment of this dream. He made some statements about the beginning of the dream, perhaps referring to his parents' sexual activities, but these were casual, intellectual comments that had little meaning to him. Mainly, he drew blanks when I asked him to examine different sections of the dream. Consequently, I let him pursue whatever line of inquiry he preferred, without discussing the dream further.

This patient remained in analytic treatment of four to five times a week for over four years. As is true of any analysis, it is difficult to describe in an orderly fashion its sequence in terms of regressions, fixations, and development of the transference because of what we might call disgressions as the patient moved back and forth and even laterally on the developmental scale. However, I can identify the main movement over the course of the treatment. Such reconstructions will be mechanistic and somewhat contrived because various themes have been extracted from a complex network of feelings and infantile reactions and artificially isolated so that we can establish a sequence. This sequence was recapitulated in the panoramic dream.

This patient began his analysis by boasting about his masculine prowess. He told me about several of his macho activities in the past, such as being in the merchant marines and, later, being a paratrooper in the army. He also detailed his sexual exploits. In the transference, he compared his superior potency with mine, viewing my sexuality with disdain, as something laughable. These attitudes were forecast in the first part of the dream when he interrupted the older couple and was amused at their making love. He then ran along a path by the sea, looking with pride at his bulging thigh muscles, a phallic pride.

This bravado was a defensive facade shielding dependent yearnings, a wish to return to and fuse with his mother. The sea was a symbol for his mother, as he emphasized by pointing out the similarity of the French words for mother and sea, *la mère* and *la mer*, whereas the food stands represented the nurturing interaction and his oral needs. As he relaxed his defensive masculinity, I interpreted his competitiveness toward me as a denial of helpless and vulnerable feelings, and he began experiencing waves of hostile dependency. Clearly, he wanted to reach out to me and have me love and nurture him, a maternal transference, but he felt ashamed, humiliated, and afraid of revealing what he saw as the weak, childish, unmanly parts of his self. This pregenital transference, which also included passive homosexual impulses, and his defenses against it occupied a major portion of the analysis, as his conflict about returning to the sea or getting food at the stand constituted the major segment of the dream. I need not pursue further the parallels between the analysis and the dream except to point out that behind the pregenital transference, as we might expect, we encountered intense oedipal rivalry and primal scene material which was apparent at the beginning of the dream and from which he literally ran away.

I have explained this patient's character structure as consisting of various levels which unfolded in the transference and appeared in a panoramic dream. In the dream, the core conflict appeared at the beginning when he interrupted the older couple in the act of intercourse, a reference to the primal scene and oedipal rivalries and strivings. Next, he indulged in phallic exhibitionistic and defensive activity, as happened also in the analysis. He then regressed further to conflicting oral yearnings, and this sequence was repeated in treatment. Finally he reached down into oedipal material which, as stated, occurred in the beginning of the dream.

This patient's character was relatively well organized and cohesive. He functioned relatively well in his daily life, had satisfactory interpersonal relationships, and was moderately free of anxiety and depression. He sought treatment because he had a vague realization that he could not become intimately involved with a woman. He could easily have sexual relations, but he was concerned about not being able to become emotionally involved. He was also concerned about his career, not being satisfied with pursuing romantic masculine activities that had no stability or future. At the end of the analysis, he had firmly established himself in an academic career and had married.

Another patient, a 30-year-old scientist, had a panoramic dream the night before his first appointment. In this dream, he depicted the structure of his personality, and it predicted, quite accurately, the course of his transference. He dreamed that he was taking an ocean voyage on a ship that had a skillful and respected captain. However, somewhere during the voyage, the patient found himself in the midst of a storm. He described the ship's precarious balance and indicated that it was in serious danger of sinking. At this point, the captain became a villain because he did not care about the patient's welfare. Although the captain was basically responsible and cautious, he did not particularly care about the patient's welfare. He was interested only in saving himself. For the rest of the dream, the patient worked with the captain (the period of animosity having passed), and together they weathered the storm. As the dream predicted, after an initial idealization, the patient became quite paranoid about me and had to be hospitalized briefly. But he quickly reintegrated, and the analysis continued without any particular complications.

Panoramic dreams do not seem to occur in fundamentally fragmented personalities. Schizoid and borderline patients who frequently use splitting and projective mechanisms apparently are not capable of producing such dreams. In my experience, primitively fixated patients bring bizarre dreams, as I have described, or what can be called *fragmented dreams*, in contrast with panoramic dreams. Bizarre dreams are also fragmented.

The scientist patient had a paranoid episode that indicated that his psyche could fragment, as it mainly used projective mechanisms. However, as is so often the case with creative persons, he was also capable of complex thought activities combined with accurate and sensitive appraisals of reality, meaning that his ego could reach high levels of integration. He had the panoramic dream just reported when he was functioning in a relatively cohesive and efficient manner.

Freud (1900) stated that all the elements of a dream, what-

ever else their significance, represent some aspect of the dreamer's ego. All dreams are a reflection of the sleeper's mind. Most
dreams depict dominant themes that have been stimulated by
current events. The panoramic dream is obviously a response to
the new, perhaps frightening experience of beginning treatment. Fragmented dreams differ from both panoramic and
ordinary dreams in that they portray only part of the ego, rather
than specific processes in the context of the total mind. However, it is often difficult to distinguish a fragmented dream from
one dealing with a particular problem.

It is often impossible to discover the day residue in most
fragmented dreams. One of their characteristics is that they do
not seem to have any connection with external reality. This
problem is further complicated because these dreams may picture different parts of the ego, and this can make the dream
setting appear unified and cohesive. If studied carefully, the
various scenes in these dreams are found to be unrelated to one
another; that is, they do not belong on a similar continuum, but
this can be hard to determine.

Fragmented patients dream fragmented dreams, meaning
that it is easier to discover such dreams when we know something about the patient's ego state. For example, an agoraphobic
woman in her middle twenties constantly used splitting mechanisms to keep various facets of her life separate from one
another. The outside world was no longer part of her experience
because she confined herself to her parental home, except to
keep her therapy appointments, to which she was driven by her
father. As her treatment later indicated, she had split off parts of
herself, destructive hostile parts, and put them in the outer
world from which she could phobically withdraw. Thus, she
lived a highly constricted life with only part of her ego. Basically, she differed from the typical paranoid in that she had cut
herself off from those parts of herself that she projected into the
environment outside her house, to which she confined herself.
By contrast, the paranoid patient is always seeking the paranoid
object and in a perverse way maintains contact with it.

The agoraphobic patient never had what could be viewed
as a panoramic dream. All of her dreams dealt with specific
themes and had little if any action in them. In the first dream

that she reported, she simply sat in her living room with a strange man. They both sat very still, hardly moving, and did not talk to each other. Later in the dream, she saw herself sitting alone in the same room, but the left half of her body was missing. It was as if she were cut in half, a hemisected person. Nothing else happened. Further on in treatment she dreamed of storms and holocausts, but she was always standing off at a considerable distance.

The manifest content of these dreams indicate that there was little connection between various feelings and parts of the self. This patient produced no associations to them. She acted as if she were bringing something to me, dumping it at my feet, and having nothing more to do with it. She had concretized different aspects of her psyche and by so doing was getting rid of them. What she retained for herself was virtually unknown to the rest of the world. She revealed herself as half a person, that is, a fragmented person, who barricaded herself from all relations with the outer world.

Transference and Countertransference Implications of Dreams

Dreams occurring during psychoanalytic treatment always have some transference implications. The patient just discussed spent long periods of time saying absolutely nothing during her sessions. My few attempts to get her to talk were totally ineffective. This does not seem strange in view of the first dream, which began with her sitting in a room with a stranger and not talking to him. The stranger was myself, but she did not relate to me. In treatment, in the same fashion, she related or, rather, she did not relate to me. She withdrew into herself and hardly acknowledged my presence. This was how she had protected herself in a traumatic, even physically assaultive, infantile environment.

There are many ways in which the transference can manifest itself through dreams and by the act of dreaming. Some of the dreams I have presented demonstrate transference elements in both their manifest and latent content. However, for some patients, bringing dreams to the therapist in itself has some transference significance. These patients may unconsciously feel that they are presenting a gift to their analyst when they report a dream, regardless of its content. Or the recitation of dreams, especially long and numerous dreams, can be a resistance in that therapists are inundated with material that they cannot process.

In turn, psychoanalysts sometimes dream about their patients, and they can learn a good deal about their transference feelings from such dreams. Occasionally, therapists may feel heavy feelings of sleepiness with a particular patient and, in some instances, actually fall asleep during a session. Apart from those patients who are boring, feeling sleepy or even falling asleep may be a reaction to how the patient is relating to the therapist. For example, during a session, an analyst fell asleep and dreamed that he was in a bathtub. Water was pouring into the tub, apparently coming from nowhere in particular. The therapist literally felt inundated. He was in a state of light sleep, and as he gradually awakened, he could see that the stream of water was coming out of his patient's mouth. The therapist had felt overwhelmed by the patient's material, but he was not aware of it until he had this dream. He had only been cognizant of a vague discomfort for which he could not account. This dream is similar to the dreams that Silberer described when he fell asleep during some activity such as being intellectually preoccupied. This was, in effect, a hypnogogic dream.

Part III

CLINICAL USES
OF PSYCHOANALYSIS

Chapter 5

ANXIETY THEORY AND NEUROSOGENESIS

Clinical psychoanalytic formulations stress the importance of anxiety in the production of psychopathology. This affect is the core around which neuroses are formed. Thus, theories about the generation of anxiety are in the forefront of the development of clinical concepts.

ANXIETY THEORY

The First Anxiety Theory

When Freud first began his psychoanalytic explorations, his orientation was heavily biological. He thought in terms of aberrant inner forces that were "noxious" (a word Freud frequently used in his early papers) to the psyche, as if some poison were invading the mind and causing psychic disequilibrium. His formulations were made in the context of the psychodynamic hypothesis which concentrated on a tension–discharge sequence. His first anxiety theory dealt with the accumulation of undischarged sexual feelings (see Chapter 2) and, from a therapeutic perspective, stressed the importance of abreaction (see Chapter 7). He thus concluded that the production of anxiety was a discharge phenomenon.

Freud (1895a) based his conclusions on certain observations derived from patients, as well as from various general situations. For example, he noted the outbreak of anxiety neuroses in virgins, newlyweds, women whose husbands suffer from premature ejaculations or practice coitus interruptus, women who are intentionally abstinent, widows, and menopausal women. Freud was stressing that anxiety was the outcome of undischarged sexual tension, and he referred to sexual excitations in these instances as *sexual noxae* (Breuer and Freud 1895).

The same circumstances apply to men. Men who are abstinent for any reason, situational or neurotic, men who practice coitus interruptus, and older men whose potency is decreased while libido is increased (or perhaps relatively increased) all may fall prey to the anxiety neurosis.

The anxiety neurosis is characterized by periodic episodic bouts of anxiety, not obviously related to any specific precipitating circumstances. It is referred to as *free-floating anxiety*.

In the first anxiety theory, the production of anxiety is the outcome of a discrepancy between drive tension and the adequacy of the ego's executive techniques. Truly sexually anesthetic women and impotent men have little disposition toward the formation of an anxiety neurosis, as they presumably have a low level of libido. The factors responsible for such a low level vary.

The development of sexual feelings first involves a somatic excitation seeking conscious expression and energizing sexual ideas. Sexual needs cathect (see Chapter 2) memory traces of gratifying sexual experiences which set in motion adaptive techniques that lead to the gratification of the sexual impulse. In the anxiety neuroses, the sexual impulse never reaches those psychic levels where the memory traces and adaptive techniques reside. Consequently, there is no psychical discharge. Instead, the sexual impulse is deflected into the soma and is discharged somatically without mental representation. What is felt is anxiety rather than sexual excitation, and discharge is experienced as painful rather than pleasurable.

For some reason, Freud (1895a) believed that "alienation between the somatic and the psychical sphere" occurs more readily in women than in men and that it is harder to reconcile these spheres in women. Undoubtedly, he saw more women than men with anxiety neuroses, and he may have based his opinion partially on clinical distribution. I doubt that on the basis of today's patient population that his conclusion would find much support.

Anxiety has many physical similarities to sexual excitement, such as accelerated breathing, an increased heartbeat, venous congestion, and perspiration, although in an anxiety attack these reactions are usually more intense.

In the first anxiety theory, anxiety is discussed almost exclusively in biological and somatic terms. This theory has also been called the *toxic* theory of anxiety, emphasizing its organic attributes. Essentially, the first anxiety theory asserts that psychological processes—higher mentational activities—are not involved. Anxiety is simply defined in terms of its somatic constituents.

The Second Anxiety Theory

The first anxiety theory did not deal with the observation that anxiety is a highly complex affect. Besides its somatic components, anxiety has many subjective features. It is characterized by feelings of dread, impending doom, a sense of danger, and fear. These feelings would be hard to explain just on the basis of deflected somatic sexual impulses that have not achieved mental representation. Furthermore, other than environmental deprivation, the first anxiety theory does not explain why sexual impulses are blocked in their quest for gratification.

Freud's (1926) definition of anxiety (*angst*) was derived from a comparison with fear (*furcht*). It is similar to his distinction between an inner impulse or an instinct and an outer stimulus (1915a). Like an outer stimulus, fear will disappear when some specific action is taken. Specifically, a flight from a threatening situation or a disruptive stimulus will remove the source of discomfort. The muscular action of flight restores emotional equilibrium. This does not occur with anxiety. The feeling persists and cannot be immediately relieved by flight. Furthermore, there is nothing obvious to flee from. Freud (1926) summarized this by stating that fear is a reaction to an external danger, whereas anxiety is a response to an inner danger.

The situation is not that simple, however, as inner dangers can be projected into the outer world and manifest themselves as phobias. In that instance, conflict can be prevented by avoiding phobic situations. What is obvious from these definitions and observations is that anxiety cannot be understood simply as a deflection of sexual impulses into avenues of somatic discharge.

The inadequacy of the first anxiety theory is highlighted by the difficult question as to how dammed-up sexual feelings are related to life-threatening situations, both presumably leading to the subjective response of anxiety. Freud (1926) was well aware of the many subtle facets involved in understanding the ubiquitous affect of anxiety, as he increasingly used the structural hypothesis instead of the psychodynamic approach as a basic frame of reference. He did not give up thinking in psychodynamic terms, but he turned frequently to structural concepts to help him resolve confusing issues created by the exclusive adoption of psychodynamic principles.

Freud recognized the importance of the ego, and in contrast with the first anxiety theory, he finally postulated that the ego rather than the id is responsible for producing anxiety. He concluded that the ego feels threatened by abandonment, separation, and the loss of love, all being traumatic experiences that cause anxiety. Consequently, according to Freud, the first anxiety experience occurs at birth, which represents the first separation, the separation from the mother's body. The baby's crying is the first expression of anxiety, a theory that can be debated but that is difficult to reconcile with a theory based on accumulated sexual tension.

Freud's ideas about birth were different from those of Rank (1924), who ascribed special importance to the act of birth. Rank considered birth to be the prototypical trauma that is relived in all later anxiety experiences. Freud did not accept this hypothesis but merely noted certain phenomenological similarities in the baby's reactions and the anxiety attack.

Nevertheless, the role of trauma in the second anxiety theory is prominent, and although Freud never wanted to push sexual factors into the background, he could not ignore that dangerous nonsexual situations also were responsible for generating the affect of anxiety.

There are also difficulties in distinguishing between anxiety as a direct response to trauma and anxiety as a signal to the danger of a threatening trauma. Freud emphasized that the occurrence of trauma is the fundamental factor in generating anxiety, whereas the anticipation of trauma leads to the formation of a warning signal. This raises several questions. How much affect is involved in generating a signal? If a person contemplates or is alerted to the possibility of facing danger, are we justified in thinking in terms of anxiety? The realistic appraisal of the consequences of an external threat produces thoughts with shifts of low cathexis. Furthermore, anxiety has been defined as a reaction to a fantasied, unrealistic internal danger. Still, as I noted, internal and external trauma cannot be precisely distinguished. External stimuli activate internal conflicts, which are perceived as threatening, and the blurring of ego boundaries that is so often characteristic of primitive psychopathology makes the differentiation between outside and inside even more difficult.

These conceptual problems will to some extent be resolved by focusing on the production of anxiety in a clinical context. According to classic psychoanalytic theory, a symptom is a reaction to an instinctual impulse that creates unpleasure. An instinct can be pleasurable at one level of the psyche and unpleasurable at another. The ego may perceive such instinctual strivings as dangerous and painful.

Thus, the ego, which has frequently been described as weak and helpless against the onslaughts of the id, can now be viewed in terms of its power and ability to control the id. The ego achieves its dominance by repressing aberrant instinctual impulses. How does the ego do this?

As a perceptual apparatus, the ego receives stimuli from both the inner world of the mind and the outer world of reality. It attempts to regulate these excitations according to the dictates of the pleasure and reality principles (see Chapter 2). When it is about to be transgressed, the reality principle leads to the creation of the "signal of unpleasure," as Freud (1926) called it, which causes the ego to oppose the threatening internal stimulus.

In the context of the psychoeconomic hypothesis (see Chapter 2), the energy that initiates the repressive process is derived from the instinctual impulse that is to be repressed. In this instance, the instinct is divested of some of its energy which is then used to power the repressive process. In the first anxiety theory, instinctual energy is directly transformed into anxiety. In his revision of the first anxiety theory (1926), Freud emphasized that the ego partially decathects a dangerous stimulus or a threatening object or situation, and it uses that energy to remove itself from, or defend itself against, the outside trauma. The psyche thus initially feels anxiety.

For example, there are few speakers or actors who do not feel some anxiety, no matter how experienced they are, when facing an audience that is, to some measure, viewed as threatening. This anxiety, when moderate in intensity, serves as a stimulus that supplies the speaker or actor with additional energy, enabling him to relate to the audience more effectively. Apparently, the experience of feeling anxiety is accompanied by the generation of adrenaline which helps in dealing with what has been perceived as a threatening situation. This is a well-known phenomenon with soldiers entering battle and in personal combat or fights.

In the decathexis of internal impulses, the energy released is used to create the signal of unpleasure. This signal produces a modicum of anxiety and is known as the *anxiety signal*. This is why the second anxiety theory has also been called *the signal theory of anxiety*.

As discussed in Chapter 2, the decathexis of an instinctual impulse means that it is repressed. In order to achieve preconscious or conscious representation, the impulse must be cathected and hypercathected. The production of anxiety, a felt affect—which means it has attained conscious representation—thus would require *hyper*cathexis rather than *hypo*cathexis. Freud asked, "How is it possible, from an economic point of view, for a mere process of withdrawal and discharge, like the withdrawing of a preconscious ego cathexis, to produce unpleasure or anxiety, seeing that, according to our assumptions, unpleasure and anxiety can only arise as a result of an increase in cathexis?" (1926, p. 93). He implied that we are faced with a contradiction, for the achievement of consciousness and the production of a feeling are the outcomes of hypercathexis, and yet he had postulated that "the withdrawing of a preconscious ego cathexis" is the specific reaction to danger and is responsible for the production of anxiety.

Apparently Freud had temporarily lost sight of the stratification of the psychic apparatus. It is puzzling why he believed that a hypocathexis existed at the upper preconscious levels of the mind. Freud had specifically indicated that the instinctual impulse was in a state of hypocathexis within the realm of the preconscious. Presumably, because he viewed decathexis as the crucial process in repression, the impulse would soon be submerged to the psyche's lower levels. The energy that is liberated from the impulse remains in the preconscious, which causes a hypercathexis that is experienced as anxiety.

To recapitulate briefly, the production of anxiety begins with an unacceptable impulse, which is viewed alternatively as dangerous, seeking conscious expression, or, in terms of the psychodynamic hypothesis, striving for discharge. It is stripped of its cathexis in the preconscious, causing a hypercathexis that is experienced as anxiety. This hypercathexis acts as a signal to stimulate psychic processes that lead to the construction of defenses. This seems to be a smooth, coherent sequence as long as the level of cathexis is modulated in intensity so that it can continue operating as a signal. If it goes beyond a certain level, it is disruptive to the ego and becomes a *panic state*.

Anxiety is not created anew each time there is an internal danger; rather, the mnemic trace of a previous but similar trauma is activated. This implies that the aforementioned aberrant internal impulses are connected to external traumas. As stated earlier, traumatic events produce anxiety by stimulating internal impulses, and they are defended against by processes stimulated by the anxiety signal. The external trauma, however, becomes internalized as an encapsulated memory trace that can be energized, and it seeks conscious awareness when an associatively connected event in the surrounding world stimulates it. Thus, it is the memory of the trauma rather than an actual event that causes the generation of the anxiety signal. This is just another way of saying that anxiety is a reaction to an internal danger, whereas fear is a response to an external danger.

These distinctions are relative and arbitrary. The influence of neither the outside nor the inside can be excluded from our understanding of the anxiety phenomenon; there is a reciprocal interplay between the two. No matter how much emotional factors dominate, an environmental element always contributes to the production of anxiety. This is similar to paranoid projections that are invariably associated with some reality factor (see Chapter 6). In many instances, however, it is difficult to discover the anxiety-provoking elements of the surrounding reality.

Schur (1955, 1958) illustrated the intrapsychic consequences and the production of an internal signal after having been exposed to a potentially dangerous outside situation. He used the example of a driver of an automobile driving on a mountain road who suddenly encounters a danger sign warning him of hazardous road conditions and hairpin curves. The sign evokes a variety of reactions in the driver. If he is adept at mountain driving, he will have little if any affective response. The visual perception of the sign is the equivalent of signal anxiety, which enables him to remain calm. It recalls to him certain driving techniques and causes him to cut down his speed, but all of these cautionary measures are executed with equanimity and confidence. In most instances, such drivers react automatically without being particularly consciously aware of what they are doing. In this instance, it is difficult to view the driver's reaction as being motivated by anxiety, as everything is done in such a smooth, nonanxious fashion. The process and sequence of reacting to a signal and mobilizing adaptive techniques are, however, the essence of the second anxiety theory.

Another driver may feel some anxiety or may momentarily be aware of some concern. He may not be familiar with mountain driving, although he often has driven on similar routes. He may or may not consciously recall how he handled the situation in the past, but he knows what to do. His anxiety therefore disappears as he sets himself the task of facing this dangerous stretch of road. Here, it is clear that the anxiety, rather than the sign, functions as a signal, although it is the sign, an external warning of anticipated danger, that begins the process of coping with a potentially traumatic set of circumstances.

The third possibility refers to an inexperienced driver who is already anxious before he sees the sign. He is afraid that he will have an accident and perhaps does not feel adequate to accept the responsibility for the safety of his passengers. The danger sign may increase his anxiety to the extent that if he continues driving, he will certainly have an accident. Perhaps he will stop, refusing to go farther, as he feels functionally paralyzed and immobile. He could be on the verge of panic, meaning that the anxiety, instead of being modulated as a signal, has become overwhelming.

These examples are mechanistic in that they ignore the interaction of an external danger with a specific intrapsychic constellation. Perhaps the driver has a mild phobia about heights, based on sexual conflicts. The symbolic meaning of heights and mountains may refer to certain conflicting and forbidden sexual strivings. The sign may also have symbolic significance and help stimulate inner conflict that in turn generates anxiety. If this inner conflict is not too intense, then anxiety in the form of a signal will be produced, and psychic equilibrium will be restored as adaptive mechanisms are used.

Reconciliation of the First and Second Anxiety Theories

Despite his constructing the second anxiety theory, Freud did not give up the idea that anxiety was the outcome of a traumatic state in which the ego feels helpless and vulnerable in the face of accumulated libidinal tension that cannot be discharged. Jones (1931) coined the term *aphanisis* to connote this state of helpless vulnerability, a state of complete impotence and loss of sexual expression, accompanied by feelings of dread and inchoate terror. If we think in terms of structural factors, such a vulnerable ego is held together so precariously that it does not have sufficient organization and cohesion to generate feelings. The tension resulting from an accumulation of libido causes disruption and loss of integration so that the same libido can no longer be felt in a structured fashion.

Psychoanalysts recognize that the ego's operations vary depending on its state of development. Adaptive techniques are acquired throughout the course of emotional development (see Chapter 3), and so those found in later stages are lacking during early stages. Thus, it could be expected that the production of anxiety during primitive mental states would be a vastly different process than what occurs during later, more sophisticated ego organizations. In order for anxiety to function as a signal, it requires a highly differentiated ego with firm boundaries.

Initially the ego is relatively undifferentiated and depends principally on the caretaking person to achieve inner regulation. The mother acts as a modulating shield for potentially disruptive outer stimuli (see Chapter 3) and as a gratifier of instinctual needs who soothes her child's inner tension and agitation. At this early stage during the neonatal period, the infant can be overwhelmed by inner feelings if the mother fails to gratify or soothe him or her.

The child's disruptive reactions do not at first seem to be examples of anxiety, as they do not have the organization that we ordinarily attribute to affects. Rather, we witness a disturbed, perhaps tantrumlike, state which seems purposeless and psychologically meaningless. Rather, it is a demonstration of psychic disintegration. After approximately 6 months of age, there are distinct changes in the manifestations of emotional decompensation.

Children at this later period of infancy are still relatively defenseless. They have acquired sufficient structure, however, to have distinct affective responses. From 2 months on, they smile in an object-related fashion, indicating pleasure with someone else's presence. Children may also feel sad and, when disrupted, display the manifestations of anxiety that we, as adults, can identify as such. If no attempts are made to care for and soothe such infants, the anxiety response may intensify so that it loses the quality of being a discrete affect. If it is contained by a caretaking person, it will resemble a frightened state that gradually disappears.

This manifest behavior that resembles the affect of anxiety cannot be explained on the basis of the signal theory of anxiety. We can conclude this simply from the intensity of the child's response. The child's reaction is both more intense and more global. Furthermore, such infants are unable to restore equilibrium by constructing defensive adaptations; they have to rely on someone in the external world to reestablish their homeostasis, something that they apparently cannot do on their own because they do not have the resources.

The first anxiety theory, however, gives us a suitable conceptual frame to help understand these disrupted early ego states. The ego feels overwhelmed by accumulated tension based on unfulfilled needs and the lack of soothing experiences. We need not be concerned as to whether we are, in fact, dealing with sexual tension in such an early psychic state, in view of Freud's broad concepts regarding sex. Remember that Freud wrote about the involvement of libido during the autoerotic stage, a stage that precedes the formation of object relationships (see Chapter 3).

This discussion should have made clear that as with many other psychoanalytic concepts, we can view the anxiety theories as being on a continuum. At the primitive end of the spectrum we can apply the first anxiety theory, with its emphasis on accumulation and discharge. The second anxiety theory is appropriate on the other end of the continuum, as it focuses on the evocation of a signal and the mobilization of adaptive techniques to restore emotional equilibrium.

NEUROSOGENESIS AND NOSOLOGY

Classical psychoanalytic theory is supported by a biological foundation. Because Freud was trying to make some sense out of the many confusing clinical phenomena he observed, he tried to place them in a familiar perspective so that they would not continue baffling him. Consequently, his early ideas about the neuroses were couched in the scientific language of his milieu, as was his metapsychology (see Chapters 2 and 3). He thought primarily in terms of energic shifts and tension discharge processes, and so his diagnostic scheme was based on such principles.

Freud's scheme is a simple and brief diagnostic classification that in no way competes with the current *Diagnostic and Statistical Manual* (DSM-III). Psychoanalytic clinicians—because of their concentration on the unconscious and the inner workings of the mind—are not particularly involved in diagnostic classification. Surface traits and constellations of behavior are not our principal interest, because we focus on intrapsychic processes and defects in psychic structure. Still, it is important to make some diagnostic distinctions to help us assess ego strength, motivation, existing capacities, and reality testing so as to determine whether psychoanalytic treatment is feasible (see Chapter 7).

Freud (1895a) began by separating the *actual neuroses* from the *psychoneuroses*, the actual neuroses being physiological processes and the psychoneuroses referring to disturbances of emotional equilibrium that are the outcome of intrapsychic conflict. The actual neuroses consist of neurasthenia and the anxiety neurosis, and the two psychoneuroses are hysteria and the obsessional neurosis.

This classification was modified when Freud (1914c) became aware of the existence of narcissism. He then divided psychopathology into the *transference neuroses* and the *narcissistic neuroses*. The transference neuroses also refer to hysteria and the obsessional neurosis, whereas the narcissistic neuroses consist of depression and schizophrenia. Freud based this classification on treatability. The transference neuroses can benefit from psychoanalytic treatment because they form transferences, but the narcissistic neuroses cannot be analyzed because they are incapable of making transference connections (see Chapter 7). These assessments have not been confirmed by current clinical observations.

The Actual Neuroses

These two types of neuroses are not, according to Freud (1895a, 1898) the outcome of intrapsychic conflicts. There may be defects of psychic structure in such patients, but Freud did not concentrate on that aspect of psychopathology. He instead dealt primarily with accumulations of libido that never reach psychic representation.

It must be clarified that the English translations of these two neuroses, "neurasthenia" and the "anxiety neurosis," are inaccurate. In German these are called *Aktualneurosen*, the word *aktual* meaning topical in the sense that what is happening is related to the current situation rather than to past, buried memories.

The anxiety neurosis has already been explained in terms of the first anxiety theory. To summarize, libido accumulates but never reaches higher mentational psychic levels. Instead, it is somatically discharged and felt as anxiety. The damming up of libido is not explained as the consequence of repression because of intrapsychic conflict. Rather, Freud focused on external and capricious circumstances, all of which are related to the unavailability of satisfactory modes of sexual expression, as might occur in prisoners, widows, or women subjected to coitus interruptus. Psychic determinism does not seem to have any role in the production of the actual neuroses.

Neurasthenia is characterized by listless feelings, fatigue, and all of the symptoms and signs of low and depleted levels of psychic energy. The psychiatrists of the late nineteenth century described this syndrome as a lack of energy and a general rundown condition, emphasizing that the basic cause of this disorder was constitutional weakness.

Freud accepted the organic basis of neurasthenia. He believed, in contrast with the anxiety neurosis, that it was due to excessive sexual discharge. Excessive masturbation was its leading cause. The patient's libido was constantly being drained, and the patient was driven to a state of physical and emotional exhaustion. Freud did not discuss either of the actual neuroses in terms of infantile trauma or developmental vicissitudes, and such patients would not be likely candidates for psychoanalytic treatment. Rather than exploring internal processes, treatment would be directed to the patient's actions in the environment. For the anxiety neuroses, appropriate avenues of sexual discharge are required, whereas patients suffering from neurasthenia have to curb their sexual excesses. It is obvious, however, that the situation is not that simple (see Chapter 8).

The Psychoneuroses or the
Transference Neuroses

At the time that Freud was fitting the actual neuroses into a conceptual scheme, he was also forming hypotheses about the psychoneuroses. His first papers on the subject stressed their etiology and relationship to defenses. He concentrated on the transference aspects later when he directed his attention specifically to the transference phenomenon (1912a, 1914b). While examining the psychoneuroses, hysteria, and the obsessive-compulsive neuroses, Freud (1894, 1896) devised an approach to both diagnostic classification and neurosogenesis. He was now dealing with emotional problems that involve higher mental systems, in contrast with the total biological emphasis of the actual neuroses.

Freud discovered that certain defensive constellations are characteristic of particular neuroses. Displacement, conversion, and erotization, for example, are defensive processes commonly found in hysterical patients. Isolation, undoing, and reaction formation define the obsessive-compulsive neurosis. Freud also noted that the different neuroses have specific fixation points of psychosexual development to which they regress (see Chapters 3 and 6). Obsessional patients are partially arrested in their development at the anal stage, and hysterics supposedly have not resolved oedipal problems, the fixation point being at the phallic stage that precedes the oedipal period and the final genital stage (see Chapter 3).

Freud concluded early in his writings that sexual factors are the chief elements in the etiology of the neuroses (Breuer and Freud 1895). He believed that an actual trauma, a seduction, was responsible for the formation of a neurosis. In hysteria, the child, usually a little girl of 3 or 4, is seduced by a relative, most likely an uncle, but later Freud implicated the father (1896). This seductive experience, according to Freud, was the sine qua non of hysteria. In a similar fashion, a seduction is responsible for the formation of the obsessive-compulsive neurosis, only it occurs later, at around 7 or 8, and the child, usually a boy, is the aggressor. The symptoms are formed later around the feelings of self-reproach created by the forbidden sexual experience. Freud also believed that the passive victim of 3 or 4 can become the aggressor at 7 or 8 and seduce a younger child, as the victim had been earlier in his childhood.

These precise etiological connections with specific experiences of the past seem to be contrived oversimplifications. To base the formation of such complex entities as the neuroses on a single event is incongruous in view of the many facets of experience and background that are involved in the formation of the personality, either normal or emotionally imbalanced. Freud soon recognized that what his patients had reported to him as actual events were, in fact, fantasies. That is, the patients wished that they had been seduced as children, an observation that reinforced Freud's ideas about infantile sexuality but discredited his seduction hypothesis, which he soon abandoned (1905b).

The concept of specific trauma receded into the background, and the neuroses were explained on the basis of psychodynamic conflicts. Hysterics are primarily oriented around oedipal issues. In the case of the male hysteric, sexual feelings are repressed because they are equated with incestuous longings that conflict with the superego's moral prohibitions (see Chapter 2). The patient suffers from intense castration anxiety which causes him to renounce his wish to possess his mother sexually. A certain class of women unconsciously represents his mother, and he has similar inhibitions concerning them. (I shall enumerate these symptoms in the next chapter, as they are the subjective and behavioral consequences of defensive processes.) Freud gave a detailed analysis of a hysterical neurosis in the case of "Little Hans" (1909a). He traced the development of Little Hans's phobias to castration anxiety, and the horses he was afraid of were symbolic representations of his father.

Relationships Among Neuroses

Freud included three entities under the rubric of hysteria: anxiety hysteria, conversion hysteria, and phobias. These neurotic constellations are closely related to one another, and the same patient may shift from one condition to another or even demonstrate the manifestations of all three at the same time. They belong on the same continuum.

Anxiety hysteria is characterized by free-floating anxiety

that can, unlike the anxiety neurosis, be linked with mental content. These patients repress sexual impulses and experience anxiety as external situations stimulate them and they threaten to return from the repressed (see Chapters 2 and 6). The anxiety hysteric is not, however, the innocent victim of circumstances. On the contrary, these patients are provocative and seductive and create their sources of temptation. Anxiety is a reaction to forbidden sexual impulses that are, following the experiencing of this affect, repressed once more. As I shall explain in the next chapter, no other defense besides repression is involved. The conflict between sexual temptation and the prohibiting forces that are stimulated by the threat of castration is handled within the core of the psyche as repressive forces gain ascendancy and equilibrium is restored. Anxiety will occur episodically as sexual forces gather strength from both the biological buildup and self-created temptations.

Conversion hysteria surprisingly lacks anxiety, *la belle indifference*, as Charcot in Paris and his followers observed. The conflict is the same as in anxiety hysteria, that is, a clash between sexual forces and the inhibitions created by castration threats. Instead of repressing forbidden and dangerous feelings back into the id, they are moved toward the external world but stop at the periphery of the self, the somatic apparatus. Conversion is the name of this defensive process and will be examined in the next chapter. In any case, the conflict is somaticized at the interface of the psyche and the surrounding world. Thus, there is a path connecting anxiety hysteria to conversion hysteria on which the conflict moves forward from the core of the psyche to the periphery. If it continues from the periphery into reality, then we will encounter the familiar phobia. An internal danger has become an external danger.

The obsessive-compulsive neurosis is based on a conflict concerned with destructive feelings. These patients are overwhelmed by intense anal-sadistic impulses that have to be controlled. Apparently there was considerable strife during the anal phase that stirred up intense hostility in the child (see Chapter 2). This neurosis is concerned with maintaining control of inner rage, which is achieved primarily by stripping hostile feelings of their affects. Obsessive-compulsive patients present a superficial demeanor of calm, equanimity, and order, so as to control their inner disruption and their urges for disorder, an outcome of anal-sadistic wishes to soil.

As discussed in the next chapter, these patients have cruel, sadistic superegos that are also instrumental in determining the development of symptoms. These include the manifestations of the defense of undoing, a defense that is stimulated by superego pressure. The rituals and inhibitions characteristic of the obsessive-compulsive neurosis can be traced to internal prohibitions that are initiated by the superego. Freud (1909c) gave a comprehensive clinical description of this neurosis in the case history of his famous patient, the Rat Man. He also examined anal character traits and obsessive-compulsive processes in two shorter papers (1908, 1913b).

Something similar can be outlined for the obsessive-compulsive neurosis, as occurs in hysteria, which is a continuum that leads to a paranoid psychosis. The concept of such a continuum is reinforced by certain clinical phenomena. Some obsessive-compulsive rituals and techniques of avoidance are so bizarre that it is difficult to distinguish them from reactions to a delusion. For example, one obsessive patient lifted his foot very high off the ground whenever he took a step. This was a gross and bizarre exaggeration of the compulsive ritual of not stepping on sidewalk cracks. When asked about this peculiar gait, he stated that he saw a row of babies lying on the ground. He therefore carefully lifted his feet so that he would not step on them. He did not actually believe that there were babies on the ground, but he behaved as if there were. Later, however, that patient became frankly schizophrenic with many paranoid features.

Many obsessive patients have a paranoid orientation, indicating that the boundaries between the inner world of the mind and external reality are not well established. Federn (1933, 1952) believed that how much an object is included in the ego sphere, that is, is with ego feeling, determines whether it will be perceived as internal or external. Internal objects receive greater cathexis from the ego and lower psychic levels than do external objects that are primarily cathected by the system perceptual-consciousness (see Chapter 2). The obsessive-compulsive patient's chief defensive adaptation is to decathect destructive feelings, a process that is called *isolation* or *intellectualization* (see Chapter 6). If the process of decathexis continues further, then what began as an inner destructive feeling will be perceived as being in the surrounding world and will become attached to an external object. This is what occurs in the paranoid patient. The patient's hostility is denied as belonging to the self and is attributed to another person, who is perceived as destructive and a persecutor. Rather than a movement through the psychic apparatus, as occurs when anxiety hysteria is converted into a phobia, there is a progressive internal decathexis that changes the clinical picture of an obsessive-compulsive neurosis into a paranoid psychosis.

In closing this section, I wish to remind the reader that psychoanalysts do not use diagnostic labels with precision and that Freud was not always clear about diagnostic distinctions. For example, he considered the anxiety neurosis as one of the actual neuroses. In the continuum of the various forms of hysteria, he used the label *anxiety neurosis* for what I have referred to as *anxiety hysteria*. Anxiety hysteria, in Freud's classification, is synonymous with phobic states. This is obviously imprecise, however, if we accept Freud's formulation and wish to remain consistent within his frame of reference: An actual neurosis, insofar as it does not involve mentational elements, cannot form a transference. Therefore, it would be incorrect to count anxiety neuroses as one of the transference neuroses.

Consequently, I reserve the term *anxiety hysteria* for those cases of hysteria that do not have somatic symptoms and that readily form transferences. Conversion hysterics are rare, although phobic states are fairly common, and as Freud stressed, they readily transfer their feelings onto the therapist in psychoanalytic treatment. These entities are good examples of transference neuroses.

On the other hand, we begin to encounter obscurities and difficulties when we pursue the continuum from the obsessional neurosis to paranoia. Again, the diagnosis of paranoia is imprecise. First, Freud (1914c) wrote about *paraphrenia*, which was synonymous with psychosis. Then he adopted Bleuler's (1911) term *schizophrenia*. He formed theories about psychoses in general when he discussed the Schreber case (Freud 1911b), a patient who was a clear example of paranoia and schizophrenia. In many clinical descriptions it is difficult to tell whether Freud was dealing with a paranoid character or schizophrenia. It is clear, however, that the patients he studied ordered their lives around projections (see Chapter 6).

Next, the continuum from obsessions to paranoid projections crosses the boundary between the transference neuroses and the narcissistic neuroses. This would indicate that we can also postulate a continuum between the transference neuroses and the narcissistic neuroses, although Freud implied that the differences between these two categories of psychopathology are qualitative rather than quantitative. The propensity for transference implies a different type of character structure than those of patients who, according to Freud, are unable to make transference projections.

The Narcissistic Neuroses

The narcissistic neuroses are grouped together because they supposedly do not form transferences and therefore cannot be analyzed. As mentioned, Freud considered depression and schizophrenia to be examples of the narcissistic neuroses. Whatever the dominant theoretical orientation, it has to be consistent with the empirical data, and the data do not support the thesis that neither depressives nor schizophrenics form transferences. On the contrary, depressed patients can feel intense and clinging, dependent feelings toward their therapist, and schizophrenics are noted for their propensity to project parts of their self and feelings into their therapists. Whether these intense transferences are therapeutically manageable is another question, but it is incorrect to state that the narcissistic neuroses cannot be analyzed because of their lack of transference.

Depressed patients are much involved with themselves, with their feelings of inadequacy and unworthiness, and often with their somatic disturbances. As Freud (1917c) pointed out, they have turned their libido toward themselves, and they have little contact or interest in the outer world. This represents a particular type of narcissistic withdrawal.

Freud (1917c) distinguished between depression and

mourning, depression being a form of psychopathology and mourning a normal reaction to the death of an emotionally significant person. In depression the attachment to the lost love object remains, and the libido that was formerly directed to that person is now turned inwards, concentrating on the introject of the lost love object. The ego state associated with this intro-jected libido is characterized by painful feelings of inadequacy and low self-esteem. This libido is markedly ambivalent, and whatever hatred was felt toward the lost love object is now turned toward the self and experienced as disruptive self-hatred. Depressed patients, however, by bemoaning their condition and histrionically displaying their inner torment and misery, make uncomfortable those trying to care for them. Their self-hatred causes others to feel attacked. The introjective process becomes a means for directing hostility outward as well, and this is never clearer than when a depressed patient commits suicide. There is a Japanese saying that the worst act of destruction that an enemy can commit is to kill himself on your door-step.

Normal mourning is a reaction to the actual loss of a loved one. In melancholia or depression, there may not be any visible external loss. There may be a symbolic loss or no loss at all. In some instances the situation is paradoxical. The onset of depression may correspond to a favorable event, perhaps an inheritance or a promotion. Durkheim (1951) many years ago noted that the incidence of suicide increased whenever there was a gross change. Suicides rose when economic conditions changed from prosperity to depression, but they also increased when the reverse occurred, depression to prosperity. The same thing happened when there was a change from war to peace and peace to war.

These observations indicate that depressed patients harbor strong guilt feelings. Because of a harsh superego and intense ambivalent reactions, success, instead of being gratifying, is a source of conflict. To be gratified means to destroy or to be destroyed. Freud viewed melancholia as the outcome of an oral fixation, in Abraham's (1924b, 1927) terms, an oral-cannibalistic focus in which the source of nurture, food, is annihilated as it nurtures.

To recapitulate briefly, depressed patients have strongly dependent but highly ambivalent ties to their caretakers. This ambivalent dependency is generalized to include many other relationships and situations. Whenever anything upsets the equilibrium of this dependent relationship, introjective defenses are activated, and the patient regresses to the ambivalent phase of the oral stage of psychosexual development.

In the past, melancholia was considered to occur mainly in an older age group, such as middle-aged adults, whereas schizophrenia was associated with youth. Besides changes in the external world as stimuli for the onset of depressive episodes, certain periods of life and biological changes are often accompanied by episodes of depression. We frequently hear about mid-life crises, and during menopause, depression is a frequent occurrence, the diagnosis of *involutional melancholia* being quite common.

Even with the gross biological changes that occur during menopause, however, other variables cannot be ignored. This is the time of life when the structure of the family changes. Children have grown up and leave home. The mother is no longer able to continue in her role of taking care of dependent children. The activities that made her feel needed and important no longer serve as significant sources of self-esteem. Therefore, the middle-aged woman is particularly susceptible to depression.

Recently, certain types of depression have been determined to have a strictly biological etiology. This means that no emotional factors, or just a few, contribute to its etiology. These patients supposedly have periodic depressions that do not correspond to any environmental events; that is, the depression is not related to any disturbances in object relationships. Sometimes, depressive episodes alternate with bouts of manic excitement, and this is known as a *manic-depressive* state that can reach psychotic proportions.

If the assertions of biological psychiatrists are correct, there are certain types of depression and manic states in which psychic determinism does not play a significant role. Still, it is difficult, after observing these patients, to place them in a strictly organic context. Their personalities in general are emotionally unstable, and in their nondepressive or noninsane periods, they are disturbed persons who have problems managing their lives. Their perceptions are often bizarre, and their reality testing is poor. It is possible that these gross characterological disturbances can be explained on the basis of a neurochemical imbalance, but it seems that the biological approach has to be somewhat forced. Something as complicated as the human character—with its subtle perceptions, complex adaptations, and its propensity to draw on past experiences and learned responses— does not lend itself easily to regulations and controls that depend solely on a chemical balance in a closed system that excludes interactions with the external world. Once the outer environment is allowed to enter the world of etiological sequences, then we are introducing an interpersonal variable that will eventually lead us to psychic determinism.

The second of the narcissistic neuroses, schizophrenia, is a psychosis that has been studied extensively from a biological perspective. There has also been considerable examination of its psychodynamics, but because Freud considered the psychoses unable to be analyzed, until recently, psychoanalysts have not paid much attention to schizophrenic disorders. Nevertheless, Freud occasionally discussed the treatment of paranoid patients, and he presented us with a detailed analysis of Judge Schreber, who suffered from a florid paranoid psychosis, apparently a classical example of paranoid schizophrenia (1911b). Earlier Freud (1896) discussed his treatment of a woman who suffered from somatic delusions and ideas of reference and who felt persecuted. He diagnosed her as paranoid, but at this early stage of his career, he had not excluded psychotics from psychoanalytic treatment. He described his therapy in order to illustrate the dominant use of the defense mechanism of projection.

Freud never saw Judge Schreber but formed his conclusions from a study of Schreber's memoirs, from which he derived theories to explain the paranoid phenomenon. All psychoses (he generalized from Schreber's paranoia) begin with a withdrawal of libido from the external world. Freud referred to this withdrawal as the "end-of-the-world phenomenon" because patients in the beginning phase of a psychosis feel that the world around them is crumbling. That is how Schreber described it. As

Schreber's attention (in Freud's language, libido) became concentrated on the self, the external world became blurred and hazy and appeared bizarre.

Freud pointed out that the end-of-the-world phenomenon can be experienced as explosive and catastrophic and can be accompanied by panic. Many of the violent episodes of acute psychoses are the consequence of an abrupt withdrawal of libido. What precipitates these "breakdowns" is usually unclear because the intensity of the patient's reactions tend to blot out what may have been significant—perhaps symbolically—events that upset the patient's equilibrium to the extent that he had to massively withdraw. When we have been able to discover the precipitating circumstances, they are usually reminiscent of infantile traumas, either directly or symbolically. Somehow the psychotic system, usually containing delusional elements, that maintains psychic equilibrium is threatened and undermined and loses its adaptive capacities which were probably quite tenuous to begin with.

The withdrawn libido is felt as painful. On its path from the external world to the internal world of the psyche, it may linger on the periphery of the ego, the soma that is at the boundary of inside and outside. As libido accumulates in the soma, it creates a state of dammed-up tension that can cause pain and somatic delusions. Schreber described such a state, and Freud saw it as the basis of *hypochondriasis*. Hypochondriasis will be accompanied by considerable agitation if the patient does not bind his disruption in a delusional system that concentrates on bodily structure and functions. These delusions can be quite bizarre, such as the belief that the intestines are rotting or that the body is being invaded by bugs carrying atom bombs that are periodically exploded. Often such delusions are followed by organic signs; for example, the invaded patient develops an excruciatingly painful neurodermatitis.

The next stage is a *megalomanic* phase in which the libido retreats further, from the soma into the interior of the mind. This is a state of heightened narcissism that is characterized by grandiosity and feelings of omnipotence. The external world is mainly ignored, and such patients concentrate exclusively on their exalted self or their relationship with personages, such as

Schreber's relationship with God. Many schizophrenics remain
fixated in this megalomanic self-containment. They cling to
their delusions of grandeur, regardless of the sordid circumstances that may surround them or the menial positions they
may have been forced into. I have seen schizophrenics in state
hospitals scrubbing floors or collecting garbage but never
shaken in their belief that they were exalted emperors or gods.

Freud recognized that his formulations were schematic.
The orderly progression from the withdrawal of libido to megalomania is seldom seen in such a clear-cut sequence, but Schreber's description of his feelings apparently fit in well with Freud's
hypotheses. Ordinarily, the beginning phases of the psychotic
process are not easily observed, but then, very few patients have
Schreber's literary talents and capacity for self-expression and
self-observation. The difficulty of observing the stages that
Freud outlined is compounded by the inner turmoil and disruption that these patients experience. Even the megalomanic
phase can be intensely painful and fraught with conflict as other
elements, such as rageful destructiveness and guilt, burst onto
the surface. The loss of contact with the external world can be
felt as annihilation.

As explained in Chapter 2 in the context of the psychoeconomic hypothesis, the damming up of libido is usually painful.
Therefore, the ego makes what Freud called restitutive attempts
to reestablish contact with the surrounding milieu. The libido is
projected back into the external world, and this constitutes the
delusion which, according to Freud, repairs the "rent" with
reality. Schreber's dammed-up libido included homosexual
as well as destructive feelings, homosexual feelings that were
overtly expressed in his megalomanic, delusional constructions.
He believed that he had been turned into a woman, and that
God had intercourse with him. He wrote about many complex
details involving "rays" and "nerves" that implemented his exalted position with God.

Within this grandiose context, Schreber was able to accept
his homosexual orientation. When dealing with actual persons in
the real world, however, Schreber was immensely threatened
by his latent homosexuality and had to construct elaborate projective defenses that are the essence of paranoid ideation. For

example, Freud felt that there was evidence to indicate that Schreber had homosexual impulses toward his psychiatrist but that he had to deny them or, more specifically, to oust such feelings from the ego sphere. Schreber projected his feelings into the doctor. Instead of acknowledging "I love him," he changed this by means of projection to "he loves me." To carry this one step further, Schreber changed the feeling into its opposite. Rather than "he loves me," he changed this into "he hates me," and his psychiatrist thereby became his persecutor.

Schreber was also jealous of his therapist and suspected that he was having an affair with his wife. This attitude, as is true of all pathological jealousy, can also be attributed to homosexual impulses. This formulation requires only that the projected thought "he loves me" be changed into "he does not love me, he loves my wife," again involving denial and a change of object from Schreber to his wife. Freud recognized that the (male) paranoid patient often identifies with his wife or lover and that by having someone else seduce her, he is vicariously gratifying his homosexual impulses. Because this gratification is unacceptable, he must become angry at his "rival" and denounce him.

Many of these ideas are still useful for our current understanding of the psychoses. There is less stress, however, on the projection of unacceptable homosexual impulses. Paranoid patients who are active homosexuals are not uncommon, and they cannot be analyzed on the basis of the denial of homosexuality. Rather, the feelings involved are archaic and primitive and are concerned with cataclysmic destruction. Most paranoid patients have difficulty controlling their overwhelming feelings of hostility which they have to project and which cause splitting of the ego. In some instances these projected destructive impulses are eroticized, but whatever the homosexual preoccupation, the underlying hostility is the primary disruptive feeling.

Freud's theory of the paranoid psychosis does not stress structural defects, although it does not disagree with theories about severely disturbed patients that concentrate on defects in psychic structure. Freud's concepts regarding breaks with reality, hypochondriasis, and megalomania have proved useful, no matter what the basic theoretical orientation has been. For example, Federn (1952) did not accept that a psychosis is the outcome of increased amounts of libido, but he did agree that megalomania and hypochondriasis are the outcome of increased ego feelings as connections with the outer world are disrupted. However, he emphasized that the ego of the psychotic patient was defective, resulting in a diminished rather than an increased amount of libido.

Freud did not actually state that there was an *absolute* increase of ego libido—which we can also refer to as narcissism—in the psychoses. He had already written about diminished and depleted libido in neurasthenia. He did not present the psychotic patient as a person who lacks energy relative to the external world. Indeed, Schreber was an extremely energetic, successful, and famous person, and the other paranoid patients that Freud described were not at all withdrawn or worn down, as we might expect of a patient who lacks libido. So, although Freud wrote about a balance of psychic energy, in which libido is distributed between the self and the outer world, he did not specifically consider quantitative factors, as Federn did.

Pushing aside clinical observations for the moment, the distribution of libido in paranoia (and I am now using the term loosely) points to increased libido in one sphere, the soma or the mind, relative to a lesser amount that is directed to external reality. This does not mean that there is increased libido when compared with the healthy narcissism of the well-balanced normal ego. To be fancifully concrete, let us assume that a well-adjusted psyche contains ten ergs of libido, five of which are invested in the self and five of which flow to external objects and situations. By contrast, the psychotic patient may have only four ergs of psychic energy at his disposal, three ergs directed to the self, and only one erg toward the surrounding milieu. Three times as much libido is attached to self as compared with what can be used for relating to the outer world. In terms of the percentage of distribution, a three-to-one ratio, this type of mental equilibrium would be based on a highly narcissistic orientation. Compared with the so-called normal ego, however, we can see that this psychopathological narcissistic orientation contains less ego libido: five ergs, in our fictional qualitative system, to three ergs. From the viewpoint of absolute amounts

of energy, the healthy ego has more narcissism than does that of
the psychotic patient, however, not at the cost of renouncing the
external world of reality. Still, the problem remains, and now
we cannot continue ignoring clinical observations, that psychotics do not have the low energy levels that Freud attributed to
neurasthenia, at least not all psychotic patients, and certainly not
those who have fixed paranoid orientations. Other types of
schizophrenics, such as simple schizophrenics, appear depleted,
apathetic, and listless, but they do not have the florid and noisy
symptoms of hypochondriasis and megalomania.

As I stated in Chapter 2, of all the metapsychological viewpoints, the psychoeconomic hypothesis has received the most
severe criticism. Many clinicians consider the concept of psychic energy fanciful. Here, we have seen that dealing with it
exclusively in quantitative terms creates problems because conceptual consistency cannot be reconciled with clinical data.
Thus, there must be more to the amount of "ergs" involved in
the energic exchanges and distributions that we have been discussing that will cause us to add other dimensions to the concept
of libido. As we add qualitative elements to psychic energy, we
are broadening its scope to more than a vector that can be
visualized as an arrow pointing to either the outer world or the
self. It is reasonable then to believe that qualitative factors are
important, perhaps much more so than the quantitative distinctions of Freud's formulations.

The psychotic patient is defined as a person who has lost
contact with reality, but this is a metaphor that Freud took
literally. What is meant is that these patients have a distorted
view of the surrounding world. Freud was aware of this when
he explained that Schreber and other similar patients attempt to
repair the "rent" with reality with a delusional system. This,
however, occurs after libido has been withdrawn and represents
the end stage of the psychotic process. Nevertheless, many
psychotics are actively engaged with the external world; it is the
quality of their orientations that may be bizarre.

As can readily be seen, nosology does not have a significant
role in psychoanalytic theory or practice. Psychoanalysts, as do
all clinicians, require some system of classification so that they
can have an anchor on which to order their thinking about the

various types of patients they see. They also require diagnoses to determine the appropriate treatment. To this extent, they are following a medical model.

Freud simplified the problem of psychoanalytic treatability: the transference neuroses can be treated, and the narcissistic neuroses cannot. We now know that this is both inaccurate and oversimplified. Even though Freud was referring to specific clinical entities, he focused even more closely on a specific quality of these disorders, the capacity or lack of capacity to form transference, in order to determine whether analysis was possible. He then made this quality the basis of his diagnostic system.

Clinicians find that patients may or may not be able to relate to the psychoanalytic setting, regardless of their formal diagnoses. There is some correlation in that very severely disturbed patients are less likely candidates for psychoanalytic treatment than are patients with better-synthesized and more flexible egos. Nevertheless, the factors that determine whether a patient can be treated are not necessarily connected to the diagnosis. Concretely oriented patients, that is, patients who are not psychologically minded and have no concept of psychic determinism are very difficult, if not impossible, to analyze. These qualities may also be found in neurotic patients who have a good, if not rigid, grasp of reality and who function quite well in the external world. On the other hand, many severely disturbed patients have a keen awareness of the inner world of the mind and have an intuitive grasp of psychic determinism. They frequently relate well to the psychoanalytic approach, although they may be very difficult to treat (see Chapter 7).

Chapter 6

DEFENSES, ADAPTATIONS, AND SYMPTOMS

DEFENSES AND SYMPTOMS

The mode of the psyche's relating to both the inner and the outer world is dependent on what defenses and adaptations it has at its disposal. Early in his development of theories about psychopathology (see Chapter 5), Freud (1894, 1896) defined the psychoneuroses on the basis of the defenses they used. His concept of defense was elaborated in the context of the psychodynamic hypothesis.

The task of the ego is to keep aberrant, unacceptable id impulses outside the sphere of consciousness, where they may achieve the mobility and the executive techniques needed to obtain satisfaction. The psychic process by which this occurs is known as *repression*. Repressive forces operate on an unconscious level in that patients are unaware that they are repressing, in contrast with *suppression*, when a patient deliberately and consciously withholds impulses, thoughts, and feelings (Breuer and Freud 1895).

Repression is a central part of the theory of defenses. It is both a defense and the aim of defenses. Defenses are mental mechanisms that are set in motion by anxiety (see Chapter 5) which in turn is a reaction to an internal danger. The aim of all defenses, according to psychoanalytic theory, is to achieve repression. Defenses protect the psyche from being overwhelmed by threatening and destructive unconscious impulses that have broken through the barriers of repression, the *return of the repressed*. These impulses are re-repressed.

Repression is thus a core defense. It has been located in an unconscious portion of the ego, perhaps not too far from the id. It is viewed as a force, a countercathexis. Defenses are abstract mechanisms that are difficult to visualize without describing them phenomenologically. They should also be placed in the ego sphere, but at a slightly higher stratum than where repression resides. Somehow they will set the repressive process in motion.

Symptoms are the behavioral and subjective manifestations of defense mechanisms. Psychoanalysts are aware that symptoms have a purpose, that they are external signs that the psyche is trying to maintain a state of emotional balance. They cannot simply be suggested away without upsetting psychic equilibrium. The therapeutic psychoanalytic attitude stresses that patients will continue to have symptoms as long as they need them; that is, until basic conflicts are resolved which then would permit them to function with fewer repressive barriers. Once symptoms are no longer necessary, the psyche can adapt more easily and flexibly to the external world.

What is the difference between an adaptation and a defense? An adaptation is part of the ego's executive apparatus and is instrumental in obtaining gratification of instinctual needs. A defense to some extent performs a similar activity, which blurs the distinction between defenses and adaptations. A defense, beside maintaining repression, that is, defending against an instinctual impulse, is at the same time involved in seeking gratification of that impulse. Every defense represents a compromise formation between gratification and repression or inhibition.

As long as there is a compromise formation and some gratification is obtained, a defense can be considered to be an adaptation. Perhaps the distinction between a defensive and a nondefensive adaptation is only a matter of degree and depends on the amount of repression versus gratification that is involved. Ideally, the best adaptation would involve no repression, and the psyche could function in an uninhibited but realistic fashion with the least expenditure of energy—energy that is not consumed in constructing defenses and maintaining repression.

These distinctions imply that there is a continuum between defenses and adaptations. Although psychoanalysts disagree on the significance of defenses relative to one another and on the characteristics of specific defenses, most clinicians agree that defenses can be arranged along a hierarchical sequence. They may, however, disagree on where a particular defense belongs in this sequence or even on whether a phenomenon or process is, in fact, a defense, but the principle of hierarchy has been established.

The number of defenses, like the number of instincts, varies. As with instincts, many processes that have been considered defenses can be broken down into more elemental mechanisms. This is interesting because some defenses seem to be reactions to particular instinctual needs and also to be characteristic of specific developmental levels.

The list of defenses in the following table are fairly well accepted by the majority of psychoanalysts. They are ordered

Defenses
1. Rationalization
2. Repression
3. Displacement
4. Identification
5. Conversion
6. Isolation or Intellectualization
7. Reaction Formation or Overcompensation
8. Undoing
9. Negation
10. Projection
11. Dissociation or Splitting
12. Denial

with the principle of hierarchy in mind, so that the more sophisticated, realistic defenses characteristic of a well-structured ego are at the top of the list. The defenses farther down the list are more primitive and are associated with early developmental stages. Many of the defenses in this table include other, more elemental processes. For example, in order to project, the psyche must first use splitting mechanisms. Thus, a significant person in a patient's life may, regressively, be split into a good and a bad object. Then the bad object is extruded from the inner world of the mind into the external world of reality. This is considered a defensive operation, and the process is projection.

Before proceeding, I want to point out that I have not listed regression as a defense, because I believe that all defenses operate more or less in a regressive context. Early in his career, Freud (1900) described regression from three different frames of reference: formal, topographical, and temporal. Formal regression refers to a reversion to early patterns of adaptation; topographical to activation of the deeper (spatial) and primitive parts of the mind, such as the system Ucs dominating the Pcs; and temporal to a shift from current modes of relating to those of the past. Obviously, defensive adaptations fit well in that they belong to the past, primitive developmental phases and involve the deeper layers of the psychic apparatus. Thus, regression represents a different order of abstraction than do defensive interactions. The latter refer to perceptions, actions, and modes of relating, whereas regression describes a quality of psychic processes that can be analyzed from Freud's three viewpoints.

Freud (1894, 1896) formulated defensive operations in terms of reactions to id impulses, although the impulses did not always refer to needs. For example, in the last section of his article "Further Remarks on the Defence Neuropsychoses" (Freud 1896), he discussed a case of paranoia and the mechanism of projection. He described how this woman rid herself of certain unacceptable feelings, which included rage, a reaction to frustration, and conflict about wishes and needs, in this instance, sexual needs. Again, defenses are not only reactions to id impulses but also are often reactions to reactions to such impulses. It is important to ascertain that defenses are not simply confined to maintaining psychic balance by seeking compromise gratifications for pressing demands that would otherwise be disruptive. Defenses such as projection and dissociation, considered to be somewhat primitive on the hierarchical scale, primarily involve psychic structure and are often reactions to painful endopsychic registrations of traumatic experiences and destructive introjects rather than unacceptable sexual impulses.

Other defenses, such as denial, involve modes of relating to the outer world because the psyche cannot cope with certain segments of it that would be overwhelmingly destructive. Rationalization, on the other hand, is concerned with maintaining self-esteem. Explanations that are called rationalizations are in accord with the aspiration of the ego ideal. Having been threatened, the self-representation once again achieves harmonious stability as it is reconciled with the ego ideal. Freud first attempted to postulate a series of defensive operations as reactions to intrapsychic conflict, that is, within the context of the psychodynamic hypothesis. Today, clinicians generally view defenses as attempts to achieve homeostasis, as the psyche relates to both the internal world, which includes more than instinctual impulses, and the threatening aspects of external reality. These extensions of Freud's hypotheses can be included within the framework of the structural hypothesis. The maintenance of self-esteem as it affects the stability and cohesiveness of the self representation, an important psychic structure, depends on defense just as much as on the gratification of instinctual impulses.

In the earlier discussion of the relationship of defenses and adaptations, I implied that the closer to an adaptation a defense is, the higher it will be on the hierarchical ladder. Again, the most important criterion determining whether a defense is relatively sophisticated or primitive is the amount of reality testing that is retained. When comparing the two extremes on the table, *rationalization* at the top and *denial* at the bottom, this becomes obvious. Rationalization, as the most sophisticated defense, distorts reality only minimally, if at all. It chooses to consider only certain segments of interactions and to deemphasize others. A person who uses rationalization, and nearly all of us do, explains his or her behavior in a socially acceptable manner in order to maintain self-esteem. For example, a student fails an examination. He attributes his failure to a variety of face-saving reasons, explanations that we recognize as rationalizations. He may protest that he had too many responsibilities, which prevented him from studying as much as necessary for the examination. It could well be that he was in fact burdened in this fashion, and so he is not departing from reality. His only distortion might be that he is magnifying the significance of such circumstances in bringing about his failure in the examination. There may be more significant reasons for his poor performance that run counter to his ego ideal. He may have been lazy, or the material may have been too difficult for him. He may have felt inadequate to compete with his classmates. There may have been many other reasons for his failure, but none was acceptable to him. He thus distorts reality only in the sense that he does not point to many factors that are not immediately evident. The student who rationalizes therefore chooses the least-threatening elements to support and explain his failure.

By contrast, denial is a blotting out of reality. It is not just ignoring subtle connections, as rationalization is; rather, external percepts that are obvious to the average onlooker are disavowed; that is, they are not perceived by the person, usually a psychotic patient, who uses denial as a principal mode of relating to the external world. By directly eliminating sectors of reality, the mechanism of denial leads to gross and bizarre distortions of the surrounding environment. For example, a mother may continue nursing her dead baby as if it were still alive. She may cling to its body, denying its death, or she might find a doll and treat it as if it were a live baby. Charles Dickens described the macabre situation of the rejected bride who kept the wedding table, with all the settings and food, intact for years, not accepting that the groom was not ever going to appear. In these instances a person clings to a belief that is vital to maintaining psychic integration, a belief that is threatened and contradicted by events in the external world. Whereas persons who rationalize need to protect their self-esteem, those who use denial as a principal adaptative orientation are struggling with the necessity of protecting themselves from total psychic collapse.

The difference between the amount of reality testing that is compatible with rationalization and the lack of it that is characteristic of denial is clear enough. These defenses represent extremes, and as is true of extremes in general, distinctions are fairly easy to make. The spectrum of defenses found between the two ends of the continuum are much more difficult to evaluate in terms of their psychopathological significance and how effective they are in maintaining rational contact with the external world. Their effectiveness, indeed, has important implications for therapeutic accessibility.

Although this discussion will stress the role of these defenses in the context of emotional illness and their connections with specific early phases of development, readers need not conclude that they are suffering from severe psychopathology if some of their actions and thoughts seem to correspond to certain defensive configurations. All of us, to some extent and at some time or another, use all of the defense mechanisms listed in the table. What steers us in the direction of psychopathology is whether a particular defense represents our dominant mode of relating to the external world or our primary adaptive process to preserve emotional balance and psychic integration. In these instances a defense has become the central element of a characterological matrix.

Freud emphasized the inner life of the mind and so paid less attention to how patients reacted to other persons or behaved in general. He did not ignore what we would today refer to as the object relations aspects of the developing or stabilized ego, but he did not dwell on them. He treated defenses in the same fashion, in that he focused on how they maintained repression or handled id impulses but did not study them as techniques of relating or adapting to interpersonal relationships and the exigencies of the external world. In this respect, it is interesting that Freud did pay attention to *repression*, which I have placed next on the table after rationalization.

It may seem that I am confusing frames of reference by placing repression on a list with other defenses whose purpose is to maintain repression. However, there are clinical instances in which repression is achieved without any defensive superstructure. That is, in order to construct defenses, the ego undergoes specific alterations or calls into play certain mental processes that define a particular defense. Apparently, in some patients, no such changes occur, but the repressed material is once again pushed into obscurity, apparently without any special efforts or defensive techniques.

The patient that I discussed in Chapter 2 who repeatedly forgot her dream is a good example of this type of repression. She related to me a dream that clearly depicted an erotic transference. She avoided associating to it, because she did not want to expose her transference feelings, which she perceived as dangerous for many reasons. When I brought her attention back to the dream by repeating it to her, she became internally agitated, as evidenced by the physical sensations of the room whirling around her and the couch turning, and then she totally forgot the dream. Other than her momentary physical turmoil, she used no special adaptations to shut the dream out of awareness.

This propensity to "selectively forget" is found in some hysterical character types and in the more general population, as Freud (1901) pointed out in "The Psychopathology of Everyday Life" when he described tendentious lapses of memory. The forgotten content is undoubtedly relegated to the system Ucs. because no matter how hard such persons try to remember, they cannot bring the item into consciousness. Later, it may erupt in what seems to be a spontaneous fashion, although with patients this does not happen often unless the analyst, with some transference interpretations, has paved the way for its recovery.

Sometimes it is difficult to distinguish between denial and what we might phenomenologically call repression. The chief difference is that in denial an external percept is disavowed, whereas in repression, something perceived from the internal world is no longer remembered. These patients do not necessarily deny having had a thought, feeling, or dream, as happened with my patient; they simply cannot remember it. Rather than eliminating a part of external reality, they cannot bring a portion of internal reality into conscious awareness. The latter implies far less serious psychopathology than does the former.

Different levels of emotional development are associated with specific defenses. Although psychosexual theory was not constructed with the concept of defense in the foreground, it is conceptually consistent that the most primitive levels of development would have the least-developed reality-testing functions. The rationale for viewing defense in terms of a spectrum from primitive to sophisticated is strengthened when empirically observed defenses, arranged in an hierarchical continuum on the basis of their reality-testing properties, are found to be characteristic of psychosexual stages of development that can maintain conceptual consistency only if they are sequentially arranged in a similar fashion.

Because the concept of defense presupposes conflict, developmental phases must be examined in terms of psychopathological distortions if, as they prove to be, they are connected with specific defenses. The hierarchy of defenses can easily be juxtaposed with the hierarchy of psychopathology. Briefly, rationalization is found in a more or less normal psyche; repression, displacement, and conversion are typical of hysteria; isolation, reaction formation, undoing, and sometimes negation characterize the obsessive-compulsive neuroses; introjection is found in depression; projection and splitting mechanisms are characteristic of paranoid states and psychoses; and denial is found in severe psychotic states. Again, I wish to remind the reader that these equations should not be taken out of context. An occasional use of any of the listed defenses does not permit the clinical observer to make any inferences about diagnosis.

SPECIFIC DEFENSES

A defense is simply a mechanism, an abstraction that has no meaning or clinical relevance unless it is considered together with its behavioral manifestations. Various constellations of behavior can be conceptualized in terms of one or a combination of these mechanisms. In turn, it is possible to reduce some defensive operations into more elemental components, but the levels of abstraction characteristic of the defenses in the table seem to be fairly easily elaborated so that they can be clinically useful.

Displacement

Displacement is a commonly used defense found in a broad variety of personality types. When it is connected with psychopathology, it is chiefly associated with the psychoneuroses, especially hysteria, but it occurs often in obsessive-compulsive neuroses, character disorders, and the psychoses. It is nearly a ubiquitous defensive technique.

Displacement requires little internal rearrangement. As stated in Chapters 2 and 3, every instinct has a source, aim, and object. The mechanism of displacement is a change of the object that satisfies the instinct, or the object that is the target of an unconscious feeling. The latter can include destructive, dependent, and erotic impulses. In displacement the main feature is the *substitute* object. Numerous mundane events illustrate this defensive phenomenon. For example, after an argument with his wife, a man kicks his dog. He takes out the anger that he felt toward his wife on an innocent animal, an anger that he did not dare take out on her. He may even be consciously aware of what he was doing but often he is not.

The choice of the substitute object is important. It must in some way be related to the original person, perhaps symbolically. The dog in the preceding example may be an apt representation of the wife from the husband's viewpoint because he may well consider his spouse to be a bitch. Animals are frequently used as substitute objects, often representing children. Childless women, for example, may have household pets that they treat as babies, inasmuch as they are cuddly and can be held or caressed. The pet appears to be an appropriate choice to make up for what may be felt as a lack or to represent a safe wish fulfillment inasmuch as actually having a child may create too much conflict.

Displacement leading to the use of substitute objects may or may not be associated with psychopathology. There are other examples of displacement in which the connection to emotional illness is unmistakable. For example, in phobias, there is always a substitute object that either resembles the actual feared object or has somewhat obvious symbolic connections to it. Freud

(1909) described a 5-year-old phobic child, "Little Hans," who had a fear of horses. In Little Hans's unconscious, horses stood for his father, whom he feared because he was afraid of being punished by him for his visible oedipal sexual attachment to his mother. Horses were convenient in that Little Hans could avoid encountering them by not venturing outside the house and avoiding certain streets in which many horses were likely to be found. He could not avoid his father, and having to remain at home because of his phobia kept him close to the desired mother. For Little Hans, horses were especially appropriate because as he indicated in a drawing of a horse's head, this horse did, in fact, resemble his father, as Freud noted when he examined this drawing. Horses are also big, powerful creatures with large penises similar to what Little Hans and most little boys observe in their fathers. Thus, horses had some resemblance to the father and had certain characteristics in common with him. They were also symbolic in that they represented a threatening masculinity.

In other phobias, such as agoraphobia and the fear of falling, the symbolic element is prominent, and the neurosis cannot be understood without knowing its significance. Freud always attributed a sexual meaning to phobias, such as the fear of falling's being a "fallen woman." It can readily be seen that to some extent the content of the displacement is related to the sociocultural milieu. Because horses are no longer commonly found on our streets and the connotation of "fallen woman" is largely unknown and has little impact, these phobias are rarely seen. Agoraphobia, however, is not unusual and will be examined later.

In some clinical instances, the choice of substitute object is bizarre. A colleague told me of a patient who had a strong attraction to the inner tubes of used tires. He would cut slits into them, wide enough to insert his head, and then breathe the air from the inside of the inner tube until he felt giddy. The entering of the inner tube, to him, represented returning to the womb, but this was a rather grotesque method of reenacting a primitive, infantile wish. Perhaps this wish's primitive qualities account for the bizarre displacement. On the basis of this behavior, it is easy to conclude that this patient was suffering from

severe emotional problems and might well have been schizophrenic. This is an extreme example and places the mechanism
of displacement in a psychotic context.

Freud (1900) divided the mind's operations into primary
and secondary processes. The secondary process is a logical,
orderly, controlled reality-attuned process characteristic of the
personality's higher levels, whereas primary process is associated with primitive mental operations typical of the psyche's
early primitive levels. In terms of the structural hypothesis, the
primary process belongs to the id and the secondary process to
the ego. It must be stressed, however, that these mental operations are found in all psyches, in both psychopathologically and
nonpsychopathologically oriented minds.

The operations of the primary process, according to Freud,
consist of condensation, symbolization, and displacement. Condensation is a phenomenon that combines two or more feelings,
thoughts, or impulses. It may also be related to visual images in
which several images are superimposed on one another, as may
happen in dreams. Freud (1900) introduced the idea of the
primary process in "The Interpretation of Dreams." Here, I wish
to stress that displacement is closely related to symbolism. Thus,
displacement, a mechanism that is included in the table of defenses, is found in all psyches, as it is an element of the primary
process, a universal operation.

For the most part, however, displacement operates on the
higher levels of the psychic structure. There may be little connection between displacements based on understandable similarities and symbolism and the bizarre displacement of the
patient who was fixated on inner tubes. The only common
denominator may be the displacement onto a substitute object,
but this is only a surface similarity and does not indicate similar
psychic processes operating at deeper levels of the personality. I
believe that generally, displacement mechanisms are characteristic of higher levels of psychic integration.

Identification, Incorporation, and Introjection

Similar to displacement, identification is both a mechanism of
defense in the traditional sense as well as a process that is found

in all psyches. I discussed the role of identification in normal development in Chapter 2. Its defensive function can be important to maintaining psychic stability, as the identificatory process takes various forms.

Freud emphasized the role of identification in hysterical and depressed patients. Both little girls and little boys identify with the parent of the same sex for defensive reasons and as an aspect of normal development. As this happens at around the oedipal phase, it is sometimes difficult to distinguish between what belongs to a neurosis and what is inevitable for the achievement of a sexual identity. A little boy, for example, may identify with his father because he wants to usurp him in obtaining his mother's affections. This seems to happen so regularly that it is difficult to view such interactions as examples of psychopathology. On the other hand, such types of identification occur often in certain hysterical character types. As a psychopathological process, identification is accompanied by other defenses, especially displacement.

The role of identification in depressed states is of paramount importance. Still, this is puzzling because depression can assume both severely neurotic and psychotic proportions. Freud classified depression among the narcissistic neuroses along with schizophrenia, whereas he considered hysteria to be a high-grade neurosis, an example of a transference neurosis (see Chapter 5). Thus, we have an example of a defense's being associated with levels of psychopathology that are far apart on the hierarchical spectrum and the developmental sequence. Furthermore, as it is associated with normal development, identification is also an essential ingredient of the mourning process which is both ubiquitous and closely related to depression.

The concept of identification creates special difficulties that call to question our theories about hierarchical sequences as they apply to both defense mechanisms and the various forms of psychopathology. We also must ask whether the concept of identification is precise enough.

Identification has been defined as the process by which the self-representation is formed as it takes over the characteristics of another person in the external world who is emotionally meaningful to the subject. The internalization pertains to the general personality of the other person—rather than just to specific attributes or particular functions, such as caretaking, of what in psychoanalysis is referred to as the external object. From the viewpoint of psychic structure, identification is a fairly high-level interaction.

Melanie Klein (1946) was the first to hypothesize the mechanism of *projective identification*, which combines two defenses, projection and identification. This is conceptually confusing because identification belongs to the upper end of the hierarchical ladder, whereas projection is closer to the bottom end. Klein viewed projective identification as a rather primitive mechanism often designed to rid the psyche of inner disruptive and destructive forces, usually conceptualized as bad introjects. They are projected into the external object, and then after they have been rearranged and refined, divesting the projected elements of their destructive qualities, they are once again internalized, expanding the self representation in a positive fashion.

It might be advantageous to refer to all phenomena pertaining to something in the outside world that is made part of the inner world as *internalization*. Identification is a particular form of internalization that is specifically concerned with consolidating the personality by patterning it after some person in the surrounding world, a person on whom one is dependent or perhaps has idealized to some extent. This means that the child who is making an identification adopts the same attitudes, personal philosophies, and mode of relating of the person with whom he or she is identifying. This happens with children as part of normal development, presumably reaching its peak during the oedipal phase. However, it can also occur later in life at almost any age, and the identificatory process can undergo psychopathological distortions and regression.

For example, a male patient may have identified with his mother rather than his father, because he fears the masculine role. The father may have been especially threatening, and the mother may have been highly seductive. The latter may lead to incestuous temptation that serves only to intensify castration anxiety to an unbearable degree. To resolve this oedipal dilemma, the child therefore makes a feminine identification, which could mean that he wants a passive homosexual relationship with his father to protect him from his dangerous sexual rivalry with his father. This was the situation with Freud's famous patient, the Wolf Man (1918). Identification in this context is related primarily to the acquisition of a sexual identity, and in the case of the Wolf Man, the pathological distortion of this process was associated with an obsessional neurosis which later turned out to be more closely related to a paranoid character structure.

Again we are faced with a situation in which a defense that had been attached to a high-level conflict is also found in more severe forms of psychopathology. However, as is true of displacement, identification is found in a variety of nonpathological situations, although the distinction between a pathological and a nonpathological state is often difficult to make in psychoanalysis, and is often irrelevant. A common example of identification that does not seem to have any particular significance is as follows: I recall watching my fellow residents in the lunchroom, most of them chief residents on other services—internal medicine and various surgical specialties. Having been an undergraduate medical student in this hospital, I have been exposed to most of the chiefs of service, all of whom had distinctive if not powerful personalities. After a few minutes of conversation with some of these chief residents, and occasionally by simply observing them, I can easily guess whom they are working for, as they had taken over the mannerisms, gestures, and verbal habits of the senior staff members. In some instances, they kept them even after they had finished their residency and had made their own mark in the professional world.

Whether identification in these examples concerns a sexual identity or refers to the acquisition of a professional *modus operandi*, it is still an interaction that focuses on general personality characteristics, that is, the more holistic elements of character structure rather than the discrete parts and segments that are the outcome of part–object relationships.

Many aspects of the outer world or object relationships can be internalized, but for the sake of clarity, some of these interactions should not be considered to be examples of identification. Schafer (1968) defined two other processes of internalization that help us maintain a hierarchical perspective: incorporation and introjection.

Incorporation is associated with the earliest developmental stages. It is first evident when children barely, if at all, differentiate the internal world from external reality. They take in elements of their surrounding milieu that reestablish homeostasis and provide soothing and nurture. These interactions somehow become part of the self. They form endopsychic registrations and lead to the acquisition of psychic structure (see Chapter 2). Incorporation is the basic psychic process in many of the phenomena that Klein and her followers studied, interactions with part–object breasts that are internalized being a prominent example. This is obviously a developmental phenomenon, but in states of severe regressive decompensations, incorporation can become a primitive mode of relating to what is perceived as a threatening external world.

I recall a depressed patient who experienced a regression of psychotic proportions while in treatment. He had been overwhelmed by some life situations in which he had experienced a modicum of success. His sadistic superego could not tolerate his achievements and the adulation he received. Consequently, his depression intensified and was accompanied by feelings of helpless vulnerability and panic. He also felt extremely needy and would moan and groan about how miserable he felt and how much emotional sustenance he required just to survive. His behavior became quite primitive.

For example, some sessions were dominated by oral material. This patient would go into endless detail about how he would like to "swallow" everything and everyone around him. On one occasion he snapped his teeth at my ankle, as I had my legs on a hassock near the couch on which he was lying. He would have bitten me if I had not reflexively pulled away. He stressed his intense desire to devour me, to fill himself up with me, so that he could use my internalized strength to vanquish all the evil, disruptive forces inside him. Only by incorporating power and "goodness" could he master sadistic, controlling introjects and prevent them from "tearing" him apart and robbing him of the "last vestiges of identity." He also stressed the nurturing elements associated with literally devouring me—a cannibalistic preoccupation that eventually achieved some capacity to solace him.

This patient illustrates the primitive archaic qualities of

incorporation as the internalizing process is set in motion in the interest of psychic survival. The open expression of cannibalistic impulses would ordinarily occur in the context of a psychotic regression, and this was to some extent true of my patient. However, he was able to function outside my consultation room, and his deep regression was confined to the treatment setting. His impulses to incorporate, although minimally acted out, remained chiefly in the realm of fantasy, and he was able to gain some security from the transference aspects of our relationship. Instead of literally incorporating me, he had fantasies of my being inside him, and he was able to carry me with him in his daily life to counteract his sadistic superego and malignant destructive introjects.

Relatively recently, clinicians have had patients who have adopted incorporative defenses and made them into characterological adaptations. I am referring to *obesity* and *bulimia*, the latter often being associated with *anorexia nervosa*. We have learned that these patients' psychopathology is usually the outcome of a primitive ego state that prominently uses incorporation as a mode of coping with the external world. In some cases of obesity and many of bulimia, it is as if these patients want to put the entire world inside them. By so doing they can control it, make it predictable, and not feel dependent and vulnerable. Control is also in the forefront of the psyches of patients suffering from anorexia nervosa, in that they attempt mastery by denying that they have any needs, even the need for sustenance and nurture.

It is evident that although incorporation is directed toward bringing into the psyche various elements and persons of the external world, it is quite different from identification. The difference concerns the content of the internalization. The internalizations that are the outcome of incorporation are primitive because they are concrete representations of benign or threatening forces and are unchangeable; that is, they are not assimilated into the psyche and become amalgamated and integrated into various ego subsystems. In treatment, for example, the analyst is often idealized as the powerful good object and is incorporated as a protector. Bad objects are admitted into the psyche so that they can be destroyed or controlled.

Schafer (1968) also distinguished *introjection* from identification and incorporation. Introjection is also an internalizing process that, in the psychic hierarchy, could be placed somewhere between them. The content of the internalization and its fate within the psyche are once again the features that differentiate the three mechanisms of incorporation, introjection, and identification.

The first dim perceptions of external objects are percepts of part objects. The mother, for example, is not viewed as a person in her own right, a personality distinct and apart from the child, as occurs when identification takes place. Instead, during introjection, the external object is perceived only in terms of its function in the caretaking process. The differences in sensory percepts that occur during incorporation and introjection are just a matter of degree, and so absolute distinctions are difficult to make. The percepts of an ego state that is operating at the level of introjection are somewhat better structured and are much less amorphous or magically oriented than are those found when incorporation is the prominent internalizing modality.

The fate of what is internalized during introjection is somewhat different from what is internalized during incorporation and identification. What is taken into the ego seems to move from a global incorporation to a discrete introjection and finally, in identification, to an amalgamation, that is, an assimilation in which what has been internalized is no longer specifically distinguished. As might be expected, the content of the introjective process is the introject, a term that Ferenczi (1909, 1955) introduced. If we accept that children at some early developmental phase relate to the outside world only in terms of inner needs, then what is primarily perceived is the response to such needs. Correspondingly, the sensory system registers the need-satisfying interaction that constitutes the introject. When we speak of the maternal introject, we are not referring to the mother in terms of her emotional makeup; rather, we are describing a function, the maternal caretaking function that, in the introject phase, consists of a well-delineated endopsychic registration with discrete boundaries of its own.

As the psyche continues to develop, the introject acquires

other qualities, besides being a *functional introject*. It may become helpful in acquiring adaptive techniques, or it can be threatening and destructive. Eventually it loses its introject status as it becomes more fully amalgamated in the self representation and contributes to the identity sense.

The introject is unique in that it has firm boundaries and does not, in a manner of speaking, blend into the surrounding psychic tissue. Klein (1946) described good and bad introjects that represent what she called internal objects. These introjects can undergo many changes. They will often be walled off from the rest of the ego if they are experienced as destructive and, as such, remain encapsulated as a foreign body. During normal development, however, introjects lose their introject status; that is, they lose their boundaries and contribute to the differentiation of psychic structure.

These theories about internal objects and introjects appear to be mechanistic and concrete and of little clinical relevance. Klein has often been attacked for anthropomorphizing various parts of the psyche and confusing the manifestations of fantasies for psychic processes that can be explained etiologically. Nevertheless, many of her ideas have been modified, and today are incorporated into object relations theory (see Chapter 8).

Freud (1917c) was aware of the significance of introjects, as he indicated in his ideas about mourning processes and melancholia. He was not, however, too precise in his terminology, as he did not distinguish between identification and introjections. Certain psychic phenomena are best understood in terms of inner forces that represent emotionally significant persons affecting psychic equilibrium; in other words, they are most efficiently conceptualized as introjects.

A middle-aged man lost his father during the latter part of his analysis. While in treatment, he had worked out some of his tremendous ambivalence toward him, but his reactions to his father's death were more intense than we had anticipated. He felt quite depressed and had a series of dreams in which his father would walk into a room looking sad and distraught. Nothing in particular happened. His father would just stand there, looking lost, unhappy, and perplexed. The patient did not know how to respond, but he felt an intense need not to let his

father out of his sight. The patient's associations confirmed
Freud's formulations about melancholia in which he concluded
that the patient clings to "the lost love object." My patient had to
bring his father into the room, his own ego, and keep him there,
distinct and separate. Nothing happened, which meant that the
patient was paralyzed by his father's presence. He could not do
anything, and this was reflected both in his accomplishments in
his daily life and in his analysis.

It is easy to view the father's appearance in the dream as an
introject with discrete boundaries that interferes with the ego's
efficient functioning. A later dream further justified this viewpoint. The patient dreamed that as usual, his father walked into
the room but his facial expression had changed, and he no
longer was confused or depressed. Instead, he smiled, and then
his body broke up into small fragments. They became smaller
and smaller until they were no longer visible. The patient's
depression regarding his father's death lifted immediately after
the dream, although it had been becoming less intense some
weeks before it. He also stopped having this recurring dream.

This last dream seems to be a graphic depiction of how an
introject—in this case, the paternal introject—loses its boundaries and its introject status and becomes absorbed into the ego.
This sequence is compatible with Freud's ideas about the mourning process. The lost love object is finally relinquished, but
elements of it may be retained as the bereaved person retains
some of its characteristics which become part of the mourner's
personality. What begins as introjection eventually is transformed into identification.

Internalizing processes can be adaptive in that they add
some dimension to the ego and expand the range of the self
representation. They are defensive in that they usually protect
the psyche from being overwhelmed by destructive impulses, as
they originate either within the psyche or in the external world.
Freud did not pay particular attention to the influence of the
outer world, except to consider its traumatic potential or its
impact on the production of psychosis (1924a, 1924b). Anna
Freud (1936), however, described an interesting use of identification as a defense, especially for patients dealing with persons
whom they perceive as dangerous. Anna Freud called this *identification with the aggressor.*

Often, when people find themselves threatened by someone who is capable of doing considerable harm, they identify with that person. As with all identifications, a patient may take over the character traits of another person and make them his own. This can occur in special instances, when the psyche has a need to protect itself against unacceptable destructive feelings toward a particular person, as well as against a fear of retaliation, which usually takes the form of castration anxiety. The clearest examples of identification with the aggressor, however, are connected to the fear of survival.

For example, when given trustee status, concentration camp victims often became more cruel than their sadistic guards were. They treated their fellow prisoners as they had been treated and, in many instances, took over the mannerisms and the contemptuous attitudes of their captors. The purpose of such a turnabout is obvious in view of the inmates' horrible circumstances, in which their survival was precarious. The prisoners were deprived of their sense of autonomy, and so if they had an opportunity to fill up their rapidly emptying self representation, they would seize it. Not only would they fill up their emptiness, but the newly acquired identity put them on the side of strength and power rather than helplessness and vulnerability.

There are many less striking, more mundane examples of identification with the aggressor, such as an employee's acting like the tyrannical boss toward his subordinates. This is the typical psychology of the martinet and is a special instance of the identification I described earlier concerning residents aping the mannerisms and attitudes of the senior staff members.

Conversion

Conversion was one of the earliest defenses that Freud described (Breuer and Freud 1895). Today, examples of conversion are rare, but this defense illustrates qualities characteristic of all defenses. A conflict between a sexual impulse and opposing forces is converted into a somatic dysfunction, a situation typically found in conversion hysteria. Because hysteria is fairly high up on the hierarchy of emotional disorders, conversion is also at the upper end of the scale, as depicted in the table. It is placed higher than the defenses of isolation, reaction formation, and undoing that are typical of the obsessive-compulsive neurosis. The obsessive-compulsive neurosis is considered to be a more primitive neurotic constellation than is hysteria, and so it is conceptually consistent that conversion would be considered a "higher" defense than are isolation, reaction formation, and undoing.

The status of hysteria as a high-level psychoneurosis has been questioned, to the point that many clinicians doubt that hysteria, as Freud saw it, actually exists. Most patients who have been initially diagnosed as hysterics reveal either a psychotic core or a relatively severe character disorder. Thus, to be consistent, conversion should no longer be an example of a fairly sophisticated adaptation. Indeed, so-called hysterics appear naive, concrete, and nonpsychologically minded. The conversion of a mental process to a somatic symptom—that is, reversion to the soma—may in itself be indicative of primitive psychic processes. Certainly, patients who often somatize are difficult to treat from a psychotherapeutic perspective. Although often suggestible, they do not do well with reassurance, hypnosis, or persuasion.

Somatic symptoms, nonetheless, often cleverly symbolize a compromise between the repressed impulse and repressing forces. The taboos regarding sex that prevailed during Freud's time are no longer as significant in our society, perhaps helping explain why conversion symptoms are seldom encountered, especially in sophisticated cities. Such symptoms are not unusual in less-developed nations or in the backwoods, mountains, or outlying areas of our country, indicating that the cultural variable is important to determining what defensive adaptations the psyche will employ. This makes sense because defenses, although they are constructed to preserve intrapsychic balance, nevertheless contribute to the way that the ego reacts to the external world and must conform to some of the exigencies of reality. If the psyche is facing a sexually repressive reality, then it must react accordingly. A conversion is particularly appropriate to specific, nonpsychological, unsophisticated environments that lean heavily on superstition and magical thinking.

To repeat, somatic symptoms may take forms involving

sensory phenomena—for example, anesthesia, blindness, deafness, and motor dysfunctions, such as paralysis of limbs, loss of equilibrium, and convulsions. The organ involved is symbolic of the conflict and often is a substitute for the penis. This is an instance of displacement, and in conversion, we usually encounter an *upward displacement*, that is, feelings involving the genitals are transferred upwards to the arms or eyes, for example.

There are other reasons besides symbolic appropriateness that a specific part of the body is selected for the conversion process. A part that has been weakened in some way becomes the point in which the libido is concentrated. If an arm has been paralyzed because of an organic affliction such as poliomyelitis, then even after it has recovered, that arm will be the likely target for somatization. The limb represents the point of least resistance, and therefore the most susceptible to being used in a regressive fashion.

Isolation, Reaction Formation, and Undoing

Isolation, reaction formation, and undoing are typically found in our urban sociocultural milieu, perhaps because they are associated with obsessive-compulsive neuroses and character traits and our culture has often been described as having an obsessional base. Our cultural heritage stresses order, cleanliness, and thrift and encourages not permitting emotions to dominate or rule our actions. We are trained to have intellectual relationships to a task-oriented outer world, and so the defenses of isolation, reaction formation, and undoing fit in well.

Isolation is a defense that protects the psyche from being overwhelmed by emotions. It allows an inner impulse to reach consciousness, but it is deprived of feelings. As psychoanalysts would say, it is decathected, as it loses its cathexis (see Chapter 2). Without its affect, the unacceptable impulse is rendered harmless, and this is especially important, as such impulses are usually sadistic. In treatment we encounter patients who can express the most destructive feelings imaginable in a calm, unemotional fashion.

When patients use isolation—or intellectualization as we sometimes refer to this defense—we are aware that their understanding of our interpretations is shallow and superficial and has little or no impact on their behavior or outlook. They strip all feeling from what otherwise might be intense emotional issues. These patients "intellectualize" away everything.

In addition to decathecting feelings or potential insights, we are sometimes confronted with a temporal isolation. Sometimes a thought must be expressed simultaneously with another thought in order to generate affect. If only one component of a thought is expressed and the other one is delayed until later, that is, pulled out of context, the affect that would have been attached to the combination of thoughts will be lost. I recall a patient describing her husband as a vile, loathsome creature, but not exactly in those terms. Rather, she presented a litany of his wrongdoings vis-à-vis his business associates and stressed his duplicity and cheapness. She also added that this had had little effect on her; in fact, she was gaining considerable advantage from his financial successes. She then changed the subject, leaving the topic of her husband for about 15 minutes. When she returned to her feelings about him, she confessed not liking him but could not specify on any aspect of his personality to justify her negative outlook. In the past she had described many incidents that would justify anger, but she was not feeling any anger. I reminded her of what she had said earlier, which she acknowledged, but again she repeated that it did not matter.

In another session this patient again repeated a similar litany. I intervened by commenting that for some reason she did not want to face the extent of the rage she felt toward her husband and pointed out some of her negative comments about how he treated her. I added that her criticisms of me, such as not being interested in her, preferring other patients, and feeling that she was a silly scatterbrained woman, were remarkably similar to her criticisms of her husband. She felt a tremendous urge to change the subject and then had a fantasy of a time bomb with a 15-minute fuse. She knew that she had plenty of time to defuse it but that I was not allowing her to do it. Suddenly she felt angry toward her husband. I need not pursue further the transference implications of this vignette or its genetic antecedents. I simply wish to stress that by temporarily isolating various perceptions of her husband, this patient was able to protect herself from the impact of her anger. The time factor separated two elements that, if they had remained contiguous, would have forced the patient to face her rage.

Isolation keeps matters in the realm of the intellect rather than in the sphere of emotions, which is why it is most often referred to as *intellectualization*. Besides being a defense mechanism, intellectualization is an attribute of normal thinking. To think clearly, the mind must keep emotions under control so that it can integrate percepts, organize ideas, and take into account the limitations imposed by reality. Affects could interfere with the pursuit of logical operations. In creative endeavor, however, the primitive parts of the psyche apparatus, including affects, participate in the innovative achievement.

Reaction formation leads to the repression of the forbidden impulse by replacing it with its opposite. It is more familiarly known as *overcompensation* and is an example of how a defense incorporates what is being defended against. Frequently, even casual observers recognize intuitively what overcompensating people are defending themselves against. Reaction formation is involved with those obsessional aspects that are the outcome of violent inner forces seeking discharge. Thus, the task of reaction formation or overcompensation is to control these inner disruptive forces, which invariably are based on hostile destructive impulses, or according to Freud, anal-sadistic drives. Regardless of how well defended these personality types may be, their underlying rage and sadism are evident and are felt by the persons who have to deal with them.

Occasionally we find a man or woman involved in a cause, a humane endeavor, who espouses sound and sensitive principles but does it in a manner that arouses mistrust and even hostility. The cloying sweetness of some "do-gooders" can be devastating and infuriating, because the recipient of such "kindness" feels attacked, overtly or covertly sensing the attacker's underlying murderous rage. "Killed with kindness" is an apt expression of the situation in which basic sadism becomes interwoven with an overcompensatory preoccupation that takes the form of an obsession. This was evident some years ago when a powerful, well-organized antivivisection group tried to get a law passed forbidding animal experimentation. Publicly, these antivivisectionists verbalized tender, compassionate feelings for the lives of the animals they were trying to save. They stressed humanity and how sacred life was, even that of a dog. However, in stressing their *violent* opposition to vivisection—a just and, interestingly enough, nonhostile cause from their viewpoint— they expressed hatred for the physiologists and other scientists using animals as research subjects. The antivivisectionists wrote threatening letters to famous academicians, going into endless detail as to what they would do to them, tortures and mutilations such as castration and disembowelment, and many of these letters employed the foulest language imaginable. I have encountered obsessional patients who could conjure cruel fantasies and express the most violent thoughts with a saintly mien and a beatific expression on their faces. As with the antivivisectionists', theirs was a righteous anger devoid of affect and in the interest of a good cause.

Overcompensation occurs in many milder forms than these. At times we may feel guilty about some thought, feeling, or action and we may bend over backwards, so to speak, to make up for our negative feelings, regardless of whether they are conscious or unconscious. We may then tend to do something to offset our guilt-provoking activities by making psychic compensation. This may consist of bringing a gift, such as flowers after a lovers' quarrel. Overcompensation sometimes becomes difficult to distinguish from the next defense to be discussed, undoing.

Undoing refers primarily to actions rather than feelings and attitudes, which refer predominately to reaction formation. However, actions designed to atone for guilt-laden attitudes or behavior obliterate such distinctions. The differences may be quantitative in that the behavior and actions attributed to the defense of undoing are more complex and ritualistic than those associated with overcompensation. The compulsive aspect of the obsessive-compulsive neurosis or the obsessive-compulsive character can be understood mainly in terms of undoing.

Undoing is another example of a mental mechanism expressing an unacceptable impulse and prohibitive forces. As with isolation, there is a temporal separation between the two. The forbidden feeling or impulse is expressed or acted out, and then the prohibitive forces make up for or "undo" the anticipated consequences of the previous action. The forbidden feeling consists of a hostile attitude or an act intended to be destructive. The response of undoing usually takes the form of a ritual of atonement or expiation. Both the hostile act and the atonement for it may be symbolically disguised, and patients may be totally unaware of their behavior's significance. In fact, they may be annoyed by it because it seems bizarre and pointless. Nevertheless, they feel driven to perform the ritual, because if they do not, they will become overwhelmed with anxiety. Patients are puzzled by and often irritated because this ritual requires a good deal of work and takes up so much time. In fact, as Freud (1909c) discussed in his treatment of his famous obsessional patient known as the Rat Man, because of a persistent fantasy about rats, the patient may be practically paralyzed in his daily functioning, as both the ritualistic actions and the thoughts crowd out all other activities.

Freud gave us an interesting example of undoing. While aimlessly walking down a country road, the Rat Man casually kicked a stone into the middle of the road, giving no particular thought to his action. As he walked on, he started thinking about what he had done. He then reflected that if his beloved in her carriage came down the road, the wheel of the vehicle would hit the stone, thereby overturning the carriage and killing her. He then became anxious, retraced his steps, and, in an attempt to undo this anticipated murder, kicked the stone off the road. Feeling under less pressure, he contemplated what he had just done and concluded that all of this was, indeed, very silly. In an attempt to dismiss his preoccupations he once again kicked the stone into the middle of the road. As we might expect, the whole sequence repeated itself, and so it went on endlessly, virtually rendering the patient unable to do anything else.

Undoing can occur in less striking circumstances than those of the Rat Man. It may be a fairly pedestrian phenomenon. All of us have been plagued by doubts as to whether we have turned off the stove or locked the door, so much so that we are driven to return and make certain that we have taken care of such mundane matters. More often than not we discover that we have done what we could not remember doing. Sometimes even after checking we are again overcome by the insecurity that perhaps we have once more been remiss and might possibly return a second or third time. In the third time, we are probably confronted with manifest psychopathology. Still, at one time or another, almost all of us have had a nearly uncontrollable urge to determine whether we have taken proper safety precautions.

These common reactions are similar to what the Rat Man experienced. If we had, in fact, not turned off the gas or locked the door, we would fear that we had created a dangerous situation. If not ourselves, we would be putting something or someone in jeopardy. This represents the same sort of hostile, destructive attitude as the Rat Man's fantasy that the stone he kicked in the middle of the road would kill his beloved by causing her carriage to overturn. That is, our unconscious intent is destructive. The obsessive rumination indicates our inner conflict. Part of us has an unconscious wish to create havoc, and another part, which incorporates the superego, feels guilty and wants to make reparation, that is, undo the possible harmful consequences of our wishes, as acted out by our neglect in taking safety precautions. Like the Rat Man, we feel driven to be protective, but our hesitation and uncertain belief that we are being foolish—in our case because we feel that we have not been remiss—are signs that we want to be destructive. This vacillation between hostile impulses, subjectively perceived as hatred, and the desire to be caring and protective, a manifestation of love, is known as *ambivalence*, which is characteristic of obsessive-compulsive preoccupation and symptomatology.

Negation

Negation is another common defensive adaptation. It is perhaps one of the most obvious defenses, but confronting a person who has often used this mechanism produces the greatest resistance to accepting what to most observers seems self-evident. Negation (see Freud 1925b) allows the unacceptable impulse or thought to reach consciousness, but it is then disavowed as being part of the self. For example, a patient will state that I, the therapist, might believe that he felt in such and such a way about a situation or had a particular thought or reaction but that it is decidedly not the case. Indeed, it had never occurred to him. The fact that he is verbalizing thoughts and feelings that "never occurred to him" does not strike him as a contradiction. As long as he disavows the thoughts as his own, he can admit them to consciousness. Usually, however, after he has been confronted and his initial resistance has been overcome, the patient can accept that whatever is brought up belongs to the inner world of the mind.

In therapy, clinicians often are faced with a special instance of negation related to associations to dreams. For example, a patient may have a dream in which someone other than the patient is attacking someone else. Perhaps the person attacked is a poorly disguised version of the therapist, so thinly disguised that the analyst ventures a transference interpretation, to the effect that the patient wished to attack the therapist or is experiencing some feelings of hatred toward him. The patient then corrects the analyst by naively protesting that he was not the attacker and refers to the other person in the dream, whereupon the analyst may point out that the patient created the dream and, in a sense, is responsible for everything that goes on in the dream.

The patient's initial reaction is an example of negation in that he negates having hostile, destructive feelings. By using displacement, the patient attributes the feelings to someone else but is, in the manifest dream content, aware of the negative feelings directed toward the analyst. However, they do not belong to the patient, the usual belief associated with negation. In this example, the defensive process is carried one step further: instead of being simply disavowed, these feelings are attributed to another person. The latter instance is an example of displacement, in which, again, various defenses are operating in conjunction with one another.

Is negation associated with any particular form of psychopathology, in the same way that reaction formation, isolation, and undoing are adaptations typical of the obsessive-compulsive neurosis? I believe that it is a less specific adaptation that can be compatible with many psychic configurations. All defenses can from time to time operate in all different types of personalities, but when they do, they bring out certain characterological features that might not have been prominent pre-

viously. For example, if a person reacts on the basis of the
psychic mechanism of undoing, his behavior will assume obsessive-compulsive characteristics that it might not have exhibited
in the past, at least to the same degree.

Does something comparable happen with negation? I believe that negation represents a fundamental psychic process
that is characteristic of the operations of the mental apparatus in
general. It is not necessarily a reaction to destructive feelings, as
seems to be the case with the obsessive-compulsive neurosis, or
to sexual feelings, as has been postulated for hysteria. It is
primitive in that it denies the existence of mental content, but it
is sophisticated in that such psychic elements gain admission to
the sphere of consciousness. They are simply not recognized as
belonging to the self, being treated as if they were foreign
bodies. These "foreign bodies" are not just impulses and needs;
they can be connected with feelings of self-esteem.

I recall a colleague's dream in which his self-esteem was
threatened because he was using negation. It was threatened in a
fashion, however, that was reassuring, as occurs with examination dreams.

As a medical student, my colleague dreamed that he was
being given an oral examination by an esteemed professor in
physiology. This student had done research before going to
medical school and already had a Ph.D. in physiology. In his
dream, however, he was being asked questions that to his con-
sternation and embarrassment, he could not answer. He could
still remember the questions he had been asked and the fact that
he did not have the knowledge—so he was convinced—to
answer them. In the dream, the professor became infuriated at
the student's ignorance and, in a contemptuous, condescending
manner, gave him the answers that he "did not know." My
colleague felt very foolish during the dream, a feeling that
persisted after he had awakened. I heard this dream many years
after he had had it, and my colleague still felt foolish about his
performance during the dream examination. Having a Ph.D. in
physiology, he felt that he should have been able to answer the
questions. He still believed that this information had not been
available to him and that the professor gave him the right
answers which he now remembered.

When I pointed out the obvious, that it was his knowledge that the professor was expounding, as he alone had created the dream, he was astonished. At first, he was tempted to argue with me, denying that he knew anything, but quickly he recognized how ridiculous his position was. In actuality, there was no professor lecturing to him. He had created the whole interaction, but his beliefs before our discussion and his tendency to protest were based on negation. Why he had to maintain such beliefs beyond the reassurance qualities of a typical examination dream is another question that would require careful analysis to answer.

Projection

Projection has been widely explored in the clinical setting and has been associated with fairly primitive forms of psychopathology. It can be viewed as an extension of undoing if we follow a particular sequence beginning from the inside of the psychic apparatus. Mental elements move from the inside to the outside. They traverse from the Ucs to the Pcs and finally to Pcpt-Cs. Once such elements reach consciousness, they may be handled defensively. If they are disavowed within the sphere of consciousness, then we are witnessing negation. On the other hand, if they are pushed further along the path from inside to outside, they are moved into the outer world, and this is known as projection.

Thus, projection can be viewed as the defensive continuation of a process in which mental content originating in the psychic apparatus is not considered as being part of the self. Although with negation, there is simply a disavowal, with projection what is being denied is said to emanate from the outer world. More specifically, the person who projects does not take responsibility for his own feelings; instead he attributes them to someone else. Because what is being projected is basically unacceptable to the subject, the segment of external reality that has become the receptacle of the projection is experienced as disruptive. This receptacle is usually a person who is viewed as being hostile and destructive, as he or she has taken over the subject's murderous feelings. The content of projection usually consists of destructive impulses, and they are often attributed to an emotionally significant person, an external object that has become a *paranoid object*. The projection of hostile feelings occurs regularly in a paranoid psychosis or character structure; in fact, it defines these emotional constellations.

People who use projection as an adaptative modality have the same beliefs as do dreamers who negate, but they are awake. The fact that they are not sleeping leads us to conclude that they are projecting rather than negating. Paranoid patients blame an external object rather than themselves for having destructive or homosexual feelings. With negation, dreamers portray someone other than themselves as harboring unacceptable impulses or as having behaved in a destructive fashion. Because this occurs in a dream state, however, it is in the psychic sphere and therefore constitutes negation. Patients who project, because they are awake, have established boundaries between the inner and the outer world. Consequently, what is inside is viewed as being outside, and in fact, a situation in the outside world complies with the projective process. I have spoken of this interaction between the outer and the inner world as *environmental compliance* (Giovacchini 1958), in much the same way that Freud (Breuer and Freud 1895) wrote about *somatic compliance* in the production of hysterical conversion symptoms. In the paranoid state there is always some degree of environmental compliance, in that the receptacle of the projection bears some similarity to what is projected. Clinicians are aware that there is always a kernel of truth in a paranoid delusion. That is, the targets of the patient's accusation harbor feelings similar to those projected into them.

Not all projections are connected with paranoid processes. Projection regularly occurs in analysis and is an integral part of the transference. Patients project into the analyst attitudes and feelings that were initially directed toward infantile objects. They also project various psychic structures and introjects. The psychic structure usually is the superego, and the analyst is given the role of an outside conscience. The patient fears the therapist's critical judgments and may try to win approbation and approval. In this instance, introjects refer to good and bad internal objects, as Klein (1946) described.

The projection of a bad internal object is typical for paranoid patients. They harbor introjects within themselves that are perceived as dangerous and destructive. These are residues of early traumatic object relationships (see Chapter 3). They are experienced as threatening, as patients believe that they can destroy good internal objects which in turn are the precipitates of satisfying and nurturing object relationships. Some patients need to protect these good objects by getting rid of their bad objects. The resultant clinical picture is paranoid.

Other types of projection do not necessarily create paranoid configurations. For various reasons, such patients project good rather than bad internal objects into the therapist. I recall a middle-aged commercial artist who constantly reviled himself. He had low self-esteem and felt inadequate and useless. Actually, he was somewhat renowned in the area of his artistic specialty and, unlike most of his fellow artists, was able to make a relatively good living from his work. Nevertheless, he had a low opinion of himself and his abilities, and this was reflected in his appearance.

When I first saw him, he was dirty and disheveled and had an offensive odor. He viewed himself as a garbage disposal unit, and that is how he smelled. I, and the patient that followed him, found the stench unbearable, and so I had to make it a condition of treatment that he take a bath. The patient complied, and instead of being angry, as I had expected, he expressed gratitude for my setting limits to the manifestations of his self-deprecatory attitudes. It seemed that as he was tearing himself down, he was building me up. This gradually happened as he turned to me for evaluations of specific works of art or comparisons of a particular school with another. He was treating me as an authority in his area of expertise. He was asking me for judgments that he was much more capable of making than I was. As I saw this develop, I was puzzled.

It became apparent that he was "giving" me his talents and expert judgments. These represented the good parts of himself, parts that he did not acknowledge. In fact, he did his best to hide them. Eventually, I interpreted that he needed to endow me with his strengths, special knowledge, and creative evaluations. His initial response was to deny that he possessed anything positive, but his associations over a period of several weeks confirmed my interpretation. He talked about my being a safety

deposit box, a place that protected valuables. He accepted that
he was using this safety deposit box, which indicated an admission—for the first time he could remember—that he might have
something that was valuable enough to be protected.

He protected the good parts of himself by projecting them
into me. He did not trust them to himself because he had no
faith in his ability to keep good and bad parts separated. The
latter would destroy the former. On the other hand, he was
certain that I could control the bad parts of myself and render
them harmless. Therefore his talents were safe as long as he was
able to project them. Instead of viewing me as a paranoid
object, he had idealized me.

This is an example of a rather novel use of projective
mechanisms, but one that we are encountering more frequently,
or perhaps recognize more often, as we learn more about patients suffering from primitive mental states. Although this type
of projection first serves as a defensive maneuver, it can also
become a vehicle for progressive changes within the psyche as it
attains heightened self-esteem and higher levels of integration. I
discussed projective identification earlier in this chapter, a defensive process that can also set the developmental process in
motion once again, especially if it had been fixated at a primitive stage because of the crippling effects of psychopathology.
After projecting insecure aspects of the identity sense into the
analyst, these patients take them back into their own ego in a
more cohesive, integrated form. Having passed through the
therapist's psyche, they have acquired further differentiation,
balance, and resiliency. The analyst has imbued them with an
increased capacity for synthesis and security. Thus, the patients
build up their self representation by an integrative "passage," by
a projection, and then, through identification, by taking back in
a modified form what they have projected and identifying with
some aspects of the therapist's self representation.

Dissociation or Splitting

Dissociation or splitting is a psychic mechanism that often operates in conjunction with projection. It refers to a disruption of

the psychic apparatus in which the ego loses its cohesive synthesis. Rather than operating as an integrated unit, it becomes fragmented, and the various parts of the ego seem to function independently of one another.

Freud (1938) discussed fragmentation in terms of its defensive meaning, although much earlier he had identified this mechanism as characteristic of hysteria (Breuer and Freud 1895). Freud considered Janet's pronouncement that hysterics are characterized by their propensity to dissociate, but he viewed it as a sign of weakness and condemned these patients as being morally degenerate. Freud disagreed with Janet's judgmental attitude and preferred to understand his patients in terms of intrapsychic conflict. Breuer, however, made formulations similar to Janet's, but without being critical or moralistic.

Breuer believed that hysterical patients do not react appropriately to a traumatic incident. They do not discharge their tension by experiencing anxiety. Instead, the traumatic incident becomes encapsulated and walled off from the rest of the ego. According to Breuer, such patients are in a *hypnoidal* state while being traumatized. The trauma is incorporated during this hypnoidal state and remains in the psyche as a foreign body. It is divorced from the main psychic current and removed from the sphere of consciousness. The task of treatment was to bring the hypnoidal state into consciousness, to experience it with the anxiety that properly belongs to such a frightening event—what Breuer called abreaction and catharsis—and once again to reestablish the unity of the ego.

Freud at first paid lip service to Breuer's ideas, but because they did not pertain to intrapsychic conflict and the role of sexuality, he gradually abandoned them. Nevertheless, the concept of coexisting but nonconnected ego states is explicitly acknowledged in Breuer's hypotheses and has become an explanatory base by which we understand commonly encountered psychopathology. Perhaps the most obvious use of dissociation is found in patients who have been diagnosed as *multiple personalities*. These patients were not too rarely seen in Freud's and Charcot's time, and within the last few years, more such patients seem to be coming to our attention. Whether we are dealing with hysterical fragmentation or schizophrenia is debatable, but the fact that their personalities are fragmented into independent components is unmistakable.

As defensive adaptations, splitting mechanisms are characteristic of primitive mental configurations and early states of developmental fixation, especially when they are combined with projection or projective identification. However, in some instances, it is difficult to discover the splitting mechanisms' adaptive and defensive qualities, as they appear to be the consequences of psychic disintegration. A defense ordinarily attempts to maintain equilibrium and establish some degree of psychic synthesis. When the psyche fragments, it loses cohesiveness as it regresses or disintegrates into a state of disorganization. Thus, the distinction between splitting as a defense and as a manifestation of psychic breakdown is not always clear-cut.

Splitting, dissociation, and fragmentation are terms that have often been treated as synonymous. With splitting phenomena, regardless of whether we refer to them as dissociation or fragmentation, we need only determine the qualities that distinguish a disintegrative from an adaptive process, as this distinction is clinically significant.

The chief differences between defense and disintegration is stability. The various parts of the psyche that have become disconnected have achieved some degree of equilibrium. The split-off portions of the ego have a synthesis and organization of their own. This is clear in patients with multiple personalities, in which each separate person that periodically appears has a well-developed identity and seems to represent a whole person. Other less striking patients who use splitting defenses may not have the same type or extent of synthesis as do multiple personalities, but the various parts of the psyche are firmly organized and fixed. Because of such dissociations, there are limitations as to how these character types relate to others. A relationship, for example, must be limited to fairly specific interactions. The split-off portion is less than the whole, although this may not seem to be true in multiple personalities. This is reflected in how the psyche functions in the external world. It is not relating and coping on the basis of all its resources but is limited to a particular segment of the ego.

Patients suffering from primitive mental states frequently form intense transferences. They may passionately idealize or vehemently hate their therapists, and this seldom can be mitigated until significant therapeutic progress has been made. However, the patient may switch from a strong positive to a strong negative attitude, and the reverse can also occur. At times, these changes may appear to be capricious, but both stances represent rigid, constricted viewpoints to which the patient tenaciously clings. They are based on the influence of the introjects of a part of the ego that has become dominant in the perceptual system. The ego can perceive in only a limited fashion, only in terms of extreme polarities. Because of its fragmented state, the ego cannot take into account other viewpoints that have become split off into other parts of the ego that are not, at the time, operative. To put it schematically, the ego is split in two, one part containing the good objects and the other the bad objects. Good and bad cannot be combined in an attitude of ambivalence. In some instances, these internal objects cannot be projected into the same person.

The same person can become the receptacle of projected good and bad objects, but in an alternating sequence. The split ego may need to manifest both sides of the dissociation, and this may be difficult to accomplish in the analytic setting.

The patient relates to the analyst on the basis of the dominant ego state, which in a dissociated ego represents a segment of the mind that is, according to Freud, separated from the "main ego current." I recall a patient who vacillated between idealizing me and seeing me as a hateful, inadequate person who hated him. The negative transference finally dominated and caused him to discontinue treatment. He became involved with a consciousness-raising group that he had idealized while he was still in treatment with me. He had extolled the benign attitudes of various members and praised their virtues and sensitivities. He spoke of them as if they were a community of saints. As might have been predicted, he became disillusioned with them and began seeing them as rather nasty persons who preferred talking about life rather than living it. Finally, he returned to treatment and was able to personify his two varying attitudes as stemming from "Black Bart" and the "White Angel." He viewed these various parts of himself as separate identities, but the cleavage was not as great as is found in patients with multiple personalities. Rather, he knew that he was just one person with various facets to his personality.

There are other psychic processes that could be considered defensive adaptations. The list I compiled could be longer, but I chose to include only those mechanisms that are generally accepted by most clinicians. I discussed rationalization and denial initially because they represent extremes. The reader might wonder why I omitted *sublimation* and did not place it in the same area as rationalization.

SUBLIMATION

I did not include sublimation among the defenses because I do not believe that it is a defense in the traditional sense. It is a socializing adjustive process, but it does not lead to repression, and so it is not considered to be a defense, nor does it have any psychopathological connotations.

Sublimation is a psychic process by which a sexual drive is transformed into a nonsexual impulse. It is primarily a desexualizing mechanism that leads, according to the psychoeconomic hypothesis, to discharge. However, it has also been associated with destructive impulses. Through sublimation, what initially might have been antisocial behavior is converted into socially acceptable behavior. The instinctual impulse, although transformed, is fully gratified, which does not occur to such a degree with defenses.

Defenses require an expenditure of energy that drains the available reservoir that powers the ego's integrative and executive systems that cope with inner needs and the exigencies of the outer world (see Chapter 2). Defenses thus interfere with the general efficiency of the psychic apparatus. Sublimation, on the other hand, is supposedly a creative activity accompanied by an efficient use of energy, which leads to an enhancement of self-esteem. None of this occurs with a defensive interaction.

The commonly given example of sublimation is that of artists whose infantile, anal impulses to smear feces is expressed in their paintings, in which they smear paint onto a canvas and produce beautiful paintings. In this instance, anal impulses have been sublimated. Another popular example is that of surgeons who have elevated their sadistic mutilating impulses to a procedure that involves cutting into the human body, but with the purpose of restoring health rather than committing murder.

These examples, and the latter one in particular, are frequently accompanied by signs of inner struggle and emotional pain rather than being simply gratifying creative acts. Artists and surgeons often suffer from a crippling emotional disorder, frequently of an obsessive-compulsive nature. This is observed especially in surgeons and calls into question the normative quality of sublimation.

Some analysts (Waelder 1960) doubt that true sublimation exists. That is, it is doubtful whether a sexual instinct can be gratified by a nonsexual activity. Furthermore, we can question whether any impulse can be nondefensively satisfied by interactions or products different from the inner needs that have been stimulated. The object that is related to the instinct can be changed through displacement, but can any other activity be used as a substitute? Certainly if a person is hungry and requires food, nothing else will do. Is it any different with sexual and hostile impulses? I have explained that destructive feelings can be replaced by their opposites by persons who use reaction formation as a defense. In these instances, the impulse is repressed, but this is not supposed to happen with sublimation. It is difficult to distinguish between sublimation and reaction formation, however, and what we have labeled as sublimation may actually be reaction formation.

Chapter 7

TREATMENT

TREATABILITY

Some of the issues pertaining to treatability as well as several other technical issues have been discussed in various parts of this book, especially Chapter 5. However, they will be repeated here and expanded, because they deserve emphasis and belong in the context of the subject of this chapter.

Psychoanalysis as a technique of treatment has been traditionally limited to a small and select group of patients. Freud reserved his method of treatment for those patients he diagnosed as having transference neuroses (see Chapter 5)—patients who form transferences, hysterics and obsessional neuroses. These are supposedly persons with good ego strength, who will respond to interpretations by acquiring insights that will enable them to resolve their intrapsychic conflicts. Patients who do not respond in this fashion are also unable to form transferences. These are the more severely disturbed patients who have narcissistic neuroses.

Psychoanalysis was thus reserved for patients who had intrapsychic conflicts but a fairly intact psychic apparatus. Those suffering from structural defects were excluded because of their impulsivity, their lack of capacity to control inner impulses, and their inability to distinguish past from present. This last inability precluded the working through of transference, because in treatment patients had to recognize eventually that their feelings about the therapist were repetitions of past infantile attitudes that were not related to the current setting or situation. Such patients had to be able to conform to the rules governing the therapeutic relationship. They had to be able to tolerate a certain degree of frustration, as the analysis meant not giving in to inner infantile needs and had to be conducted in an atmosphere of abstinence.

The patients that Freud treated early in his career who led him to make hypotheses about treatability and technique of treatment do not seem to have been fundamentally different from the patients he later judged to be unsuitable for psychoanalytic treatment. Reichard (1956) studied some of the patients that Freud described in "Studies on Hysteria" (Breuer and Freud 1895) and concluded that instead of being classic examples of persons having transference neuroses, these patients in fact had moderately severe character disorders, in some instances with fairly obvious psychotic cores. Other patients that Freud treated and that supplied the data on which he based his conclusions regarding various neuroses were classified as having transference neuroses and therefore amenable to psychoanalytic treatment. With additional data collected from follow-ups, Freud's sanguine outlook regarding the "high level" of neuroses cannot be substantiated. I am referring to the Dora case (Freud 1904), Little Hans (Freud 1909a), and the Wolf Man (Freud 1918).

When Dora was an old woman, she was interviewed in Boston and she revealed that she suffered from much more than a hysterical neurosis. She apparently had severe character problems, and although not overtly psychotic, she was sufficiently intrusive that she made miserable the emotionally significant persons around her. Dora was described as cantankerous and narcissistically preoccupied to the degree that she could not relate in a feeling and humanistic fashion to anyone. Her symptoms had been far from contained, as Freud had concluded, when she was an 18-year-old adolescent. As an elderly adult, she did not have definite symptoms (see Chapter 6) but instead related to the external world in a manipulating and sometimes maladaptive fashion.

Little Hans demonstrated a course somewhat similar to Dora's. What initially appeared to be a clear-cut phobic neurosis seemed to have been transformed into a character problem in adulthood. I spoke to a psychoanalyst and an ophthalmologist who knew him personally when he was a stage director at a famous opera house. They reported that he was an impulse-ridden character who was sadistic toward women. Again, these later descriptions indicated that as an adult, Little Hans went beyond the boundaries of a conventional phobic state. Freud did not actually treat Little Hans; Hans's father, an early disciple of psychoanalysis, did, but Freud supervised him.

The Wolf Man, probably Freud's most famous psychoanalytic patient, was first diagnosed as having a severe obsessional neurosis. At the beginning of treatment, he was almost totally functionally paralyzed and had undergone intense traumas, such as losing his fortune and his aristocratic rank during the Russian Revolution. Freud treated him for several years, finally setting a termination date that forced the treatment to end. Some years later it became apparent that the Wolf Man required further treatment, and so Freud sent him to Ruth Mack-Brunswick. At the time the Wolf Man was obviously psychotic; he had somatic delusions centering on the size of his nose, and he had some paranoid ideation. His treatment with Dr. Mack-Brunswick and the further course of his life demonstrated that he had many psychotic features (Brunswick 1928), although he also had considerable strengths that enabled him to endure many adversities, such as his wife's suicide and his own Nazi persecution.

Freud must have felt that these patients could withstand the conditions and abstinence that psychoanalysis, as he practiced it, demanded. His chief goal was to make the unconscious conscious. To achieve this, he had to overcome the patient's resistance to gaining access to the deeper layers of his personality, a resistance that reached its peak in the transference interaction. If his patients could not overcome this resistance or were incapable of forming transferences so that the resistance could be faced and vanquished, then they could not be treated. As I pointed out in Chapter 5, Freud's diagnostic system divided emotional illness into transference neuroses and narcissistic neuroses, which indicated whether or not the patient could be treated. But when Freud was not particularly focused on diagnosis, he did not hesitate to treat patients that, according to his later criteria, would not have met his conditions.

For example, Freud treated a woman who was paranoid and had ideas of reference, delusions, and hallucinations (1896). Indeed, he advised psychoanalysts not to be bound by rules or preconceived notions that would restrict clinical endeavors: "Successful cases are those in which one proceeds, as it were, without any purpose in view, allows oneself to be taken by surprise by any new turn in them, and always meets them with an open mind, free from any presuppositions. The correct behavior for an analyst lies in swinging over according to need from the one mental attitude to the other . . . " (Freud 1912c, p. 114).

RESISTANCE AND FREE ASSOCIATION

Freud (1913a) compared psychoanalysis to a chess game. The clinician can make some statements about opening gambits and end moves, but it is impossible to formulate rules about the game beyond the beginning and before the end. During the middle part, strategy is difficult to postulate and generalize because there are too many imponderables. Nevertheless, Freud felt that there were certain indispensable techniques, designed to facilitate the overcoming of resistance so that the unconscious can become conscious. Early in his career, Freud stressed the importance of resistance (see Chapter 2). Hypnosis did allow him access to a patient's unconscious, but it obliterated all traces of resistance. The hypnotized patients made their unconscious conscious for the therapist, but not for themselves. The therapist's later telling them about what they had learned may have been of some intellectual interest for the patient, but there was little sense of conviction or emotional response. If there were resistance, it undoubtedly entered the picture at this time, a resistance to what the therapist was trying to convey.

Freud was therefore dissatisfied with hypnosis. By accident (see Chapter 2), he discovered another method of gaining access to a patient's unconscious without hypnosis. During rounds, he stopped to see a patient who had been receiving a massage. The patient's thoughts kept wandering as she verbalized them, and Freud later was struck by the fact that he had learned as much about her as when she was hypnotized. This episode was responsible for the discovery of free association. By allowing patients to express whatever came into their mind, Freud was able to learn about their unconscious. The patients produced what he called *derivatives of the unconscious,* which could be pieced together, thereby producing valuable information about id processes. I do not believe that Freud's definition of free association as he instructs the patient could be better stated:

> One thing before you start. What you tell me must differ from an ordinary conversation. Ordinarily you rightly try to keep a connecting thread running through your remarks and you exclude any intrusive ideas that may occur to you and any side-issues, so as not to wander too far from the point. But in this case you must proceed differently. You will notice that as you relate things various thoughts will occur to you which you would like to put aside on the ground of certain criticisms and objections. You will be tempted to say to yourself that this or that is irrelevant here or is quite unimportant, or nonsensical, so that there is no need to say it. You must never give in to these criticisms but must say it in spite of them—indeed, you must say it precisely *because* you feel an aversion to doing so. . . . So say whatever goes through your mind. Act as though, for instance, you were a traveller sitting next to the window of a railway carriage and describing to someone inside the carriage the changing views which you see outside (1913a, p. 135, emphasis in original).

Freud's patients, however, were still reluctant to verbalize their thoughts freely. Freud (Breuer and Freud 1895) then asked the patient to lie down. He then pressed his finger against the patient's forehead and asked him to tell him whatever thoughts came to mind connected to the time when the patient's symptoms first occurred. The patient usually answered that nothing came to mind. Freud then tried again, with the same result. Nevertheless, he kept asking the patient to reveal his feelings and thoughts until finally the patient was able to tell Freud that something had entered his mind. What astonished Freud was that the patient eventually admitted having had that thought or feeling even the first time that Freud pressed his finger against his forehead, but had decided that it was either too trivial or embarrassing. This conscious suppression was based on resistance.

Freud believed initially that resistance is a conscious phenomenon because the patient is aware of suppressing thoughts and feelings. It is striking that patients defied the authoritarian therapist. Usually they follow the doctor's orders, especially during those mid-Victorian years when the physician had considerably more prestige and authority than is the situation today. Furthermore, from a realistic viewpoint, it makes no sense that a patient who turns to a therapist for help should not follow a precedure that promises him relief from oppressive symptoms. This was a curious phenomenon that had to be dealt with in the treatment setting. Though the patient knows he is suppressing, he does not know why. That is because the motivations for the resistance are unconscious. As Freud learned, there is an inherent resistance to facing unconscious material (see Chapter 2) that is intensified by specific intrapsychic conflicts. His patients' reactions were responses to these conflicts that, in turn, were the outcome of unacceptable inner impulses.

When Freud abandoned hypnosis, he also gave up the pressure technique and adopted a procedure that most modern psychoanalysts have found useful. The patient is simply asked to lie down on the couch and to free associate. The analyst explains what he means by free association in the same manner that Freud defined it. Asking the patient to free associate is, in psychoanalytic circles, referred to as "following the fundamental rule" (*die Grundregel*), which is considered to be the essence of the psychoanalytic treatment process. The aim of treatment is thus to prevent the patient from deviating from the fundamental rule.

As happened with the pressure technique, patients have

resistance to free associating. Although considerably modulated from what occurred when Freud used the pressure technique, treatment was still a struggle, a battle between patient and therapist. The analyst was supposed to use all of his influence and prestige to pressure patients to give up their resistances to free associating.

Resistance takes other forms besides the suppression of associations. Patients can create situations that will cause them not to have any associations during treatment. For example, the tension that ordinarily builds up between sessions and serves as an impetus for free association can be discharged in behavior that has been labeled *acting out*. This behavior may serve as an outlet for unconscious impulses that, if contained, would be verbalized during analysis in the form of free associations. These productions, known as *significant material*, represent id derivatives and are valuable to the therapeutic process.

Freud did whatever he could to stop his patients from acting out. He tried to convert their actions into recollections (Freud 1914e), and he actually forbade his patients to become involved in certain activities. Again he felt strongly that analysis had to be conducted in an atmosphere of abstinence. He reprimanded his patients for masturbating and generally advised them not to make any important changes in their lives, such as changing jobs, leaving their spouses, or getting married. In some instances, he prohibited any sexual activity. In regard to making important life decisions, it must be remembered that the early analyses Freud and his followers conducted were very short when compared with those today. They lasted only a matter of months, seldom over a year. The analysis of the Rat Man, considered to be fairly long and extensive, took 11 months (Freud 1909c), whereas modern analyses are counted in years rather than months. Many analysts still believe in the rule of abstinence and attempt to impose conditions for analysis. In general, I believe that throughout the years analysts have become more flexible and are likely to view what in the past was called acting out as the manifestations of defensive psychopathological adaptations that should be analyzed rather than arbitrarily prohibited.

Freud also insisted that his patients lie down on the couch, a practice that most psychoanalysts still follow. Freud (1913a) confessed that he did not like being stared at for 8 hours a day and acknowledged that this maneuver was for his benefit. Most therapists would agree with Freud, although some prefer to have their patients sit up.

There is more to lying on the couch than catering to the analyst's comfort, however. The patient's not being able to look at the therapist places the treatment relationship in a unique frame of reference. In ordinary social relationships and interchanges, the participants look at each other. They can read each other's faces and then respond appropriately. They choose what they are going to say rather than responding spontaneously, and they judge their reactions consciously or unconsciously from the clues they receive from being able to observe each other. The focus of the relationship thus is on the external qualities of the interaction and is governed by secondary process thought processes (see Chapters 2 and 3). In this type of relationship, there are no free associations, and intrapsychic processes are pushed into the background, the exact antithesis of the psychoanalytic interaction.

Visual images are important to maintaining a hold on the external world of reality. Incoming stimuli must be processed, setting the ego's integrative capacities in motion and shifting attention from the inside world of the unconscious and the primary process to the outside environment and the secondary process. Experiments in sensory deprivation are exaggerated examples of perception's being allowed in only an inward direction, in that the field of external perceptions is blocked. Because of this blockage, thoughts, internal images, and feelings emerge, sometimes reaching the intensity of an hallucination; that is, because visual contact with reality is diminished or absent, primary process thinking and imagery dominate. This is equivalent to free association, but it is a much more intense disruptive process that is therapeutically counterproductive.

The loss of visual contact that occurs with lying on the couch is far from absolute, but it allows patients to redirect their perceptions to the inner world of the mind. Furthermore, whatever thoughts they have about the analyst are easier to express because they do not have to face him. Patients have greater freedom to allow fantasies to emerge and revise their inner percepts of the analyst to reflect their psychopathologically distorted adaptations. (This distortion is transference, which I discuss shortly.) The point I am now stressing is that lying down on the couch has technical advantages in that it promotes an intrapsychic orientation and the development of transference.

Unearthing the psyche's deeper processes requires that the treatment maintain continuity. If too much time elapses between treatment sessions, it often will be more difficult for the patient to enter an intrapsychic frame of reference. It is as if the hold on reality becomes harder to loosen if the patient does not have frequent sessions. The defenses against free association seem to gather strength as the time between appointments lengthens.

Freud recommended that psychoanalytic patients be seen daily. Because he wanted to have his Sundays free, he scheduled appointments for six days a week. Although Freud believed that his patients had good ego strength and suffered primarily from intrapsychic conflicts, his recommendations about frequency of appointments are especially apt for the treatment of patients suffering from defects in character structure. Many such patients have problems relating to their inability to hold and maintain a mental representation of a supporting person that will help them achieve psychic balance. They cannot retain introjects (see Chapter 2) without the actual presence of the person embodied in the introject. The image of the analyst is also difficult to internalize, and this inability disturbs the continuity of the analytic process or interferes with whatever integrative benefits it might otherwise have. Frequent sessions help maintain a focus on the treatment relationship. Seeing the patient every day is an ideal that is seldom attainable, usually because of time and expense. Most analyses are conducted less frequently, four or five times a week. Some practitioners believe they can achieve an analytic relationship by seeing the patient two or three times a week. These are still debatable and arbitrary issues, and Freud himself eventually stopped seeing patients six times a week, but this was a matter of expediency rather than due to a scientifically reasoned conclusion.

Kardiner (1977) related that in 1922 he wanted to be analyzed by Freud, who was at the time in the process of setting up his schedule. Freud had available 30 hours a week, which meant that on the basis of six weekly sessions, he could accept five patients. There were, however, six persons, Kardiner and some British analysts, who were seeking treatment. Freud suggested referring one of them to a colleague, but none was willing to give up the opportunity of being analyzed by Freud. Anna Freud overheard this discussion and suggested that instead of her father's seeing five patients six times a week that he see six patients five times a week, and that is how the frequency of appointments was reduced.

Freud (1911–1914) made many recommendations regarding analysis. He advised not taking notes during the session, was adamant about charging for missed appointments, and cautioned against accepting friends or relatives as patients. Freud admitted, however, that these were his personal preferences and that some analysts might find another mode of relating more suitable.

INTERPRETATIONS

The principal tool of psychoanalytic treatment is interpretation. Because the therapeutic relationship is centered on a personal interaction, communication of insights is the main mode of helping patients resolve their problems. Making the unconscious conscious, the stated goal of psychoanalysis, occurs through free association and verbal interchanges, the latter consisting of interpretations.

There are different types of interpretations, the most therapeutically effective being interpretations of the transference. Freud (1912a) believed that the patient's resistance reaches its peak when transference feelings break into the flow of associations. Contemporary psychoanalysts do not emphasize the resistive aspects of the transference as much as Freud did, but they agree that transference interpretations are important for therapeutic resolution (Gill 1979, 1983).

Analysts sometimes make interpretations that do not seem

to include transference elements. They may interpret patients' associations in terms of feelings directed to other persons in their life, such as a spouse, a child, a parent, or a boss. These usually are infantile feelings, but they are not overtly related to the analyst. Often, these interpretations appear to help the patient effect psychic synthesis, although it can be debated as to how much true insight results from them. It has been argued that at most they lead to intellectual insights. These in turn can create resistances to the acquisition of emotionally meaningful and therapeutically useful revelations that help resolve intrapsychic conflict. When patients have received benefits from such interactions, they have been attributed to the analyst's warm interest and supportive attitudes. Classical analysts believe that the therapist should confine his interpretations to the analysis of the transference, but this is far from a settled question.

Interpretations of other persons' attitudes and behavior toward one another seem to be the least therapeutically relevant interpretations. They do not deal with the patient's motivations and sometimes are nothing more than gossip couched in psychoanalytic jargon. Occasionally, however, they do strengthen the relationship between the patient and the analyst so that significant transference material can emerge and be analyzed.

Finally, there is another type of interpretation that, on the surface, does not seem to be an interpretation. I refer to it as an *interpretation of the analytic setting.* I can best illustrate it by giving an example from Winnicott's (1972) account of an analysis (see Giovacchini 1972). Winnicott's patient, a young professional man, told him about some success that he had recently had. The patient was especially pleased because he was usually depressed and experienced life as futile and hopeless. For the first time in many years, he felt good about his accomplishments and about himself, and he enthusiastically shared his triumph with Winnicott. Winnicott, apparently, did not respond according to his expectations; he did not show enough feeling to satisfy the patient. The patient then complained that he, Winnicott, was not sufficiently involved with him or concerned about his welfare. He was bitterly disappointed.

Winnicott stated, "I made an interpretation"; that is, he explained to his patient that he did not get as enthusiastic as the patient did, but then, he did not feel as depressed and as miserable, either, but kept his feelings and responses within certain limits. I find it curious that Winnicott introduced his reply with the phrase "I made an interpretation" because there is nothing in what he said that obviously resembles an interpretation. Rather, Winnicott was explaining his reactions and not saying anything about the patient's feelings and motivations. Whatever insight he was conveying was about himself and not the patient. Nevertheless, at some level, Winnicott viewed what he said as an interpretation.

I believe that Winnicott was correct and that what he said was equivalent to a transference interpretation. His reply referred to his reactions as an analyst which means that he was defining the analytic setting. He indicated that his responses were not as enthusiastic or as depressed as his patient's, that any expectations beyond these boundaries were created by the patient's projections. Winnicott thus had established a norm, the limits of the analytic setting, and any reactions outside these limits belonged to the patient.

The definition of the analytic setting frequently means the limits of what is acceptable within the therapeutic frame. In some instances, it may sound as if the therapist is imposing prohibitions, and perhaps he is, but their impact is created by their transference implications.

For example, a patient, a young attorney, wanted to be psychoanalyzed. He indicated that he was eager to have a "classical" analysis because he traveled in a psychoanalytically sophisticated group, many of whose members had been analyzed. His life was also rigidly constructed because of his relatively severe obsessive-compulsive symptoms.

During the first two sessions he spontaneously gave me a chronologically well organized, detailed history. On the third session, I asked him to lie down because I was beginning to believe that he could go on forever reciting his history. Because he had indicated that he wanted a classical analysis, I was mildly surprised when he balked at my suggestion that he use the couch. Nevertheless, he reluctantly placed himself on the couch, lying there motionless and stiff.

He then resumed talking, in a slow and monotonous voice,

amplifying on what he had been discussing when he was sitting up. Halfway through the session, he abruptly sat up, faced me, and, in a prosecuting-attorney voice, demanded that I give him a "report" of where we were in the treatment, how far we had gone, and what our goals were. I was momentarily thrown off balance by his sudden and unexpected confrontation. I did not answer but motioned with my hand that he lie down once again. He did, but he was furious as he continued with his history, reluctantly accepting that I was not going to respond to his demand.

In the next session, he protested that he needed feedback and denounced my silence. I deliberated as to how to respond. I felt that to grant his request would disrupt the analytic setting. I did not want to relate to him on the basis of the content of his material. On the other hand, I was beginning to believe that my silence was becoming a weapon in a power struggle. I could envision a tug-of-war, the patient tugging away in a struggle to make me talk and I stubbornly resisting his efforts. Obviously, this was an intolerable situation.

My dilemma was intensified when I considered interpreting his demands in terms of intrapsychic forces. Such interpretations, if I had understood the underlying processes better, rather than just on the basis of mere speculation or intellectual jousting, would have been appropriate. On such short acquaintance, however, I could not be certain about the correctness of my understanding and, even if I could, whether the timing was proper. More important was my intent in making such an interpretation. Would it be to give the patient an integrative insight based on my unambivalent understanding, or would it be an attempt to get him to give up his demands and to stop harassing me? Clearly, it would have been the latter.

I finally took a stance. As the patient's frenzy continued, I told him that I saw my role as that of his analyst. I was not there to give spot reports, make summations, evaluate progress, set goals, or make predictions about prognosis. My function, as I saw it, was to analyze him, that is, to learn from him how his mind worked and eventually to share my understanding with him. I added that I had been under the impression that he had understood this, as he had come to me because he knew I was a psychoanalyst and he was specifically seeking a classical analysis. If he insisted on having his demands met or seeking a procedure that followed a different protocol, I would be glad to refer him to someone who was willing to conform to his wishes. I would also be glad to continue my relationship with him, and he was still free to say or feel anything he wanted. The patient grunted but decided to remain with me. From time to time, he continued making the same demands, but he never sat up and he did not feel the same frenzy. The treatment atmosphere was different because the air had been cleared in such a way that my psychoanalytic equanimity was not disturbed.

What I had done was define the analytic setting. I had specified what I was willing and not willing to do. Winnicott did the same thing when he discussed his feelings. I pursued a similar principle in that I outlined the parameters of my role as an analyst. By so doing, I was emphasizing that the patient's reactions were not the outcome of the frustration of realistic expectations; rather, he was responding to inner pressures associated with his neurosis. These forces stemmed from infantile needs which when expressed to me constituted transference. At that time, I was unable to be specific about their content, but the patient was soon able to understand that they were manifestations of defensive adaptations and to see that there was a discrepancy between his wish to be analyzed and his demands. My definition of the analytic setting made him realize that his demands were unrealistic and that their sources resided within himself and were related to intrapsychic conflicts. My pronouncement had an integrative effect, as it reestablished an analytic frame of reference and strengthened the holding environment.

When dealing with rigid or primitively fixated patients, a definition of the psychoanalytic setting seems to be required more frequently than it might be with patients who have better-structured psyches. Perhaps these latter patients, because of their sharper and more cohesive ego boundaries, are better able to separate inside from outside and to determine what stems from within themselves and what emanates from the outer world. This makes it easier for them to recognize transference because they can distinguish infantile reactions and perceptions from a realistic appraisal of the analyst. Some other patients find it difficult to make such a distinction.

The definition of the analytic setting states the boundaries in the therapeutic framework and clarifies the way to transference interpretations. It may not exactly be an interpretation if interpretations signify only verbal content. If we expand the concept of interpretation to the introduction of the intrapsychic viewpoint and do not restrict the process to verbal exchange (nonverbal interpretation), then we can understand why different types of interpretations may be useful for certain types of psychopathology.

For example, some contemporary analysts value interpretations of the current interaction between patient and therapist and tend to minimize the significance of genetic interpretations. A *genetic interpretation* explains a current reaction or feeling as the outcome of a past relationship. It refers to an infantile relationship with a significant person such as a parent or a sibling as being similiar to the patient's relationship with the analyst. The analyst interprets these feelings as properly belonging to that person of the past.

Analysts who object to genetic interpretations point out that they divert attention away from the immediacy of transference feelings. The analyst is, in effect, saying: "You don't feel this or that way toward me, you really hate your father." In many instances, pushing the present back into the past can serve as a defense for the analyst against painful countertransference feelings. The analyst is sidestepping the impact of the patient's feelings by removing them from the present context. By so doing, these affective states are no longer sufficiently cathected so that they can be subjected to the working-through process. For these reasons, some contemporary analysts, especially those who work with primitive mental states, insist that the only meaningful interpretation is a transference interpretation confined to the participants—the patient and the therapist—in the consultation room.

How does an interpretation promote therapeutic resolution? Freud believed that it mainly gave the patient understanding and, by overcoming resistance, brought unconscious material and memories into consciousness. The constrictions owing to repression and the energy bound in the defensive process would be released, allowing the patient greater psychic freedom and permitting him to give up his symptoms.

THE THERAPEUTIC SETTING

Communications between analyst and patient occur in a specific setting that can be divided into two components, a *foreground* and a *background*. Interpretation in the classical sense is a foreground activity designed to foster insight, whereas the background consists of the holding environment from which the patient derives support. This model is similar to the early mother–infant nurturing interaction, which can also be viewed as having a foreground and a background.

For example, the mother both nurtures and soothes her child. She furnishes food, a foreground activity that is a response to inner needs. The feeding, however, has to occur in a harmonious setting. The devoted mother makes the nurturing experience as pleasant as possible, holding her child tenderly and creating a calm, nondisruptive, protective atmosphere. Under these circumstances, inner needs are experienced as potentially pleasurable.

In treatment, for interpretations to be effective, they also must be delivered in a propitious context. The patient must have trust and confidence in the analyst in order to be able to accept his interpretations. If what the analyst conveys to the patient is to have "nurturing" value, it must occur in a calm, soothing setting. Interpretation has traditionally been the substance of the analytic interaction that leads to the resolution of intrapsychic conflict or, when dealing with patients suffering from primitive mental states, to the acquisition of psychic structure. In view of our current experiences with patients, however, we must explore more thoroughly the role of the background, the holding environment (Winnicott 1952b, 1954).

The treatment of severely disturbed patients has caused some analysts to question whether interpretation is the significant factor in the treatment process (see Giovacchini and Boyer 1983). Instead, they attach the greatest importance to the holding qualities of the therapeutic setting and minimize the value of the interpretation. To these analysts, improvement results from the supportive qualities of the therapeutic frame. These ideas have created considerable controversy regarding the question of what can be rightfully called psychoanalytic treatment.

If the foreground—that is, the interpretive aspects—of the therapeutic relationship plays only a minimal role, and the background—that is, the supporting qualities—gains dominance, then are we practicing analysis or supportive psychotherapy? The purpose of supportive psychotherapy is to reinstitute defenses that have broken down and thus are no longer able to serve as adaptations. Through reassurance, persuasion, and encouragement, the therapist attempts to help the patient cope with the exigencies of the environment. To a large measure, this occurs by building up self-esteem so that the patient can develop enough confidence to come to grips with his problems. Thus, supportive psychotherapy is radically different in procedure and intent from psychoanalysis.

A basic difference in supportive therapy is the therapist's involvement with the patient's reality. By contrast, in psychoanalysis, the analyst confines his relationship with the patient to intrapsychic phenomena and avoids making value judgments about the patient's behavior. The insights gained in the consultation room are the significant treatment elements. Whether these insights are derived solely from the nurturing foreground and whether they have to be explicit verbal statements are still open questions.

Another salient distinction between supportive psychotherapy and psychoanalysis is that the former seeks to reestablish the prebreakdown status quo, and the latter strives for higher levels of psychic integration and character change. Any form of treatment that achieves such fundamental changes deserves to be called psychoanalysis, because such improvement can come about only with increased understanding, an understanding based on psychoanalytic principles. When successful, the treatment of severely disturbed patients results in the acquisition of psychic structure and sometimes in the resolution of intrapsychic conflicts. Following treatment, some patients progress from a character disorder, defined by defective psychic structure, to a psychoneurosis in which intrapsychic conflicts are prominent. Some clinicians attribute this type of improvement to the holding environment and its soothing benefits rather than to the structure-promoting qualities of interpretations.

There is no doubt that the more emotionally disturbed the patient is, the more significant the holding environment will be, and the less effective the verbal interpretations will be. The holding environment and the potentially beneficial effects of interpretation, however, are not separate activities but are closely interrelated.

TRANSFERENCE AND COUNTERTRANSFERENCE

The psychoanalytic relationship obviously differs from an ordinary social relationship. Freud cautioned analysts against analyzing friends or relatives, although he is reputed to have treated his daughter (see Bertin 1982, p. 159). He believed that a personal relationship with a patient hindered the therapist's objectivity and the development of the transference.

Freud also recommended that analysts maintain a certain degree of anonymity. They should be mirrors that reflect the patient's feelings. Freud (1913a) described the therapist's role by using two metaphors. He viewed analysts as surgeons who must be dispassionate in dissecting the psyche. To be effective, they must maintain a sterile field which, in psychoanalysis, means not letting their feelings "contaminate" their objectivity. They must be relentless in their pursuit of unconscious elements and not let their feelings stand in their way, no matter how much their patients may demand some overt response from them. Freud also referred to analysts as telephone receivers that unscramble messages and put them into a coherent and understandable form. Both metaphors eliminate any human elements and concerns that are basic to close and helpful relationships.

Thus, to Freud, analytic treatment was primarily a method of discovery, and because it can be effective only with the development of the transference, the analyst's role is as a listener. Analysts develop a way of listening that is the counterpart to free association, an attitude of *evenly suspended attention* (Freud 1912c). This is an extension of Freud's advice that analysts listen to their patients without any preconceived notions and be prepared to be surprised at every turn in the material. Analysts are advised to suspend their secondary process and to allow their attention to hover. As they listen to their patient's associations, they should allow derivatives from their own unconscious to surface and to link these to some of the patient's productions. This procedure eventually leads to insights which will, in time, be conveyed to the patient.

Regardless of Freud's beliefs, many analysts, myself included, do not feel that the mirror, telephone, and surgeon analogies represent a stance that would be effective in treating most of the patients that today seek psychoanalytic help. The analyst's noninvolvement can easily be interpreted by patients as neglect or disinterest or understood as condescension and depreciation. Patients often feel that they are being treated in the same way as they were by neglectful and assaultive persons in the past. This is more true of patients who are suffering from severe emotional problems than of better-integrated patients who have been diagnosed as psychoneurotics.

We assume that we know what is meant by analytic neutrality. Still, does it have to include qualities that are inappropriate for the treatment of certain groups of patients? Must the neutral attitude be equated with noninvolvement and superficially resemble indifference and emotional distance? How is it then compatible with the treatment process?

In classical psychoanalysis, analysts should reveal as little as possible about their feelings or personal life. When they stray from this position, they are revealing countertransference feelings, which Freud (1910a) believed to be detrimental to therapy. He recommended that the presence of countertransference justified further analysis for the therapist, to work out the conflicts responsible for those feelings.

Countertransference reactions cover a wide range. They may vary from finding patients extremely attractive to loathing and hating them. Indeed, some patients are either appealing and likable or obnoxious and intrusive, and having some personal reactions to them is only natural. Still, most analysts can submerge such responses with their clinical interest and concern. They tend not to pass judgment but find the patient's character traits to be subjects of interest and analytic investigation. They represent the manifestations of character structure and psychopathology. Sometimes, however, analysts find themselves reacting.

What is countertransference? To this day, the term has not been uniformly defined. Some analysts consider it to be a response to the patient's transference projections. For example, Racker (1968) wrote about two types, which he called *concomitant* and *concordant*. The former is the analyst's identification with the patient's infantile feelings and vulnerabilities as they are manifested in the transference. In general, this could be thought of as a positive response, an empathic interaction that has therapeutic potential. A concordant response, by contrast, is oppositional. The therapist feels uncomfortable as the receptacle of the patient's projections and so resists them. This may take many forms, such as feeling disrupted, uncomfortable, or angry. These may not be consciously perceived responses, but they will be expressed either overtly or covertly.

Other clinicians prefer to view any untoward response by the therapist as a countertransference. The distinction is that the term countertransference is not limited to a reaction to transference elements. What is meant by untoward, however, is not always easy to determine, and what stimulates the analyst's feelings is also far from evident. Furthermore, disturbing responses to the patient are not necessarily related to the analyst's infantile past.

An alternative way of regarding countertransference is to consider that all of the therapists' reactions have countertransference elements, in the same way that all of the patient's feelings and thoughts have transference implications. Everything we experience contains, in varying proportions, elements from all levels of our psyche. The contributions of the deeper primitive levels as they are directed toward an external object, either the patient or the analyst, can be justifiably referred to as a countertransference and a transference, respectively. Thus, we do not have to distinguish responses that lie outside the sphere of transference or countertransference.

If we accept that everything involves transference and countertransference, this still does not mean that we can interpret all of the patient's material on the basis of its transference significance. The transference contribution, that is, the participation of the primitive levels of the personality, may be so minimal that it cannot be used for therapeutic advantage. If a patient is late because, as she claims, she had a flat tire, it may not be appropriate to interpret her need to control the therapeutic setting as a hostile negative transference. This may well be a correct interpretation, but it would not benefit the therapeutic process.

There are too many other factors stemming from the external world that can explain the patient's behavior so that focusing on sources within the unconscious will appear absurd, especially to the defensive patient. Though all transactions between patient and analyst contain transference and countertransference elements, only those in which such elements dominate over the contributions from reality can be woven into an interpretative framework.

Some countertransference reactions are universal, whereas others are typical of specific characterological constellations and intrapsychic conflicts. I have labeled the former as homogeneous countertransference responses and the latter as idiosyncratic countertransference responses (Giovacchini 1985). Homogeneous reactions have infantile elements, but they are expected, and most of us would react in a similar fashion. Certain types of behavior are objectionable to practically every therapist, extreme examples being the dangerous patient who threatens the analyst's life. Most of us would feel sufficiently disrupted and anxious that we could not continue to function as an analyst. This is a realistic response, but it also has unconscious, infantile elements.

In other instances, the analyst may react in an exaggerated or unique fashion to what most of us would consider as fairly innocuous. This would be an example of idiosyncratic and psychic imbalance. A simple example of an idiosyncratic response is the analyst who felt uncomfortable with a woman patient to the degree that he had to refer her to someone else. Later, on reflection, he discovered that he was reacting to the fact that she physically resembled his mother, something he was unaware of when he saw her. If a therapist has many and intense idiosyncratic reactions, then it might be wise to follow Freud's (1910a) advice and seek further analysis.

WORKING THROUGH AND
THE REPETITION COMPULSION

It is generally agreed that the essence of the psychoanalytic treatment process is the mechanism of *working through*. Although most psychoanalysts could define working through, many disagree as to the actual mechanisms involved. Working through is a complex process that must be elaborated and connected with other psychic mechanisms such as the repetition compulsion and phenomena like childhood amnesia and screen memories.

The time during which crucial traumas occur is subjected to *childhood amnesia*, that is, early infantile experiences that are repressed. *Screen memories* are memories that have distorted a childhood experience or event. Often, they are "cover memories" that are remembered in lieu of other, more emotionally significant but conflicting memories. Although unusually sharp and vivid, these memories deal with apparently trivial and banal events, as sometimes occurs in the manifest context of dreams. They are compromise formations between repressed and repressing forces (Freud 1899).

According to Freud (1914e), what is essential from childhood is retained in these memories, and so their analyses become vital to therapeutic resolutions or working through. Because clinical psychoanalytic theory stresses that the etiology of neuroses resides in childhood experiences, the analyses of screen memories that help retrieve memories of traumatic infantile events could be an essential part of the treatment process.

Memories supposedly refer to actual events, although screen memories represent distortions of childhood experiences. We often wonder how much is fact and how much is fantasy, although in treatment, most analysts tend not to be concerned with what actually happened. They try to look at the patient's material as if it were a fantasy that reveals how the mind functions or malfunctions. Freud referred to fantasies as internal acts that can be analyzed, in contrast with external acts (sometimes referred to as acting out) that are barriers to analysis and working through. *Acting out* is behavior that puts internal conflict into external action. By so doing, it makes unavailable the memory of past significant events, thereby preventing them from being resolved. Freud also considered actions in terms of their repetitive qualities and viewed working through as being part of converting repetition into remembering.

Freud (1914e) implied that there is much more to the analytic process than just a struggle between remembering and defensive forgetting. He stated that as the patient works through inner problems, something may be remembered that never could have been forgotten, because it was never conscious. For the purpose of the treatment, it does not make any difference whether the recovered memory was ever conscious.

These statements sound strange unless we think in terms of psychic structure and developmental stages (see Chapter 3). Possibly the impact of the traumatic environment had its damaging effects before the psyche was sufficiently structuralized so that it could form endopsychic registrations (memories, introjects, or mental representations) of the disruptive milieu. The level of ego organization is prementational and unable to form mental representations of percepts. The effects of trauma are felt from the beginning, although they may be phase specific and have their chief impact on a particular developmental phase or psychosexual stage. Nevertheless, when treating patients suffering from primitive mental states, we invariably recover or, better stated, help construct memories, in the sense that they were never part of the patient's experience because they were not subjectively perceived. When the resistance to conflicting unconscious elements that can be expressed by such memories is overcome, the patient will accept them, even though he or she cannot recall them.

The interplay between remembering and repetition through behavior represents the polarities of analyzing and activities that are contrary to analysis. Repetition serves as a resistance, but when it is directed toward the analyst, it can be understood as an example of the repetition compulsion.

Even though transference can be a resistance to analytic progress, it is necessary in order to bring transference feelings into the treatment so that they can be analyzed. Even though repetition constitutes a similar resistance, it must be brought into the transference interaction as the repetition compulsion in order to be resolved. Freud summarized this interplay of resistance and analytic work as follows: "It cannot be disputed that controlling the phenomena of transference presents the psychoanalyst with the greatest difficulties. But it should not be forgotten that it is precisely they that do us the inestimable service of making the patient's hidden and forgotten erotic impulses immediate and manifest. For when all is said and done, it is impossible to destroy anyone *in absentia* or *in effigie*" (Freud 1912a, p. 108).

The *repetition compulsion* is both a childhood adaptive pattern—though it often appears to be self-destructive—and an intrinsic quality of instincts (see Chapter 2). The child needs to repeat a traumatic event in order to master it, to convert a position of passive vulnerability into active mastery. For our patients, it is a maladaptive pattern because it is frequently self-destructive. When it expresses itself in actions toward the therapist, it has become incorporated into the transference.

Working through also leads to states of higher ego integration and so is a structure-promoting experience. In the analytic relationship, both structural organization and the resolution of intrapsychic conflict begin early in the analytic relationship. At first, improvement depends more on the background of the holding environment, or the therapeutic alliance as Zetzel (1956) called it, than on the foreground of the interpretative interaction.

Talking to a sympathetic, calm listener is in itself a structuralizing experience that helps resolve conflicts. Thus, the analytic setting promotes organization, even though it is also the vehicle that simultaneously allows regression and disorganization. Although patients are encouraged to be spontaneous and not to structure their thoughts, the verbalization of feelings and the recall of memories and experiences occur in a sufficiently coherent manner, so that they serve as communications that the analyst can understand as belonging in a specific context. Gradually, as patients keep free associating, the material will develop certain repetitive patterns that the analyst will recognize, but most likely the patients will not be aware of them.

In fact, some analyses consist of a seemingly endless repetition of the same theme. For example, I have seen many patients, both men and women, who constantly complain about their spouses, and this can go on for many years without any changes in the material or the patient's attitudes. What slowly evolves is a connection between these persistent and rigid current orientations and similar patterns in the distant past. The present is often an adult replica of a past relationship, the patient's repeating a relationship with some significant person in the infantile world. This is an example of the repetition compulsion.

It is often uncanny how faithfully the present recapitulates the past. I can cite examples of wives of alcoholic husbands who complain vociferously of how they are mistreated, even beaten by cruel and indifferent husbands who are irresponsible, poor providers, sadistic, and unfaithful. These wives lament their fate, but the few wives I have seen in treatment did not leave their husbands. Paradoxically, the marriage endures unless for some reason the husband stops drinking and reforms (see Giovacchini 1958). In this instance, the wife may begin to drink excessively.

This is a repetitive pattern, as can be deduced from the patient's background. The parents of the wife of the alcoholic have had an almost identical relationship with each other as the patient has with her husband. Her father has usually been a brutal alcoholic, and her mother has remained, on the surface anyway, a passive, long-suffering victim.

To illustrate how close the present is to the past, I cite the example of a patient who was repeating to an astonishing degree with her husband her mother's relationship with and attitudes toward her husband. The patient's father and husband both were raised in impoverished circumstances. Each aspired to recognition and wealth, and they were ruthless in their pursuit of success. Both achieved their purpose, but they were so relentless and single-minded that they neglected their families, leaving their wives to raise their children.

The similarities between the patient's family and her parents' family even extended to its composition. They both consisted of four children, two older sons and two younger daughters in the same age sequence. The oldest sons in both families had been diagnosed as schizophrenics and had been institutionalized on and off for long periods of time. The other children all had serious problems; some were drug abusers and alcoholics, and those who were married were unhappy with their spouses.

My patient had resolved that she would not lead the self-sacrificing, humiliating life that her mother had. She had vowed that she would never put up with a husband who ignored her and had innumerable extramarital affairs. Yet, she now admitted that she found herself in exactly the same circumstances. She had identified with her mother to the extent that the role she assumed determined her total orientation toward the world. She was desperate and unhappy and complained about her husband's behavior, but it was clear that she could not leave him. In turn, he was furious at his nagging wife, but he made no effort to separate or get a divorce. It was obvious that they were tied to each other by constricting, neurotic bonds.

These patients are fairly frequently encountered in psychoanalytic practice. Usually it is the wife who seeks treatment, and the all-pervasive, marital relationship can be understood as a manifestation of the repetition compulsion. My patient was repeating the traumatic constellation of the parents' marriage and identifying with her mother's masochistic position in her current relationship with her husband.

In treatment, as was the case with my patient, the transference eventually involves the repetition of a masochistic pattern. The therapist represents both the husband and father, invoking accusations of not caring about the patient, not understanding her needs, and being interested in and fond of other patients at her expense. These complaints, which sometimes intensify to the status of a verbal attack, may evoke disturbing countertransference reactions. Nevertheless, regardless of the analyst's feelings, the patient's material is relatively easy to understand once the transference is dominated by the repetition compulsion. This can be considered the beginning phase of the working-through process, and so the analyst must survive this transference state. The patient's material and the analyst's responses are essential ingredients of the curative process.

Working through is not a unilateral process. The analyst's countertransference feelings can either initiate or delay the process of resolution. Through transference projections, therapists are equated with important persons from the patient's past. They have a definitive role within the framework of the repetition compulsion. They must accept that role and yet not participate to the extent that the patient either demands or expects. Therapists' countertransference orientations determine how much they will use their feelings to understand the unfolding of the repetition compulsion or, if those feelings become disturbingly intense, how much they precipitate behavior toward the patient that makes the transference feel as if it is a part of the patient's reality.

Valenstein (1983) discussed several categories of psychic functioning dealing with sensory and motor responses. According to him, working through involves the action system, meaning that as insights lead to states of higher ego integration, they cause alterations in the action system that may change some behavioral patterns. This often occurs in the treatment setting, sometimes indicating progress and other times disrupting the working-through process. The latter type of behavior is usually called acting out.

Reality-adapted behavioral change is a consequence of working through, whereas acting out is considered a therapeutically counterproductive resistance. These distinctions, however, are difficult to make and are not necessarily absolute.

The analytic setting causes the patient's material to structuralize sufficiently that definitive patterns emerge. These patterns organize themselves under the pressure of the repetition compulsion, with the analytic setting acting as a catalyst. The analyst often reacts, because of evoked countertransference feelings, in a fashion that is consistent with the role projected onto him, as the transference dictates. If the therapist's feelings overwhelm his objectivity, then the treatment will be at an impasse. As discussed, Freud imposed the rule of abstinence, demanding that patients suppress certain types of behavior he felt created resistances and impasses. He admitted, however, that some actions can be valuable because they bring "a piece of life" into the treatment. Still, it is extremely difficult to distinguish actions that will be beneficial from those that will be harmful.

Giving in to certain instinctual impulses by seeking to gratify them can be considered acting out, whereas other types of behavior cannot. Other types of behavior refer to complex action units, including many facets of the psyche in which executive and integrative ego systems operate in a judicial, superego-controlled, reality-adapted fashion. Id impulses are also involved, but they do not express themselves as directly as in acting out. Nevertheless, despite secondary-process taming, primary-process elements may erupt as the repetition compulsion gains momentum and brings the past into the present transference context.

Patients suffering from characterological problems have difficulty in achieving a balanced view of the external world and in constructing structured and integrated ego boundaries. The movement from the internal to the external world has occurred in a defective fashion. In treatment, as part of the working-through process, the course of development is reversed, and the repetition compulsion can be reenacted in the transitional space (see Chapter 3). This is best illustrated with clinical examples that contain delusions, as delusions involve radical alterations of the external world. Examples of psychotic patients often highlight processes that occur in the psychoanalytic treatment of less-disturbed patients.

Feinsilver (1980) wrote about transitional play as being essential to the treatment of some patients. The example he used was of a schizophrenic woman who had delusions of an influencing machine similar to the one Tausk (1919) described in his classic paper. She believed that Feinsilver manipulated parts of this machine in order to torture her. When she accused her therapist of maltreating her, he humorously responded that he was being paid to cause her anguish, that this was what he was supposed to do. The patient must have understood that he was stating that he was making himself available for her projections. He was also conveying that he dealt with them in a playful manner, taking them out of the realm of grim reality. The patient responded by being amused and intrigued with his response, and this helped her considerably in understanding that she needed her projections and so was able to experience them in a nonanxious setting.

Delusions vary in their tenacity and disruptiveness. Some delusions are so fixed in patients' minds that they nearly replace reality. Other delusions are more loosely organized and allow elements of the current reality to enter them. These I have called *transitional delusions*, and they often are experienced as amusing rather than grim.

One patient believed that various ancient philosophers and poets would periodically visit him. They usually came after he had been reading their works, and they simply continued the discourse the book had started. He felt flattered because of their attention and believed that he had learned enough from them to write fairly good poetry. In other instances, he developed delusions characterized by megalomania and direct communications with God. I concluded that this was an example in which a transitional delusion degenerated into a typical delusion as the patient's psychopathology dominated.

In treatment, working through changes the direction of the transitional delusion on the pathway to a psychotic organization. Aberrant impulses and parts of the self that have contributed to delusional replacements of reality are brought back into the transitional space, where they are subjected to psychic operations characteristic of that mental area. For example, Feinsilver's (1980) banter with his patient helped convert a grim delusion into a subject for playful scrutiny.

A paranoid patient who had benign auditory hallucinations offers another example. He had become extremely paranoid about me, and during a particular session, he emphasized how afraid he was of me. He was convinced that I was being paid a vast sum of money by the Mafia to pick his brains and destroy his mind. He meant "pick his brains" literally, as if I were going to open his skull and drive an ice pick into his brain. He was very angry and frightened to the point of panic. Quite spontaneously, I asked why the Mafia should have to pay me anything to pick his brains when that service was included in his fee. As first, he was astonished, and then he chuckled and finally laughed. He replied that I really enjoyed my work, and I countered by stating that working with him was very instructive and that I was learning a lot. He was greatly pleased, and his previous fear, anger, and suspiciousness disappeared. Instead, he started reviewing the context of both malignant and transitional delusions with an impish glee, as evidenced by such questions as "Did I really do that?" or "Did I really have such bizarre thoughts and beliefs?" He was amused by the intricacy of his ideas and fascinated with their primitive qualities and gaps of logic.

This was a crucial session because we could return to some of the questions he had raised and to conclusions during later phases of treatment. He continued having delusions that emphasized the paranoid transference, but they were not as intractable or as intense and they no longer disrupted him or our relationship. My response indicating my willingness to be the recipient of transference projections allowed him to join me in what I consider to be the transitional space and to examine our interaction. I conceptualize our location as the transitional space because the atmosphere became light and playful and involved with illusions and fantasies rather than delusions.

Winnicott (1953, 1967, 1971) believed that the transitional space is an area in which the infant exercises omnipotent control and develops into the space that contains play, illusion, and the "cultural experience." From the viewpoint of omnipotence, children, at first, have the illusion that they are the source of their own nurture. Later, they enjoy this illusion, and this is when the capacity for organized play develops. From these transitional activities, ego boundaries become integrated, and the child begins to recognize and relate to the external world. In working through, something comparable happens. The distorted external world is moved back into the transitional space where it is reacted to and evaluated in terms of illusions and play rather than delusions. The transference–countertransference aspects of the repetition compulsion are examined in this area, and the consequences of the understanding gained from this examination significantly affect how the external world is perceived and reacted to.

There are some similarities between this back-and-forth movement and Freud's ideas (1911b) about the production of the paranoid psychosis. Freud postulated that patients first experience an end-of-the-world phenomenon in which libido is withdrawn from the external world and put back into the psyche. If this is sufficiently intense, the world will be decathected to the extent that it no longer exists for the patient. This happens in catatonia. In regard to the paranoid process, Freud believed that the delusion represents the libido's return to the external world, an attempt to repair the "rent" with reality caused by the initial withdrawal of libido (see Chapter 5).

Freud did not hypothesize in terms of a transitional space, but his concepts definitely involved back-and-forth movements between the inner and the outer world. The transitional space can be viewed as the factor that determines whether the movement from one space to another will lead to psychopathology or to psychic structure and integration as a consequence of successful working through. Basically, this means that the reality created by psychopathological distortions becomes part of a fantasy system and as Freud repeatedly pointed out, fantasies have a tremendous impact on the achievement or disruption of psychic equilibrium.

The interaction of play and illusion in the transitional space does not imply frivolity, though humor and wit may be involved. It is, nevertheless, a serious exchange between patient and therapist aimed at bringing grim distorted reality into the realm of the intrapsychic. This is the essence of the working through process, and it is relevant for nonpsychotic as well as psychotic patients.

Nondelusional patients also distort reality in that they externalize the infantile ambience. The repetition compulsion is in many subtle ways reenacted in the external world. In this sense, it is similar to a delusion because it replaces a common reality with a private reality. During an analytic relationship, the patient to some extent shifts his infantile focus from the external world to the analytic ambience. Once the patient can view these constructions in a transference–countertransference frame of reference, both the analyst and the patient are working in the transitional space.

Working through transforms concrete actions and attitudes into metaphors. My patient was an extreme example in that he believed that I would actually pick at his brain. When we discussed our relationship as if it were a fantasy, he could think of picking brains as a learning experience. This happens with other patients in less discernible ways: what the patient believes becomes a conjecture and an abstraction.

In summary, the treatment process is not unilateral. The analyst's responses can either set it in motion or impede its development. In some instances, both the patient's and analyst's psychic survival are at stake.

I have emphasized the spatial qualities of working through and have located the process in the transitional space. This is the area of play, fantasy, and illusion, a space that is the seat of creativity, and, as Winnicott (1967) stated, "the location of the cultural experience." The psychoanalytic experience is a creative endeavor in which concrete and grim orientations and actions are converted into metaphors that, in turn, expand the operations of perceptual and executive ego systems. How some of these changes occur is still very much a mystery, but the treatment of patients fixated at primitive mental states is a fruitful area that will help us fill in many gaps in our understanding.

Part IV

EGO PSYCHOLOGY AND OBJECT RELATIONS THEORY

Chapter 8

FROM ID PSYCHOLOGY TO EGO PSYCHOLOGY

As stated in the preface, the integration of ego psychology into classic psychoanalytic theory has not yet been achieved. To some extent, I have attempted to effect such an integration in both theoretical and clinical chapters as I compared various basic psychoanalytic hypotheses with current views about the same areas of observation and exploration. At best, this comparison may represent upward extensions, that is, slight modifications because of the acquisition of new clinical data, and the establishment of a continuum. For the most part, however, there is no conceptual sequence; rather, there seems to be a quantum jump between early and later formulations.

In psychoanalysis, the acquisition of new data does not lead smoothly to the creation of new theoretical approaches. As Freud himself demonstrated, a patient can be observed and then evaluated from an id-psychological perspective, or the same patient can be formulated on the basis of characterological features and defects based on an ego-psychological model (see Reichard 1956).

Eventually, even within a fairly coherent and internally

consistent theoretical system, the investigator will become aware of psychic processes that are awkwardly positioned in the conceptual framework as clinical data clamor for explanations. This is not necessarily new clinical data. It may be that because of increasing experience it has become familiar rather than entirely new. The same can be said about psychic processes. As discussed in Chapter 2, Freud was faced with just these dilemmas as he increasingly recognized some of the awkward weak spots of the topographical hypothesis. Regarding clinical data, he could not explain the unconscious sense of guilt within a topographical framework, and, as for psychic processes, there was no comfortable place to fit repression into such a scheme. He thus needed a new model that placed the ego in the forefront, even though it has to serve three masters (the id, the superego, and the outer world). Thus, he constructed the structural hypothesis which represents the formal beginning of ego psychology. I state formal because previously Freud had written articles about character structure, concentrating primarily on description since he had not yet pulled together a new model of psychic anatomy.

With the structural hypothesis in mind, analysts seem to be encountering different clinical phenomena. Instead of patients' concentrating on sexual inhibitions and avoiding material that would evoke painful guilt feelings, they complain about how alienated they feel and that they cannot cope with the exigencies of the outer world. Most of the patients we see today are concerned with problems of adaptation. They have problems concerning self-esteem and are confused as to who they are and where they belong in this world. These difficulties are related to the ego's executive system and the identity sense which is embodied in the self representation (see Chapter 3). Undoubtedly, the manifestations of psychopathology are, to some measure, related to sociocultural factors, but I believe that our theoretical set also contributes to how patients present themselves or, more precisely, to how we view them. Of course, we do not create the patient's symptoms, but our selective receptivity encourages them to reveal specific parts of themselves.

Freud emphasized the oedipal model, and at times it

seemed that he forced his patients into a Procrustean bed, an impression received from accounts of his analyses written by his analysands (Bertin 1982, Kardiner 1977). In these reports and in Freud's own writings as well, he focused exclusively on incestuous wishes and the subsequent castration anxiety (see Freud 1909a, 1909c). Within the last several decades, clinicians have been unable to maintain this same focus, as our systems include structural factors in addition to hypotheses about conflicting drives and superego retaliation. Patients seem to be emphasizing material that can best be explained in terms of ego subsystems, their integration, and how they are synchronized with each other.

ORIGINS OF THE EGO

In Chapter 3, I compared Freud's ideas about the development of the ego as a differentiation of the id and Hartmann's theories about an undifferentiated id–ego matrix. I shall explore Hartmann's concepts further, as many analysts consider him to be the leading advocate of ego psychology. His theories about the ego and its construction and functions have influenced analysts in the United States, particularly in the East, for many years, although recently his ideas have received considerably less attention.

Hartmann's work represents a transition from a classical id psychology to current theories about character structure and psychopathology. With his colleagues Kris and Lowenstein, Hartmann wrote a series of papers in the early volumes of *The Psychoanalytic Study of the Child* that stressed ego operations but were based on a conceptual model that relies heavily on psychoeconomic principles (see Chapter 2) and dual-instinct theory that constrasts libidinal and aggressive impulses (see Chapter 3). They discussed the ego concept in terms of fluctuating levels of psychic energy and balance between libidinal and aggressive impulses. Contemporary ego concepts, however, do not subscribe to the psychoeconomic hypothesis, as instincts and the id are not considered to be the sources of psychic energy. Furthermore, the balance of instinctual forces that occurs with the polarity of sexual and aggressive instincts is not a prominent feature of most current orientations.

Earlier, Hartmann (1939) published an extensive monograph, *Ego Psychology and the Problems of Adaptation*, that covered numerous aspects of ego development and its pivotal role in determining how the psyche will adapt to both internal needs and external demands. Hartmann viewed the psyche at the beginning of development as consisting of an id–ego undifferentiated mass that underwent separate lines of development, a departure from Freud's view.

In essence, Hartmann was postulating two different types of psychic substance, id and ego, intermeshed with each other in a primordial vat. As they structuralize further during the course of development, they become separated from each other. The id and ego become stratified, the ego representing the upper levels of the personality as they interface with the outer world. As a model of development, this progression seems awkward.

It is even more difficult to understand the structuralizing and differentiating processes. The ego's progressing from an unstructured to a structured state makes sense, but how does the id structuralize? The id differs from the ego in that it represents unstructure. So if it acquires structure and organization, then it is no longer id but has become ego.

Hartmann's ideas are similar to Kohut's (1971) separate lines of development. Kohut confined his formulation to the development of narcissism and object relations. He believed, as Hartmann did, that these were independent lines of development, a dual-track theory. Here, too, there seems to be considerable conceptual confusion. If we define narcissism as ego libido, then Kohut's dual-track theory must mean that ego libido develops separately from object libido. This means that there are two types of libido, for if there were just one type, how could there be separate lines of development? At least, Hartmann postulated different instincts attached to the id and ego which in some measure must affect the qualitative elements of the energy attached to them. The discrepancy in Hartmann's formulation, as stated, involved id structure, a contradiction in terms and a confusing oxymoron. Kohut created his contradiction in regard to energic issues.

No surviving energic hypothesis has proposed two types of energy. More pertinent, a separate line of development for object relations and narcissism ignores any reciprocity between the two processes. It does not eliminate the possibility of reciprocity, but it does minimize its relevance as a developmental impetus. If it included a mutual influence of ego libido and object libido, a dual-track theory would be superfluous and meaningless. Furthermore, how can narcissism, which refers to energizing the ego, be an aspect of psychic development? The ego develops and so do its functions such as relating to external objects, but how does a process, a direction of psychic energy, undergo development and differentiation? This is another conceptual fallacy.

Freud's developmental scheme makes sense and is compatible in many respects with biological postulates and the findings of neonatologists (see Chapter 2). Specifically, he stressed a line of development that proceeds from the global to the discrete, and for the most part, he confined this progression to psychic structure rather than energy or mental processes. An example of psychic structure is the formation of the ego from an undifferentiated id. The influence of external objects as a protective barrier is involved in development from the beginning, and the significance of object relations in the acquisition of psychic structure becomes more important as higher levels of psychic integration are reached.

Freud's formulations stress that the external environment is involved in the acquisition of psychic structure and differentiation. In optimal circumstances, a positive feedback sequence is established. As the ego achieves higher states of integration, it is able to deal with external objects in a more sensitive, sophisticated, and intimate fashion. Thus, the psyche is enabled to derive greater satisfaction, make meaningful identifications, and generally profit from increasingly gratifying relationships. The psyche acquires further structure and develops efficient adaptive techniques that in turn lead to a continued expansion and depth of involvement with helpful and caring persons. With psychic trauma and psychopathology, the reverse often occurs, and instead of this benign sequence, we witness a negative feedback, a vicious circle that frequently leads to withdrawal from the external world.

Hartmann's ideas (1952, 1953) about the origins of the ego do not, by any means, exclude the role of the surrounding world, but they do not emphasize it, either. In this regard he is similar to Melanie Klein, although I would expect that most of Hartmann's followers would strongly disagree. Hartmann emphasizes that there is an innate developmental progression that is begun at birth, starting with a differentiation and structuralization of the ego and id. He mentioned that this development must occur in the context of an average expectable environment, but he did not elaborate on the processes between the inner and outer worlds.

NEUTRALIZATION

Hartmann and his followers discussed psychic progression and structuralization in an energic frame of reference (Hartmann 1950, 1955, 1964; Hartmann et al. 1946, 1949). They postulated a refinement of energy from raw, unbound primary process energy to tamed, bound secondary process energy, which is referred to as *neutralized energy*. The confluence of sexual and aggressive drives somehow leads to the production of neutralized energy.

The process of neutralization is dependent on the combination of sexual and nonsexual instinctual urges. The nonsexual component neutralizes the sexual. Similarly, the eroticism of the sexual instinct tames the destructive components of the aggressive instinct. The blending of the sexual instincts and the nonsexual aggressive instincts produces neutralized energy that is in the service of adaptation and psychic structuralization. The desexualization of a sexual instinct has been called sublimation, and it is difficult to understand how Hartmann's formulation differs from Freud's in this regard. The deaggression of the aggressive instinct, however, represents a new theory.

From a theoretical viewpoint, the concept of neutralization can be appraised in the same way that the psychoeconomic hypothesis in general has been (see Chapter 2). It can also be challenged as to whether it helps explain psychic development and the construction of various ego subsystems that determine how the psyche relates to and copes with the external world. For example, how can two primary process–dominated instincts, such as sexual and aggressive instincts, combine and create a secondary process–oriented energy? The confluence of two primitive elements produces a structured, integrated, reality-adapted secondary process energic current. This is a gratuitous production of structure from nonstructure, a reversal of the second law of thermodynamics. Although Hartmann probably did not intend to contradict such a fundamental law, he implied that the combination of basic instincts is a structuralizing process occurring in a closed system.

These types of conceptual dilemmas will be created if we remain exclusively in an energic frame of reference, that is, if we deal only with concepts of psychic energy and exclude other intrapsychic processes and functions. Primary process operations can acquire secondary process accretions and refinements by being subjected to integrative experiences. These can be helpful and gratifying interactions with benign and caring persons, or in a well-developed ego, higher psychic operations can spontaneously elevate the primitive parts of the personality. The latter regularly occurs in creative activity. In other words, the acquisition of higher forms of energy cannot be an isolated process; it has to be explored within the broader framework of the total psychic apparatus. The participation of object relationships and the influence of the outer world cannot be ignored.

PRIMARY AND SECONDARY AUTONOMY

Hartmann believed that some structures in the ego are independent of the drives and that many structuralize further without the participation of instinctual elements. He was referring to functions such as sensory modalities, motor coordination, and other activities related to synthesis, differentiation, and integration. Perception, apperception, and cognitive capacities all are within the purview of primary autonomy.

Kris (1950) stated that although these are autonomous activities, they can nevertheless become instinctualized and thereby lose their autonomous status. This is most striking when an ego function becomes eroticized and drawn into the sphere of intrapsychic conflict. Hysterics offer good examples of how an ordinary motoric activity such as walking can become eroticized and lead to the symptoms of astasia-abasia (a condition characterized by a lack of balance and inability to walk). The sensory apparatus is also frequently involved, as evidenced by patients suffering from hysterical deafness or hysterical blindness.

There are many clinical situations that support the concept of the instinctualization of ego functions. They can be understood as regressive experiences in which a secondary process controlled adaptation regresses to earlier instinctual modes of functioning. But in order to regress, there has to be a fixation point to which psychic elements can return. According to Hartmann's ideas about primary autonomy, there is no such fixation point. Nevertheless, in treatment, clinicians frequently discover traumatic episodes that are responsible for disturbances of development and fixations to primitive—that is, instinctually dominated—adaptive patterns. These fixations are the outcome of psychopathology, and it can be argued that emotional disturbances disrupt the maintenance of primary autonomy.

The concept of primary autonomy once again forces us into the framework of a dual-track hypothesis. It dictates that there are separate lines of development for instinctual elements and ego structures that have been designated as autonomous. The former are initially powered by primary process–oriented energy, whereas the latter undergo maturation being fueled by neutralized energy. This introduces a developmental schism and implies that development occurs in a fragmented fashion. That is, various parts of the psyche move along as if they were isolated entities and not interdependent.

During the early stages of growth, maturation and emotional development have been conceptualized as a hierarchical continuum, a differentiation from a global amorphous state to better-differentiated, discrete ego subsystems that are coordinated and integrated with one another. This hypothesis has proved to be clinically useful and has helped us understand regressed states and certain forms of severe psychopathology in which the patient seems to have lost most of his integrative capacities. Some very disturbed patients behave as if their egos are primitive and amorphous and totally lacking in autonomous ego structures. They seem to be operating with only a minimum of secondary process psychic operations and are characterized by lack of control and nonfunctioning regulatory mechanisms. Paradoxically, although many of these patients are fragmented and use splitting defenses (see Chapter 6), they display a unified psychic apparatus.

Instead of conceiving the psyche as being compartmentalized from the beginning, it is more consistent with both clinical and developmental data to view higher, sophisticated, secondary process psychic structures as representing upward extensions and differentiations from an initial unstructured foundation that is malleable and responsive to stimuli and nurture. On the pathway to emotional maturation, there may be a series of nodal points and stages from which structures emerge as separate from one another, and then, perhaps at a higher level, they once more coalesce. These structures may be associated with developmental spurts and serve as an impetus for accelerated growth. These are the *psychic organizers* to which Spitz (1959, 1965) referred.

The developmental process is complex and still largely unknown. It may be, as Hartmann indicated, that during the neonatal stages some psychic structures are better developed than others are. This is undoubtedly the case with the sensory system, but as has repeatedly been proved, even such modalities as vision must develop (Herrick 1956) through interactions with the outer world. Although neonatologists (Brazelton 1963, 1980, Emde 1980, Klaus and Kennel 1982) are discovering that infants are capable of making fairly sensitive perceptions and discriminations much earlier than had been suspected, there is still increasing differentiation throughout the course of physical and emotional maturation. If neonates do not receive proper stimulation, elemental functions such as vision, hearing, and speech will not develop normally. This has been experimentally confirmed, especially with the visual apparatus, with laboratory animals. For example, monkeys who have been blindfolded since birth, later when the blindfolds are removed, will not be able to see in an organized sense. Some are functionally blind. There have also been natural experiments with humans, situations in which later in life vision or hearing has been restored. Sometimes they see only flashes of light rather than well-constructed images, and sounds and speech have to be learned, never achieving the same ordinary clarity that the average person enjoys.

Hartmann's concept of primary autonomy may have some value at a descriptive level as we observe the development of psychopathology. Even under the most traumatic infantile circumstances, most children learn how to hear, walk, talk, and be continent. Nor are these functions usually lost during regression. This would indicate that there is some degree of independence between some sensory and executive ego systems and other functions such as reality testing, the maintenance of control over instinctual forces, and the coherence of thought processes.

We know, however, that even these seemingly autonomous or, better stated, stable and resistive functions can succumb if the trauma is sufficiently intense. Spitz (1945) wrote about infants whose physical needs were taken care of but who received no emotional sustenance. These children were in an orphanage and placed in cribs that were in small cubicles enclosed by walls that did not reach to the ceiling but that were high enough that the child could not see over them. The children were fed on schedule but not otherwise related to, except to be changed occasionally and dressed with fresh clothes. These children never smiled, talked, or even cried. In fact, most of them failed to thrive and were dead by the end of the first year. Some of the details of their fate are vague, but it is certain that the trauma of emotional deprivation had a disastrous impact on all of their psychic and physical functions. In this instance, there did not seem to be any autonomy of physical and psychic needs. They both proved vital to survival, making it difficult to separate them along different developmental lines.

There also are examples of severe regression that involve

these receptive and communicative modalities. These are extreme situations in which the patient is incontinent, babbles incoherently, and seems to have lost his capacity for thinking and reality testing, indicating once again that it is clinically more appropriate to view various ego functions as part of a total integration that in psychopathology has broken down or has developed defectively.

The concept of secondary autonomy is easier to integrate with clinical and developmental data. Hartmann believed that certain functions or adaptations can be deinstinctualized and thereby achieve an independent, autonomous status which he labeled secondary autonomy. During treatment, the psychic processes involved in the conflict, may become, so to speak, disengaged and thus enhance the activities of the ego as it relates to both the inner and the outer world. This is often experienced as the overcoming of a compulsion or inhibition.

For example, a middle-aged male patient with a handwashing compulsion was obsessed with cleanliness and regulated his life with fixed schedules, compulsive neatness, and order. He had to wash his hands 50 times a day, and he showered at least 3 to 4 times a day. This took up so much time that as a consequence, he led a very constricted life. He was afraid to go to parties or to attend meetings of more than two persons. Entering a room with closed doors was particularly awkward because he had a phobia about touching doorknobs. Thus, his life was a combination of obsessions, compulsions, phobias, and inhibitions.

This patient's analysis was long and difficult because, as one might expect, of his rigidity. Nevertheless, he made tremendous improvements, and this was reflected in his behavior. In the beginning, he had been nearly paralyzed from a functional viewpoint. He had not been able to work because of his phobias and compulsions. After several years of treatment, his compulsions had become much less intense, and he was able to get a job and do rather well. Over a period of time, as his analysis continued to progress, he became adept at his work and was considered a valuable employee.

His behavior did not radically change, however. He still washed his hands frequently and, on occasion, showered more than once a day. He continued to be neat and orderly, perhaps to an excessive degree, but his activities did not have the same urgency and driving qualities that they did when he first sought treatment. Indeed, instead of letting them constrict his life, he was able to use these character traits in his work. That is, they were transformed from a liability to an advantage.

Because his behavior was modulated and reality-attuned, it can be conceptualized as having acquired a secondary process orientation. It was no longer controlled by primary process dominated drives and led to activity rather than inhibitions and passive withdrawal. In a sense, his behavior had become independent of the primitive layers of his personality, indicating that it had achieved a degree of autonomy.

From a theoretical perspective, secondary autonomy is difficult to distinguish from other, seemingly similar processes. If we assert that this patient's compulsive acts and inhibitions were the outcome of conflicting sexual impulses, then divesting them of their instinctual sources means that they have been desexualized. This would then be a description of sublimation (see Chapter 6). As I stated earlier, a neurotic symptom can become a useful adaptation. If he had been a surgeon, this patient's hand-washing compulsion might not even have been recognized as a compulsion and would have lost its idiosyncratic significance as it became part of his daily work routine.

From an energic viewpoint, secondary autonomy cannot be distinguished from neutralization and sublimation. It can also be confused with reaction formation, which, as discussed in Chapter 6, is almost impossible to separate from sublimation. Sublimation, neutralization, and primary and secondary autonomy are abstruse concepts with little clinical utility.

Hartmann's writings are remarkable in their absolute theoretical purity. He did not discuss clinical material, thereby forming his hypotheses without the benefit of supporting data. Nevertheless, he introduced a frame of reference, that of ego psychology, that has become extremely useful to modern clinicians, especially those interested in extending psychoanalytic treatment to patients whose psychopathology can be understood principally as structural problems in an ego-psychological context rather than on the basis of drives in an id-psychological frame.

DEPENDENCE AND INDEPENDENCE

In classical psychoanalytic theory, dependency is considered to be an attribute of the oral drive, a derivative and manifestation of early pregenital impulses (see Chapter 3). Although the infant is both physically and emotionally dependent throughout the course of development, this orientation is considered to be an attribute confined to orality. As it continues to persist during later developmental stages, it is supposedly the oral component of the total drive organization that is responsible for this character trait.

Independence has been given a similar drive status, but it belongs on the other end of the psychosexual spectrum (see Chapter 3). It is the outcome of the attainment of genitality that follows the resolution of the Oedipus complex. From the viewpoint of id psychology, independence is a sophisticated elaboration of the genital drive.

Obviously, these formulations are incomplete. They ignore chronological and sociocultural factors that cannot be overlooked when discussing dependence and independence, which clearly represent a relationship with and attitude toward emotionally significant persons. They cannot be placed in the unilateral context of psychosexual drives. Furthermore, if we remained exclusively in such a frame, the child would achieve independence during adolescence, which may happen in some cultures but not in ours.

As clinicians continue to work with dependent patients, they are becoming increasingly aware that they are dealing with an orientation that reflects the total ego organization. The influence of oral fixation is acknowledged, but the integration and efficiency of ego executive systems in an adaptive context also become significant. The personality's dependent core, analogous to the psychotic core that many British psychoanalysts emphasize, needs to be recognized in our clinical formulations. We must do so because of the types of patients that seek our help.

As I have frequently noted, patients do not often present discrete symptoms. Rather, they complain about their adjustment to the external world; that is, they stress their adaptive failures. They often feel alienated, are unable to function both in their work and socially, cannot fathom the purpose of their lives, and do not know where they belong or their goals and purpose. These are characterological problems (see Chapter 9) and are difficult to conceptualize on the basis of id–ego conflicts, as Freud did.

The dependent orientation is often foremost in many of our patients. It may not be, however, immediately evident. It represents a character trait that is the outcome of defective ego development, but whether a character trait or an intrapsychic conflict, the psyche can construct defenses to protect the patient from painful and crippling feelings of inadequacy. These are overcompensatory maneuvers associated with specific syndromes. Thus, independence in these instances also represents an ego orientation, but it is a defensive superstructure defending against a fundamental core dependency.

Patients who are primarily dependent and those who use compensatory independence present vastly different clinical pictures, although their basic personalities are similar in many ways. An extreme example of a dependent patient was a woman in her early forties who suddenly became a widow. She had lost her parents several years ago, and shortly before seeing her therapist, her husband was killed in an airplane crash. The shock generated by this unexpected disaster stunned her to the degree that she could no longer function. She could not carry on her everyday activities, which were minimal, and became bedridden. She would lie in bed day and night, moaning, groaning, and screaming and literally tearing out and eating her hair. A friend forced her to see a psychiatrist and had to practically carry her to his office. She did not resist having a consultation; she simply did not have the energy to get there on her own. She had no resources and had regressed to such an infantile state that she could not do anything, even feed herself.

The patient's family had been moderately wealthy, and she had been given all the material luxuries. Her father had been a business tycoon and was never at home. Her mother apparently had been a helpless, vulnerable woman who could not take care of the house or children. During the patient's childhood, her mother frequently spent months at a time in a local sanitarium. Her absence made no practical difference, however, as the care of the children and house was left to a fairly sizable group of servants. The mother had her own personal maid who took care of her as a nurse might an invalid or handicapped patient.

The patient followed her mother's dependent pattern. She could not do anything for herself, nor did she try. Her environment at that time could support her dependency because it was able to provide for all of her concrete needs. She had never felt any deprivation, but she was aware of having been a sad little girl who was easily frightened of new situations and uncomfortable in groups. The only longing she could acknowledge was that she missed her father, as he was seldom home, and when he was, he paid very little attention to her, being preoccupied with either his business or his mistresses.

Despite her timorous, always-anxious demeanor, she was quite popular in school. Possibly this was because she was unusually pretty, and her tense and insecure manner added to an aura of attractive delicacy and fragility. She always had a group of companions around her. She, however, attributed her popularity to her family's prestige and social standing. Her parents were not the richest in the community, but her mother came from a wealthy and famous family. Her father was also well known and had done extremely well financially.

In treatment, she lamented how unhappy she had been throughout her life and how helpless, inadequate, and ugly she felt. She stressed her neediness and feelings of misery and loneliness. The maids that looked after her caused her to feel frustrated. She wanted to be close to her father and eagerly sought his attention, but according to the patient, he turned his back on her. She pleaded, begged, and cajoled for his affection, but he had no time for his bothersome little daughter.

The patient married a man who was in many respects similar to her father. From fairly modest beginnings he had made giant strides in the financial world and was respected and feared by his colleagues. He was also reviled because he was unscrupulous and merciless in his business negotiations. He was pleased that he had married into such a famous family and that his wife had social graces and was attractive. This helped him achieve success, but other than using his wife to fulfill his ambitions, he had little personal regard for her. Like her father, he devoted himself exclusively to his work and his mistresses. His wife knew this, but she clung to him, begged succor, and slavishly gave in to his every whim. Sometimes he was brutal in his rejection of her.

In the analysis, it became obvious that this patient was repeating her childhood in her adult life. She had identified with her mother, and her husband was clearly a father surrogate. Why she persisted on such a self-destructive course is still not entirely known, although such masochistic behavior is commonly encountered as the outcome of a sadistic superego or an attempt to master infantile traumas through the repetition compulsion (see Chapter 7). It also became apparent that her helplessness, vulnerability, and dependence represented a mode of relating, an adaptive style, that permitted her to satisfy inner needs and manipulate those around her.

This patient had not shown much reaction to the death of her parents. This is understandable, inasmuch as she had practically an identical relationship with her current family as she did with her parents. When her husband died, however, her world collapsed. She reacted as if she had been deprived of her only support. Although in reality, her husband nearly ignored her, he had nevertheless become the symbol of her salvation. She was emotionally dependent on him in the same way that she relied on her wealth to sustain her. She could hire people to take care of her and furnish her with companionship.

The patient was never alone. She carefully planned her days and overscheduled herself. She had every weekend planned 18 months in advance and knew where she would be on New Year's Eve for the next 5 years. She also knew the schedules of several close friends so that she could get in touch with them whenever she needed them. Most of the time, she traveled and dined with an entourage.

She remained in treatment for over 15 years, having formed, as might be expected, an intense dependent relationship with her analyst. Although there were many extreme regressions characterized by moments of total helplessness, she never required hospitalization. She had occasionally begged to be hospitalized, but the analyst dealt with these supplications from a transference perspective. He was able to demonstrate to her how she was able, though perhaps painfully, to control relationships through her dependency. It was interesting and, to some extent, puzzling that despite her clinging, she was able to draw people to her. In part, this was because of her wealth and prestige, but many of her companions seemed to genuinely like her. As her treatment progressed, she became less frenetic about her dependency, and at the end of therapy, she had gained considerable autonomy, although she continued to rely heavily on others to manage the practical aspects of her life. She remarried, but she trusted her lawyer and used him as a confidant more than she did her husband.

Dependency in this patient manifested a generally infantile character. It also had specific meanings that pertained to her identifying with her mother and her father transference to her husband, but it was primarily the outcome of an executive ego style. Indeed, much of the psychopathology that clinicians see is characterized by a dependent ego organization or defensive superstructures designed to defend against the vulnerability that accompanies such an infantile orientation.

Many patients vigorously repudiate any dependent feelings and overtly or covertly assert that they do not need to rely on any situation or person. On the surface, they appear to be the total antithesis of the woman just described. In treatment, their autonomous attitude proves to be a facade, a false front superimposed on the surface of a personality that is marked by low self-esteem and a lack of organization. Such patients, however, manage their lives and relationships in such a way as to maintain this facade.

These personality types are commonly seen and have introduced us to groups of patients that were not often seen in the past. Women suffering from anorexia nervosa, for example, seem to be appearing, if not exactly in epidemic proportions, at least in numbers that have attracted the public media and have been the source of discussion in many panels and forums. These patients are also being extensively studied in numerous research projects. It is still not decided whether this is a new form of psychopathology or a syndrome that is, like many others, coming out of the closet. Some patients with eating disorders are ashamed of their symptoms, particularly the sequence of bulimia and vomiting, and so have avoided revealing them to family, friends, or physicians. In the past, perhaps because of inner resistance and shame, anorexics did not seek professional help, but because of more liberal and receptive current attitudes, women, and a smaller group of men, are less timorous about revealing the manifestations of their psychopathology. There is still considerable resistance, but it is related to the general defensive character of a personality that needs to disavow all needs.

The psychopathology of patients suffering from eating disorders is highly complex, and few homogeneous factors have yet been discovered that would give us a uniform conceptual basis for a specific syndrome. An ego-psychological perspective, however, permits some generalizations. For example, it is conceded that patients suffering from anorexia nervosa have an infantile personality. Rather than openly displaying their dependence, as occurred with the patient just discussed, these patients vehemently deny any dependent needs; in fact, in extreme cases, they deny the existence of any needs. They construct a false self that has the appearance of total autonomy, often to a delusional extent. Particularly, they often believe they have complete control of their inner world and no need whatsoever for the outer world.

These anorectic patients are obviously orally fixated but are not conflicted, in the ordinary sense, about oral instincts, as described in the context of psychosexual theory. Rather than a conflict about needs, there is a denial of having any requirements that they themselves cannot fulfill. For example, if they have no nutritional requirements, they are omnipotently self-sufficient. A person who does not have to eat is remarkably free and has the exhilarating sense of freedom and control, as is depicted in elusive dreams (see Chapter 4). True, most anorexics are not elated or do not radiate a feeling of freedom because they have not been able to attain what to them is an ideal state. Their psychopathological adaptations have failed to achieve their purpose, and we usually see them in a state of psychic disequilibrium in which some of the underlying depression, helplessness, and misery have emerged. Psychopathology founded on omnipotent control cannot help but fail and can lead only to a tenuous and precarious equilibrium.

The question that naturally arises is what factors are responsible for the ego's openly displaying its infantile dependent organization and for constructing a defensive superstructure driven to deny the existence of any needs, as happens with anorectic and other severely disturbed patients. How the drives are experienced, that is, the degree of pain attached to inner needs is the chief determinant as to whether the ego can acknowledge needs or has to deny them. This situation, however, has to be understood in terms of the ego's reactions rather than as the outcome of intrapsychic conflicts, as is customary in an id-psychology context. The orientation of the personality's higher levels creates painful responses to instinctual pressure. Indeed, these responses can be so intense that they threaten the ego's integrity and cohesiveness.

PAINFUL INNER NEEDS AND THE SENSE OF ALIVENESS

Patients who find their inner needs to be intensely painful have to construct defensive superstructures, the most elemental—as occurs in anorexia nervosa—leading to their total denial. Other patients are filled with a pervasive sense of deadness, which blunts the pain of inner agitation and permits them, at one level, to interact with the external world. This deadness is a protective device, an ego adaptation designed to maintain a defensive equilibrium. Within the ego's repertoire of controls is something similar to a governor or a thermostat that regulates the intensity of feelings produced by the id forces and drive impetus. The ego modulates them and, by so doing, keeps them manageable.

Flarsheim (1975) offered an excellent example of a patient,

a young woman in her twenties, who illustrated how she used a feeling of deadness to protect her from painful needs. She also suffered from anorexia nervosa and, on several occasions, was on the edge between living and dying. Not only did her body lack vitality, but her demeanor was equally lifeless. She was depressed, a depression that was accompanied by listlessness, motor retardation, and apathy. What seemed to be withdrawal was not typical of the overtly painful reactions of the ordinary depressed patient. She was sad, however, and often saw herself walking around and being enveloped by a large cloud of sadness. The patient reiterated that her life was painful, miserable, and incomprehensible.

The history of this patient's background helps us understand why she had to construct a protective layer of deadness, why she had to develop an ego that generated minimal amounts of energy just to barely activate perceptual and executive systems. This was reflected in her low-keyed approach and view of the external world. As a newborn baby she was told that she had been fussy and unsoothable. Her mother hired a nurse who had a reputation for making infants manageable and well behaved in several months. Her method was simple and apparently effective. The child was fitted with special gloves so that she could not suck her thumb. The nurse responded to her immediately when it was evident that she needed something, but she did not satisfy the need manifested. For example, if the baby were hungry, the nurse would change her diaper. Conversely, if she needed changing, she would be fed.

Thus, the patient perceived her inner needs as painful and disruptive. These needs are, however, basic to survival. A person's sense of aliveness is the outcome of experiencing needs and satisfying and fulfilling relationships with caretaking and loving persons who nurture, protect, and gratify. This patient had had just the opposite experience, in that living, as it was represented by her internal requirements, had become unbearable. Consequently, she had to deny totally the existence of any need or to deaden it. This feeling of deadness had become an ego adaptation to enable her to tolerate life. Paradoxically, feeling dead represented a method that kept her alive or that made life minimally tolerable. To achieve such a feeling of deadness—a mood state that is more primitive than is the melancholia of depression—it has to be incorporated in a relationship in order to make contact with the external world. To succeed in establishing a sense of aliveness, a feeling about the self has to be directed to the world one lives in. This most often occurs by forming a state of fusion with another person who uses feelings of deadness in a similar fashion. This patient also had such a relationship. It appeared to be a living relationship, but it was supported by the subjective sense of being dead. The latter was hard to describe beyond simply being a state of existential void.

Another patient, a middle-aged woman, reported a fantasy that involved her therapist. Her analyst had ruefully commented that psychoanalysts were becoming an extinct species and someday would be exhibited in museums. Undoubtedly, he had a depressed core, but it made it easy for the patient to fuse with him. She conjured up an image in her mind of a stuffed figure of her therapist sitting in his usual chair and of a similarly stuffed specimen of herself lying on the couch that she used. Both of them were displayed in a glass exhibit case in a natural history museum. They looked quite real and very much alive, but they were dead, the products of a taxidermist. By being dead, they could be preserved forever in a surface state of aliveness. Her analyst would survive as a therapist, but to do so he needed a patient. She felt that her sense of existence depended on her being a patient, that is, finding a role that would help her construct an identity and make her life bearable. According to this fantasy, their existence was determined by the connection established through the treatment relationship. From the patient's viewpoint, her attachment to the therapist involved fusion mechanisms and represented a pathological symbiosis.

Fusion mechanisms operate both in ordinary development (see Chapter 3) and as psychopathological defensive adaptations. As the aforementioned patient illustrated, it is a basic adaptation in that it preserves a fundamental sense of aliveness. This is a global achievement that entails the total personality rather than specific segments, as occurs with most defenses against instinctual impulses (see Chapter 6). The integration of the whole ego is often maintained by a relationship with a person in the external world with whom the subject has fused.

This represents a defensive and frequently a precarious equilibrium (see Chapter 9).

SPLITTING MECHANISMS AND SPECIAL TREATMENT PROBLEMS

Splitting, dissociation, and fragmentation, as discussed in Chapter 6, are defensive mechanisms that refer to the same group of phenomena. These terms have been used interchangeably and need not be differentiated from one another because in the psychoanalytic and psychiatric literature they are usually treated as if they are synonymous. Clinicians have emphasized their adaptive functions and role in psychopathological development. Dependence and independence have been discussed as attitudes and ego orientations as well as modes of relating to the external world. Fragmentation is a psychic mechanism manifested in general attitudes toward reality and relationships with emotionally significant persons. Focusing on such ego mechanisms is the outcome of clinical necessity. The patients we most frequently encounter are best conceptualized in an ego-psychological frame of reference and invariably cause us to consider the role of dependent attitudes and dissociative mechanisms (see Chapter 6 for clinical examples of patients who use splitting mechanisms).

The ego-psychological context has widened the significance of ego mechanisms such as fragmentation as they contribute to psychic stability and determine various characterological constellations. Kernberg (1975, 1980) and Klein (1952), as discussed in Chapter 6, wrote about the role of splitting processes in keeping good internal objects separate and protected from bad internal objects. Kohut (1971) introduced the terms *vertical splitting* and *horizontal splitting*. When dealing with processes that affect psychic structure, it can be helpful to introduce spatial concepts.

The point remains, however, as to whether metaphors or constructs such as horizontal or vertical offer a new understanding of splitting mechanisms. Vertical splitting creates a picture of an ego that is split down the middle from top to bottom, similar to cutting the corpus callosum, separating the left from the right brain. As Freud (1938) put it, various parts of the psyche are separated from the main ego current, and this is easy to conceptualize spatially as the two parts move away or become unconnected from each other. Specifying this fragmentation as vertical, however, merely sharpens our image of the process.

Distinguishing vertical from horizontal, however, is significant because it distinguishes fragmentation from another process, repression. Horizontal splitting is not really splitting, even though Kohut asserted that it was. That is, segments of the ego cannot be visualized as split off from one another when we use the spatial metaphor or horizontal cleavage. If we draw a horizontal line through the ego which, by definition, must be placed at the upper end of the psychic apparatus, then we are separating the upper from the lower levels. The lower portion, which has little access to the upper portion, then contains more id than ego, and the opposite is true for the upper portion. This is the model Freud constructed for repression rather than fragmentation, as repression belongs to a higher level of ego sophistication.

Fragmentation is an ego process that uses ego elements of varying degrees of differentiation. If the less-differentiated parts of the psychic apparatus are included in the splitting processes, then we will be, according to the structural hypothesis, introducing the id. This leads to a contradiction because it is impossible to conceptualize the id as being fragmented. Fragmentation is not something that happens to the id; it is an intrinsic quality, of the degree of organization. Again, by definition, the id is characterized by its lack of differentiation and organization. Because it is relatively amorphous, it does not contain discrete and separate parts. To fragment assumes a degree of organization in which previous wholes have been broken down into component parts or in which psychic structures that have been synthesized and coordinated with one another begin to function independently.

Fragmentation is therefore a process that can occur only at ego levels. Winnicott (1954) distinguished between unorganization and disorganization, unorganization being a nonpathological state characteristic of early stages of development, and disorganization signifying a regressive process from a previous state of differentiation and cohesive unity. When that unity is disturbed, the ego once again achieves organization—not as a cohesive whole, but within its component parts. Then we are dealing with the process of fragmentation.

Although the spatial model has some use, it is conceptually erroneous to juxtapose a horizontal beside a vertical axis. The concept of splitting does not lend itself to such simplistic treatment. It is similar to attempting to explain three-dimensional anatomy with stick figures, as they would simplify to the point of extinction. The subtlety of ego processes, likewise, is lost in the oversimplification and conceptual confusion of the metaphor of horizontal splitting.

Ego psychology pertains to the relationships among various psychic structures as well as to psychic functions. Rather than connecting a function with its instinctual base, the ego-psychological approach focuses on the operations and functions of ego subsystems as they interact with one another and with the external world. As we move back on the developmental scale to primitive ego levels, structure and function become increasingly intertwined and difficult to separate (see Chapter 3). It is such early ego states, representing either a developmental stage or psychopathological regression, that use splitting mechanisms to maintain their emotional balance. Thus, splitting occurs in the functional realm, and we can postulate that there is a fragmentation of function as well as structure. This not only means that how the ego adapts to the outer world can be subjected to fragmentation but also that its capacity for receptivity can be affected. The reactions of the ego to the ministrations of caretakers, for example, may be pathologically distorted.

This type of functional impairment has important clinical and technical implications. Because the operations of splitting defenses may be carried to a psychopathological degree, the psyche is faced with conflict, but it is not between opposing instinctual impulses, nor is it restricted to the intrapsychic realm. Rather, a splitting of functions has created an ego conflict that is manifested in its relationships toward the outer world. In treatment these difficulties are reflected in the transference, as these patients face problems that emphasize their inability to profit from potentially positive experiences. They do not view their analysts as whole persons but focus narrowly on some segment of their personalities that is colored by their projections. From a therapeutic perspective they present unique technical problems (see Chapter 7).

For example, a single schizoid young man in his middle twenties had been in treatment for about two years. He had started therapy somewhat idealizing his analyst, having read some of his works and feeling quite positive about them. Gradually, his attitude changed to the degree that he completely reversed his orientation. After two years of treatment, he was critical and disparaging, and the interpretations that he previously found helpful he saw now as useless and meaningless.

In the meantime, he had started reading the works of another analyst who was on cordial terms and even collaborated with his therapist. Without telling his first analyst, he went to see his colleague but did not tell him that he was currently in treatment. He set up a schedule with the second analyst, and they began seeing each other. He did not, however, want to discontinue with his first analyst, and so he kept his other treatment secret. Nevertheless, to his first analyst he praised his second analyst, and to his second analyst he disparaged his first analyst.

After approximately six months, as his hostile feelings continued to escalate, this patient announced his intention of terminating his relationship with his first analyst. He also confessed that he had been seeing someone else and intended to remain in treatment with him. He did not see any point in having two analysts, especially as the first analyst was useless and perhaps even harmful and the second analyst was skilled, understanding, and sensitive to his needs. On this note he stopped going to the first analyst and devoted himself solely to the second analyst, whom he had obviously idealized.

Being exclusively in treatment with one analyst, however, did not help maintain the idealization. On the contrary, after a few months, he began finding fault with the second therapist and rediscovering virtues in his first analyst. This intensified to the degree that he stopped seeing the second analyst and returned to his first analyst. He was once again accepted for treatment, and as might have been expected, the positive transference once again changed into a negative transference. The patient predictably started talking about another switch of therapists. The first analyst tried to convince the patient that he was acting out a pattern in which he was interchangeably splitting the therapists into good and bad objects, as they represented different facets of his self representation. The analyst viewed it as an inability to sustain ambivalent feelings in which both love and hatred can be directed toward the same person. He was implicitly urging his patient not to act out by terminating and starting anew; rather, he was encouraging him to work it out with him. The patient understood the logic of what he had heard but still insisted on leaving.

This time, however, the second analyst refused to see him and recommended that he work out his problems and remain where he was. The patient was disappointed at being rejected and so went to see a third therapist with whom he remained for two weeks. All in all he saw 18 therapists and had consultations in other cities as well as in the place he lived. He finally settled on a relatively young analyst who has been able to keep him in treatment for two years with the help of an older colleague whom he consults as a supervisor.

This patient is interesting from many different viewpoints. Mainly he represents a treatment problem, and it is still difficult to ascertain what would be the best approach. Should the first two analysts have allowed him to seesaw back and forth between them, or should he have been refused treatment and forced to remain with the first analyst? These are questions that cannot yet be answered. Still, apart from technical considerations, is there something about the ego structure of this and similar patients that might give us some clues to the treatability or the limits of treatability?

Such defensive and primitive dissociative ego processes occur in patients who had a traumatic maternal relationship. Often, the mother–infant bonding was defective or nonexistent. The nurturing interaction suffered an early trauma which had a splitting impact, inasmuch as it is in itself a dissociative phenomenon. This means that the caretaking person related to the infant in a fragmented fashion. A notable example is the nurse who responded to needs other than what the child was experiencing.

The patient just discussed had had a traumatic maternal relationship. He focused primarily on two interrelated elements: his mother's propensity to create chaos and her unpredictability. Somewhat similar but not identical to the nurse who "cured" children of their fussiness, this patient's mother related immediately to his physical needs. She was unable to soothe him or to provide a tranquil and comfortable environment that would make the nurturing experience pleasurable. There was no synchrony between nurture and soothing. What should have developed into a cohesive experience never achieved the degree of unity that would cause the child to feel secure and develop the trust and confidence that his needs were enjoyable and capable of being gratified.

At these early neonatal stages, there is a dissociation of functions that interferes with the later acquisition of coherent structures. This situation is similar to the fixations of psychosexual development discussed in Chapter 3. The ego is fragmented from the beginning of its development. Consequently, later ego systems are relatively isolated from one another, but they have, nevertheless, acquired some degree of unity. In regression, the fragmenting process becomes prominent and often achieves the status of an adaptive modality. This is identical to what I stated in Chapter 6 regarding the construction of defenses and symptoms. The most advanced ego position is vulnerable and, in the face of stress, regresses to its fixation point. Rather than regressing to a particular earlier ego state, with the patients I have just discussed, it regresses to a former and familiar functional mode, meaning that various functions and needs, such as nurture and soothing, operate independently of one another. This is far from being a compatible state, but the patient can survive by splitting those functions that ordinarily operate as a unit.

Fragmentation is a method by which the ego can protect itself from disintegration. Many patients' fears pertain to the terror of psychic dissolution. Such patients are overwhelmed by existential crises, and the defenses they construct are designed to hold them together, to prevent total structural collapse. To

use fragmenting processes to protect the ego against disintegration seems paradoxical, but it does represent an effort to control
the chaos that would otherwise dominate the clinical picture. In
a sense, the dissociative process slows the rapidity and intensity
of the psychic dissolution, and as it achieves a defensive equilibrium, it establishes a state of *organized disintegration*. In these
instances, breaking the ego into functional units prevents further
disorganization; that is, the regressive process is controlled and
halted. A partial state of disorganization achieves sufficient stability and cohesion to hold the ego steady, so to speak, reaching
an equilibrium that permits it to maintain varying amounts of
coordination within the psyche and between the inner and the
outer world. This may be a precarious adjustment, but it is an
adjustment in which some sense of identity and autonomy is
preserved.

A dissociated ego is frequently characterized by bizarre
behavioral constellations, which are often best described as
paradoxical reactions. The latter are due to a splitting of both
sensory perceptions and motor responses, as I have already
described. They are usually related to the patient's orientation
toward soothing and nurture. As was discussed in Chapter 3,
some persons can be soothed by situations that most of us would
find disruptive, such as noisy, smoke-filled discotheques and
other jarring settings. These nonsoothing circumstances are
calming for patients who use splitting mechanisms, because
they are recapitulations of early soothing interactions. What the
child experiences initially as agitation later becomes encapsulated in the ego sphere and acquires a defensive purpose. By
means of this encapsulation, this fragmented ego protects the
rest of the ego, "the main ego current," as Freud (1938) called it.
The fragmented ego directs its activities to the outer world
which, in turn, absorbs its agitation as it is incorporated into the
ambience. This is possible because soothing has become dissociated from nurturing, an example of fragmentation at the receptive level.

Elsewhere (Giovacchini 1979a, 1986) I described how the
fragmentation of soothing and nurturing manifests itself clinically, in a patient who adopted a defensive stance against various segments of the external world. This patient was an adoles-

cent girl who had a vulnerable, dependent, anxious mother who had tended to overfeed her as a baby and handled her awkwardly and clumsily during the feeding. The baby was swung in a wide arc and literally thrown in the crook of her mother's arm as a bottle was shoved into her mouth. The mother felt that she had to be an active participant, which consisted of making clacking sounds and poking and pinching her baby with her free hand. It was no wonder, although the mother could not understand why, that the child soon exhibited signs of terror as mealtime approached.

As an adolescent, the patient had a recurring fantasy. She saw herself sitting in her locked automobile parked on a sheet of ice in her high school parking lot. Because it was reserved for faculty, students were not allowed to park there. She therefore was breaking the rules as she sat there nonchalantly smoking a cigarette, and her pleasure was enhanced as two burly, angry, and frustrated police officers vainly tried to break into the locked car. She found it amusing that they were unable to do so.

This patient was generally known as a distant and aloof person who did not permit emotional intimacy. Most of her peers either disliked her or were irritated by her. The latter group seemed to be aware of her basic neediness and felt sorry for her, but they felt frustrated because the patient would not allow them to help her. As discussed in Chapter 3, they absorbed her inner agitation, as was illustrated by her consecutive experiences with two young psychiatrists.

In treatment, she reenacted her recurring fantasy. She would sit in the consultation room, her legs provocatively crossed, blowing smoke in the therapist's face and saying nothing. Both of her successive therapists felt intensely agitated, an agitation that was finally transformed into sexual excitement. Each became so alarmed that he had to discontinue her treatment, and the patient, each time, left with the feeling of having vanquished him, an exhilarating feeling of triumph. In her own way, she enjoyed these experiences just as she enjoyed getting drunk and noisy discotheques. These all were soothing situations.

Thus, for this patient, the fragmentation of a disruptive experience that, at one level, was meant to be soothing was split off from the rest of the psyche. This split-off portion then manipulated the outer world and erected an insulating barrier that overcompensated for the poor protective shield, Freud's (1920) *reizschutz*, that the patient's mother supplied. At the same time, the patient succeeded in transmitting her agitation to concerned persons who were trying to make emotional contact with her.

To pursue this interplay between structure and functioning in primitive mental states as it is involved in splitting mechanisms, let us return to the young man who moved back and forth between two therapists. This patient is probably an example of a person who could not deal with whole objects. Apparently, he had to split objects into good and bad and alternately assigned these roles to two therapists. The therapists represented alternately soothing and nurturing modalities. As an object, the bad therapist became associated with adequate, if not pleasurable, nurturing. What on the surface appeared to be reactions toward objects in analysis proved to be based on early interactions characteristic of the mother–infant relations. The patient treated each therapist as if he represented either the nurturing or the soothing aspect of his mother. Because these two qualities had become dissociated from each other at the beginning of his life, he was not able to bring them together sufficiently to direct them to just one therapist.

Generally, fragmenting processes involve the splitting of functions, internal and external objects, and parts of the self. These are not separate and distinct activities: There is a hierarchical continuum between function and structure, the latter being subjectively perceived as belonging to either the self or the object world, topics that will be discussed in the next chapter. The dominant ego state in the transference context will determine whether the functional or the structural element is in the forefront. Usually, the patient deals with the therapist as a person, attributing particular good or bad qualities to him or her, but with further regression, the traumatic elements of the mother–infant interaction emerge as the patient reexperiences the pain and disruption of inadequate mothering. In regression the analyst is transformed from a person into a function.

As Freud constantly stressed, id psychology was a conceptual base that enabled him to construct a rational therapeutic system. Although some psychoanalysts would debate various parts of the treatment procedure, especially in view of the types of psychopathology that confront them today, most would agree that within the id-psychology framework, Freud's recommendations regarding treatment are consistent with his theoretical model and that his basic premises, such as psychic determinism and interpretation of the transference, have stood the test of time (see Chapter 7). The patients just discussed in an ego-psychological context raise technical questions that may lead to some modifications of technique that, in my opinion, would not make significant inroads into these premises. The predominant use of splitting defenses creates, as I have described, bizarre clinical situations that are generally unfamiliar to most analysts. For example, the two analysts drawn into the various fragments of their patient's ego were in a quandary. They did not know whether they both should treat him or insist that he remain with just one therapist and work out his problems in just one therapeutic setting, advice that is frequently given to patients who seek consultation because they are not satisfied with how their treatment is progressing.

Because they do not accept them for treatment, most analysts have not had much experience in dealing with patients whose splitting mechanisms cause them to seek another therapist or move from therapist to therapist. That is, analysts reject such patients as being untreatable, and from a psychoanalytic viewpoint, they often are correct. Nevertheless, these patients suffer and seek help—often from psychoanalysts because despite their resistances, they still have faith in the psychoanalytic process and method. This is an interesting paradox that we occasionally encounter in primitively fixated patients who operate principally on the basis of splitting mechanisms. According to Freud's criteria, they are not good candidates for analysis, but sometimes they pursue it, seeking a therapist who will accept them. If they succeed, they may adapt well to the treatment process, or they may create situations similar to those presented.

We have to ask ourselves whether we have helped create a situation that we view as an intense resistance and sometimes an unresolvable impasse. Perhaps if the therapists had accepted the patient's demands—in this instance, not trying to prevent him from seeing another analyst but instead indicating a willingness to see him if he chose to return and acknowledging his right to see whomever he pleased—the treatment setting might have been preserved. The first analyst could interpret the infantile roots and resistive aspects of the patient's intentions to terminate treatment, but without trying to stop him. As stated in Chapter 7, interpretations represent insights, not prohibitions. With two therapists involved, the therapy had degenerated into a struggle to keep the patient from wandering off. Perhaps nothing therapeutic could have been accomplished with these analysts because of the tense atmosphere that had been created. Indeed, the patient seemed to settle down with the younger analyst he later saw.

The training of a psychoanalyst implicitly stresses that analytic treatment is strictly a one-to-one relationship. Having another person participating in the treatment is inconceivable in a classical analysis, as the transference would be diluted or contaminated. If a patient cannot accept an exclusive relationship with the analyst, then he cannot be analyzed. I thus ask again whether the patient's unanalyzability is not partially iatrogenic.

For example, a 30-year-old man also could not direct all of his feelings toward one therapist. Unlike the patient just reported, he did not want to leave the "bad" analyst. Instead, he had found two analysts and alternately idealized one and denigrated the other. He insisted, however, on continuing his treatment with both of them, realizing that his feelings would change, and so he wanted both of them to be "on hand." The analysts were uneasy about this arrangement. They conferred with each other, with the patient's permission, and decided that he would have to choose one of them. The patient protested, but both analysts remained firm.

Trying to abide by their decision, the patient chose one but after two weeks changed his mind and switched to the other analyst. This pattern repeated itself two or three times until finally the therapists once again had to take a stand. They told him that if he left one of them, he could not ever return. Fearing that the analysts were intractable, the patient became frantic.

After one session with one analyst, he called up the other therapist to make an appointment and promised that he would not
again try to change back. The therapist relented, but again after
only one session and in a state of mind bordering on panic, the
patient called the analyst he just left for a consultation to review
his situation. This time, he was refused. The patient pleaded and
protested, but he was not given an appointment.

Finally, the patient found a third therapist who apparently
was not concerned about the patient's propensity for seeking
more than one therapist. In fact, shortly after beginning treatment he went to a colleague of the third therapist, who was
willing to see him whenever he wished. His primary analyst, as
he was called, did not object, taking the attitude that the patient
had the right to see anyone he wanted to. This arrangement
worked out well in that the patient and therapists were comfortable, and after six months, the patient discontinued, on his own,
his therapy with the second therapist and continued with his
primary analyst.

The first pair of therapists, as they now realize, were trying
to force the patient to do something that he was incapable of
doing. They were, in a sense, demanding that he give up his
chief defensive modality, splitting. Whatever idealization and
denigration meant, this patient was not able to direct all of his
feelings toward one person. He had not yet reached the developmental position that would allow him to construct an ambivalent relationship. His ego was not sufficiently unified and cohesive for him to interact with the outer world without
fragmenting external objects. Thus, the two therapists were
insisting that he behave in a fashion that went beyond his level
of emotional development and integration.

Some patients who use dissociative defensive adaptations
do need two therapists to relate to different facets of their
psychic apparatus. A woman in her early thirties, for example,
required a therapist to whom she related on the basis of higher
ego levels and experienced the vicissitudes of erotic intrapsychic conflicts in the transference. She also saw another therapist
with whom she fused and whose feelings she tried to incorporate in order to develop feelings of her own. In this way, she was
using her therapists to relate to different levels of her personal-

ity, separating the more advanced ego states from the primitive stages. This separation is not exactly an example of fragmentation in the technical sense, which asserts that the fragmented components belong to the same level of organization. Still, this patient lacked a cohesive ego organization, and even with her primary therapist who, as a transference figure, represented higher psychic levels, she displayed the manifestations of splitting. She directed some of her feelings about him and others toward emotionally significant persons in the external world. This also happened with the other therapist, with whom she fused. She also attached herself to others from whom she expected "to learn how to feel." By relating to each therapist on the basis of different psychic levels, this patient projected parts of her self and her infantile expectations into the analyst in a fragmented fashion. Rather than splitting the whole ego, she dealt only with parts of the ego. This, however, must occur generally with splitting mechanisms because such primitive processes are characteristic of early developmental phases and regressed ego states.

The classical analyst could ask whether a treatment relationship with multiple therapists can be considered to be psychoanalytic treatment. That is, if psychoanalytic treatment is defined by only one therapist, then obviously the therapy of the patients discussed here cannot qualify as being psychoanalytic. If, on the other hand, we focus on the process and the technique of each therapist, there are no discernible differences between what occurred in their treatment and in more traditional treatment.

CONCLUDING PERSPECTIVES

As is true of id psychology, ego psychology can also be viewed as a continuum that includes classical formulations at one end and novel structural considerations at the other end. Ordinarily, psychoanalysts limit the term *classical* to Freud's formulations, but this is a difficult perspective to maintain because Freud, as we have seen, modified and changed some of his seminal ideas, particularly those involving the seduction hypothesis (see Chapter 2) and anxiety theory (see Chapter 5). Nevertheless, it is misleading to think of formulations in the realm of ego psychology as classical.

Still, there are great differences between Hartmann's relatively early ideas about autonomy, adaptation, and the neutralization of drives, for example, and recent theories that focus on ego processes, psychic configurations, and orientations. Hartmann's ideas, as in id psychology, continue to revolve around the drives. In later theories, however, instinctual elements, although not ignored, recede farther into the background. Ego psychology has caused clinicians to focus on interactions with the external world rather than to view reality as a constant that becomes involved with various elements of the psychic apparatus that can be considered to be variables or as inconstant. In a sense, classical concepts seem to deal with intractable, immutable factors, such as instinctual impulses and certain exigencies of the environment, as they react to one another in an adversarial fashion. By contrast, recent ego-psychological hypotheses concentrate on variability in both the internal and the external world. These may lead to either enhancing or destructive consequences as the two worlds interact with each other.

Hartmann emphasized adaptation, but as Freud did, he remained almost exclusively in the intrapsychic realm. The psyche must adapt to reality and learn how to cope with its exigencies. Hartmann, however, did not pay much attention to reality itself. The early ego psychologists simply accepted the existence of reality as a generality and did not define the specificity of ego and outer-world interactions, conflicts, or mutuality (see Freud 1924a, 1924b). Thus, adaptation was discussed as an ego process that was principally derived from instinctual needs rather than as a technique of coping with specific age-appropriate or age-inappropriate demands of the surrounding milieu as the psyche moves from the infantile environment to the adult world.

The purview of psychoanalysis is the intrapsychic realm, which is the frame of reference around which all interactions revolve. To so-called nonclassical ego psychologists, however, the characteristics of the external world have to be understood as factors that determine how psychic structure is acquired and adaptive techniques are constructed. The ego patterns of dependency and the use of dissociative mechanisms can be traced to particular facets of early transactions with the infantile milieu. These processes are studied mainly from an intrapsychic perspective, but external influences also are considered, especially as they are incorporated into the ego sphere. The maternal relationship, as it succeeds or fails in nurturing and soothing, must be understood in detail and in terms of the mother's psychopathological needs as she relates to her child. This represents an object relations perspective, which is essential to the study of both character development and psychopathology, topics that will be examined in the next chapter.

Chapter 9

CHARACTER STRUCTURE AND OBJECT RELATIONS

In order to understand character psychopathology, the concept of character has to be defined. Although there are not, as yet, precise diagnostic distinctions outlining distinct forms of structural psychopathology, there are, nevertheless, certain guidelines that will enable the clinician to roughly separate various clinical conditions that are commonly encountered. These guidelines are not sufficiently developed to constitute a nosological system (see Chapter 5) nor can they be until psychoanalysts have reached a consensus as to what is meant by character or character structure. This has been minimally discussed in the context of the structural hypothesis (see Chapter 2), but it requires further elucidation if we wish to separate various forms of characterological defects and psychopathology.

DEFINITION AND CLASSIFICATION
OF CHARACTER

Freud discussed character in various contexts. He expanded his ideas about psychosexuality in describing character types that are the outcome of fixations on particular psychosexual stages, such as oral (1905b), anal (1908), and phallic characters (1923b). He postulated that these patients develop certain styles and traits that are extensions of symptomatic defensive patterns. Ego-dystonic symptoms become converted into ego-syntonic traits that represent basic adaptive or characteristic patterns of coping with both the inner and the outer world. For example, obsessive-compulsive patients' anality expresses itself in impulses to soil and smear feces. These patients institute defenses such as reaction formation to defend themselves against such feelings. This causes structural alterations in the ego that shape the executive system's *modus operandi.* In this instance, the defense of reaction formation leads to a propensity for orderliness and perhaps frugality and stubbornness (see Chapter 2), orientations that become attached to all adaptive interactions and are manifested as character traits. This is an example of how a psychodynamic conflict can cause structural changes at higher levels of the psychic apparatus, characterological configurations that affect how a person relates to the outer world.

Freud also discussed "character types" met in psychoanalysis (1916) which are differentiated from one another according to how they relate to the external world. For example, he wrote about patients who "are wrecked by success" or about narcissistic character types who need to be loved and admired. These patients' lives are marked by repetitive patterns of behavior that are often frustrating and self-defeating.

As mentioned in Chapter 8, Freud was interested in how the ego expressed itself in terms of adaptations and object relations as it relates to the outer world. He first mentioned the attachment to external objects when he juxtaposed ego libido alongside object libido (see Chapter 2 and Freud 1914c). In this regard, Freud can be considered to be the first object relations theorist, although admittedly, he did not concentrate on the external world nor investigate the reciprocal qualities of the interaction between the psyche and the external world.

Many clinicians and theorists use the terms *ego* and *psyche* interchangeably. The psyche includes all levels of the psychic apparatus, whereas ego refers to a particular portion of the mind with specific qualities and particular functions. Still, there is some advantage in thinking of the whole psyche, rather than just a segment of it, interfacing with the external world. As id, ego, and superego contribute to the structure of character and determine its perceptions and adaptations, the whole person is involved with the environment in which he must survive and grow.

Thus, character can be conceptualized as a *supraordinate* structure that incorporates elements from all levels of the psyche. It is an organization that signifies the style of relating rather than the substance or method of interaction. Character connotes structure only loosely, as it cannot be assigned a specific location in the psyche. It is the outcome of a conglomeration of ego subsystems, but it is multifaceted and is also shaped by superego dictates and driven by id impetus. Our model of the mind is an abstraction, but the concept of character is a higher-order abstraction that has proved to be clinically useful.

As frequently noted, the psychopathology most often encountered can best be explained as being based on defects in characterological organization rather than on id–ego conflicts in a psychodynamic context (see Chapter 2). Gitelson (1958) was one of the first psychoanalysts to deal with ego defects as constituting a particular form of psychopathology, and he identified specific types of characterological constellations as being associated with them. This may have been the first attempt to define clinical entities that had not yet been included in psychoanalytic diagnostic classifications. Such patients' symptoms are not typical of those of the actual neuroses or the transference and narcissistic neuroses.

Gitelson explained a particular character type on the basis of an ego defect. Since then, many investigators have made the ego their central focus in clinical investigations. This in turn justified the construction of a specialized branch of psychoanalysis known as ego psychology, although, as repeatedly emphasized, the mind can never be investigated by dissecting only a portion of it and isolating it from the whole.

Some patients, Gitelson noted, seem to function quite well in a restricted environment. In fact, some of them are highly successful and may achieve considerable distinction and financial reward. If they are removed from what to them is a familiar and protective setting, they may emotionally collapse; that is, they may be overwhelmed by panic and become completely helpless and immobilized. Gitelson believed that such persons suffer from an ego defect that he called a *hypertrophied ego*, meaning that it is especially well adapted to cope with a milieu that others might find overwhelming. Therefore, removing these persons from that environment, really an arena, to more conventional and less trying surroundings makes their adaptive techniques inoperable. The ego is designated as hypertrophied because it has the strength, perhaps the superstrength, to function in a highly competitive world. It is, however, a limited, constricted, and rigid ego that can thrive only in a particular setting, as it lacks the flexibility to adjust to changes or to react appropriately to unforeseen events. I have described such patients as seeking an environment that resembles the infantile world with which they have learned to cope (see Chapter 3 and Giovacchini 1967), because it is in tune with their primitive defensive adaptations. The external world supports the ego's executive system, an interaction that preserves psychic equilibrium.

Patients suffering from hypertrophied egos have not been classified as a separate entity. Although such hypertrophied egos represent a character type, they are part of a psychic constellation that may vary considerably among different patients. Can we specify an axis to use as a reference point to classify patients suffering from character defects? As discussed (see Chapter 5), precise diagnostic distinctions are not particularly important to psychoanalysts, because they are more interested in psychic processes than in phenomenology, which is the basis of the current diagnostic system as described in the DSM-III. Still, as is true of the psychoneuroses and the psychoses, categories dividing different types of characterological disorders do help clinicians order their thinking and systematically observe their patients.

Because the concept of character depends on the qualities of adaptive techniques as they determine relationships with the outer world, primarily object relationships, the axis we are seeking might refer to how effectively or ineffectively the psyche adjusts to the surrounding environment. It is clinically useful to construct a hierarchy ranging from patients who have generally withdrawn from the external world and who are unable to survive on their own to patients who can adjust fairly easily. Gitelson's category of patients with hypertrophied egos would fit somewhere in the middle of this scale in that they can manage their survival very well but with an uncompromising rigidity. Other factors should also help us separate the various character disorders and place them in a hierarchy of psychopathology that involve differing degrees of ego integration. Ego integration is associated with specific developmental levels which also help establish how adaptive techniques are constructed and will function in the external world to obtain gratification of inner needs.

The variables used to establish a psychoanalytic nosology are also applicable to patients suffering from character disorders. In Chapter 5, I emphasized that psychoanalytic diagnoses do not depend solely on phenomenology, that is, clusters of behavior and specific symptoms. Rather, they are derived from several interlocking frames of reference, such as the level of developmental fixation, the specific intrapsychic conflict, and the defenses that are used to deal with the anxiety caused by that conflict. Within the framework of ego psychology, similar variables are used to determine types of characterological psychopathology, but because structure is in the forefront of pathological processes, there is a somewhat different emphasis. For example, intrapsychic conflict, though not ignored, is not used as much as an explanation as are other variables. Levels of emotional development are important to the studies of character disorders, but specific defenses that are manifested by discrete symptoms are not frequently encountered. Most of these patients do not complain of or manifest specific symptomatic patterns. Instead, they complain about how they are adjusting to their environment, where they are going, the purpose of their life, and where they fit in the scheme of things. They are afraid and feel alienated from society, indicating that they are not in harmony with the external world. The combination of fixation at an early developmental level and particular failures of adaptation are the principal variables that determine specific types of structural psychopathology and enable the clinician to classify these emotional disorders.

The broadest distinction the psychoanalyst makes is between the psychoneuroses and what have been loosely referred to as character disorders. The latter designation emphasizes psychic structure by referring to character, and the word "disorder" indicates that there is a defect in character structure, a structural problem. Under this rubric are included different but related types of psychopathology of varying intensity. Ego psychology has not yet been sufficiently organized, nor do psychoanalysts agree on how to label and formulate the various entities that comprise the character disorders. Most analysts would agree, however, that borderline patients and narcissistic personality disorders are important and common forms of psychopathology that involve developmental and adaptational failures (Kernberg 1975, 1980, Kohut 1971). Some clinicians (Boyer 1961, 1983, Giovacchini 1979b, Searles 1963, 1965) include the psychoses in the category of character disorders.

I have found that formulating a continuum of psychopathology based on the quality of object relations is useful for understanding patients and, to some extent, for anticipating transference development in treatment. From the primitive end of this continuum to that of the more advanced states, I have included the following emotional disorders: schizoid states, borderline states, character neuroses, and affective disorders (Giovacchini 1979b). These types of psychopathology are distinguished from one another according to their capacities to function in the external world and how they perceive and relate to external objects. This object relations axis is the central hub around which the various types of character organization can be clustered.

For example, *schizoid states* are fixated at prementational states of ego development (see Chapter 3). Such persons have what could be considered a minimum of psychic structure, and so their relationships with the external world are meager and impoverished. Their main defensive adaptation is withdrawal, and in treatment they avoid becoming engaged in the therapeutic relationship. In many respects, their environment seems incomprehensible to them, inasmuch as their sensory and executive ego systems are fixated at such a primitive level that it does not have sufficient organization and boundaries to perceive the nuances and relate to the complexities of the outer world. The psychoanalytic situation may, at first, appear beyond their capacity to integrate, and the therapist may feel that analysis is impossible because of the lack of transference. Still, in many instances, if the therapist realizes that the so-called lack of transference is in itself a transference phenomenon, in that the patient is dealing with the analytic situation in his characteristic defensive fashion, that is, schizoid withdrawal, it is possible to deal with it therapeutically. This is a defense transference, and if the patient is allowed to withdraw comfortably, he may eventually develop enough security to reveal other parts of the self.

The borderline states will be discussed in some detail in the next subsection because it deserves a separate focus. There are many controversial opinions about borderline patients. I include them here as part of a continuum and view these patients as having progressed slightly farther on the developmental scale than have the patients suffering from schizoid states. Borderline patients have moved up from a prementational phase to a somewhat amorphous but psychologically oriented ego organization. They have some adaptive techniques and do not use withdrawal mechanisms as extensively as do schizoid patients, but they do not function well because their adaptive techniques are not sufficiently sophisticated to deal with the exigencies of the external world. I cited clinical examples of such patients in Chapter 2 when discussing the adaptive hypothesis. Here, I shall only repeat the words of the patient who said that he lived in a world of calculus complexity but had only an arithmetic mentality to deal with it. By contrast, the schizoid patient does not even have an arithmetic mentality. In treatment, the borderline patient's dependency may be immediately manifest, and he may demand to be protected and taken care of. There are, however, many other possible reactions, and frequently these patients are suspicious and distrustful. They may doubt the analyst's constancy and competence, just as they doubt their own.

The next group is the character neuroses. These patients have complex adaptational patterns directed toward certain

segments of the external world. Gitelson's formulation of the
hypertrophied ego would apply to patients suffering from character neuroses, although not all patients with character neuroses
have hypertrophied egos. Many of these patients have not been
able to achieve an autonomous ego, and frequently in treatment
we discover that they are still fused with destructive maternal
imagoes. They may have constructed defenses against the effects (such as fear of annihilation and devastatingly low self-
esteem) of such a fusion. These are usually narcissistic defenses.
These patients protect themselves from a fundamental lack of
self-esteem and a frightening involvement with external objects
and avoid becoming engaged in intimate but terrifying relationships. Other patients suffering from character neuroses state
their inadequacies directly, and their anxiety is manifest. This
latter group are likely to complain of feeling alienated.

The affective disorders follow and are the last group of the
hierarchy I have outlined. These are the depressions that Freud
(1914c) considered to be one of the narcissistic neuroses, the
other being schizophrenia (see Chapter 5). These patients have
developed fairly sophisticated modes of adaptation and can
relate to external objects in an ambivalent fashion (see Chapter
3). Their internal object representations and their attitudes toward the self are ambivalent as well.

The clinical entities that I have just outlined are not generally accepted or understood. Indeed, there is much confusion
regarding classification, especially of the character neuroses and
borderline states.

Alexander (1927, 1961) many years ago used the diagnosis
of neurotic character to designate a group of patients who have
defective superegos and act out in an antisocial fashion. These
are the psychopathic personalities of the past and the sociopaths
of today. Psychopathic personality has a pejorative connotation,
however, and so the term has been dropped. I recall, however,
that some clinicians believed that *character neurosis* meant the
same as *neurotic character* and *psychopathic personality* and
therefore viewed such patients in the same negative light. There
are some sociopathic types that can be classified as having
character neuroses, but this does not mean that all character
neurotics are sociopaths or neurotic characters.

The term *character disorder* has also been used loosely and confused with the terms I have just discussed. Rather than being considered a general category separating a group of patients who display structural psychopathology from those who have psychoneuroses, it has been used as a diagnosis for a particular clinical entity. The same dilemma is found in id psychology, when clinicians apply the term *narcissistic neurosis* to classify a patient rather than a group of disorders.

The psychoses, as mentioned, are a form of character disorder, but they do not belong on the aforementioned continuum. This is partially because of the incompleteness of the model, but it is because the structure of psychosis requires explanatory dimensions and variables other than those used to explain other character disorders.

BORDERLINE STATES AND NARCISSISTIC PERSONALITY DISORDERS

I shall discuss borderline states and narcissistic personality disorders in a separate section because in the last several years they have received considerable attention in psychoanalytic circles. Various prominent clinicians have studied these conditions, and there is considerable disagreement and controversy as to how they should be viewed, especially the borderline states (see Masterson 1976).

Masterson (1976) and Rinsley (1982) view borderline patients as being fixated at the stage of separation–individuation (Mahler 1972); Searles (1963) focuses on fusion mechanisms; and Grotstein (1981), Ogden (1982), and Kernberg (1975) emphasize the use of splitting mechanisms and projective identification. Not all of these formulations are mutually contradictory; on the contrary, some can be reinforced by others, but many of these authors have focused on obscure diagnostic distinctions. For example, Masterson's theories indicate that borderline patients are much higher on the developmental scale than I indicated in the preceding section.

Initially, the word *borderline* was used to describe patients who have psychotic episodes but who are not actually psychotic

(Knight 1953). This means they are not rigidly and intractably psychotic, as is true of many schizophrenics. Borderline patients ordinarily have a nonpsychotic organization, a certain degree of psychic stability, but can easily go into a psychosis and just as easily recover from it.

All the groups of patients that I described in the preceding section are phenomenologically borderline. They are prone to occasional decompensations characteristic of psychotic breaks. None of these decompensations, however, has the durability of a schizophrenic psychosis. True, from the perspective of a patient's mental status, a variety of character types would qualify for the designation of borderline.

Kernberg believes that borderline patients have a stable organization that can temporarily lose its stability. At deeper levels, these patients suffer from intense destructive impulses that are handled by splitting mechanisms. Otherwise, the internalized bad objects would devour the inner good object representations. This is manifested by the psyche's lack of cohesion, leading to contradictory ego states and ways of relating to the external world, depending on whether the ego is dominated by good or bad internal objects.

The use of primitive defenses such as splitting causes a developmental fixation at a stage before the synthesis of good and bad objects. Kernberg used Melanie Klein's frame of reference and views borderline patients' psychopathology as located at a stage before the achievement of ambivalence (see Chapter 3). If good objects must be separated from bad objects in order to protect them, then we are describing a situation that Klein (1946) called the *paranoid-schizoid* position. Throughout early development (0 to 2 months), according to Klein, internal object representations are polarized into good and bad. The bad are then projected into segments of the external world which are experienced as retaliatory, persecuting, and destructive. The good objects remain in the self and are also reflected in caretaking external objects that nurture and protect. Splitting defenses are characteristic of this primitive orientation. Following Kernberg's hypotheses, the borderline patient's psychopathology is based on the paranoid-schizoid position.

To summarize Klein's sequence, the paranoid-schizoid position is followed by the *depressive position*, which occurs at around 6 months (Klein 1935). At this time the ego has achieved some synthesis of good and bad objects and is able to reconcile the existence of both loving and destructive feelings. The same object, whether internal or external, can be both loved and hated, an ambivalent orientation. Klein postulated that the paranoid-schizoid and depressive positions represent, for example, the fixation points of psychopathology, paranoid states, and manic-depressive episodes, as well as the course of ordinary emotional development. Kernberg also contended that splitting and projective mechanisms are characteristic of the earlier phase. Klein felt that the *manic defense* was a specific defense against the turmoil created by the depressive position.

In regard to the borderline state, it is apparent that Kernberg, as Klein, did not focus on the significance of object relations or, more specifically, on the interaction of the patient with the external world or the influence of emotionally significant persons on emotional development and the construction of psychopathology. As I pointed out (see Chapters 6 and 8), splitting and projective mechanisms are characteristic of early forms of psychopathology, but this does not explain why they should be considered to be typical defenses for borderline patients, unless clinicians wish to define borderline patients on the basis of their having splitting and projective defenses. This is not a feasible correlation, however, because there are other types of psychopathology, some more severe than that of the borderline, in which these defenses are prominent. Paranoid schizophrenics and other paranoid states are good examples of patients who, in fact, were responsible for the formulation of these pathological mechanisms. They are examples of fixed psychotic organizations that are the antithesis of the borderline state.

Taking into account the influence of the environment, Masterson (1976) and Rinsley (1982) stressed that borderline patients are fixated at Mahler's (1972) stage of separation–individuation. Masterson, in particular, focused on the mother's participation in blocking emotional growth. He concluded that the mother rewards infantile fixations and punishes attempts at development and integration. Although this model seems to be in the context of object relations and to emphasize the process of psychic structuralization, it actually concerns reward and punishment—somwhat similar to conditioning and behavioral modifications—and does not explore the subtleties and nuances of object relations as they impede or enhance psychic integration.

Ego psychology has not yet attained a conceptual base that will help us understand the interactions between the inner world of the mind and the external world involved in processes of growth and individuation or pathological distortions of the structuralizing sequence. At the most, we can point to general categories of interactions, such as good or bad, nurturing or depriving, or reward and punishment, as Masterson has done. Masterson explored the interface between the ego and the outer world, whereas Kernberg and Klein limited their observations to the inner world.

Abend and colleagues (1983) concluded after a four-year study conducted by the Kris study group of the New York Psychoanalytic Institute that the differences between borderline and psychoneurotic psychopathology are quantitative rather than qualitative. Furthermore, they emphasized that such patients do not constitute a specific diagnostic category. Instead, the so-called borderline condition is a general classification that includes a wide spectrum of emotional disorders and character structures.

Again, we are faced with how to define this borderline condition or borderline state. If we focus on the phenomenon of moving in and out of a psychosis, then I believe that Abend and his colleagues are correct. Still, the character structures involved are so diversified that it seems inappropriate to base such an important diagnostic distinction on just a phenomenological variable. This is the reason that I designated as borderline the group of patients following the schizoid state on the developmental scale.

The patients that I call borderline are borderline in two respects. They fill the phenomenological criterion of borderline, as do all the other patients with character disorders, but in addition, they are borderline in how they adapt to the external world. The patient who said that he had an arithmetic mentality but lived in a world of calculus complexity beautifully illustrates how the ego's executive system cannot cope with the exigencies of the external world because it is not equipped to do so. Such patients can make only borderline adaptations. Thus, the borderline patients that I have described are defined from two vantage points, a phenomenological and an adaptational perspective. The latter includes the object relations frame of reference, as it represents transactions with the outer world and external objects.

How does this classification of borderline compare or contrast with Kernberg's? Can such a character organization contain the good and bad objects and the intense destructive feelings that Kernberg described? I do not believe that the internal object representations that Kernberg characterized as typical of the borderline state are compatible with the inner world of the psyche for the patients that I call borderline. The group that Kernberg studied relate to the world in a psychopathological manner, but not necessarily marginally. They do have some well-developed ego executive techniques and in some instances can be highly successful. They do not always feel alienated or afraid and often enough are quite at ease with certain segments of their environment, which they may even exploit. They therefore are borderline only in a phenomenological sense.

Some of these patients, however, could easily be fit into the group that I call character neuroses. Moreover, I do not believe that Kernberg was describing a homogeneous group, for he pointed out that some of these patients can be treated by the psychoanalytic method and others cannot. The latter are patients who are overwhelmed by oral-cannibalistic impulses and consumed by greed. This distinction concerning treatability clearly indicates that Kernberg attributed different degrees of psychopathology to the general category of borderline.

Kernberg explored patients whose character disorders can best be described as a character neuroses. Various parts of the self are at variance with others, resulting in *structural conflicts*. If classification, however, were the only issue, it would not matter whether we referred to such patients as borderline or character neuroses.

The significant differences between these two types of psychopathology concern the points of developmental fixation and the issues of treatability. The borderline states that I described are fixated at levels of an amorphous ego organization and have not developed adequate executive techniques to cope with the external world. The character neurotics, or borderlines as Kernberg would prefer, are somewhat more advanced developmentally, as they have acquired part–object relations and have been more or less able to relate to those segments of the external world that are in tune with their adaptations. These psychic orientations predictably lead to different types of transference reactions, which determine the course of treatment. This does not mean that character neurotics are easier to treat than are borderline patients; they just present different therapeutic situations and transference–countertransference reactions based on specific aspects of their character structure. Borderline patients, particularly, are characterized by their neediness.

Nonetheless, these distinctions should not be taken too literally, because in the clinical setting, clear-cut examples of psychopathological entities are seldom found. Rather, clinicians find much overlapping of diagnostic categories, and the dynamics and structure of the patient as well as the evolution of the transference include many levels of the psyche and qualities that belong to various types of emotional disorders. The reason for making a diagnostic judgment—and some psychoanalysts doubt that there is any—is to help the clinician find dominant patterns of adaptations and defenses that permit conclusions about character structure and give some order and predictability to the treatment process. Predictability, however, is not easily achieved when dealing with a complex human personality and when faced with unforeseen events: as Freud (1912c) stated, the therapist must be prepared to be surprised at every turn in the patient's material.

Patients suffering from character neuroses have fragile and vulnerable self representations. They are overwhelmed with feelings of inadequacy and painful low esteem. Two antithetical patterns of behavior and orientations are the outcome of such a poorly constructed self representation. Both are commonly seen in clinical practice, and a patient may vacillate from one position to the other.

Some of these patients openly and directly reveal their inadequate selves and negative self-evaluations. They feel alienated. They are obsessed with their feelings of unworthiness and constantly blame themselves for feeling intimidated and inadequate. In many instances, it is clear that they have been performing at a superior level, but they do not seem to be aware of it. For example, a young lawyer complained that he had been a constant failure at school and had learned nothing. He was afraid that he would never be able to get a job because it was apparent how professionally worthless he was. His therapist was astonished when he learned that his patient had made law review and had been the class valedictorian. He had easily passed his bar exams, but he still persisted in viewing himself negatively and critically.

Most patients are not so talented and successful. Their vociferous proclamation of inadequacy is reflected in their repetitive failures, but even in these instances, clinicians sense that they are dealing with inner conflict that affects performance. Feelings of inadequacy are the manifestations of such conflicts and often represent defenses against losing control of omnipotent and destructive impulses.

Other patients construct defenses, know as narcissistic defenses, against their basic vulnerability and feelings of inadequacy. For years, these have been known as *narcissistic personalities*, but in the last 15 years, Kohut (1971) has referred to them as *narcissistic personality disorders*, implying that he was looking at a group of patients from an entirely new perspective.

This character type has been familiar to both professionals and nonprofessionals for centuries. Some of these persons have become leaders and through their charisma have gained immense power. They have been recognized by their sometimes ruthless ambition for fame, prestige, and power and the sometimes obvious fact that they are overcompensating for some real or imagined defect. If we put narcissistic defenses on a continuum, the borderline qualities of these patients—referring to going in and out of a psychosis—will be prominent. The megalomania of the paranoid patient seems to be an extreme example of a narcissitic personality disorder. The differences between flamboyant, delusional patients and nonpsychotic narcissists are obvious, but some patients are unquestionably psychotic and yet do not seem to be too different from others considered to be nonpsychotic. The line is often hard to draw, and many patients who appear in most respects to be sane sometimes reveal that segments of their personality are organized around a psychotic pattern.

For example, Eissler (1958) concluded that Goethe suffered from an encapsulated psychosis. Though Goethe was a literary giant, he could not understand Newton's theories about light. He particularly abhorred the conclusion that white light is a composite of all the colors on the spectrum. Goethe fiercely hated Newton for sullying the purity of white light, and his reactions were so intense that they could easily be recognized as paranoid. Goethe had apparently endowed a physical phenomenon with spiritual, moral, and aesthetic qualities, and he felt that Newton's findings were personal assaults on his integrity and ideals. These data suggest that Goethe was a narcissistic personality who could function at the highest creative levels, even though he might have had a psychotic core.

A young man in his twenties illustrated how a delusion could become woven into attitudes and behavior that seems to be reality oriented. This patient verbally attacked his therapist because he did not prevent him from having a one-night sexual liaison with a lesbian. He had intense feelings about what he had done and about the therapist's lack of protection. He insisted that his behavior was self-destructive, that it would ruin him. The intensity of his reactions were strange in view of what he considered to be his dereliction.

There was, however, some justification in his accusations. He was the eldest son of a wealthy family that had some very famous ancestors. He had to live up to extremely high standards, and if his behavior with the lesbian were made public, he would be ridiculed and disgraced. This seemed to be an unlikely consequence, but perhaps some eyebrows might have been raised in the exclusive club that he frequented.

The patient's remorse was based on reality-oriented circumstances and hypersensitivity. Although the extent of his response was bizarre, on the surface, it did not appear to be the outcome of a psychotic core. Actually, it turned out that he was feeling the manifestations of a delusion, a delusion that was realistically organized. He later revealed that he believed that he was the Messiah and had a divine mission to accomplish on Earth. Soon he would have disciples gathering around him, but if they learned about his liaison with a lesbian, he would lose his exalted status.

He had harbored this delusion of divinity for many years, but until recently, it had not created any special difficulties for him. In fact, in a sense, it had served him well as a narcissistic defense that acted as an overcompensation for feelings of inadequacy and lack of accomplishment. He was officious, condescending, and arrogant, and he capitalized on his illustrious family name. Still, his narcissistic orientation, although an offensive character trait, did not seem particularly unusual. He had hidden his delusion well, but as he revealed it in the treatment setting, it became clear that his superficial arrogance was the secondary process–toned derivative of a fundamental psychotic megalomania.

Kohut (1971) believed that the psychopathology of narcissistic personality disorders was related to a stage of arrested development that involved the formation of an idealized self. He did not clarify the exact nature of this developmental sequence, but apparently sometime after the infant's development has reached the stage of primary narcissism, the child forms a *grandiose self* and constructs an *idealized parental imago*. Apparently, the child does not receive sufficient mirroring to establish a solid, healthy narcissistic core and so later has to construct defenses to secure his narcissism. Mirroring means being admired so that the infant feels valued and develops confidence and self-esteem.

From the way in which Kohut stated his thesis, we have to assume that the infant passes directly from a stage of primary narcissism to a narcissistic phase in which the grandiose self and the idealized parental imago dominate. Kohut placed this phase within the realm of primary narcissism, clearly a conceptual inconsistency. This quantumlike jump from a preobject phase of primary narcissism to a sophisticated and structured self representation, as indicated by the formulation of a grandiose self, and from an amorphous ego to an ego that relates to external objects in a highly discriminating and structured fashion, as it would with the formation of an idealized parental imago, ignores the continuity of development and its gradual hierarchical stratification, as occurs with progressively integrating experiences with the outer world. To move immediately from a position in which the outer world is not perceived as separate from the self to one in which it can organize complex and structured configurations such as grandiosity and idealized parental imagos represents a gross conceptual fallacy. Furthermore, it disregards how introjects are acquired and how they contribute to the formation of the self representation. Kohut's theories are extreme examples of adultomorphization, as he demonstrated by placing grandiosity in the context of primary narcissism.

Melanie Klein has been criticized for attributing to infants psychic processes and functions that are far beyond their capacities and level of psychic integration. For example, she believed that the superego exists during the first months of life, not a rudimentary or an embryonic superego, but a powerful, sadistic one that is well differentiated. From this perspective, she was in accord with Catholic doctrine that stresses the dogma of original sin. Freud and Winnicott, to some extent, also assumed that the infant's mind is capable of fairly sophisticated attitudes and affects.

Freud (1914c) viewed narcissism as a quality of the first three or four months of life, and Winnicott (1953) wrote about omnipotence and primary psychic creativity as being characteristic of the transitional space, a psychic phenomenon that precedes the recognition of the surrounding world and external objects. It is difficult to understand how a preverbal infant can sustain such complex feelings and orientations as grandiosity and omnipotence. "His majesty the baby" that Freud (1914c) wrote about is a role that the parents assign to their baby as they seek to recover their lost narcissism.

Regressed states in treatment and the characterological manifestations of narcissistic personalities reveal narcissistic defenses and megalomanic preoccupation that are associated with early ego states. The processes of both symptom formation and regression (see Chapter 6) include various developmental levels, and qualities and functions that are acquired during later stages and are drawn back into the regressive stream. Therefore, what we observe is not the initial developmental state but a mixture of early primitive elements and later acquired functions and attitudes such as narcissistic orientations, grandiosity, and megalomanic expectations. If these formulations represent the rationale for a therapeutic approach, as Kohut believed, then the clinician is operating on erroneous and misleading principles. Freud and Winnicott, by contrast, confined their formulations to developmental phases and did not implicate them directly in constructing a theoretical framework for the treatment process.

Kohut believed that narcissistic personality disorders were fixated at the stage in which grandiosity and the idealized parental imago were formed. Such patients' narcissism is, in a manner of speaking, arrested in its development because as children, they have not had adequate empathic experiences or received the proper mirroring, that is, admiration, that would contribute to self-esteem and narcissistic self-confidence. Thus, the therapeutic task is to supply empathy by making empathic interpretations and supporting, by means of mirroring, the patients' need for grandiosity. Eventually, the therapist will have to introduce reality when he believes that such patients are strong enough for such a confrontation.

Apart from the obvious contrivance, role playing, and manipulation involved, this approach is based on the naive assumption that the psychopathology of narcissistic personality disorders consists of simply an arrested developmental phase and that the therapist's task is to restart the developmental process, by providing the patient with growth-promoting experiences that were missing or inadequate during infancy. The structuralizing effect of transference interpretations is not given much weight in Kohut's therapeutic approach, although it is not totally ignored.

The role of narcissism in the production of psychopathology has not been ignored by psychoanalysts, and it was taken into account even in the earliest classical psychoanalytic formulations. Freud (1911b, 1914c) was well aware of its contributions to both the psychotic and the nonpsychotic processes. He was familiar with how it was involved with character structure, and as discussed, he even designated a diagnostic category known as the narcissistic neuroses (1914c). The study of borderline and narcissistic patients, however, emphasizes the consequences of the lack of defenses or the use of overcompensatory narcissistic defenses. True, developmental fixations and arrests are important determinants of characterological psychopathology, but the clinical situation is much more complex than simply a linear halt of development. Many psychic structures must be examined, especially those involved with incorporative functions and the formation of the self representation.

OBJECT RELATIONS AND PSYCHIC STRUCTURE

Object relations theory is supposedly an important subdivision of ego psychology. I say supposedly because the significance of external objects in determining psychic health or psychopathology was implicitly (Freud 1905a) and explicitly (Freud 1914c) stated relatively early in the history of the psychoanalytic movement. If we accept that ego psychology began with the construction of the structural hypothesis (Freud 1923a), then the early theories about object relations, such as those that describe the balance between ego libido and object libido, belong to the realm of classical psychoanalysis. These are, however, arbitrary distinctions, and psychoanalytic theory has evolved around the axis of a smooth continuum, so that it is impossible and irrelevant to determine where classic theory ends and ego psychology begins. It is simply a matter of clinical necessity that we pay relatively more attention to the ego and its substructures as they relate to and cope with the surrounding world.

The study of early infant–mother relationships, known as the *longitudinal approach*, has been popular for many years. As Mahler (1972) proved, much can be learned from direct observation, especially if the mother–child dyad is followed throughout the child's emotional development. This is a phenomenological approach that concentrates on the overt manifestations of object relationships and permits inferences to be made as to how they determine various psychic processes that either impede or encourage emotional integration and character development. The sequence can be observed when the subject is followed from infancy through childhood to adolescence and adulthood.

Mahler formulated a series of developmental phases that have both clinical significance and implications for developmental psychology. Unlike most developmental sequences, Mahler's focuses on the object relationship itself, stressing its qualities that justify making it a separate phase. Mahler listed the following phases: separation–individuation, the practicing phase, and rapprochement.

Before separation–individuation, the infant relates to objects in only a rudimentary fashion. Mahler believes that before individuation, the mother–child dyad is characterized by symbiotic fusion. The child and mother constitute a unit and do not have a separate sense of being. The infant's ego boundaries are not yet formed, and the outer world is not perceived as separate from the self. This is actually a preobject state. According to Mahler, this state of symbiotic fusion occurs between the ages of 3 to 6 months.

The term *symbiosis* requires clarification. The concept was first articulated by De Bary (1879), a biologist, who described how certain species depend on one another for their survival. The examples of sucker fish acting as guides for blind sharks as they feed on the remnants of their host's meal or birds that pick food out of the teeth of rhinoceroses to the benefit of both species are frequently cited. What these examples stress is mutual dependence. This relationship is markedly different from parasitism in which the dependence is unilateral. One member of the dyad also becomes attached to the other for survival, but often at the detriment of the other. The mother–child dyad only approximates symbiosis because although the infant depends on the mother for survival, the mother can survive without the child. The early mother–child caretaking relationship therefore seems to be more of an example of parasitism than of symbiosis. If we are thinking only in terms of physical survival, this is certainly true.

Human interactions, however, have to be viewed in terms of emotional survival as well as physical survival. Fairly healthy mothers are intensely attached to their children. Winnicott

(1956) coined the expression *primary maternal preoccupation*, which he believed was biologically oriented. This state of total involvement begins at the end of pregnancy and lasts for several weeks. The mother is intensely enmeshed with the baby's needs, but it is apparent that her psychic equilibrium depends on being close, even biologically, to a child who is still an extension of herself. According to Winnicott (1957), this attachment is something that only a woman can understand. He stated: "I am a man so I can never really know what it is like to see wrapped over there in the cot a bit of my own self, a bit of me living an independent life, yet at the same time dependent and gradually becoming a person" (p. 17). The mother's preoccupation is more than an emotional state or orientation. It has an instinctual element that is set in motion with conception and pregnancy. Winnicott further stated in regard to primary maternal preoccupation: "It gradually develops and becomes a state of heightened sensitivity during, and especially toward the end of, the pregnancy. It lasts for a few weeks after the birth of the child. It is not easily remembered by mothers once they have recovered from it. . . . I do not believe that it is possible to understand the functioning of the mother at the very beginning of the infant's life without seeing that she must be able to reach this state of heightened sensitivity, almost an illness, and to recover from it" (Winnicott 1956b, p. 302).

Winnicott's description of primary maternal preoccupation is similar to current descriptions of bonding, especially in his proposal that the mother feels herself in the infant's place so that she can intuitively respond to its needs. Modern investigators (Klaus and Kennel 1982) have been quick to point out, however, that they face a dilemma in deciding how much emphasis they should give to the importance of parent–infant contact in the first hour of the child's life. Klaus and Kennell stressed that despite the lack of early contact—as dictated by rigid hospital rules and routine in the last 20 to 30 years—most mothers become bonded to their babies. They acknowledge that humans are highly adaptable and that there are many routes to attachment. They are obviously trying not to make some mothers feel guilty, and they have considerable data to support their viewpoint.

The way that a mother responds to the infant's needs determines how its psychic structures will evolve and how its developmental path will reach the goal of mature whole–object relationships. Problems in bonding are reflected in how the baby's psychic apparatus achieves the integration to establish internal equilibrium and relate to external objects. How much of a biological component bonding contains and how dependent it is on early mother–infant contact are questions that require further exploration. In the clinical realm, the quality of the infantile caretaking relationship appears to be crucial to the quality and equilibrium of psychic structure. This is especially apparent in the study of adopted children.

The phenomenon of bonding and the emergence of maternal behavior depend on many poorly understood variables. It has been demonstrated in animals that virgin rats have to overcome their fear of a pup's odor before they can mother, whereas the natural mother has no such fear and can begin mothering immediately (Rosenblatt 1969). The questions that these studies raise concern the emergence of the maternal instinct and its dependence on pregnancy and parturition, as Winnicott claimed in his description of primary maternal preoccupation. The infant may also act as a stimulant for the production of hormones that help create a maternal orientation. There is undoubtedly a complex interplay of factors that converge to produce an intuitive, nurturing, structure-promoting, caretaking relationship. The treatment of adopted children offers data that permit us to make inferences about the failure to establish bonding.

It is unwarranted to make generalizations from the study of psychopathology, and adopted children seeking treatment must, in some way, be emotionally disturbed. Still, in some instances, the extent of later psychopathology does not seem to be understandable as the outcome of infantile traumas. That is, there seems to be a marked discrepancy between the deprivations and frustrations of childhood and the severity of emotional illness. Many adopted children appear to have serious problems, frequently involving acting out and delinquent behavior that is hard to explain in terms of their backgrounds. Again, I realize that we cannot apply our hypotheses to children who have not sought therapy, but the findings are sufficiently striking that they may lead to insights into the so-called biological components of maternal behavior.

The behavior of some adopted children reinforces Winnicott's ideas about the importance of primary maternal preoccupation to optimal or even adequate mothering. For example, a woman in her early thirties had unsuccessfully tried for many years to get pregnant, and so she finally adopted a child. She received the baby one hour after birth, and she and her husband were absolutely delighted to finally have a baby in their home. The mother was in analysis at the time, and although she had problems, they were not, according to her analyst, particularly severe. Certainly she functioned well and was considered to be charming and attractive. The husband, though not in treatment, was known as a stable and warm person. The marriage had been relatively serene until the adoption of this daughter.

The baby was apparently disturbed from the moment she entered the household. She was diagnosed as being colicky, and there was little anyone could do to make her feel better. Despite the child's discomfort, she walked and talked early and showed considerable curiosity as she explored the surrounding world, but even these seemingly positive activities created a tense and uneasy state in her parents.

Although the child had high scores in her aptitude and intelligence tests, she was always at the bottom of her class. She failed several subjects and was almost totally unable to understand the simplest mathematical principles. By contrast, she was excellent in history and world literature because she had a keen memory, but she still got poor grades, as she rarely completed her assignments. She did not get along with her classmates, and her poor academic performance made her unpopular with her teachers.

She was so unhappy during her childhood that her parents arranged to place her in treatment. She formed an attachment to her therapist, who believed that the relationship helped fill a sense of emptiness she felt. He admitted that his patient had a strange mental state, because it seemed that her parents had shown unusual tolerance, and their devotion to their daughter remained firm and constant.

Despite her good relationship with her therapist, this patient's adolescence was a nightmare. She relied heavily on drugs, drank excessively, and was promiscuous. She was expelled from school and had to be sent to a special facility for emotionally disturbed and learning-handicapped children. At the age of 16, she stopped going to school because she felt that it was a waste of time and that the faculty really did not know what to do with her. Residential treatment facilities had been recommended several times, but she had threatened to run away if she were placed in one of them. She finally got a job as a waitress, and for about a year, that is, up until the age of 17, she had a relatively quiet period.

Her promiscuity, however, continued, and she became pregnant and contracted gonorrhea. She had an abortion and was treated for gonorrhea, but six months later she was again pregnant and had another abortion. Three years later she tried to kill herself by overdosing on barbiturates. Afterwards she became anorexic and would occasionally cut herself. Now she lives in a halfway house but from time to time is hospitalized in a psychiatric ward for months at a time.

The subtle nuances and traumas that may have been characteristic of her childhood could have very well eluded us. Still, the data that were collected did not come just from what the parents reported and were not restricted simply to observation and phenomenology. The mother was in analytic treatment at the time their daughter was adopted, and she continued seeing her analyst throughout her daughter's childhood. The discrepancies between the mother's character structure and what was learned about the husband and their child's antisocial, destructive, and self-destructive acting-out were enormous.

Current theories indicate that the daughter is suffering from a schizoaffective disorder that has cyclical features, a mental orientation that has almost totally impaired her capacity to function and that is hard to understand on the basis of her relationship with her parents.

Perhaps, as was suggested by a prominent child analyst, this patient is a "bad seed," a basically constitutional and genetic disorder. Such a suggestion is the outcome of desperation, for we are unable to understand her in terms of psychic determinism. The influence of the past is excluded in this biologically oriented explanation. Still, as the current research keeps stressing the importance of bonding as an almost instinctive reaction, the phenomenon of primary maternal preoccupation gains prominence. If primary maternal preoccupation begins at conception and is developed throughout gestation and parturition, then there will be difficulties in mothering an adopted child. These are nebulous issues that require further exploration.

Early bonding paves the way for the establishment of the symbiotic phase as well as for the formation of object relations. Mahler (1968) believes that the symbiotic phase begins when the infant is approximately 3 months of age. I assume that she means that the child enters the symbiotic phase then, but this does not necessarily mean that the mother begins to find herself fused with her infant at that time. If she is in the throes of primary maternal preoccupation, it is likely that in terms of her mental operations, she constructed a symbiotic tie to her baby soon after birth when she formed a bond with him. In fact, Winnicott would place the onset of the mother's symbiosis much further back, sometime after conception.

Symbiosis as a psychoanalytic concept is somewhat different from the relationships between animals. Symbiosis is a visible interaction between the participants, and each is aware how the other species is ministering to specific needs. This is not so, of course, between mother and child. The infant cannot be thought of as being aware of anything in a structured sense, at least not at the same level as the mother perceives and feels. Thus, the mother can perceive herself as being in a state of symbiotic fusion long before the child is aware of the external world as being sufficiently separate from the self so that he can fuse with it.

Mahler (1968) and Mahler and colleagues (1975) placed such early stages in the sphere of primary narcissism (see Chapter 3). She distinguished two subphases, the first occurring during the first few weeks of extrauterine life, which she calls the stage of *absolute primary narcissism* and is marked "by the infant's lack of awareness of a mothering agent" (Mahler 1968, p. 10). Mahler then distinguished the subphase of the *symbiotic stage proper*, beginning at 3 months. At this stage, although the child is still developmentally oriented on a primary narcissistic axis, he begins to directly perceive the external world. The child is somewhat aware of need satisfaction and begins to recognize vaguely that it is coming from "a need satisfying part object— albeit still within the orbit of his omnipotent symbiotic dual unit with a mothering agency, toward which he turns libidinally" (Mahler 1968, p. 10). Mahler considers this stage to be one of partial primary narcissism.

Mahler also adultomorphized in regard to the child's perceiving a "need-satisfying part object . . . within the orbit of his symbiotic dual unity" during the phase of primary narcissism. She qualified her position by stating that she was not discussing absolute primary narcissism: "not such an absolute primary narcissism" (Mahler 1968, p. 10), but it is conceptually inconsistent to think in terms of gradations of primary narcissism. Once an organism proceeds beyond not being able to distinguish the external world to a dim awareness of need-satisfying part objects, it can no longer be considered as being in a state of primary narcissism. To formulate object relations in a phase that has been defined as objectless is inappropriate and confusing. It is an extreme example of attributing qualities and functions to early ego states that cannot support such a level of relatively advanced psychic integration.

The point is that the child begins the developmental journey toward the formation of object relationships and self and object representations after having passed through a symbiotic phase. The mother, on the other hand, has already achieved the capacity to have object relations and has well-structured self and object representations when she reverts (Winnicott would say regresses) to a state of symbiotic unity. Symbiosis, for the mother, is a psychic phenomenon in which self and object representations fuse with each other, in this instance the object representation of the child, which, to a large measure, is endopsychically registered before the child is born. By contrast, the infant is directing its psychic energy to the outer world in order to perceive it as partially separate and to internalize the mother as a source of nurture and need satisfaction. The child is making the caretaking person part of himself, and this—in an ego-psychological frame—constitutes symbiotic fusion. The infant is not aware or concerned about reciprocity. The mother, on the other hand, more closely approximates a state of true symbiosis, in that she both gives and receives. In giving to her child, she is deriving benefits of her own that enhance her self-esteem and lead to levels of higher psychic integration. Although fusion mechanisms are involved, they operate in the context of well-differentiated and advanced ego states.

Mahler (1968) observed that during the height of symbiosis, at around 4 to 5 months, infants become more outwardly directed, that they seem to shift their attention from their bodily parts to their mother. Their facial expressions are more differentiated and expressive. This beginning involvement with the external world becomes progressively elaborated as they turn toward outside stimuli and then return to the mother as if they were seeking her protection or validation. This activity heralds the emergence from symbiotic fusion as infants move forward developmentally to attain separation–individuation, a movement known as the *hatching phase*, a beginning subphase of the process of separation–individuation. According to Mahler, the hatching phase ordinarily occurs at around the eighth month and is associated with the start of locomotion.

The hatching process occurs with an increasingly differentiated sensorium, as the system perceptual-conscious continues to develop under the sway of maturational and developmental forces. Infants' interest in the external world widens as they, at the same time, feel safe in the symbiotic context of nurturing and protection. As their outwardly directed attention evolves, infants use the mother as a reference point, as one with whom they can check back. On the one hand, children want to behave autonomously, but they do not want to be outside the sphere of the mother's support. This is exemplified in the expression "Mother, I would rather do it myself," but the dependence on the mother is nevertheless obvious. This is known as the *practicing subphase* of separation–individuation, which occurs from 10 to 16 months of age.

The hatching subphase is equated with the birth of an individual. During the practicing period, autonomous ego functions (see Chapter 8) rapidly develop. The pleasure in functioning serves as a developmental impetus that compensates for the partial object loss that is inherent in the achievement of autonomy. The practicing period lasts until around 18 months, when toddlers feel elated and powerful, believing in their omnipotence, as Mahler (1968) stated, an omnipotence derived from incorporating the mother's magical powers as the toddlers view them.

I believe that the chronological period that Mahler called the practicing subphase is the developmental stage during which the subjective attributes of narcissism first appear, and not during the early months of life when secondary narcissism reputedly follows primary narcissism. In the regressive process, the toddler's narcissistic orientation is drawn into the regression and becomes a dominant feature of a much earlier ego state. Nevertheless, it belongs to a much later phase of development. I believe that many psychoanalytic theorists and clinicians have overlooked the distinction between traits that belong to higher levels of development and qualities that are characteristic of early developmental stages; in other words, they have overlooked the distinction between fixation and regression. Consequently, their formulations are adultomorphic, as has been discussed.

As would be expected, the ego state characterized by feeling powerful and elated has to be brought in tune with reality. Therefore, the next 18 months of life represent a period of vulnerability. Reality testing develops as toddlers further internalize relationships with external objects, and their sense of omnipotence under optimal circumstances becomes tamed into healthy self-esteem and confidence. Because of a more realistic orientation, children no longer have to deny the importance of the mother, as occurs during the practicing period when they need to emphasize their autonomy and invulnerability.

The need to ignore the mother gradually decreases and is replaced by a wish to share their experiences with her. This occurs when children are better able to be separate and actively involved with the external world. This is known as the *rapprochement subphase*, which is ushered into the developmental sequence at around 18 months of age and lasts for about three years, when children enter the triangular relationship of the Oedipus complex, develop a superego, and begin to consolidate a sense of identity (see Chapter 3).

In contrast with the practicing subphase, during which children must move away from acknowledging a need for support in pursuing autonomous activities, during the rapprochement period, toddlers actively solicit approval for their endeavors. Their attitude is best characterized by the boast "Look mother, no hands!" Whereas previously, the narcissistic orientation seemed to be firmly fixed, during the rapprochement subphase, children seek "emotional refueling," as Furer (1964) stressed.

The final phase in Mahler's chronological sequence culminates at around 3 years of age when there is a beginning consolidation of the identity sense that is not as dependent on the confirmation of external objects and situations. According to some child analysts (Fraiberg 1969), at around 18 months, children have developed *object constancy*.

Object constancy means that children can maintain an introject (see Chapter 2) or a mental representation without the reinforcement of the presence of an external object. There are various opinions about when this capacity develops, but object constancy is usually considered to develop at 18 months (Piaget 1937, 1952). When discussing object constancy, various clinicians and investigators may not be referring to the same phenomenon. For example, Spitz (1959) believes that it occurs much earlier, at around 8 months and that it can be considered in the context of stranger anxiety (see next section). He implicitly demonstrated that there are gradations of object constancy, that this capacity gradually develops and differentiates. External percepts are internalized with varying degrees of permanency. At 8 months, according to Spitz, the presence of a stranger evokes the mental representation of the mother that can then be contrasted with an external image that does not correspond to the maternal mental representation. This produces anxiety, but it does not mean that the mother imago can be always activated without her presence or with the absence of internal needs. The evocation of memories is dependent on certain conditions such as inner needs or the presence of strangers.

Anna Freud (1965) coined the expression *libidinal object constancy*, which also has a connotation slightly different from object constancy or *evocative memory*, as it has also been named. She specifically focused on the relationship of the infant with the mother, a relationship that has progressed beyond the mother's being used as a source of gratification and nurture once libidinal object constancy has been achieved. She postulated that the child can now cathect the mother, regardless of whether she gratifies or frustrates him. The mother is now recognized as a person in her own right, apart from being simply a caretaker.

Mahler's developmental sequence can be challenged, but psychoanalysts generally have not been critical of her ideas. There have been reservations about her methodology, especially in regard to how much can be learned from direct observations, a phenomenological frame of reference characteristic of the longitudinal approach. Perhaps Mahler's detailed formulations go beyond the data of observation. Some of her conclusions are also derived from the study of clinical material, usually children, but there are also clinical situations with adult patients that lend themselves to explanations based on some of her developmental hypotheses. For example, in regard to the practicing period, a patient treated his analyst as if he were the mother who had to be in the vicinity but not specifically acknowledged. He spent session after session virtually analyzing himself. He viewed his behavior and associations in terms of their unconscious determinants and frequently made genetic connections. If the analyst ventured an interpretation, the patient would seem to ignore it.

Although the patient ostensibly paid no attention to his therapist, he became upset if the therapist had to miss an appointment for any reason. The patient depicted the way he felt about his treatment in a fantasy: He thought of an electronic bug that he had read about in a magazine in the analyst's waiting room. This apparatus, which looked like a big beetle, freely roaming around several rooms. It could not, however, wander too far away from a source of electricity. Periodically it had to return to that source, plug itself in, and recharge its battery so that it could once again obtain energy for its travels. This patient saw himself as this bug, and although true to form he did not acknowledge it, the energy source represented the treatment process. During this phase of analysis, the patient could be conceptualized as reliving the practicing subphase in the transference interaction.

These data do not by themselves justify the construction of a hypothesis such as the practicing subphase, but they are suggestive and can be fit into such a conceptual frame. In a similar vein, there are numerous examples of psychopathology that can be explained on the basis of a defect in establishing object constancy. A woman in her early thirties gave me a wooden statuette during her first week of therapy. She insisted that I keep it in an alcove by my chair and made this a condition for treatment. The statuette was about 16 to 18 inches tall, was obviously a woman, but with no arms, and the face had no features. It was bumpy and amorphous. The impression was of a primitive emaciated figure, but I felt that it had artistic merit. It reminded me of a Giacometti sculpture.

Clearly, the statuette represented the way in which the patient viewed herself. It had no mouth, a reflection of the patient's belief that she was incapable of being nurtured. The absence of arms went along with the patient's belief that she had no one to embrace or to be embraced by; no one had ever been around during her childhood to hold and soothe her. She could not recall ever being gratified or having anyone nearby that was more interested in her welfare than in his or her own.

She began treatment by asking me when I would be taking my next trip. She had to know all the details of my prospective travels. When I told her, she became furious that I was going to abandon her, even though the trip was still six months away. She filled her sessions by complaining about how she was going to be deserted. She demanded my constant presence and made a similar demand of the few close friends she had. She had to know where they could be located, and for reasons that I only imperfectly understand, they did not seem to resent her intrusiveness. When I finally did leave the city, she became angry and had to have a detailed account of my itinerary. She did not call me either on that or subsequent trips, but she still had to know where I would be at every moment so that she could, as she put it, form a picture of me in her mind. She lamented how hard it was to retain such an image.

I had expected that she would feel some relief when I returned, but just the opposite was true. She was just as angry, if not more so, when she had her first appointment after my absence. I later learned that sometime after I left, she had lost her mental representation of me, and so she found it painful to integrate me into her ego once again. It was as if I were a foreign body that could not be smoothly incorporated into her psyche. That was one of the reasons that once she had been able to form an intrapsychic image of me as a therapist, it was so difficult to have me leave her, because she knew that she could not hold a mental representation without its being periodically reinforced by my physical presence. This did not always mean that she needed my whole person; a detached part of myself such as my voice on a telephone-answering machine sufficed to keep her stable between sessions.

I was impressed by the intensity of her need for external reinforcement that enabled her to tenuously maintain psychic equilibrium. This is exemplified in the following incident: I unexpectedly had to make a fairly long trip, but it was so arranged that it did not interfere with her schedule. I saw her six days a week. I was going to leave shortly after her Saturday morning appointment and to return the following Sunday evening in plenty of time for her Monday afternoon session. To spare myself her verbal abuse, I decided not to tell her about my trip, and I rationalized that it would not make any difference to her because her sessions would not be interrupted.

To my amazement, when she walked into my consultation room that Saturday morning, she asked, "Where are you going?" I must have weakly replied something to the effect, "What makes you think that I'm going anywhere?" She then looked at me sternly and said, "You are better dressed than usual, and that is not for me. Furthermore, you have the look of anticipation of a man who is going to do something outside his routine." I was completely taken by surprise and somewhat angrily retorted that because I was not interfering with her schedule, it should make no difference whether I did or did not take a trip. She ruefully shook her head and replied that I simply did not understand, whereupon I exclaimed that she expected me to remain in one spot twenty-four hours a day, seven days a week. She calmly said, "Of course." I believe I then understood how elusive external percepts were for her and how difficult it was for her to internalize any relationship, especially one that could lead to security.

Her giving me the statuette represented an attempt to keep an external percept of herself within my perceptual sphere. At one level, she assumed that I had the same ego defect that she had, that I would not be able to hold a mental representation of her without the reinforcement of an external object. Although I believe that my capacity for evocative memory is well developed, I felt somewhat disturbed when she, on occasion, angrily took the statuette away. She always returned it, but the last time she took it I remained calm and unconcerned. We both understood that she had reached a stage of ego integration that allowed her to internalize relationships and that she now had the capacity for object constancy. In a sense, neither one of us needed the statuette any longer.

OTHER OBJECT RELATIONS THEORIES

It is difficult to be comprehensive when discussing object relations, because so many different authors have written on this subject, often without specifically identifying their topic. As to be expected, there is much overlapping, and frequently a supposedly "new" theory is a series of statements, garbed in a different language, that merely repeat well-known and well-established concepts. For example, Harry Stack Sullivan's school of interpersonal psychiatry uses an elaborate terminology to describe well-known psychoanalytic principles and functions such as reality testing (consensual validation), primary process and transference (parataxic distortion), and the self representation (the self system), carefully avoiding such terms as narcissism and the unconscious. Nevertheless, Sullivan had keen clinical insights and in his writings indicated a sensitive and understanding approach to his patients.

I have mentioned Kohut and Kernberg (see Chapter 8) in another connection and need not explore their ideas further. Kohut's theories and therapeutic principles have had a significant and controversial impact on psychoanalysts in spite of having been severely criticized (Giovacchini 1979b). Whether his influence, as eloquently voiced by his followers, continues, remains to be seen. I suspect that as students of psychoanalysis gain a broader perspective of ego psychology and character structure, to a large measure a historical overview, Kohut's ideas will be realistically evaluated.

Alexander's and French's (1946) innovations regarding psychoanalytic technique may represent a paradigm in the form of a sequence of responses to pronouncements that claim to revolutionize our understanding of and approach to clinical situations and to replace classical principles. At first—at least at the Chicago Institute for Psychoanalysis—Alexander and French were hailed as discoverers that would change psychoanalytic treatment. They allegedly had presented a major breakthrough that would permit us to treat a broader range of patients both more economically and more practically. Instead of psychoanalytic treatment's being a final approach, everything could now be considered to be a variable. The number and length of sessions, whether the patient would lie down or sit up, the sex of the therapist, and even the analyst's response to the patient's transference projections were variables that had to be determined in the context of specific psychopathology. The therapeutic interaction was called the *corrective emotional experience*, which dominated the therapeutic armamentarium rather than the interpretation of the transference (Gill 1979). Basically, the Chicago "school" minimized the importance of intrapsychic factors—in the same way that Kohut diminished the significance of drives—and replaced them with interpersonal interactions. On the surface this seemed to be more of an object relations approach.

After the initial fervor and enthusiasm, Alexander's and French's recommendations were soberly examined and found to have little relevance to the psychoanalytic process. Today "corrective emotional experience" is practically a pejorative expression. What promised to be a breakthrough was disappointing, and the covert movement away from intrapsychic factors and the spontaneous unfolding of the transference created a treatment relationship that proved difficult to construct. The therapist had to know how to react properly to the patient's transference projections and to manipulate them correctly for therapeutic resolution. Without some omnipotence, this is an awesome task.

Kohut's theoretical inconsistencies (see Chapter 8 and Giovacchini 1979b) and therapeutic principles have also affected our treatment philosophy. True, ego psychology generally does not emphasize drives to the extent that classical theory does, but in focusing on the acquisition of psychic structure, it still stresses intrapsychic factors. In regard to treatment, Kohut believed that the patient's development is arrested at a narcissistic phase that is defective or defensive in the construction of a grandiose self and the idealized parental imago. There has been a deficiency of narcissistic mirroring and empathic experiences in the patient's past, traumatic constellations that have led to developmental fixation, low self-esteem, and the lack of a cohesive self. The therapist's task is to make up for these infantile deprivations by making empathic interpretations and mirroring, which means admiring, to compensate for the lack of narcissistic supplies in the past. Eventually, the therapist has to introduce reality, but by that time, the experience of treatment will have been sufficiently positive that the patient will have acquired the ego strength to relate to the external world with less constricting, compensatory narcissistic defenses.

This brief description points to the treatment plan that has little resemblance to the working-through process as we understand it (see Chapter 7). Although it mentions "empathic interpretations," the interpretative process and how it leads to internal changes (they are labeled simply *transmuting internalizations*) are not clarified. Rather, the effects of the therapist's manipulations through mirroring are the main factors that account for improvement. Similar to Alexander and French, Kohut and his followers emphasize an interaction rather than making the unconscious conscious and the working-through process that accompanies the acquisition of insight within a transference context (Gill 1979).

Ego psychology and object relations theory do not minimize the importance of intrapsychic processes and the role of insight within the frame of emotional reliving in acquiring higher levels of psychic integration. On the contrary, many theorists have found ideas about object relations and psychic development indispensable to their understanding of the patient's transference projections and their own countertransference responses. They recognize that some patients project both primitive parts of the self and disruptive instinctual impulses in the transference interaction, an understanding that leads to structure-promoting interpretations.

Fairbairn, Melanie Klein, and Winnicott made contributions to object relations and early development that have been the most influential in constructing contemporary concepts that contribute to our therapeutic outlook. I have throughout this book discussed some of Melanie Klein's and Winnicott's formulations. I will, in the case of Klein, briefly summarize her contributions after introducing Fairbairn. Both of these authors have been incorporated in many clinicians' thinking without giving them recognition. In fact, Klein has been frequently attacked in the United States especially, while she has gained considerable recognition south of the border. In England and the United States, she has been quite controversial, although in one form or another her ideas have been adopted, particularly by child analysts. Winnicott has been gaining increasing acceptance throughout the years.

Many other writers have made valuable contributions— such as Balint (1955, 1959), Bion (1963), Greenacre (1959, 1960), Guntrip (1961), Jacobson (1959, 1964), and Lewin (1950)—but I shall not discuss them specifically. Rather, the writers that I have chosen have certain similarities in that we can construct a continuum between various facets of their views about the acquisition of internal structures and external relationships.

Fairbairn's Theories

W. R. D. Fairbairn, a Scottish psychoanalyst, was one of the first analysts to believe that there were inherent weaknesses in the libido theory. He stressed that the classical drive theory was inadequate and had to be replaced by an object relations approach. His impressions were based on clinical material that led him to revise the psychopathology of the psychoses and psychoneuroses (Fairbairn 1941). His ideas were both revolutionary and controversial when he first proposed them. Today, he does not evoke particularly strong reactions, as some of his hypotheses have been incorporated in what has been sometimes referred to as the British school of object relations, which includes such analysts as Balint (1955), Guntrip (1961), Rosenfeld (1965) and Winnicott.

Fairbairn arrived at his conclusions after studying what he called schizoid states. He defined them as primitive ego states in which objects are not yet perceived or are dimly constructed in a preambivalent fashion. The schizoid orientation was then followed by a manic-depressive ambivalent constellation that corresponds to Abraham's oral-cannibalistic phase (see Chapter 3). At this juncture, Fairbairn departed from Freud and Abraham in outlining his developmental sequence. He rejected the anal and phallic stages, and this, I believe, is Fairbairn's unique but debatable contribution.

Fairbairn accepted Abraham's two oral phases, the oral-dependent (schizoid) and the oral-cannibalistic (manic-depressive) phases, and the final genital phase. He explained that whereas the oral phase seeks nurture and the genital phase seeks genital or sexual discharge, it is not biologically consistent to place preoccupation with defecation (anal) and urination (phallic) at the same conceptual level. Feces and urine are not objects sought by instincts or inner needs, as are breasts and genitals. Consequently, Fairbairn concluded that the so-called anal and phallic phases are artifacts. His theory is an object relations theory, and therefore, the object that produces satisfaction and psychic equilibrium is central to his conceptual scheme. He repeatedly stated that the goal of libido is seeking an object.

At first, placing the search for an object as a primal impetus does not make sense either conceptually or behaviorally. Infants seem to strive for nurture, reestablishment of equilibrium, pleasure, and survival. These endeavors intuitively strike us as being basic, biologically directed goals. Pursuing object attachment for its own sake appears to be inconsistent with the neonate's lack of physical and psychic differentiation.

Recent findings in the field of neonatology indicate that some differentiation and contact with the outer world occur very early, within the first few days of life (Stern 1985). This could mean that processes geared toward homeostatic balance and survival are associated very early with interactions with external objects. They may not be specifically recognized as caretaking persons, but through overlapping sensory modalities, the child may quickly equate satisfying experiences with forces outside the immediate sphere of the rudimentary somatic self. Overlapping sensory modalities refers to the neonate's capacity to retain sensations in one modality, such as tactile, when another one is stimulated, such as vision, signifying that reactions with the outer world have an early influence on the acquisition of comfort and on psychic structure. This once again stresses the importance of objects that can be sought primarily because they are recognized (perhaps on a biological intuitive basis) as vital.

Fairbairn (1954) divided objects into acceptable and unacceptable objects, which are handled differently in various neuroses. Anal and phallic are, according to Fairbairn, rejective techniques in which objects are extruded from the ego. Anal is a much more primitive rejective technique than is phallic, and even within the anal sphere, there are gradations that account for the severity of the psychopathological state. For example, the paranoid patient uses primitive anal techniques in that the rejected object is totally hated, whereas the obsessive patient, who also uses anal techniques, extrudes objects toward which he also has giving feelings and concern.

In regard to psychopathology, Fairbairn postulated that most neuroses have a schizoid core and that the adaptive and defensive techniques employed to deal with this early ego state determine the manifestations of emotional illness. He emphasized that the libido is not genital but that the genital has been libidinized and that this also applies to other psychosexual levels such as anal and phallic. A primitive ego has a limited number of modalities to libidinize, whereas higher states of ego integration have at their disposal a variety of adaptations characteristic of different levels of psychosexuality.

Fairbairn's emphasis on objects, similar to other early object relations theorists, did not focus on the quality of the object relationship, that is, what psychic processes characterized the interaction. As discussed, he viewed development from a different frame of reference, which strongly emphasized transactions with the outer world without specifically exploring the nature of those transactions. Fairbairn paved the way for later clinicians who focused on the psychotic core that seems to characterize the borderline conditions that we commonly encounter. He also indicated that many patients whom we have regarded as high-grade psychoneurotics, that is, patients who were believed to be displaying problems centering on conflicts regarding oedipal issues, were also examples of basic schizoid orientations. Fairbairn did not accept the Oedipus complex as a universal phenomenon; rather, he viewed it as a sociocultural artifact. The neo-Freudians (Horney 1937) followed in his footsteps.

Fairbairn's system ignored many essential factors that pertain to subtle elements of psychic structure and differentiation of the inner world of the psyche and the outer world of objects. The word *object* is an abstraction for an actual person who inhabits our reality. Jacobson (1959, 1964) recognized this when she put all objects in the category of object representations inside the psyche and then distinguished among internal object representations, external object representations, and the self representation. Sandler (1960) also emphasized the intrapsychic aspects of object relations. Both Jacobson and Sandler, however, tried to conceptualize within the frame of drive theory, whereas Fairbairn preferred to concentrate on adaptation to the outer world rather than on inner needs.

Melanie Klein's Theories

Perhaps Melanie Klein has been the most controversial person in psychoanalysis. She gained prominence in England but almost split the British Psychoanalytic Society. In Mexico and South America, she has been the most respected psychoanalyst since Freud, whereas in the United States she has been virtually ignored. Recently, however, she has gained some recognition among child analysts and those clinicians who work with patients suffering from primitive mental states. When Klein's formulations are taken out of context, they are often valued and integrated into our clinical models, whereas when they are examined within the Kleinian system, they have been severely criticized. I will only briefly allude to her basic tenets and the critiques, particularly those of Kernberg (1972) and Lindon (1972).

As is true of many ego psychologists, Klein did not pay much attention to the dynamic aspects of intrapsychic conflict. In fact, she ignored it, but unlike others, she did not minimize the role of instinctual factors. Klein restricted her concept of conflict to a clash between life and death instincts (see Chapter 3). This would seem to indicate that Klein's ideas were not related to the influence of the environment and the role of objects. This is partially true in that her clinical and theoretical descriptions did not include any of the specific interactions with emotionally significant persons, but she constantly stressed the interplay of objects, internal and external, good and bad. For Klein, instincts had acquired the qualities of structure (see D'Alvia et al. 1984). She equated the projection of instinctual impulses and parts of the self (Klein 1952).

At birth, according to Klein, there is an excess of death instinct over life instinct, which leads to the formation of the polarity of good and bad internal objects that are also considered parts of the self. This preponderance of destructive forces is reinforced by the neonate's envy and greed, qualities that are present since birth in Klein's developmental scheme (Klein 1952). Envy is a reaction of neonates in their helpless state to powerful caretaking objects. They resent and envy the other person's power over them. Greed is an accompanying emotion and is the consequence of the neonates' desire to wrest away that strength and make it their own. At the same time, they suffer from guilt because of their harsh superego.

These hypotheses have caused many critics to protest that they are the quintessence of adultomorphization. Today, as discussed in Chapter 3, postulating the existence and effects of the death instinct is sufficient reason to reject Klein. To add a preexisting superego (which fits well with the Catholics' concept of original sin) and to attribute such complex feelings as greed and envy to a neonate seems to violate the basic principles of hierarchical stratification. Many have protested that these formulations represent the products of fantasy rather than their causes. Nevertheless, a thorough understanding of the products of fantasy can be clinically useful, one reason that Klein has continued to appeal to many psychoanalysts. As she expanded on the development and fate of objects, her clinical contributions increased in value.

According to Klein, because of continued instinctual diffusion, good and bad objects become further polarized. The ego uses splitting mechanisms to protect itself against what is becoming unbearable tension. Thus, bad objects are projected into the outside world, and good objects are retained. This is the *paranoid-schizoid* position, which occurs at around 2 months of age (Klein 1946). Similar to Abraham's (see Chapter 3) and Fairbairn's formulations, the paranoid-schizoid position is conceptualized as a preambivalent orientation, as the objects involved are either good or bad; they cannot be both or something in between.

As the child continues to develop, internal and external objects are structured in a more sophisticated fashion, and what was formerly projected is now reintrojected. The distinction between good and bad objects recedes into the background, and the same object is now endowed with both love and hate, an achievement that signifies the acquisition of the capacity to feel ambivalent. This occurs at around 6 months, and because of the internalization of ambivalent object choices, it is known as the *depressive position* (Klein 1935).

The adaptive task of the depressive position is to gain control of self-destructive forces that stem from the negative impetus of ambivalence. Just as splitting and projection are the characteristic defenses of the paranoid-schizoid position, control and mastery are the means of reestablishing equilibrium during the depressive position. These modes are exemplified in what is called the *manic defense*, which, if intensified to psychotic proportions, is manifested by manic symptoms, such as megalomania, hyperactivity, euphoria, and grandiose delusions. Ordinarily, the manic position is expressed in a more restrained, modulated form. Whereas the paranoid-schizoid position leads to a characterological orientation that stresses passivity and withdrawal (though there may be compensatory belligerence), the manic position involves aggression and active engagement with the external world.

Klein did not emphasize distinctions between pathological and nonpathological orientations. She described the paranoid-schizoid and the manic positions and their corresponding defenses as if they were part of the normal developmental sequence. She also viewed them as the foundations of psychopathology in general, implying that all human behavior is based on what essentially are mental mechanisms associated with psychotic processes. This mixture of psychopathology and ordinary development led to considerable criticism and caused many clinicians to reject altogether Klein's ideas.

Perhaps, psychoanalysts are beginning to be more moderate in their evaluation of Klein. If her calendar is ignored, that is, if the sophisticated psychic processes that she attributed to the first months of life are moved forward on the developmental timetable, her theories become plausible. Furthermore, taking them out of the context of ordinary developmental processes and understanding them as psychopathological distortions leads to insights into the psychic mechanisms involved in severe emotional illness. Clinicians who deal with primitive mental states are now overtly or covertly accepting many of Melanie Klein's concepts.

Winnicott's Theories

Winnicott started his professional life as a pediatrician and then became a psychoanalyst. His early experience with children strongly influenced his thinking as a psychoanalyst, and because psychoanalysts are becoming increasingly interested in the early months of life and focusing on mother–infant relationships, Winnicott's ideas have gained status and relevance. In the last several years, he has been generally accepted, even though there have been, as expected, some reservations. He has been frequently criticized because he is difficult to understand and his hypotheses are not well structured or clearly stated. Readers may admire and enjoy his poetry, but it sometimes obscures rather than enlightens.

Nevertheless, Winnicott demonstrated the significance of the mother–infant bond and dyad as it contributes to the formation of character and the structuring of object relations. He emphasized the importance of early interactions and their role in the development of the identity sense and the acquisition of a true self. He stated, "There is no such thing as a baby" (Winnicott 1952a, p. 99). He added that a caregiving person will be near the baby, a bit of poetry that is hard to forget as it beautifully clarifies that the essence of the child is based on the mother–infant duality. Neither mother nor child can exist in isolation in a healthy setting.

This book has relied heavily on Winnicott's ideas, perhaps more so than on any other psychoanalyst's, with the exception of Freud. Here, I will review those of Winnicott's hypotheses that I believe can be fit into a developmental sequence that belongs in an ego psychological frame of reference and is based on developing object relations. This was not necessarily Winnicott's intent, but his ideas nevertheless lend themselves to such understanding. I am referring particularly to his concept of the transitional phenomenon (Winnicott 1953) and the "use of an object" (Winnicott 1969).

Winnicott's concept of the transitional object and phenomenon is poorly understood. It is frequently thought of as representing a transition point between the internal and the external worlds when the child begins to establish object relationships. This is true, but much more is involved, especially in terms of the acquisition of internal structures that eventually are responsible for constructing the self representation. An exploration of the transitional phase as a developmental stage may cause us to revise our ideas about the role of symbiosis in the course of emotional differentiation. Following Winnicott, Mahler's (1972) theories about hatching from the symbiotic fusion to achieve separation–individuation recede into the background.

The transitional phase can be equated with the beginning of organized mentation. Before it we can think of an amorphous prementational phase followed by an ego that has a dim awareness of perceptions from the external world (see Chapter 3). It has not yet recognized that there are objects that are not part of the self. This is not, however, a fusion state, because for fusion to occur the object first must be recognized as being separate from the self.

Winnicott's model is spatial. He postulated the existence of three spaces: (1) the inner space of the mind, (2) the transitional space, and (3) the external space of the outer world. The transitional space is a space that, for children, belongs to the inner world but, for adults or the observers, is part of the outer world. Reconciling these antithetical viewpoints causes us to see these two spaces as overlapping, and this area of overlapping is designated as the *transitional space*.

The transitional space represents an extension of ego boundaries, but to children it belongs to the inner world. To infants, any object that resides in the transitional space belongs to them and is under their omnipotent control, according to Winnicott. These objects are known as transitional objects, and they can be cuddled and caressed or treated roughly and manhandled. In any case, they are valued possessions that provide security and soothing.

I have already questioned adultomorphic formulations, those attributing to the immature infant such complex orientations and actions as omnipotence and manipulation. Still, the concept of control can be retained if we think of it as a feeling of trust and confidence that inner needs will be gratified. Winnicott referred to this mental state as an illusion that causes children to believe that they are the source of their own nurture. To attribute illusion, that is, a false belief, to a 3-month-old child may also be an adult's reconstruction based on subjective responses rather than on the infant's capabilities.

What Winnicott described might be more accurately referred to as the precursor to illusion. The child with a well-developed transitional space, that is, a child who has extended his ego boundaries to encompass segments of the outer world, may form something akin to a belief that he is capable of self-gratification. This occurs if the mother can respond to his needs as soon as the child perceives them, that is, a mother who is intuitively in tune with the infant's needs. The mother's immediate response supports the illusion that the child is the source of his own nurture. Whatever happens, the infant who has received optimal mothering can be gratified and soothed by the mother and the transitional object that clearly is part of his domain.

At this early stage the child's perception of the outer world—or, better still, of the influence of the outer world on his well-being—is only rudimentary. With further emotional maturation, the position of the external world becomes clearer as it is better recognized, and objects become structured as ego boundaries are further consolidated. The child begins to acknowledge both the existence and the importance of the nurturing mother. It is as if the transitional space momentarily recedes as reality enters the picture. Regarding the fate of objects, some of them have to move out of the transitional space into the surrounding world.

Winnicott stated that the illusion of controlling objects in the transitional space is gradually and partially relinquished. Whereas at one time the child had the illusion of being the source of his nurture, an orientation that Winnicott called *primary psychic creativity*, he later enjoys and plays with the illusion of being totally self-sufficient. This is the beginning of fantasy activity.

As is true of Klein, we can question Winnicott's timetable and wonder whether we can place illusions and the construction of fantasy at the age of 3 or 4 months, although neonatologists' observations, as mentioned, keep pushing various mental activities and perceptions further and further back on the developmental course.

Until the child has sufficient integration to acknowledge the existence of a world outside the self and have trust and confidence in its caretaking aspects, he has to maintain an attitude of self-sufficiency. This attitude is largely determined by the infant's neurophysiological and emotional immaturity. The infant cannot, during the early phases, understand the significance of the milieu in supplying nurture and soothing, because he is not yet able to separate inside from outside. Observations of and experiments with infants have taught us that during the first few weeks of life, the neonates can discriminate some objects in the external world and retain sensory (tactile) impressions of them. According to many investigators, infants cannot, however, differentiate parts of their body from external objects.

To repeat, Winnicott believed that as long as the transitional space dominates, the child does not make such a differentiation. To do so would mean relinquishing control over the object, the same control the child has achieved over his body, and letting it go free, so to speak, as he begins to perceive the object as separate, autonomous, and part of the external world. Winnicott then made the curious statement (1969) that once infants relinquish the object, they feel that they have killed it. Apparently once the object leaves the transitional space, it is first perceived as destroyed. Winnicott believed that it therefore had to be destroyed before it could be found again.

This theory is related to Winnicott's hypothesis (1956a) about what he called the *antisocial* tendency. The latter is a clinical phenomenon manifested by delinquent or antisocial behavior. Children or adolescents act in a way that cause others to hate them. If handled correctly, this hatred can be adaptive because if the patient can be objectively hated, then it is possible that parts of the self can be found that are capable of being loved. This would establish a relationship with the outer world based on positive nurturing rather than negative destructive elements, but object contact begins with destructive (antisocial) interactions, according to Winnicott.

This is still another example of hypotheses about psychopathology being directly applied to the developmental process, particularly to the construction of object relationships. If we remove the destructive factor from Winnicott's concepts and view the object as simply moving from the transitional space into the outer world, then we will have established a sequence of development that will help us understand the structuring and differentiation of the external from the internal world. Perhaps there is a sense of loss when what is essentially a narcissistic position is relinquished, but this need not include the feeling that an important person or object has been killed. This would be conceptually inconsistent and an adultomorphic construction.

Viewing the recession of the transitional space as the path to the formation of object relationships pushes into the background the role of symbiotic fusion with the mother as an essential developmental stage. As mentioned, in order to effect a fusion, the infant must have some awareness, albeit dim, of the external world. According to Winnicott, from the child's viewpoint, the object has to be in the external world, outside the transitional space, before there can be a symbiotic fusion. This means that such a fusion can occur only after there is some differentiation between the inner and the outer world, and therefore it cannot be a preliminary stage that leads to the structuring of individuation and object relations. From the object relations perspective that considers interactions in the transitional space to be significant for emotional development, the role of symbiosis is less important as a developmental impetus. It is a process associated with later emotional states in which some form of object relatedness has been established.

Fusion states can be either the outcome of psychopathology or the essence of intimate and enhancing relationships, but in both situations the psyche has attained a fairly sophisticated degree of integration. The transitional space persists during these later phases, during which symbiotic ties can be formed. The transitional space does not disappear during the course of development, nor do relatively primitive types of object relations such as symbiotic fusion become entirely replaced by later objective and sensitive responses to external objects. Fusion states can be rewarding for both participants, as the valued parts of the self are enhanced by being discovered and rediscovered through the process of fusion and with support from a caring person.

Throughout life, the transitional space recedes and expands, depending on whether the ego is in touch with the inner self or is involved in making reality assessments. Winnicott was probably referring to the qualities of the transitional space during later emotional stages when he stressed that it is the seat of illusion, fantasy formation, and the location of the "cultural experience" (Winnicott 1967). Thus, the transitional space is elemental in a wide spectrum of psychic processes, ranging from primitive psychic differentiation to sensitive, intimate, and creative interactions that encompass our cultural endeavors.

Ego psychology shifts the focus of control from id levels to higher integrative systems within the ego sphere. Freud (1923a) introduced this focus when he stated that the ego had to serve three masters, the id, the superego, and reality. Although it serves these masters, it also controls them, as Freud emphasized in his metaphor of the horse and rider (1923a). The horse represents the powerful id, and the rider, the ego, is small and weak compared with it, but by exerting the proper pressures, he leads the horse to do as he wishes.

The essence of psychoanalytic treatment also lies within the ego sphere. Freud (1933, p. 80) explained: "Where id was, there ego shall be." Explorations and increased understanding of the formation of object relations and the developmental process widen our knowledge of psychopathology and point to the therapeutic direction that will lead to the acquisition of psychic structure, a therapeutic achievement, as it represents an expansion of the ego.

REFERENCES

Abend, S., Porder, M., and Willick, M. (1983). *Borderline Patients: Psychoanalytic Perspectives*. New York: International Universities Press.

Abraham, K. (1916). The first pregenital stage of the libido. In *Selected Papers of Karl Abraham*, pp. 248–280. London: Hogarth Press, 1955.

—— (1921). Contributions to the theory of the anal character. In *Selected Papers of Karl Abraham*, pp. 370–392. London: Hogarth Press, 1955.

—— (1924a). The influence of oral erotism on character formation. In *Selected Papers of Karl Abraham*, pp. 393–407. London: Hogarth Press, 1955.

—— (1924b). A short study of the development of the libido viewed in the light of mental disorders. In *Selected Papers of Karl Abraham*, pp. 418–480. London: Hogarth Press, 1955.

—— (1927). Notes on the psychoanalytic investigation and treatment of manic depressive insanity and allied conditions. In *Selected Papers of Karl Abraham*, pp. 137–157. London: Hogarth Press, 1955.

Alexander, F. (1927). *The Psychoanalysis of the Total Personality*. New York: Nervous and Mental Disease.

―――― (1956). *Psychoanalysis and Psychotherapy.* New York: Norton.

―――― (1961). *The Scope of Psychoanalysis.* New York: Basic Books.

Alexander, F., and French, T. (1946). *Psychoanalytic Therapy.* New York: Ronald.

Alexander, F., and Selesnick, S. (1966). *The History of Psychiatry.* New York: Alfred A. Knopf.

Aristophanes (1955). The plays of Aristophanes. In *Great Books of the Western World.* Chicago: Encyclopedia Britannica.

Balint, M. (1937). Early development states of the ego. In *Primary Love and Psychoanalytic Technique,* pp. 126–148. New York: Liverwright.

―――― (1955). Friendly expanses—horrid empty spaces. *International Journal of Psycho-Analysis* 36:225–241.

―――― (1959). *Thrills and Regression.* New York: International Universities Press.

Bernard, C. (1865). *An Introduction to the Study of Experimental Medicine.* New York: Henry Schuman, 1949.

Bertin, C. (1982). *Maria Bonaparte: A Life.* New York: Harcourt, Brace, Jovanovich.

Bibring, E. (1941). The development and problems of the theory of instincts. *International Journal of Psycho-Analysis* 22:102–132.

Bion, W. R. (1963). *Elements of Psychoanalysis.* New York: Basic Books.

Bleuler, E. (1911). *Dementia Precox or the Group of Schizophrenias.* New York: International Universities Press, 1958.

Boyer, L. B. (1961). Provisional evaluation of psychoanalysis: few parameters in the treatment of schizophrenia. *International Journal of Psycho-Analysis* 42:389–403.

―――― (1983). *The Regressed Patient.* New York: Aronson.

Boyer, L. B., and Giovacchini, P. (1967). *Psychoanalytic Treatment of Characterological and Schizophrenic Disorders.* New York: International Science Press.

―――― (1980). *Psychoanalytic Treatment of Characterological, Borderline and Schizophrenic Disorders.* New York: Aronson.

Brazelton, T. B. (1963). The early mother-infant adjustment. *Pediatrics* 32:931–938.

―――― (1980). *New Knowledge about the Infant from Current Research: Implications for Psychoanalysis.* Paper presented at the May 1980 meetings of the American Psychoanalytic Association, San Francisco, Calif.

Brenner, C. (1957). *An Elementary Textbook of Psychoanalysis.* New York: International Universities Press.

Breuer, J., and Freud, S. (1895). Studies on hysteria. *Standard Edition* 2. London: Hogarth Press, 1955.

Brunswick, R. M. (1928). A supplement to "Freud's history of an infantile neurosis." *International Journal of Psycho-Analysis* 9:439–476.

Cannon, W. B. (1932). *The Wisdom of the Body*. New York: Norton.

Coppolillo, H. (1967). Maturational aspects of the transitional phenomenon. *International Journal of Psycho-Analysis* 48:237–247.

D'Alvia, G., Maladesky, A., and Picollo, A. (1984). Certain reflections concerning instinct theory in the works of Freud and M. Klein. *Revista de Psicoanalisis* 40:737–767.

De Bary, J. (1879). *Die Erscheinung der Symbiose*. Strasbourg: Trubner.

Deutsch, H. (1942). Some forms of emotional disturbances and their relationship to schizophrenia. *Psychoanalytic Quarterly* 11:301–321.

Durkheim, E. (1951). *Suicide: A Study in Sociology*. Glencoe, Ill.: The Free Press.

Edelson, M. (1983). *Hypothesis and Evidence in Psychoanalysis*. Chicago: University of Chicago Press.

Eissler, K. (1958). Goethe and science: a contribution to the psychology of Goethe's psychosis. In *Psychoanalysis and Social Sciences*, Vol. 5, ed. W. Munsterberger and S. Axelrod, pp. 51–98. New York: International Universities Press.

Ellenberger, H. (1970). *The Discovery of the Unconscious*. New York: Basic Books.

Emde, R. (1980). Levels of meaning for infant emotions: a bio-social view. In *Development of Cognition, Affect and Social Relations*, ed. W. A. Collins. Hillside, New Jersey: Erlbaum.

Fairbairn, W. R. D. (1941). A revised psychopathology of the neuroses and psychoses. *International Journal of Psycho-Analysis* 22:250–279.

——— (1954). *An Object Relations Theory of the Personality*. New York: Basic Books.

Federn, P. (1933). The analysis of psychotics. *International Journal of Psycho-Analysis* 15:209–215.

——— (1952). *Ego Psychology and the Psychoses*. New York: Basic Books.

Feinsilver, D. (1980). Transitional relatedness and containment in the treatment of a chronic schizophrenic patient. *International Review of Psycho-Analysis* 7:309–318.

Fenichel, O. (1945). *The Psychoanalytic Theory of Neurosis*. New York: Norton.

Ferenczi, S. (1909). Introjection and transference. In *Sex in Psycho-Analysis: Contributions to Psycho-Analysis*, pp. 35–94. Boston: Gorham, 1916.

—— (1955). *The Selected Papers of Sandor Ferenczi, M.D.* New York: Basic Books.

Flarsheim, A. (1975). Therapist's collusion with the patient's wish for suicide. In *Tactics and Techniques in Psychoanalytic Therapy: Countertransference.*, Vol. 2, ed. P. Giovacchini, pp. 155–196. New York: Aronson.

Fraiberg, S. (1969). Libidinal object constancy and mental representation. *Psychoanalytic Study of the Child* 24:9–47.

Freud, A. (1936). *The Ego and the Mechanisms of Defense*. New York: International Universities Press.

—— (1965). *Normality and Pathology in Childhood*. New York: International Universities Press.

Freud, S. (1877a). Beobachtungen uber Gestaltung und feineren Bau der als Hoden Lappenorgane des Aals. *S. B. Akad. Wissenschaft*, Vienna I Abt. 75,4.

—— (1877b). Uber den Ursprung der hinteren Nervenwurzeln in Ruckenmarken von Amnocoetes. *S. B. Akad. Wissenschaft*, Vienna III Abt. 75,15.

—— (1891). *On Aphasia*. New York: International Universities Press, 1953.

—— (1892). A case of successful treatment by hypnosis. *Standard Edition* 1:115–129.

—— (1893). On the physical mechanisms of hysterical phenomenon. *Standard Edition* 3:25–41.

—— (1894). The neuro-psychoses of defence. *Standard Edition* 2:41–62.

—— (1895a). On the justification for detaching a particular syndrome from neurasthenia under the description "anxiety neurosis." *Standard Edition* 3:85–116.

—— (1895b). Project for a scientific psychology. *Standard Edition* 1:281–392.

—— (1896). Further remarks on the defence neuro-psychoses. *Standard Edition* 3:157–187.

—— (1897). Letter 69 to Fliess. In *The Origins of Psychoanalysis*, 1950. New York: International Universities Press.

—— (1898). Sexuality in the aetiology of the neuroses. *Standard Edition* 3:259–287.

—— (1899). Screen memories. *Standard Edition* 3: 299–323.

—— (1900). The interpretation of dreams. *Standard Edition* 4/5.

—— (1901). The psychopathology of everyday life. *Standard Edition* 6.

—— (1904). Fragment of an analysis of a case of hysteria. *Standard Edition* 7:1–123.

—— (1905a). My views on the part played by sexuality in the aetiology of the neuroses. *Standard Edition* 7:269–281.

—— (1905b). Three essays on the theory of sexuality. *Standard Edition* 7:123–244.

—— (1907). Obsessive actions and religious practices. *Standard Edition* 9:115–129.

—— (1908). Character and anal eroticism. *Standard Edition* 9:167–177.

—— (1909a). Analysis of a phobia in a five-year-old boy. *Standard Edition* 10:1–148.

—— (1909b). Five lectures on psycho-analysis. *Standard Edition* 11:1–56.

—— (1909c). Notes upon a case of obsessional neuroses. *Standard Edition* 10:151–319.

—— (1910a). The future prospects of psychoanalytic therapy. *Standard Edition* 11:139–153.

—— (1910b). Leonardo da Vinci and a memory from his childhood. *Standard Edition* 11:59–139.

—— (1910c). The psycho-analytic view of psychogenic disturbance of vision. *Standard Edition* 11:209–219.

—— (1911a). Formulations on the two principles of mental functioning. *Standard Edition* 12:213–227.

—— (1911b). Psycho-analytic notes on an autobiographical account of a case of paranoia (dementia paranoides). *Standard Edition* 12:1–80.

—— (1911–1914). Papers on technique. *Standard Edition* 12:85–172.

—— (1912a). The dynamics of transference. *Standard Edition* 12:97–109.

—— (1912b). A note on the unconscious in psycho-analysis. *Standard Edition* 12:255–267.

—— (1912c). Recommendations to physicians practicing psycho-analysis. *Standard Edition* 12:109–121.

—— (1913a).On beginning the treatment (further recommendations on the technique of psycho-analysis). *Standard Edition* 12:121–145.

—— (1913b). The disposition to obsessional neurosis. *Standard Edition* 12:311–327.

—— (1913c). Totem and taboo. *Standard Edition* 13:1–162.

—— (1914a). The Moses of Michelangelo. *Standard Edition* 13:209–237.

—— (1914b). Observations on transference love. *Standard Edition* 12:157–172.

—— (1914c). On narcissism. *Standard Edition* 14:67–105.

—— (1914d). On the history of the psycho-analytic movement. *Standard Edition* 14:1–67.

—— (1914e). Remembering, repeating and working through. *Standard Edition* 12:145–157.

—— (1915a). Instincts and their vicissitudes. *Standard Edition* 14:109–141.

—— (1915b). Repression. *Standard Edition* 14:141–159.

—— (1915c). The unconscious. *Standard Edition* 14:159–205.

—— (1916). Some character types met within psycho-analytic work. *Standard Edition* 14:309–337.

—— (1916–1917). Introductory lectures on psycho-analysis. *Standard Edition* 15/16.

—— (1917a). A childhood recollection from *Dichtung und Wahrheit*. *Standard Edition* 17:145–157.

—— (1917b). A difficulty in the path of psycho-analysis. *Standard Edition* 17:135–145.

—— (1917c). Mourning and melancholia. *Standard Edition* 14:237–261.

—— (1917d). On transformation of instinct as exemplified in anal erotism. *Standard Edition* 17:125–135.

—— (1918). From the history of an infantile neurosis. *Standard Edition* 17:1–123.

—— (1920). Beyond the pleasure principle. *Standard Edition* 18:1–65.

—— (1921). Group psychology and analysis of the ego. *Standard Edition* 18:65–145.

—— (1923a).The ego and the id. *Standard Edition* 19:1–60.

—— (1923b). The infantile genital organization: an interpolation into the theory of sexuality. *Standard Edition* 19:141–149.

—— (1923c). Two encyclopaedia articles. *Standard Edition* 18:235–263.

—— (1924a). The loss of reality in neurosis and psychosis. *Standard Edition* 19:183–191.

—— (1924b). Neurosis and psychosis. *Standard Edition* 19:149–155.

—— (1925a). An autobiographical study. *Standard Edition* 20:1–71.

—— (1925b). Negation. *Standard Edition* 19:235–241.

—— (1925c). A note upon the "mystic writing pad." *Standard Edition* 19:227–235.

—— (1926). Inhibitions, symptoms and anxiety. *Standard Edition* 20:75–177.

—— (1933). New introductory lectures on psycho-analysis. *Standard Edition* 22:1–183.

—— (1937). Analysis terminable and interminable. *Standard Edition* 23:209–255.

—— (1938). Splitting of the ego in the process of defence. *Standard Edition* 23:271–279.

—— (1940). An outline of psycho-analysis. *Standard Edition* 23:139–209.

—— (1950). *Origins of Psycho-Analysis: Letters to Wilhelm Fliess, Drafts and Notes, 1887–1902.* Ed. Marie Bonaparte. Trans. Eric Mosbacher and James Strachey. New York: Basic Books.

—— (1969). Seven letters and two postcards to Emil Fliess. *International Journal of Psycho-Analysis* 50:419–432.

Furer, M. (1964). The development of a preschool symbiotic boy. *The Psychoanalytic Study of the Child* 19:448–469.

Gedo, J., and Goldberg, A. (1976). *Models of the Mind: A Psychoanalytic Theory.* Chicago: University of Chicago Press.

Gill, M. (1979). The analysis of the transference. *Journal of the American Psychoanalytic Association* 27:263–288.

—— (1983). The interpersonal paradigm and the degree of the therapist's involvement. *Contemporary Psychoanalysis* 19:200–237.

Giovacchini, P. (1958). Mutual adaptation in various object relationships. *International Journal of Psycho-Analysis* 39:1–8.

—— (1967). Frustration and externalization. *Psychoanalytic Quarterly* 36:571–583.

—— (1972). *Tactics and Techniques in Psychoanalytic Therapy.* Vol. 1. New York: Aronson.

—— (1979a). The sins of the parents: the borderline adolescent and primal confusion. *Adolescent Psychiatry* 7:213–233.

—— (1979b). *The Treatment of Primitive Mental States.* New York: Aronson.

—— (1980). *A Clinician's Guide to Reading Freud.* New York: Aronson.

—— (1984). *Character Disorders and Adaptive Mechanisms.* New York: Aronson.

—— (1985). Countertransference and the severely disturbed adolescent. *Adolescent Psychiatry* 12:449–468.

—— (1986). *Developmental Defects and the Transitional Space: Mental Breakdown and Creative Integration.* New York: Aronson.

Giovacchini, P., and Boyer, L. B. (1975). The psychoanalytic impasse. *International Journal of Psychoanalytic Psychotherapy* 4:25–47.

—— (1983). *Technical Factors in the Treatment of the Severely Disturbed Patient.* New York: Aronson.

Gitelson, M. (1958). On ego distortion. *International Journal of Psycho-Analysis* 39:245–258.

Glover, E. (1930). Grades of ego differentiation. *International Journal of Psycho-Analysis* 11:1–12.

Greenacre, P. (1952). Pregenital patterning. *International Journal of Psycho-Analsis* 33:410–415.

—— (1958). Early physical determinants in the development of the sense of identity. *Journal of the American Psychoanalytic Association* 6:612–627.

—— (1959). On focal symbiosis. In *Dynamic Psychopathology in Childhood*, ed. L. Jessner and E. Pavenstedt, pp. 243–256. New York: Grune and Stratton.

—— (1960). Considerations regarding the parent-infant relationship. *International Journal of Psycho-Analysis* 41:571–584.

Groddeck, G. (1923). *The Book of the Id.* New York: International Universities Press, 1950.

Grotstein, J. (1981). *Splitting and Projective Identification.* New York: Aronson.

Grünbaum, A. (1984). *The Foundations of Psychoanalysis.* Los Angeles: University of California Press.

Guntrip, H. (1961). *Personality Structure and Human Interaction.* New York: International Universities Press.

Guttman, S., Jones, R., and Parrish, S. (1980). *Concordance to the Psychological Works of Sigmund Freud.* Boston: G. K. Hall.

Hartmann, H. (1939). *Ego Psychology and the Problem of Adaptation.* New York: International Universities Press, 1958.

—— (1950). Comments on the psychoanalytic theory of the ego. *The Psychoanalytic Study of the Child* 5:74–96.

—— (1952). The mutual influences in the development of ego and id. *The Psychoanalytic Study of the Child* 7:9–30.

—— (1953). Contribution to the metapsychology of schizophrenia. *The Psychoanalytic Study of the Child* 8:177–198.

—— (1955). Notes on the theory of sublimation. *The Psychoanalytic Study of the Child* 10:9–29.

—— (1964). *Essays on Ego Psychology: Selected Problems in Psychoanalytic Theory.* New York: International Universities Press.

Hartmann, H., Kris, E., and Loewenstein, R. M. (1946). Comments on the formation of psychic structure. *The Psychoanalytic Study of the Child* 2:11–38.

—— (1949). Notes on the theory of aggression. *The Psychoanalytic Study of the Child* 3/4:9–36.

Herodotus (1952). The history of Herodotus. In *Great Books of the Western World.* Chicago: Encyclopedia Britannica.

Herrick, E. J. (1956). *The Evolution of Human Nature.* Austin: University of Texas Press.

Horney, K. (1937). *The Neurotic Personality of Our Time.* New York: Norton.

Jacobson, E. (1959). Depersonalization. *Journal of the American Psychoanalytic Association* 7:591–610.

—— (1964). *The Self and the Object World.* New York: International Universities Press.

—— (1969). *Psychotic Conflict and Reality.* New York: International Universities Press.

Johnson, A. M., and Szurek, S. (1952). The genesis of antisocial acting out in children and adults. *Psychoanalytic Quarterly* 3:323–335.

—— (1964). Etiology of antisocial behavior in delinquents and psychopaths. *Journal of the American Medical Association* 154:814–817.

Jones, E. (1931). Fear, guilt and hate. In *Papers of Psycho-Analysis,* pp. 304–320. Boston: Beacon Press, 1948.

—— (1953). *The Life and Works of Sigmund Freud.* Vol. 1. New York: Basic Books.

Kardiner, A. (1977). *My Analysis with Freud.* New York: Norton.

Kardiner, A., Karush, A., and Ovesey, L. (1959). Methodological study of Freudian theory: 1. basic concepts. *Journal of Nervous and Mental Diseases* 11:129–168.

Kernberg, O. (1972). A critique of Melanie Klein's theory. In *Tactics and Techniques in Psychoanalytic Therapy,* ed. P. Giovacchini, pp. 62–97. New York: Aronson.

—— (1975). *Borderline Conditions and Pathological Narcissism.* New York: Aronson.

—— (1980). *Internal World and External Reality: Object Relations Theory Applied.* New York: Aronson.

Khan, M. M. R. (1964). Ego distortion, cumulative trauma and the role of reconstruction in the analytic situation. *International Journal of Psycho-Analysis* 45:272–279.

Klaus, M., and Kennel, J. (1982). *Parent-Infant Bonding.* St. Louis: Mosby.

Klein, M. (1935). A contribution to the psychogenesis of manic-depressive states. *International Journal of Psycho-Analysis* 16:145–174.

—— (1946). Notes on some schizoid mechanisms. *International Journal of Psycho-Analysis* 27:99–110.

—— (1952). *Developments in Psycho-Analysis.* Ed. J. Riviere. London: Hogarth Press.

Knight, R. (1953). Borderline states. *Bulletin of the Menninger Clinic* 19:1–12.

Kohut, H. (1971). *The Analysis of the Self.* New York: International Universities Press.

—— (1977). *The Restoration of the Self.* New York: International Universities Press.

Kraepelin, E. (1883). *Dementia Precox and Paraphrenia.* Edinburgh: Livingston.

—— (1903). *Lehrbuch der Psychiatrie.* Seventh Ed. Leipzig: Barth.

Kris, E. (1950). On preconscious mental processes. *Psychoanalytic Quarterly* 19:540–560.

Kuhn, T. S. (1962). *The Structure of Scientific Revolutions.* Chicago: University of Chicago Press.

Lewin, B. (1950). *The Psychoanalysis of Elation.* New York: Norton.

Lindon, J. (1972). Melanie Klein's theory and technique: her life and work. In *Tactics and Techniques in Psychoanalytic Therapy*, ed. P. Giovacchini, pp. 33–61. New York: Aronson.

Mahler, M. (1968). *On Human Symbiosis and the Vicissitudes of Individuation.* New York: International Universities Press.

—— (1972). A study of the separation-individuation process and its possible application to borderline phenomena in the psychoanalytic situation. *Psychoanalytic Study of the Child* 27:403–424.

Mahler, M., Pine, F., and Bergman, A. (1975). *The Psychological Birth of the Human Infant.* New York: Basic Books.

Malcolm, J. (1981). *Psychoanalysis: The Impossible Profession.* New York: Knopf.

Masterson, J. (1976). *Treatment of the Borderline Adult*. New York: Brunner/Mazel.

Meltzoff, A. N., and Moore, M. K. (1977). Imitations of facial and manual gestures by human neonates. *Science* 198:75–78.

Modell, A. (1963). Primitive object relations and the predisposition to schizophrenia. *International Journal of Psycho-Analysis* 44:282–293.

—— (1968). *Object Love and Reality*. New York: International Universities Press.

Nietzsche, F. (1937). *The Philosophy of Nietzsche*. Ed. W. Wright. New York: Random House.

Nunberg, H. (1932). *Principles of Psychoanalysis: Their Application to the Neuroses*. New York: International Universities Press.

Nunberg, H., and Federn, E. (1962). *Minutes of the Vienna Psychoanalytic Society* I and II, 1906–1910. New York: International Universities Press.

Ogden, T. H. (1982). *Projective Identification: Psychotherapeutic Technique*. New York: Aronson.

Piaget, J. (1937). *The Construction of Reality in the Child*. New York: Basic Books, 1954.

—— (1952). *Language and Thought of the Child*. London: Routledge and Kegan Paul.

Piers, G., and Singer, M. (1953). *Shame and Guilt*. Springfield, Ill.: Charles C Thomas.

Pollack, G. (1973). Bertha Pappenheim: pathological mourning. *Journal of the American Psychoanalytic Association* 21:328–332.

Racker, H. (1968). *Transference and Countertransference*. New York: International Universities Press.

Rank, O. (1924). *The Trauma of Birth*. London: Hogarth Press, 1929.

Ransom, J. (1984). Use of the passive voice. *Journal of the American Medical Association* 251:127.

Reichard, S. (1956). A re-examination of "Studies in Hysteria." *Psychoanalytic Quarterly* 25:155–177.

Rinsley, D. (1982). Object relations theory and psychotherapy, with particular reference to the self-disordered patient. In *Treatment of the Severely Disturbed Patient*, ed. P. Giovacchini and L. B. Boyer, pp. 187–217. New York: Aronson.

Rosenblatt, J. S. (1969). The development of maternal responsiveness in rats. *American Journal of Orthopsychiatry* 39:36–56.

Rosenfeld, H. (1965). *Psychotic States: A Psychoanalytic Approach.* New York: International Universities Press.

Sandler, J. (1960). The background of safety. *International Journal of Psycho-Analysis* 41:352–356.

Sandler, J., and Rosenblatt, B. (1962). The concept of the representational world. *The Psychoanalytic Study of the Child* 17:128–145.

Schafer, R. (1960). The loving and beloved superego. *The Psychoanalytic Study of the Child* 15:163–188.

—— (1968). *Aspects of Internalization.* New York: International Universities Press.

Schur, M. (1955). Comments on the metapsychology of somatization. *The Psychoanalytic Study of the Child* 10:119–165.

—— (1958). The ego and the id in anxiety. *The Psychoanalytic Study of the Child* 13:190–223.

Searles, H. (1963). Transference psychosis in the psychotherapy of schizophrenia. *International Journal of Psycho-Analysis* 44:249–291.

—— (1965). *Collected Papers on Schizophrenia and Related Subjects.* New York: International Universities Press.

Spinoza, B. (1952). *The Chief Works of Benedict de Spinoza.* New York: Dover.

Spitz, R. (1945). Hospitalism. *The Psychoanalytic Study of the Child* 1:53–74.

—— (1959). *A Genetic Field Theory of Ego Formation.* New York: International Universities Press.

—— (1965). *The First Year of Life.* New York: International Universities Press.

Sprenger, J., and Kraemer, H. (1486). *Maalleus Maleficarum.* London: Pushkin.

Stern, D. (1985). *The Interpersonal World of the Infant.* New York: Basic Books.

Sullivan, H. S. (1953). *The Interpersonal Theory of Psychiatry.* New York: Norton.

Tausk, V. (1919). On the origin of the "influencing machine" in schizophrenia. *Psychoanalytic Quarterly* 2:519–556, 1933.

Valenstein, A. F. (1983). Working through and resistance to change: insight and the action system. *Journal of the American Psychoanalytic Association* 31:353–375.

Waelder, R. (1960). *Basic Theory of Psychoanalysis*. New York: International Universities Press.

Weiss, E. (1950). *Principles of Psychodynamics*. New York: Grune and Stratton.

Winnicott, D. W. (1952a). Anxiety associated with insecurity. In *Collected Papers: Through Pediatrics to Psycho-Analysis*, ed. D. W. Winnicott, pp. 97–101. New York: Basic Books, 1958.

—— (1952b). Psychosis and child care. In *Collected Papers: Through Pediatrics to Psycho-Analysis*, ed. D. W. Winnicott, pp. 219–228. New York: Basic Books, 1958.

—— (1953). Transitional objects and transitional phenomena. In *Playing and Reality*, ed. D. W. Winnicott, pp. 1–26. London: Tavistock, 1971.

—— (1954). Withdrawal and regression. In *Collected Papers: Through Pediatrics to Psycho-Analysis*, ed. D. W. Winnicott, pp. 255–262. New York: Basic Books, 1958.

—— (1956a). The antisocial tendency. In *Collected Papers: Through Pediatrics to Psycho-Analysis*, ed. D. W. Winnicott, pp. 306–316. New York: Basic Books, 1958.

—— (1956b). Primary maternal preoccupation. In *Collected Papers: Through Pediatrics to Psycho-Analysis*, ed. D. W. Winnicott, pp. 300–306. New York: Basic Books, 1958.

—— (1957). *The Child, the Family, and the Outside World*. London: Tavistock.

—— (1967). The location of the cultural experience. In *Playing and Reality*, ed. D. W. Winnicott, pp. 95–103. London: Tavistock, 1971.

—— (1969). The use of an object and relating through identification. In *Playing and Reality*, ed. D. W. Winnicott, pp. 86–95. London: Tavistock, 1971.

—— (1971). *Playing and Reality*. London: Tavistock.

—— (1972). Fragment of an analysis. In *Tactics and Techniques in Psychoanalytic Therapy*, ed P. Giovacchini, pp. 455–697. New York: Aronson.

Zetzel, E. (1956). Current concepts of transference. *Journal of the American Psychoanalytic Association* 1:526–537.

Zilboorg, G., and Henry, G. (1941). *A History of Medical Psychology*. New York: Norton.

INDEX

Mental state, hypnoid, 19
Mesmer, F. A., 15
Metapsychology, 25–86
Modell, A., 95
Moniz, E., 11
Mortido, 126
Multiple personalities, 233–234
Mystic Writing Pad, 29, 67–68, 69

Narcissism
  primary, *see* Primary narcissism
  secondary, 94–96, 114
"On Narcissism," 76–77
Narcissistic neurosis(es), 182, 189–198, 317
Narcissistic personalities, 323
Narcissistic personality disorders, 322–328
Needs, painful inner, and sense of aliveness, 291–294
Negation, 226–229
Negative therapeutic reaction, 40
Neurasthenia, 183
Neurosis(es)
  actual, 182–183
  anxiety, 183, 188
  character, 315–316
  infantile, 85
  narcissistic, 182, 189–198, 317
  obsessive-compulsive, 186–188
  relationships among, 185–189
  transference, 182, 184–185
Neurosogenesis, and nosology, 181–198
Neurotic character, 316
Neutralization, 278–279
Neutralized energy, 278
New York Psychoanalytic Institute, 320
Nietzsche, F., 12

Noguchi, H., 7
Nosology, neurosogenesis and, 181–198
Nunberg, H., 8, 90

Obesity, 215
Object, 348
  paranoid, 230
  self, 95
  substitute, 208
Object constancy, 338
  libidinal, 339
Object relations
  character structure and, 309–357
  and psychic structure, 328–342
Object relations theory(ies), 342–357
  ego psychology and, 271–357
Object relationships, 49
Object representation, 5
Obsessive-compulsive neurosis, 186–188
Oedipus complex, 14, 49, 55–56, 104, 105–111, 348
Ogden, T. H., 317
Operations, primary and secondary process, 30
Oral character, 97
Oral-dependent drives, 97–98
Oral drives, 97
Oral-sadistic attitude, 98
Oral stage, 96–100
Orality, 84
Organ pleasure, 89
Organized disintegration, 300
Organizers, psychic, 281
Overcompensation, 223
Overdetermination, 136

Painful inner needs, and sense of aliveness, 291–294